TURMOIL IN PUNJAB

Praise for *Turmoil in Punjab*

'This is a comprehensive historical perspective and the most valuable contribution on the turmoil in Punjab ever since it began in 1978. It covers all dimensions of the ethno-national movement, the militancy, the violence, and the roles played by politicians, and state and Central executing agencies. In an insider's account of policymaking at the state level and of operations Blue Star, Wood Rose and Black Thunder I and II, the author is objective, candid and does not mince words. This book has important lessons for our political leaders, the bureaucracy, the police and the army. It is a must-read for all of them and those interested in India's domestic politics.'

—General V.P. Malik, former Chief of Army Staff

'We had to wait nearly thirty eight-years for an independent eyewitness account of Operation Blue Star, the events leading up to it and the campaign for Khalistan that followed it. Ramesh Inder Singh was district magistrate of Amritsar during the army operation in the Golden Temple and thereafter, but he has not spared anyone from the civilian or military authorities. He's covered the whole history of the Punjab troubles, from the emergence of Bhindranwale to Operation Black Thunder I and II, and then the final ruthless police campaign that ended Sikh militancy in the state. It's a gripping story of missed opportunities, misplaced courage, military arrogance and criminality, particularly gun-dealing. Some previously unanswered questions are answered but the reader is left to choose from several different explanations for Indira Gandhi's handling of the crisis that led to her assassination.'

—Sir Mark Tully, author and BBC journalist

'It must have been a painful experience for Ramesh Inder Singh to chronicle the gory events that shook India in 1984. He has tried to be unbiased in his narrative of Operation Blue Star, Prime Minister Indira Gandhi's assassination and the riots that followed in Delhi. It is a grisly tale of blood, brutal violence and high politics gone haywire.'

—H.K. Dua, former editor of *Hindustan Times*, *The Indian Express* and *The Tribune;* editorial adviser to *The Times of India*; media adviser to the Prime Minister; and member of Parliament

'This work is a tell-all account of Punjab in the 1980s. Nobody comes out untarnished—not serving officials, not senior politicians, not journalists, not commentators and, of course, not the militants. The author's contentions are persuasive since he was a ranking bureaucrat at the time and had a close-up view of the events that took place in Punjab's difficult decade. At a very critical period, he was also the district magistrate of Amritsar, the epicentre of the turmoil. His familiarity with the official rules of engagement and what actually happened on the ground, often in front of his eyes, are quite startling. The contentions in this work are drawn from available data sources but many of them, perhaps the most enticing ones, are based on the author's personal observations and experiences. Some may find these unsettling as the narration pulls no punches. The author has daringly thrown down the gauntlet, and now it's open season to take up the challenge and contest his assertions. Will anybody do it? What is assured, however, is that the reader will find this granulated, intimate account a compelling read.'

—Dipankar Gupta, sociologist

'Backed by thorough research, this is a warts-and-all account of Operation Bluestar and the rise and fall of militancy in Punjab. Ramesh Inder Singh, as deputy commissioner, Amritsar (1984–87), provided the civil administration's interface for operations Bluestar, Woodrose and Black Thunder I. He spares no one for accountability, including himself. His critical analysis of the good, bad and ugly facets of the military operations, clearly bringing out the lessons learnt, is the hallmark of the book. *Turmoil in Punjab* is a dispassionate and authentic account by an insider that fills a void in history and settles most controversies for good.'

—Lieutenant General H.S. Panag (retd)

'This is an authentic and empathetic account of Operation Blue Star. It traces the larger and immediate background and discusses its aftermath of about a decade of militancy. The insider's story told by Ramesh Inder Singh is a historical document of vital importance for contemporary India. This book is eminently readable.'

—J.S. Grewal, historian, former director of Indian Institute of Advanced Studies, Shimla, and former vice chancellor of Guru Nanak Dev University, Amritsar

TURMOIL IN PUNJAB

BEFORE AND AFTER BLUE STAR

An Insider's Story

RAMESH INDER SINGH

HarperCollins *Publishers* India

First published in India by HarperCollins *Publishers* 2022
4th Floor, Tower A, Building No. 10, Phase II, DLF Cyber City,
Gurugram, Haryana – 122002
www.harpercollins.co.in

2 4 6 8 10 9 7 5 3 1

P-ISBN: 978-93-5489-906-5
E-ISBN: 978-93-5489-909-6

Typeset in 11/15.4 Stempel Garamond LT Std
Manipal Technologies Limited, Manipal

Printed and bound at
Saurabh Printers Pvt. Ltd.

This book is produced from independently certified FSC® paper to ensure responsible forest management.

HarperCollins *Publishers*, Macken House, 39/40 Mayor Street Upper,
Dublin 1, D01 C9W8, Ireland

To Punjab and its people, to set right the record of the volcanic events, in the hope that India's diverse communities withstand divisive forces and prosper in unity and peace

Contents

PART II: The Historical Background

Preface

Even in the best of times, perceptions of an event or a situation vary. Catastrophic events in particular tend to obscure objectivity, divide people and often cause facts to fall by the wayside. Operation Blue Star and its aftermath were cataclysmic events of this nature, making India go to war with itself. The nation lost a Prime Minister, a chief minister, a former army chief, thousands of innocent citizens and some not-so-innocent ones. However, nearly four decades later, we still hear varying versions of what happened, why and how it happened. Facts are sacred, but whose facts are they? It is one person's truth against another's, your interpretation versus theirs.

In June 1984, the Indian Army marched to Amritsar—Operation Blue Star was under way. Some saw it as an invasion of the sacred space of the Golden Temple, while some others viewed it as a military operation to clear the area of gun-wielding terrorists.

Prime Minister Indira Gandhi was assassinated a few months later. Carnage followed on the streets of Delhi and elsewhere, with over

3,000 innocent Sikhs being murdered. Some believe it was genocide, while others considered it a spontaneous reaction to the murder of their beloved leader. For some, Sant Jarnail Singh Bhindranwale was a shaheed, a martyr, as publicly pronounced by the *jathedar* of the Akal Takht in 2003. Others, however, viewed him as a zealot responsible for over two decades of Punjab's turmoil, misery and mayhem.

I was an eyewitness, and at times an actor, howsoever insignificant, as this moment of history unfolded. What I saw or did—or what I failed to do—needs to be told. My conscience, more than anything else, impels me to tell my facts and my interpretation of the events that transpired over the troubled decade and a half surrounding Operation Blue Star. To leave things unsaid would be to blank out history. Therefore, I feel the need for an objective and factual account of the events and happenings. This is my attempt in the pages of this book.

In Punjab, terrorism has been eliminated decisively. However, the deep, fundamental ethno-socio-religious fault lines that led to the turmoil in the state still persist. History has an uncanny habit of repeating itself, and we have to be on guard, for only the civilizations that draw lessons from their history and move forward prosper.

Being on the rolls of the government, this is the earliest opportunity I received to publish the present work, post my superannuation as chief secretary, Punjab, and thereafter as chief information commissioner, Punjab, under the Right to Information regime. And I do not regret this interregnum because the passage of years has helped crystallize issues and cooled down tempers. In these thirty-eight years, a lot has been said and written about Operation Blue Star and the chaos in Punjab. An abundance of pop history books and documentaries and a few eyewitness accounts—mostly hearsay—have been published. Everything, however, has not been said and probably may not be said for a while, considering the sensitivity of the subject and the security imperatives.

I have, however, narrated as much as I know and chronicled it honestly. I hope, as passions mellow over time, people within and outside the establishment will be more receptive of this work. My words may displease some; however, the intention is not to hurt any feelings or apportion blame—though in historical accounts that may be unavoidable—but to initiate dialogue, open the way to introspection and, most importantly, move towards reconciliation and closure over a tragic past.

Part I

1

'Rumours Have Wings'[1]

'*Khalsa ji, kammar kus lo, samay aa gaya hai* [Khalsa ji, the time has come, gird your loins],' proclaimed Sant Jarnail Singh Bhindranwale in his clarion call imploring the Sikh community to rise against the Government of India. It was 8 or 9 June 1984, soon after the end of Operation Blue Star. Bhindranwale was on a Pakistani TV channel, sitting upright and wearing the traditional Sikh *choghah* with a *kammar kasa* or cummerbund tightly tied around the waist. I heard him live on Lahore TV, along with millions residing along the international border. Technology had enabled Pakistan to carry transmissions deep into India, compromising our territorial sovereignty. The telecast was repeated many times over, with a tacit message that Bhindranwale would make an important announcement in the days to come.

A few days later, my maternal uncle, a retired police officer, was the first from my extended family to reach Amritsar. He was inquisitive, almost interrogatory, as he said, 'Take me to the tunnel via which Sant

Ji escaped.' My denial that there was no tunnel or that the Sant was dead found no acceptance.

He countered, 'But P.C. Sethi, the Union home minister, said in Parliament that extremists were taking refuge in a tunnel in the complex.' The minister's statement was refuted by the then president of the Shiromani Gurdwara Parbandhak Committee (SGPC), Atma Singh, as late as 28 April 1984, but the rebuttal notwithstanding, the minister had set up the gullible devotee's fantasy—the tunnel, some said, extended up to the Wagah border. When I persisted with my refutation, he demanded, 'Where is Gurdev Singh? Let me speak to him. You are new to the place and do not know.'

Gurdev Singh Brar was my predecessor as deputy commissioner, Amritsar. Of the many rumours, a popular one then was that Gurdev Singh had escorted Bhindranwale to safety through a secret tunnel. For the devout, the rumours were truth. Gurdev Singh had not been seen in public since the day he imposed curfew in Amritsar on 3 June 1984. The government had not yet formally announced Bhindranwale's death, and even after it did so, the Damdami Taksal, the Sikh seminary to which Bhindranwale belonged, continued to deny it. People believed the latter, for they had seen him in flesh and blood on TV exhorting the Khalsa to revolt. And seeing is believing. This served as excellent propaganda for the Pakistani Inter-Services Intelligence (ISI) to sustain and instigate the frayed Sikh tempers.

By the middle of May 1984, Central Reserve Police Force (CRPF) troops had been deployed around the Golden Temple. The militants had set up a chain of armed fortifications encircling all strategic points in and around the temple complex. The observation posts on high vantage points gave early warning of any movement around the temple precincts. The brick-lined pigeonhole openings in the walls, sandbagged doors, windows, ventilators and pillboxes with clear lines of sight and fire had converted the temple into a hunting ground. These battlements provided a sense of security and protection to the militants, who operated in a well-controlled and coordinated manner. Obviously, an effective command-and-control structure was in position.

On 27 May, CRPF troops at Akhara Bala Nand exchanged fire with militants, a situation that was repeated on 30 May. On 1 June 1984, the CRPF closed in, firing from the rooftop observation posts built on high-rise private properties overlooking the temple, mainly houses and hotels. There was an intermittent exchange of fire starting from noon till about 8 p.m. Eleven civilians, including two women, died and more than twenty-four were injured. Bullets hit the temple complex, by one count, thirty-two in all. Curfew was imposed in Amritsar for thirty-two hours, starting 9 p.m. on 1 June. Allegedly, the firing started as unprovoked sniping by the CRPF with the objective of drawing counter fire from the militants. That would give away details of their emplacements and weaponry.

The firing coincided with the arrival in Amritsar from Meerut of Brig. N.K. Talwar, deputy commandant of 9 Infantry Division, along with the principal staff officer to the general officer commanding (GOC) of the division in the wee hours of the morning on 1 June. Maj. Gen. K.S. Brar also reached Amritsar in the late afternoon. On 29 May an advance element of 9 Division had landed at Amritsar to establish a bridge-head. An operation room was set up in the sand model room—a tin-roof large hall—at the headquarters of 15 Infantry Division based at Amritsar. Maj. Gen. Jagdish Singh Jamwal, GOC of 15 Infantry Division, held a meeting on the evening of 1 June with his senior staff officers, conveying the movement of 9 Division from Meerut to Amritsar, and reviewing the required arrangements.

Journalists had free access to the temple complex till then and it was during the exchange of fire between the militants and the CRPF on 27 and 30 May and 1 June that a foreign TV crew managed to interview Bhindranwale. They recorded the exchange of fire and the bullet marks on the walls of the temple complex, giving the impression that they were visuals of Operation Blue Star. The video recording reached Pakistan, and was subsequently telecast by Lahore TV, making it appear as though it took place on a date subsequent to the army operation on 5–6 June — Operation Blue Star.

Thanks to Pakistan, Bhindranwale was alive even in death. His clarion call moved many *jathas* (organized groups of Sikhs) from near and far to march to Amritsar. These groups were intercepted on different dates and suitably dealt with. However, some Sikh soldiers revolted too. Sporadic reports of mutiny in a few army units from areas outside Punjab poured in, as armed deserters proceeded to Amritsar from places as far as Patna, Rampur, Ranchi and Rajasthan.

What a propaganda coup! Words were proving more potent than the weapons Pakistan had infiltrated across the border. A deceptive telecast had Punjab on the boil. What did we do? In 1984, the Orwellian year, we followed in the footsteps of Big Brother and gagged all public communication. Punjab was cut off from the rest of the country, a statewide curfew was imposed, and the operation of buses, trains and private vehicles was suspended. All telephone lines were snapped. The state was declared a restricted area for foreigners.

As the soldiers moved in, foreign scribes were bundled out of Amritsar on 3 June in buses escorted by the army straight to Delhi. There was a blackout of all news; no newspapers were published or allowed in Punjab from outside for a few days. But it's an inviolable fact that the more you suppress something, the more propensity it has to spread. Rumours ran rife, some of them state-sponsored. Doordarshan and All India Radio (AIR) were still on air, but given the trust deficit, only a section of the population believed what they said.

It took the Sikh clergy nineteen years to formally acknowledge that Sant Jarnail Singh Bhindranwale, fourteenth chief of the Damdami Taksal, the fundamentalist Sikh seminary, was dead. The then jathedar of the Akal Takht, Joginder Singh Vedanti, conferred a *siropa* (robe of honour) on Bhindranwale's son, Ishar Singh, at a public gathering at the Diwan Hall, Gurdwara Manji Sahib, in the Golden Temple complex on 6 June 2003, putting an end to the myth that he was alive.

The congregation canonized Bhindranwale as a shaheed of the Sikh *quam* (community).

The delay in declaring the *shahadat* or martyrdom was deliberate. Doing so made Bhindranwale a zinda-shaheed, which can be loosely translated to immortal martyr, perpetuating his iconic command over the militant movement—helping to maintain its momentum. It also eliminated the chances of any alternative power centre to the Damdami Taksal to emerge, and at a more personal level, it facilitated Baba Joginder Singh, Bhindranwale's father, and his family to exercise hegemony over the Sikh religio-political scene. Bhindranwale became even more valuable in his demise; his death created a legend, an irrational yet hallowed myth that was to drive the ethno-religious cause for years, and which still does for some.

The mystery of my predecessor deputy commissioner Gurdev Singh's sudden disappearance, however, was short-lived. He returned to India from the US at the end of the ex-India leave he had applied for as early as April 1984. On his return, he was posted in Chandigarh, the state headquarters, so everyone could see he was back.

A likeable person, Gurdev Singh had risen to the Indian Administrative Service (IAS) from the state service on the strength of an outstanding service record. His undoing in Amritsar, however, was his outspoken nature—his public outpourings against the frisking of the civilian population at various checkposts by the CRPF may have made him popular among the hardliner Sikhs, but he became anathema to the security forces. He had a running argument with B.P. Tiwari, the deputy inspector general (DIG), CRPF.

The differences became public knowledge and weakened the command and control of the district magistrate over law-enforcing agencies. The CRPF pickets, at times, even refused to acknowledge curfew passes issued by the district magistrate and on one instance allegedly tore the curfew pass issued to a local journalist, Harbir Singh Bhanwar. This naturally resulted in a protest by local journalists to the governor on his tour to Amritsar.

The relationship between the district magistrate and the paramilitary forces did not improve, and an issue of *The Tribune* dated 2 June 1984 reported under the headline, 'Administration Helpless', and that 'the local administration is in shambles. Neither the civil administration nor the state police has much say in the prevailing circumstances. Both the senior superintendent of police (SSP) and the district magistrate are said to be demoralized . . . at one stage the district administration was completely bypassed and all orders went direct to the paramilitary forces.'

Gurdev Singh was unhappy with the way events were unfolding and had expressed a desire to be moved out of Amritsar. His request was not granted. In April 1984 he applied for a long ex-India leave to visit his son in the US. The summer Olympics was scheduled to be held in Los Angeles, California, in July that year. Gurdev Singh's credentials as a sports administrator—he was associated with the Indian Hockey Federation—and his status as a Grade 1 international hockey umpire gave him additional grounds to seek leave for the Games.

Around the same time, in May 1984, I received a call from the office of the chief secretary, K.D. Vasudeva. Laconic in style, he came straight to the point and sounded me out on the move to send me to Amritsar as a leave substitute for Gurdev Singh. The proposal, he added, was subject to Governor B.D. Pande and his adviser Surendra Nath clearing my name. I was asked to call on both of them the same day.

Pande was a distinguished civil servant who had been conferred the Padma Shri in 1977 and the Padma Vibhushan in 2000. After his retirement as Cabinet secretary, he was appointed as the governor of West Bengal, my original cadre in the IAS before I shifted to Punjab in July 1978.

On 5 October 1983, six Hindu bus passengers were singled out and shot near Dhilwan in Kapurthala district, Punjab. The Central government could ill-afford to be seen as a silent spectator and asked

Chief Minister Darbara Singh to resign, which he did on 6 October. The state was brought under President's Rule and B.D. Pande was transferred to Punjab from Calcutta (now Kolkata). He took over as governor, Punjab, on 10 October 1983. With the political buffer between the people of Punjab and the Union government gone, the seemingly onerous task of providing security to citizens directly passed on to the Prime Minister.

When I called on Pande in early May 1984, he was forthright: If I performed, I would stay on in Amritsar. Otherwise, Gurdev Singh would rejoin at the end of his leave. Pande directed me to visit the district to familiarize myself with the ground realities. He neither mentioned nor betrayed any plan or signs of a proposed operation against militants in the Golden Temple. Surendra Nath, however, mumbled in rather hush-hush tones that it was time for the administration to assert itself. I sought no details, and he gave me none. However, implicit in the unspoken words was a hint of some strong anti-militant measures.

The next day, I proceeded to Amritsar for a week-long tour of the district. Gurdev Singh was all smiles, visibly relieved to receive his designated but still unannounced replacement. We spent a few hours together, exchanging notes. Before we parted company, Gurdev Singh informed me that he had scheduled his leave from 5 June and asked me to reach Amritsar a day in advance to take over. I agreed.

The first day of my week-long tour of Amritsar district was spent in the city: I paid obeisance at the Golden Temple, Durgiana Temple and Jallianwala Bagh; took a leisurely walk around the narrow, serpentine lanes of the walled city encircling the Golden Temple complex; and visited the university and the labour belt of Khasa and Chheharta. The city seemed normal, except for the police *naka*s, or road barricades.

Pilgrims thronged the Golden Temple, and a continuous recitation of the gurbani was going on. I performed *parikrama*, the sacred circumambulatory ritual, paid obeisance at the Harmandir Sahib, the sanctum sanctorum, and received prasad. There was nothing out of the ordinary at the temple. However, as I neared the Akal Takht, I could feel an imperceptible shift. Maybe I was overtly conscious, but it seemed that we were under observation. My accompanying officers—the district development and panchayat officer and secretary, zila parishad—nudged me to move fast, cautioning me not to look towards the fortifications. We could see young men with flowing beards dressed in long kurtas and *kachera*s, the long undershorts. They were carrying kirpans slung from *gatra*s (sashes) and wielding weapons, mostly rifles or shotguns. The 'boys' of Bhindranwale were demonstratively conspicuous.

Their weapons reminded me of the only in-person interaction I ever had with Bhindranwale. In 1979, I was posted as additional district magistrate (ADM) at Faridkot, his home district. My official residence was sandwiched between the two majestic *kothi*s of the erstwhile princely state of Faridkot, where the deputy commissioner and the senior superintendent of police lived. Simranjit Singh Mann, the towering senior superintendent, my neighbour in the Police House, as his residence was called, rang up one morning to say that Bhindranwale was with him and that he would walk across the barbed wire fence partitioning our houses to see me.

The Nirankari–Sikh clash at Amritsar in 1978 had brought Bhindranwale into the limelight and catapulted him to the centre stage of Sikh politics. When he met me, he was convivial and warm, unlike his subsequent firebrand image. His remonstrance, however, was that I was stringent in the sanctioning of arms licences. His men needed weapons for self-defence, and he cajoled me to be liberal. Arms are the only ornaments Sikhs don, he said, and added, *Shastradhari bano* (Acquire firearms).'

Five years later, standing in the holiest of holy Sikh shrines, I could see that Bhindranwale had managed a substantial stockpile of arms for his men, all licensed. Simranjit had to face a departmental inquiry for the liberal grant of arms licences while he was posted as superintendent at Faridkot. His quick explanation to Harjit Singh Randhawa, inspector general, Criminal Investigation Department (CID), who was conducting the proceedings, was that he had no power to grant licences. The authority lay vested in the office of the district magistrate. The police could only make recommendations. So, he escaped action. But Simranjit was and remains a zealot. 'Bhindranwale shared an ideology with my father: a separate homeland for the Sikhs,' writes his daughter, Pavit Kaur.[2]

For the next few days of my tour, I travelled the mofussil areas of Amritsar district. Any prolonged presence at a particular place would have attracted attention and that could be risky. In those days, government officials hesitated to venture into the border belt, and never did so without an armed escort. Militants ruled the roost, and even in the cities, the State writ ran tenuously. The hardliners were in de facto control of not only the Golden Temple, but were also freely operating from some other gurdwaras, including at the Darbar Sahib, Tarn Taran, Gurdwara Shri Khadoor Sahib, Gurdwara Sahibs at Baba Bakala, at Ramdas, and about forty other gurdwaras under the management of local committees.

My position as director, rural development and panchayats, I thought, provided a perfect alibi for my presence in the rural belt. To make it appear a routine visit, I included the adjoining border district of Gurdaspur in my itinerary, where my batch mate J.S. Maini was the district magistrate, and spent a night there. The subterfuge did not work. *Ajit,* the Punjabi daily, carried news about the impending transfer of Gurdev Singh. My name was mentioned as one of the likely successors.

I returned to Chandigarh on 28 May, stopping for a cup of tea at Jalandhar with N.S. Rattan, commissioner (appeals). A Brahmin convert to Sikhism, Rattan's father had served for long years at the Golden Temple. His ancestral house adjoining the Bunga Ramgarhia overlooked the Parikrama of the temple. He had spent his formative years playing around the place and I benefitted enormously from his briefing about the goings-on in the temple complex.

My tour of the border belt exposed me to the grim reality of the 'fringe' area of India abutting the international border with Pakistan. In Chandigarh, we in the directorate of rural development and panchayats had claimed credit—and we thought it was well deserved—for conducting peaceful elections to village panchayats only a few months earlier. However, at Khem Karan, Bhikhiwind, Chabhal, Pul Kanjari and in the communities along the border belt, village after village, it was the same story—I found that the extremists had bulldozed their way to victory of their nominees under duress, in some cases unanimously. It was not for nothing that the men who ruled India before Independence often spent days and months touring the countryside, on horseback, in boats and even on camels and elephants in inaccessible areas to know the conditions in which India and her people lived.

On my trip, I too learnt a bit of history. Pul Kanjari, a small, sleepy place on the international border with Pakistan, is so named after Moran, a Muslim dancing girl. She would perform for Maharaja Ranjit Singh when he commuted between Lahore and Amritsar. One night, while crossing the local canal built by Shah Jahan to carry water from the Ravi to the Shalimar Gardens in Lahore, Moran accidently dropped her sandals in the canal and could not reach on time to perform. Ranjit Singh, distraught over the delay, ordered that a bridge be built over the canal. It is called *pul* (bridge) *kanjari* (literally meaning 'whore') because dancing girls were socially not respected those days, but Moran obviously had enough clout with the maharaja to have a bridge built over the canal.

Unwittingly, Moran was the trigger for events that set a precedent and influenced the course of Sikh history. Her liaison with the maharaja did not go down well with the then jathedar of the Akal Takht, the indomitable Baba Phula Singh, who was quick to award *tankha* (punishment) to Maharaja Ranjit Singh for the breach of the moral code of conduct. The maharaja was to be flogged with a leash. Ranjit Singh submitted himself before the *sangat*, a public congregation of Sikhs at the Golden Temple, to receive the punishment, but was spared the humiliation by a pardon.[3]

The Sikh sovereign's submission to the ecclesiastical court of the Golden Temple was to be followed by many powerful men in history, including independent India's head of state President Giani Zail Singh and Punjab's chief minister Surjit Singh Barnala. But that is for the chapters ahead.

2

On to Amritsar

IT WAS AN UNEQUIVOCAL ORDER TO RELINQUISH MY POST AS director of rural development and panchayats in Chandigarh on the afternoon of 1 June 1984. The government notification further directed that I 'take over charge of his new assignment as Deputy Commissioner, Amritsar, vice S. Gurdev Singh, IAS, on the forenoon of 5 June 1984, by curtailing his joining time'.

The transfer order gave no latitude to me or the incumbent deputy commissioner Gurdev Singh to decide the date or time of joining duty, nor did it clarify if he would join back service in Amritsar at the end of his three-month leave, as had originally been proposed. However, the post of director, rural development, was not filled and only an ad hoc arrangement was made by giving additional charge to another officer in my place. That left scope for my return to Chandigarh at the end of Gurdev Singh's leave.

On 2 June, when I reached home after an uneventful walk in Leisure Valley that adjoined my house, there was an urgent message from Chief Secretary K.D. Vasudeva. When I called him, Vasudeva directed me, 'You need to proceed to Amritsar today.' I pleaded, 'But Sir, Gurdev Singh is going on leave from 6 June and we had proposed to hand over and take over charge on 5 June. The government order also directs so.'

Vasudeva, usually congenial and accommodating, was not willing to concede more than twelve hours to me, 'Leave tomorrow morning at the latest and take charge.' There was finality in his voice as he added, 'Gurdev will be intimated.' The change in schedule put me in a spin. I hurriedly packed two suitcases and left for Amritsar the next morning.

I had no inkling that the army was on the move. There was no briefing from the state government. The chief secretary or the home secretary gave no details or reasons for rushing me to Amritsar; I had only the terse telephonic directive of the chief secretary. There was urgency in Vasudeva's voice, and I mistakenly surmised that Gurdev Singh had had another spat with the CRPF—something he was known to do—and that was the reason the government wanted me in Amritsar at the earliest. As it turned out, the situation was far graver.

Wading through police checkposts dotting the route, it took me a little longer than the usual four hours to reach the Circuit House in Amritsar. From the time of my arrival, Gurdev Singh and I were together most of the time.

In Punjab 3 June was a public holiday. 'The Hindu infidel of Goindwal on the Beas', as Jahangir called Guru Arjan Dev, was martyred on that day. In his autobiography *Tuzuk-e-Jahangiri*, Emperor Jahangir described the Guru as a Hindu masquerading as a saint, misleading the people. 'For a long time,' Jahangir wrote, 'I had been thinking that either this false trade should be eliminated or that he should be brought into the embrace of Islam . . . I ordered his possessions and goods confiscated and him executed.'[1] The Guru was brutally tortured at Lahore fort, and on his refusal to convert to

Islam, Jahangir ordered Governor Murtaza Khan to put the 'kafir' to death. Guru Arjan Dev became the first Sikh martyr.

The Guru's martyrdom day is commemorated every year since then. And 1984 was no exception. A large number of pilgrims had gathered from all over the country at the Golden Temple, at Gurdwara Ramsar and at Baba Deep Singh Shaheed, where the Guru's martyrdom is traditionally observed with deep reverence.

For some inexplicable reason, Gurdev Singh had imposed a curfew in the walled city on 3 June from 11 a.m. till 5 p.m. and then extended it from 9 p.m. the same day till 5 June. That confined a large number of pilgrims inside the temple precinct and made it impossible for the outstation pilgrims who had visited on the martyrdom day to leave the temple complex. Later, he told me that he had merely acted under the home secretary's directions.

The choice of the sacred day for deploying the army was a blunder. Some Sikh organizations never miss an opportunity to draw parallels between the launch of Operation Blue Star on the Guru's martyrdom day and Gen. Dyer's choice of 13 April, Baisakhi, for the Jallianwala Bagh massacre, both the days being of immense significance.

On 3 June, Amritsar was quiet due to the curfew. At the high-roofed colonial-style Circuit House, Gurdev Singh and I were maundering over nothing in particular, sipping cups of tea, when a motorcycle rider in army uniform arrived. He insisted on seeing the district magistrate in person and said that he carried an urgent demi-official (DO) letter to deliver. He was escorted to us. After a quick read, Gurdev Singh passed the epistle to me, muttering, 'I did not requisition him', meaning Brar. Under law, a district magistrate is empowered to call on the army for assistance to civil authorities to deal with any exigency. However, neither had Gurdev Singh requisitioned army help, nor was there any intimation from the state government about summoning the troops.

The demi-official letter was from Maj. Gen. K.S. Brar, AVSM, Vir Chakra, GOC of the Meerut-based 9 Infantry Division, addressed to Gurdev Singh. It announced the general's arrival in Amritsar as the 'overall commander of all regular army units and paramilitary forces'. The general had been assigned the duty of aiding the civil administration with the prevailing law and order situation and dealing with extremist menace. He further intimated that he had convened a meeting of the senior civil and army officers to get to know each other, and invited Gurdev Singh to make himself available at 5 p.m. at the joint operation control room set up on the premises of the HQ of Panther Division.

Now, at least we knew that the army was officially out in aid to civil authority. However, who had requisitioned the troops or what exact task had been assigned to them was not clear. We speculated about these developments and tried to figure out Prime Minister Indira Gandhi's address to the nation the night before, where she had concluded her speech calling for peace and healing of wounds.

Gurdev Singh and I, both ignorant of the behind-the-scene developments, presumed that some amicable solution to the Punjab problem was in the offing and the army had been deployed as a precaution or maybe even as a pressure tactic. Gurdev Singh had been in direct touch with S.S. Sidhu, adviser to the governor, who was perceived to be close to the Gandhis, and he was confident that the Prime Minister was keen for a political settlement of the Punjab tangle. Much later, he was appointed governor, first of Manipur and then of Goa.

We heard the name 'Operation Blue Star' for the first time from Brar in the civil–military conference at 5 p.m. on 3 June. I was yet to take over charge of the district and had no official standing, but on Gurdev Singh's asking and to maintain continuity, I accompanied him to the meeting. From the civilian side, apart from Gurdev and I, those present in the rather large but spartanly furnished control room were Chaudhary Sube Singh, SSP, Amritsar; S.R. Sharma, additional DIG, Jalandhar Range; Pandit Harjit Singh, SP, CID; M.P.S. Aulakh, IPS, from the Intelligence Bureau (IB); G.S. Pandher, DIG Border

Security Force (BSF); and B.P. Tiwari, DIG, CRPF. Seated at the head of the long table was Brar, his body language as if censuring us, the civilian officers.

Brar briefed us about the task assigned to him; the objective given to 9 Infantry Division, he said, was to clear the Golden Temple complex of Bhindranwale and the armed militants. He informed us that the entire state would be brought under curfew from 9 p.m. on 3 June, and all vehicular movement would be suspended. This was confirmed later when Gurdev Singh received a TPM (wireless) message from the home secretary, directing all district magistrates in the state to enforce the curfew, starting 9 p.m. Only cattle could traverse unimpeded.

Brar disclosed that his troops had commenced an encirclement of the temple complex, which was to be tightened the next night. Brar's pronounced commanding stance soon landed him in dissension with G.S. Pandher, a 1964 batch IPS officer of the Manipur cadre who was on deputation as DIG, BSF, Amritsar. Pandher, like Brar, was an upright officer and a stickler for rules. It was that momentary flare-up, triggered by a personality mismatch between two of them, or perhaps by the way Brar ordered Pandher around, that found the two in an argument. Brar wanted both CRPF and BSF troops deployed around the temple to intermittently fire towards the fortifications in the complex, starting from the intervening night of 3 and 4 June. The intent was to draw out counter-fire from the militants, which would give away their precise positions on the battlements and the type of armaments deployed by them before the army actually moved in.

Pandher had handled insurgency in the north-east and had seen how inquiries were invariably instituted, post facto, and therefore wanted to secure himself, should he be subsequently questioned for resorting to unprovoked firing towards the temple. There was also the question of pricked religious sensibilities. Therefore, he declined to comply with Brar's directions unless given written orders.

His stand was that the BSF would open fire only if militants first fired at BSF troops, and that his men would not intentionally resort to unprovoked aggression. Pandher wanted written orders; the general would have none of it. Their differences, in fact, highlighted the incongruity in the approach of the civil service and the army on how to handle law and order contingencies.

Losing his cool, Brar roared, 'This is mutiny.' Pandher, however, did not budge and was naturally reported by the general to his senior command with a request to shift him. The BSF and CRPF had been placed under the operational command of the army. However, it seemed that Pandher had not been conveyed the required instructions by his HQ. It was a failure of coordination.

Pandher, in any case, did not want to serve under the general and sent a wireless request to his superiors seeking permission to proceed on leave. Birbal Nath, director general (DG), BSF, who had served as SSP Amritsar in 1966–67 and later as director general of police (DGP), Punjab, did not resist the army's request.

We did not get to see Pandher again when we met for the civil–military liaison conferences the next day. He had to face an inquiry for not obeying the oral orders of the general, but was eventually cleared of all charges and went on to become DGP, Manipur, and thereafter served the Government of India as DG, Bureau of Police Research and Development. He was awarded the President's Police Medal for Distinguished Service in 1996.

The clash between the general and the DIG, Pandher, resulted in a premature winding up of the perfunctory meeting on 3 June, with a resolve to meet again. There was little discussion regarding the respective roles the different government agencies were expected to play. The details of any assistance or coordination that the army expected from the civil administration were not spelt out. Overconfidence, lack of appreciation of the on-ground conditions and a noticeable disinclination to take the district administration on board characterized the general's stance.

Pandit Harjit Singh, SP, CID, however, gave his assessment in unambiguous terms that the militants, numbering about 400–500, would put up a determined resistance and fight to the finish should the army decide to enter the temple complex. He specified that the militants were armed to the teeth and possessed automatic weapons, including machine guns, though the exact number was not known. He put the number of innocent pilgrims inside the complex at around 1,500.

Harjit Singh's family were Brahmin converts to Sikhism. A level-headed and erudite officer, he had anchored sources of information deep among the militants and one could safely rely on him for a dispassionate assessment. In the meeting, he was unequivocal in conveying his appraisal of the situation, but being mild-mannered, he did not force his point on the general, who was unwilling to believe him. Harjit Singh was also handicapped by his rank—he was just an SP, equivalent to a major in the army.

Gurdev Singh and M.P.S. Aulakh endorsed Harjit Singh's overview of the situation. The general, however, brushed aside the threat perception from the militants by saying, 'Once the militants see my *kale bhoots* [the commandos dressed in black dungarees] they will be on the run.'

Gurbachan Jagat, who was then DIG, CID, in Chandigarh, told me that he had personally briefed Lt Gen. R.S. Dayal, security adviser to the governor, Punjab, and chief of staff, Western Command, about the weaponry held by the militants and their tenacity to fight and die as martyrs. There were also media reports of the stockpiling of arms inside the temple. But due note of these cautions was not taken before launching Operation Blue Star.

Subsequent to the operation, however, the forces complained of lack of information and intelligence. Pranab Mukherjee, who was then the finance minister and a member of the sub-committee of the Union Cabinet that decided to storm the temple complex, has written, 'No one anticipated the protracted resistance.'[2] He has stated that intelligence and the army both were confident they would neutralize the militants without much difficulty, an erroneous presumption which cost the forces heavily.

I wish the army and the Central government had listened to the field officers, but then, the civilian officers were 'suspects' guilty of dereliction of duty, which had led to the militants accumulating weapons and successfully fortifying the temple complex. It was a total collapse of law and order in Punjab.

On the night of 3 June, I shifted from the Circuit House to a room at the official residence of the deputy commissioner on Gurdev Singh's invite. He had brought forward his departure from Amritsar to the morning of 4 June due to the curfew and suspension of traffic in the state. He signed the relinquishing report and my joining report as deputy commissioner early on the morning of 4 June before he got into the car to leave for Delhi. He was escorted all the way to the Punjab–Haryana border by a police pilot jeep, clearing the army and police barricades and roadblocks. He left the district and his household luggage at the official residence under my charge from the morning of 4 June.

Rumours, however, have an uncanny persuasive quality about them. Tittle-tattle had it that Gurdev Singh had been removed from his post. Mark Tully, the famed BBC correspondent, in his éclat account *Amritsar: Mrs Gandhi's Last Battle*, narrates that Gurdev Singh lifted the curfew while the army operation was on, resulting in the escape of militants from the complex. 'When news of the young men's escape reached the army, the Generals were livid. They ordered curfew to be re-imposed and immediately transferred the District Commissioner, the senior local administrator, who throughout the last months of the crisis had often seemed more loyal to Bhindranwale than to the government.'[3]

This is far from the truth. The curfew imposed by Gurdev Singh on the morning of 3 June was lifted by me, the new district magistrate, on the evening of 6 June, after due deliberation with the army. Gurdev Singh was in Delhi then to catch a flight to the US. The perils of writing history that is not based on facts are many, and there is also a missive I have for my tribe, the civil servants—if you lose credibility, almost any rumour sticks to you.

A similarly erroneous account of Gurdev Singh's transfer has been given by another journalist, Jagtar Singh, formerly of *the Indian Express*, who in his otherwise-well-researched work *Khalistan Struggle: A Non-Movement*, has written, 'At a meeting of the senior officers at Kotwali, Amritsar Deputy Commissioner Gurdev Singh Brar questioned as to on whose orders had the CRPF opened fire on the shrine. In protest, he proceeded on leave and was replaced by Ramesh Inder Singh.'[4]

The press censorship and sudden imposition of the curfew led to many rumours about Gurdev Singh. One such rumour was that he had refused to sign the requisition order to deploy the army to storm the temple, and therefore was posted out of Amritsar, and some added that he was arrested for it. This falsehood has been perpetuated for years by certain radical elements even after Gurdev Singh appeared in a joint interview with me on TV and confirmed that he was never asked to requisition the army, nor did he ever refuse to sign any order.

After assuming charge as district magistrate, I wanted to brief A.S. Pooni, home secretary, Punjab, but the telephone exchange declined to put my call through. On inquiry, I was informed that under instructions from the army, outstation calls were not allowed—not even the call of the district magistrate to the state's home secretary. When I tried to speak to the SSP and my district food and supplies officer and some other junior officials, I found that all telephone, telegram and teleprinter services in Amritsar had been suspended, even for senior government officers.

In the joint civil–army conference at the HQ of 9 Division on 4 June, I raised the issue of the disconnected telephone lines: How was I to run the curfew-bound district without communicating with my officers, both senior and junior? Brar, however, bluntly declined to restore the telephone services for at least another two or three days. I could use the army exchange in an emergency, he said. But with all other telephones dead, my connectivity to the army exchange would enable me to contact only the army hierarchy and not the civilian chain of administration. I needed to be in constant communication with my district officials, who were to act on my instructions, but there was no link with them. In the curfewed city, they were in quarantine.

The situation was even more pitiable for residents of the area, particularly those residing in the lanes around the temple complex. Exchange of fire between the militants and paramilitary forces had started from 1 June and it intensified with the army's deployment. A stray bullet killed one Prem Wati, a close relation of R.P. Chatrath, an executive engineer of the UBD Canal system, who lived near the temple. The tragedy underscored the imperative of a planned evacuation of the civilian population from the area around the temple before commencement of army action.

I raised the issue in the civil–military conference, and wanted the task of evacuating civilian residents to be prioritized. Brar agreed with me. Roadways buses were earmarked for this task and kept ready, but the extrication of civilians from the narrow lanes around the temple never materialized. There was continuous exchange of fire between the militants and the troops, and the events moved so fast that the troops had no time to organize the evacuation, which became riskier by the hour, with the two sides aggressively engaging in rapid fire. The civilians were left to their own fate.

The state government was kept informed of these developments through TPM messages sent on the police wireless network, but there was no response from the home department. The deafening silence of the state HQ and my immediate boss, the divisional commissioner, Jalandhar, I thought, was nothing but willing abnegation of civil authority. Later on, I learnt that A.S. Pooni was despondent over the army operation and had gone on leave. So had Dinesh Chandra, the divisional commissioner, Jalandhar, though for different reasons. It was only on 7 June that N.S. Rattan, the commissioner (appeals), was ordered to officiate in place of the regular commissioner and subsequently deputed to visit Amritsar.

Here I was, not even twenty-four hours into my new job, dealing with two lieutenant generals camping in Amritsar—Sundarji and Ranjit Dayal—and three major generals, K.S. Brar in the Golden Temple, J.S. Jamwal in the sub-divisions of Amritsar, Ajnala and Baba Bakala, and Shamsher Singh in Patti and parts of Tarn Taran, along with the thousands of troops that had swarmed the district, with no possibility of communication with my seniors or juniors. Punjab had turned olive green—the fauji colour—and the khaki stood eclipsed.

3

The Trigger

It was a mystery murder. The assailant had stealthily accessed the well-secured precinct of the Nirankari Mandal in Delhi, assuming cover as a carpenter. Along with his tools and timber, he smuggled in a sniper rifle, a .30 carbine, and waited. On 24 April 1980, he laid ambush on an unoccupied room of the mandal guest house. The window in the room gave him an unhindered line of sight to the vestibule where Baba Gurbachan Singh, head of the Nirankari Mandal, was to retire for the night.

As the Baba alighted from his Mercedes sedan, the assassin fired six shots, killing him on the spot and injuring two others, one of whom died later. At least two hand grenades were also thrown. In the melee that followed, the assassin quietly escaped through the window of the bathroom—he had removed its iron grill. Delhi Police took up the investigation but the crime had inter-state ramifications and was therefore transferred to the Central Bureau of Investigation (CBI).

Bhindranwale was suspected to have conspired in Baba Gurbachan Singh's murder. The CBI believed that the murder weapon was licensed in the name of Jagbir Singh, Bhindranwale's brother, and it had been acquired through a registered arms dealer in Moga, with the active facilitation of a senior police officer in Faridkot. Those days I was posted in Faridkot as additional district magistrate and was in charge of the arms licensing branch. The CBI sleuths landed up in my office and for a fortnight scanned all our records, seizing a few they suspected could be linked to the case.

Ranjit Singh, the main accused in the murder, surrendered in 1983. The trial court convicted him for life in 1993. A Division Bench of the Delhi High Court upheld the sentence. He had undergone nearly thirteen years in prison when the President of India remitted his remaining sentence in 1997. While he was undergoing the sentence, the SGPC appointed him to the exalted position of jathedar of the Akal Takht.

The roots of the Sikh–Nirankari conflict go back many decades. In the nineteenth century, Baba Dyal Das (1783–1855) had initiated the Nirankari Samparda (set-up), a puritanical pursuit within the Sikh faith. It was called Nirankari after the founder of Sikhism, Guru Nanak, who is addressed by Sikhs as 'Nanak, the Nirankari', the devotee of a formless god. The Nirankaris observed the tenets of Sikhism. However, two followers of Baba Dyal Das's movement—Buta Singh (1873–1944) and Avtar Singh (1899–1969)—broke off and set up a separate sect in 1929.

In 1947, post-Partition, both groups—the followers of Baba Dyal Das and the breakaway group of Avtar Singh—moved to India. The mainstream group shifted to Amritsar and also set up a Nirankari gurdwara in Chandigarh.

However, Baba Avtar Singh of the breakaway group shifted to Delhi in 1947 and registered a sect called the Sant Nirankari Mandal. His son, Gurbachan Singh, succeeded him in 1962. Devout Sikhs believe that the Nirankari Mandal has deviated from the tenets of the faith. The SGPC recognizes the right of every individual to profess the faith of his or her choice but holds that this right does not extend to committing blasphemy or heresy of another religion, and for this reason it holds the Delhi-based Nirankari Mandal responsible for such heterodox misconduct. The SGPC, in a white paper titled 'They Massacre Sikhs', has detailed the heretical deviations of the Nirankari Mandal from the Sikh faith.

The conflict between the Nirankaris and the Sikhs had been going on for a while, but Baba Gurbachan Singh's assassination was a direct consequence of the bloodbath enacted in Amritsar on 13 April 1978. On that day, thirteen Sikhs, three Nirankaris and two bystanders were killed in a tragedy that could have been prevented had the state machinery been vigilant.

Inexplicably, the district administration had allowed the Nirankaris to hold their annual meet in Amritsar. Given the history of Sikh–Nirankari discord, to allow a national-level Nirankari convention and permit a public procession through Amritsar, the seat of Sikhism, on Baisakhi—the day the Khalsa was created by Guru Gobind Singh in 1699—was, to say the least, begging for unrest, particularly as the Nirankaris were carrying firearms.

The undercurrents of the ongoing canonical conflict had materialized long ago in open skirmishes between the Nirankaris and a section of the Sikhs led by Sant Kartar Singh of the Bhindran Jatha. But these signals were ignored by the Amritsar administration as they permitted the Nirankaris to congregate on 13 April.[1]

Sikhs gather from all over the world to celebrate Baisakhi at the Golden Temple every year in April, and 1978 was no exception. The complex was brimming with devotees when the news of a Nirankari procession through the streets of Amritsar reached the Golden Temple. Two Sikh organizations, namely the Akhand Kirtani Jatha and the Damdami Taksal, in an impromptu decision, resolved to stage a protest. By that time, however, the Nirankari procession had passed through the town and terminated at the railway colony ground, the venue of their convention. So, about 250 Sikhs decided to march barefoot from the Golden Temple to the venue of the congregation in five jathas or groups.

Jiwan Singh Umranangal, a minister in Chief Minister P.S. Badal's Shiromani Akali Dal (SAD)–Janata Party ministry that ruled Punjab, unsuccessfully tried to persuade Bhindranwale and Fauja Singh of the Akhand Kirtani Jatha not to proceed to the railway colony. In fact, the protesters demanded that the minister direct the police to terminate the Nirankari congregation. The mild-mannered minister publicly evaded responsibility by saying that not even a Patwari would listen to him; what could one say of the deputy commissioner or the police chief? The minister also did not alert the district administration to the looming danger. The police, by then, were under the mistaken belief that the Nirankari procession had ended peacefully and all was well.

Bhindranwale stayed back at the temple while Fauja Singh led the Sikhs, mostly unarmed—though some were carrying the kirpan—to the railway colony ground. According to the account given to me by K.S. Janjua, the then district magistrate, Amritsar, Inspector Anoop Singh, assisted by about ten constables, intercepted the march about 300 yards from the venue around 12.30 p.m. He persuaded them not to proceed further and also requisitioned more police, but in the meantime stone-pelting started. At this stage, someone fired at the protesters, who charged their way forward towards the pandal. The deputy superintendent (DSP) in charge failed to control the situation with the small force at his command.

Anticipating opposition to their convention, the armed Nirankaris, some of them ex-servicemen, had come prepared. They opened fire, mostly from twelve bore guns, with deadly consequences. The outcome was a gruesome sight of blood and eighteen dead bodies.

Janjua was unaware of what was happening at the venue and received a police wireless message after the massacre was over. It was a public holiday and he was home. He quickly picked up S.R. Bunger,

IAS, additional district magistrate, and the two rushed to the spot. Gurbachan Jagat, SSP, Amritsar, had already reached the venue.

Immediately after the firing incident, Baba Gurbachan Singh shifted to the nearby Nirankari Bhavan but returned to the pandal soon thereafter and recommenced the religious discourse, as if all was normal. A few officials tried to thwart him but he carried on. Janjua climbed the rostrum, removed the microphone and forced the Baba to step down. That ended the convention. However, no arrests were made, nor any arms seized.

Chief Minister Badal was then in Bombay (now Mumbai), and he rushed to Amritsar the next day, accompanied by home secretary R.C. Kapila and Hit Abhilashi, a Janata Party minister in his Cabinet. At the Circuit House, the SGPC president, G.S. Tohra, and Jagdev Singh Talwandi, a senior Akali Dal leader, joined Badal, and inquired of the deputy commissioner as to why permission was granted to the Nirankaris to hold the meet. Janjua's explanation was that there was no disagreeable report from the CID or the district police. A written communication was received from the CID around 2 p.m. on 13 April but by then the clash had already taken place. Janjua also explained that two ministers belonging to the Janata Party had conveyed to the district administration their programme to attend the Nirankari convention, which implied that the government also had no reservations about it. Hit Abhilashi had, in fact, reached Amritsar and was waiting to proceed to the venue when the killings took place.

When Talwandi heard that Abhilashi was scheduled to participate in the Nirankari convention, he was enraged. Janjua told me that the mercurial Talwandi's right hand spontaneously reached for the kirpan, his eyes menacingly fixed on Abhilashi. Tohra and Badal calmed Talwandi down. Such were the passions and the tempers at that time. Abhilashi, however, could not escape the militants' wrath and was murdered in 1988.

Janjua was transferred out of Amritsar to the innocuous assignment of managing director (MD), Warehousing Corporation.

He was singled out because of his perceived proximity to Niranjan Singh, the deputy commissioner of Gurdaspur, which was next door.

Niranjan Singh was a leading light of the Nirankari Mandal and routinely preached his faith; in his case, the desired dividing line between his official position as the head of the district administration and a Nirankari had got blurred. The fact that he was posted at Gurdaspur, which had a history of Sikh–Nirankari conflict, is inexplicable. He was present on 13 April at the venue of the violence and rushed to Janjua's residence after the clash. It is alleged that he used his influence to ensure that Baba Gurbachan Singh was escorted to safety out of Amritsar to Delhi.

The incident set off a chain of clashes between Sikhs and Nirankaris at various places in Punjab and beyond, such as Kanpur, Delhi and Madhya Pradesh. The Communist Party of India (CPI), the Communist Party of India (Marxist) (CPI[M]), the Congress and even Akali stalwarts like Tohra and Talwandi demanded a judicial probe into the Amritsar clash. Had it been ordered, it may have defused the sentiments. However, for unknown 'administrative considerations' the state government did not order it.

The tragedy galvanized the Sikh radicals. The Akal Takht, on 10 June 1978, issued a *hukamnama*, a religious edict, to boycott the Nirankaris. It was a directive to socially ostracize them, and terminate '*roti beti di sanjh* (social relations)'. The SGPC and the Akali Dal demanded a ban on Nirankari religious books. The Punjab government outlawed the entry of Baba Gurbachan Singh into the state, but the order was set aside on 24 January 1979 by the Supreme Court.

The Amritsar killings and the subsequent developments were to change the course of Punjab's history. The radicals, steeped in the tradition of shaheedi, were ready for revenge. The perceived failure of the then governments to give justice may also have impelled them to take the law into their own hands and redeem the honour of the *panth*. Retribution and honour, after all, go together; slogans like '*Jithe lahu*

Singha da dullu, othe nishan kesari jhulu [The Kesari (Sikh) flag shall fly high wherever Sikh blood is spilt]' would now resonate through the memorial meetings that were held in various parts of the state. The selective killings of Nirankaris commenced soon thereafter.

The tragedy provided Bhindranwale an opportunity to emerge as the unchallenged numero uno of the anti-Nirankari movement. He called the Nirankaris 'Narakdharis'. He was a crusader, a committed puritanical who stood for '*Khalsa ji da bolbala*', or the pre-eminence of the panth, the Sikh community. Over a period of time, Bhindranwale eclipsed the Akalis, whose responses were modulated due to electoral constraints of not alienating non-Sikhs. The Akali Dal was in power in the state in coalition with the Janata Party that included the Jana Sangh.

Badal, a moderate Akali, came under ideological assault from fundamentalists like Tohra within his party. He was depicted as pro–Jana Sangh and pro–Morarji Desai, with the ulterior intent to retain political power in Punjab. Additionally, now he had to cope with the emerging assertion of the radical groups led by Bhindranwale, the All India Sikh Students Federation (AISSF) and a few others.

On 20 August 1978 in Amritsar, the radical groups launched a campaign to shut down Nirankari Bhavans in the state. The conflict sharpened the inter-religious feud and inter-community divisions in Punjab. The bulk of the followers of the Nirankari Mandal were and remain urban dwellers, both Hindus and mostly non-Jat Sikhs, while the preponderance of Bhindranwale's followers was rural Sikh peasantry, which forms the base of the Akali Dal.

A few Nirankaris were put on trial for the violence in Amritsar. The sessions court, Karnal, in Haryana, where the criminal case to try Baba Gurbachan Singh and others for the murders was transferred from Punjab, acquitted them in January 1980. Punjab came under President's Rule in April 1980, and Governor Jaisukh Lal Hathi did not appeal against the acquittal order of the judge. The governor's move has been imputed political motives by a few historians, as the

Nirankaris were perceived to be pro-Congress and had unswervingly backed the Emergency. The scuttling of the judicial process, however, only added to the Sikh outrage against the Nirankaris and the Central government.

From the group clashes spurred by mass emotions running at fever pitch, the conflict quickly climaxed into targeted killings of Nirankaris, their sympathizers and government officials perceived to be pro-Nirankari. In Punjab, between 1981 and June 1984, there were more than thirty-four gun and bomb attacks on Nirankaris.

The Murder

The April 1978 clash in Amritsar was followed by another murder that sent shock waves through Punjab. Lala Jagat Narain, a Chopra khatri and a Congress leader, an Arya Samaji and the chief editor and proprietor of the Jalandhar-based *Hind Samachar* group of newspapers, was killed on 9 September 1981.

Jagat Narain was scheduled to address the Nirankari congregation in Amritsar on 13 April 1978, and he had subsequently given pro-Nirankari evidence in the trial court in which he had debunked the prosecution case. His testimony helped in the acquittal of the accused.

In an obvious act of retribution, he was daringly shot dead on the national highway near Ludhiana. The two assailants, riding a Royal Enfield Bullet motorcycle (the 3-horsepower motorcycle was to become an iconic transport for terrorists in Punjab), overtook Jagat Narain's Fiat car and pumped bullets into him from a .45 PB revolver, killing him on the spot.

Why did the militants pick an octogenarian as their victim? It was a symbolic act that triggered both fear and concomitant bloodshed. Lala Jagat Narain had emerged as a symbol of Hindu revivalism and was an Arya Samaji icon. Through his biting editorials he had crusaded against the demand for a Punjabi Suba, and led a campaign prompting Punjabi Hindus to declare Hindi as their mother tongue.

When the Nirankari–Sikh issue assumed public conflict, he positioned his newspaper against the Sikh fundamentalists. His larger-than-life presence through the media organization that he owned gave the unmistaken impression that he was pro-Nirankari and against Sikh sentiments. His killing was meant to be a warning signal to others of his ilk; it was also intended to sharpen the Hindu–Sikh divide and widen the ongoing Nirankari conflict into Sikhs versus Hindus.

And that did happen. Narain's murder brought Hindus out on to the streets, resulting in shutdowns in Punjab's cities, hartals, public demonstrations, stone-pelting and even attacks on the premises of *Akali Patrika* and *Daily Ajit*, two leading Punjabi newspapers published from Jalandhar. Pillorying of the Punjabi newspapers was viewed by Sikhs as Hindu assertion of an already existing cleavage in the vernacular media of the state. The vernacular media took strong opposing stands for reasons of ideological certitude, or, as some allege, for commercial reasons to enlarge their circulation base among their respective communities.

4

Bhindranwale Arrested

In hindsight, it was a heedless and hasty move. Bhindranwale was arrested, but had to be let off within days because there was no evidence against him. His nephew, Swaran Singh, was an accused in Lala Jagat Narain's murder and the investigators suspected that Bhindranwale was a co-conspirator and abettor.

On 12 September 1981 the prosecutor procured Bhindranwale's arrest warrants from a judicial court. That was when the trouble began. The militants retaliated on 20 September, killing innocent people in Jalandhar and Tarn Taran. The Jalandhar shootout was the first incident of indiscriminate mass murders in the state. Three motorcycle-riding men opened fire in a marketplace, leaving four dead and another twelve injured. A police picket was also attacked, resulting in police firing and deaths.

Among the first to express reservation about Bhindranwale's arrest was none other than the then Union home minister, Zail Singh. On 13 September, Singh rang up Birbal Nath, DGP, Punjab, and directed him to 'reconsider the question of arrest of Sant Ji'.[1] But Darbara Singh, the chief minister, was adamant that Bhindranwale must be arrested. Besides, the court had granted an arrest warrant that had to be complied with.

Assisted by then Haryana Chief Minister Bhajan Lal, Zail Singh is said to have surreptitiously sounded Bhindranwale out about his impending arrest. That enabled Bhindranwale to slip away on the night of 13 September 1981 from Chando Kalan in Hisar district, where he was camping for Amrit Parchar to Chowk Mehta, covering a distance of more than 200 kilometres, unnoticed. By the time the Punjab Police, led by DIG D.S. Mangat, reached Chando Kalan, Bhindranwale was beyond reach. Bhajan Lal helped Bhindranwale escape from Haryana to avoid trouble in his state, while Zail Singh was settling scores with Darbara Singh, if not directly assisting Bhindranwale.

At Chando Kalan, Mangat and SSP D.R. Bhatti were challenged by Bhindranwale's followers. In the melee, two buses belonging to the Damdami Taksal were burnt. It was alleged that the police, frustrated at not finding Bhindranwale, had set them on fire. Holy Sikh scriptures kept in the buses too got burnt. The Haryana government instituted a judicial inquiry into the incident.

Bhindranwale was not the kind of person to forget or forgive, and certainly not when it came to the sacrilegious burning of Sikh scriptures. Two years later, on 21 September 1983, while Bhatti alighted from his official car and approached the stairs leading to the office of the SSP, Ludhiana, he was shot at in full public view. He was injured, but his gunman was killed. The message to the police was clear: Keep away, or else!

After the Chando Kalan fiasco, Darbara Singh, apprehensive about the police's ability to execute Bhindranwale's arrest warrant, instructed the then chief secretary, Paramjeet Singh, and DGP Birbal Nath to approach Lt Gen. S.K. Sinha, GOC Western Command, at Chandimandir for army assistance, and sought armoured personnel carriers (APCs), which the police could use at the Chowk Mehta gurdwara while carrying out the arrest. The army, however, declined the state request. The chief secretary was politely reminded that arresting criminals was the job of the police and not the army. In any case, the police had no training to use APCs, the chief secretary was told.

The chief minister, however, did not give up. He upgraded his entreaty to the Prime Minister's Office (PMO), which promptly instructed the then defence secretary P.K. Kaul to comply. Gen. K.V. Krishna Rao had taken over as army chief in June 1981 but was away on tour to Nagaland. In his absence, the army HQ conveyed the instructions of the defence secretary to the lower command. An infantry battalion based in Amritsar was alerted to move to Chowk Mehta to affect the arrest. However, Lt Gen. S.K. Sinha intervened with Gen. Rao and the move to involve the army was scuttled. The generals believed, and rightly so, that the army should not be involved in such civil affairs.

Left to handle the situation himself, it was Darbara Singh's turn to play dirty. He opted to negotiate with Bhindranwale his own surrender. J.S. Anand, the then DIG, CID, was first deputed to Chowk Mehta to confab with him. However, on seeing the DIG, Bhindranwale refused to parley with a *patit* (apostate) Sikh—Anand supported a trimmed beard and was not a *sabat surat* Sikh. A second emissary, an SP-rank sabat surat Sikh (one who sports the five Ks of Sikhism: *kesh*, *kangha*, *kara*, *kachera* and kirpan) had better luck and was successful in persuading Bhindranwale to surrender. He chose the date himself: He would surrender on 20 September.

On that day, as per his wishes, Bhindranwale was driven to Amritsar by a senior officer of Punjab state in his official car and brought back to Chowk Mehta after he had his holy dip in the sarowar (pool of nectar) at the Golden Temple and paid his obeisance.

Bhindranwale returned from Amritsar before the break of dawn. By then, a large crowd of followers had collected at Chowk Mehta. Akali leaders, including Tohra, Akal Takht jathedar Gurdial Singh

Ajnoha, pro-Congress Delhi Gurdwara Committee chief jathedar Santokh Singh and many others, also reached the venue of the public gathering—it was an opportunity to earn political capital. In fiery public speeches they espoused Bhindranwale's cause and lambasted the state government. A criminal matter pending in the court of law assumed the colour of a political slugfest.

As the rally concluded, Bhindranwale accompanied the police to the state guest house which was to serve as a detention centre. At his arrest, the large crowd at Chowk Mehta turned violent, clashing with the police and the BSF with swords and lathis. To control the mob, the police opened fire, which resulted in the death of eight persons. This set off a chain of violent events in the state, with the state government eventually caving in.

The court where Bhindranwale was produced remanded him to police custody for custodial interrogation, and during this period he was detained in government rest houses, first at Bessain and thereafter at Garhi. At the end of the period of police remand, he was confined for a few days in judicial custody at the Central Jail, Ferozepur. The officiating deputy commissioner, Shivinder Brar, had a ticklish situation at hand—Bhindranwale declined to eat jail food and insisted that be served food cooked by a Gursikh (a baptized Sikh). The jail manuals do not permit service from outside.

The ingenuity of the administration, however, was remarkable; Shivinder, the good fellow that he was, persuaded Bhindranwale to have his *garwai* (attendant) with him. The garwai was arrested under what is popularly called in Punjab 107/151 (Section 107 and 151 of the CrPC) for the possibility of breach of peace, and sent to the jail to keep Bhindranwale company. Now Bhindranwale had food cooked by a Gursikh and Shivinder had peace of mind.

The police, however, failed to find evidence against Bhindranwale. He was released unconditionally on 15 October 1981 after twenty-five days of police and judicial detention. The credibility of the government took a severe beating, and the episode also divided people on communal lines. While some viewed that Bhindranwale had been wrongly let off, others felt that he was arrested erroneously and therefore rightly released by the court. The flip-flop in the arrest and the subsequent release of Bhindranwale emboldened the radicals.

Why was he arrested if there was no or inadequate evidence against him? His release by the court and the earlier police firing at Chowk Mehta at the time of his surrender forced the state government to appoint a judicial commission of inquiry to probe the alleged police excesses. Justice Pritam Singh Pattar, a retired judge, Punjab High Court, was notified on 27 October 1981 to inquire into circumstances leading to the police firing which resulted in deaths on 20 September at Chowk Mehta. Pattar gave the police a clean chit on 9 May 1984 but the officers were kept on tenterhooks for over two years, affecting their morale, while the radicals drummed up the charge of state excesses.

After his release, an emboldened Bhindranwale toured Punjab, and even visited Delhi and Bombay with his armed followers. He went to Delhi on 21 December 1981 in connection with the *bhog* of Jathedar Santokh Singh, a pro-Congress Sikh leader who was assassinated by his political rival, Pritam Singh Sandhu, a member of the Delhi Gurdwara Prabandhak Committee. At this bhog, Bhindranwale met Zail Singh and Buta Singh, and some of them allegedly touched his feet as a mark of respect. The communist leader Harkishan Singh Surjeet was to lament that Bhindranwale stayed in Delhi with about a hundred armed followers 'as the guest of the Congress (I)-supported Delhi Gurdwara Prabandhak Committee, and in spite of the demands made by the Opposition, no effort was made to collect the unlicensed weapons. This happened right under the nose of the Central government'.[2]

Arrest of Amrik Singh

The Punjab turmoil took yet another critical turn with the arrest and subsequent acquittal of Bhai Amrik Singh, president of the All India Sikh Students Federation and a close aide of Bhindranwale.

Some unidentified Sikhs had fired at Joginder Singh Shant, the propaganda secretary of the Amritsar Nirankari Mandal on 27 June 1982. It was suspected that Amrik Singh was behind this attempt to murder. Even the police believed that Amrik Singh was out to spread terror, and therefore a decision was made to arrest him. He was to be picked up in the first week of July from Ludhiana, where he was scheduled to appear in a court case.

However, the elaborate plan to arrest him failed, as Amrik Singh did not turn up in Ludhiana that day. Chief Minister Darbara Singh, acting against his own police, 'had cautioned Amrik Singh to desist visiting Ludhiana in view of the dragnet laid by police', so disclosed the then director general of Punjab Police, Birbal Nath.[3] What Darbara Singh's motivation was in acting the way he did is difficult to say. Was he attempting a reconciliation with Bhindranwale after he had been attacked by militants on 21 January in Panchhata village?

Amrik Singh was finally arrested on 19 July 1982 in Amritsar without the knowledge of the chief minister, who was in Shimla. 'He [CM] was informed only after he [Amrik Singh] was arrested,' disclosed Birbal Nath.[4]

Amrik Singh's arrest enraged Bhindranwale and he launched an agitation for his release. Starting 19 July, fifty-one persons sat on daily dharna outside the office of the deputy commissioner, Amritsar, to seek Amrik Singh's release. Three days later, on 21 July, two more aides of Bhindranwale, Baba Thara Singh and Ram Singh, were arrested. Bhindranwale intensified the protests. He shifted to Guru Nanak Niwas in the Golden Temple to monitor the agitation, and as it turned out, stayed put in the temple precincts till death. His body was carried to the cremation ground on 7 June 1984 from the Akal Takht, where he had shifted his residence from Guru Nanak Niwas on 15 December 1983.

Earlier, on 24 April 1982, the Akali Dal had launched a morcha from Kapoori to protest against the Sutlej–Yamuna link (SYL) canal that was to carry water to Haryana, under the command of moderate

Sikh leader Sant Harchand Singh Longowal of the Shiromani Akali Dal (SAD-L). On the arrest of Amrik Singh and others, Longowal extended his support to Bhindranwale. On 26 July, he castigated the government for arresting the innocent Sikhs. This brought the two sants—Longowal and Bhindranwale—closer. To strengthen their respective agitations, they coalesced them into the Dharam Yudh Morcha. Thus, the anti-Nirankari offensive that was being spearheaded by Bhindranwale in association with the Babbar Khalsa, a militant organization, and the Akhand Kirtani Jatha, a radical religious group, now joined hands with the moderate Akali Dal (L).

There could be four possible explanations to why the moderate Akali Dal joined hands with Bhindranwale and the radical elements. First, the response to the Kapoori Morcha was tepid, despite leftist parties extending support to it. Second, Bhindranwale's shifting to the Golden Temple was viewed by Akalis as a threat to their own hegemony over Sikh affairs; thus they aimed to neutralize him. Third, the sacred space of the temple was logistically better suited to anchor the morcha; it was expected to evoke an augmented response from Sikhs. Fourth, the Akali leadership felt that the unification of Sikh forces was the need of the hour.

Jagdev Singh Talwandi, a mercurial Sikh leader heading a faction of the Akali Dal, the SAD (T), was spearheading yet another agitation, seeking the implementation of the Anandpur Sahib Resolution. On 28 July, on an appeal from SGPC president Tohra, Talwandi accepted the captaincy of Longowal and joined the common Dharam Yudh Morcha. That brought together Bhindranwale, SAD (L), SAD (T) and Tohra on a common platform. The genesis of the morcha, however, lay in the earlier call given by the World Sikh Convention in July 1981 for such an agitation to seek 'justice' for the panth.

The word *dharam* means righteous but in common parlance people interpret 'dharam yudh' as 'religious war' and not a righteous cause. For the Akali Dal, in any case, religion and politics are inseparable;

historically the Akalis have always used religious inspiration in politics to mobilize Sikhs, even when the cause is purely political and secular. The campaign for the Punjabi Suba and the opposition to Indira Gandhi's Emergency are two examples of this.

The nomenclature of the morcha—Dharam Yudh—together with the shifting of its HQ to the Golden Temple, where the Akali Dal had its office, gave the stir a sectarian imprint, despite its secular, economic and political demands. It minimized the prospects of non-Sikh participation and that eventually lent the agitation its Sikh ethno-national character.

Longowal was the designated 'dictator' of the amalgamated Dharam Yudh Morcha. He was a well-respected leader but his mild nature and affable disposition was not what dictators are made of. To make matters intractable for him, the morcha was not monolithic: It was a loose coalition of different and often competing forces that cramped and at times even challenged Longowal's authority. The disparate leaders with diverse objectives and motivations had come together to imbue a seemingly common Sikh cause and their demands with secular shades.

Ironically, Amrik Singh and Baba Thara Singh, whose arrests had brought the Sikh leadership together, were both acquitted by the court in July 1983. They remained in Gurdaspur Jail till 6 August and were then brought to Amritsar to be produced in the court. The police had planned to rearrest them after they were formally set free. However, a large crowd of their admirers had gathered outside the court. Amrik Singh and Baba Thara Singh were whisked away by the mob to the Golden Temple from the court premises, evading attempts by the heavily deployed force that had ringed the court area to rearrest them.

Sarabjit Singh, SSP, Amritsar, had deputed Surjit Singh, SP, to rearrest Amrik Singh and Baba Thara Singh when they were brought to the court, but the SP slipped away from the scene on the pretext that a senior police officer visiting Amritsar from Chandigarh had summoned him to the Guru Nanak Dev University guest house for a meeting. Sarabjit was held responsible and posted out of Amritsar. He told me that an uncomplimentary entry was made in his Annual Confidential Report (ACR) for the year, which, however, was not conveyed to him as required under the service rules. That was how he escaped unscathed.

With the release of Amrik Singh and Thara Singh, the prime reason why Bhindranwale had commenced his morcha was resolved. However, by now Bhindranwale had gained ascendency in the ethno-national movement and centrality in the fight for the Sikh cause to disengage himself from the movement at that stage. He became the driver of the movement with Amrik Singh as his chief lieutenant, who coordinated the radical elements.

The arrest and subsequent release of Amrik Singh and his companions was yet another instance of the lackadaisical administration of law and order in the state that helped fuel the Punjab turmoil.

The Water Dispute

The very name Punjab, the land of five rivers, affirms its riparian rights, its economy's extraordinary dependence on agriculture. The Central Ground Water Board and Water Resources Directorate projected (in March 2017) that in another twenty to twenty-five years the state may exhaust its underground water resources, evoking instinctive fear and consequently making every resident of the state an interested party in the inter-state water conflict.

The Kapoori agitation was a product of such fear. The Punjab Reorganization Act, 1966, had provided for the sharing of river waters between Punjab and Haryana. On 27 March 1976, while the nation was under Emergency, Prime Minister Indira Gandhi intervened to notify the inter-state water shares. Punjab and Haryana were given 3.5 million acre feet (MAF) each. However, another 8 MAF was allotted to non-riparian Rajasthan and 0.2 MAF to Delhi. The then chief minister of Punjab, Zail Singh, wrote to the Prime Minister to reconsider her decision, but his plea was ignored.

Before the award could be executed, Indira Gandhi lost the elections in March 1977. Her successor, Morarji Desai, on a request from Haryana, held a meeting with the chief ministers of Punjab, Haryana and Rajasthan but did not implement Indira Gandhi's decision, reportedly as he found the inter-se allocation to the states discriminatory. Haryana, therefore, moved the Supreme Court in 1979, seeking implementation of Indira Gandhi's award. The Akali government that had assumed office in Punjab by then also filed a suit in the Supreme Court, challenging Indira Gandhi's award and the Punjab Reorganization Act, 1966. The matter was pending in the Supreme Court for judicial adjudication, when Indira Gandhi returned to power in January 1980 and the Akali-led government in Punjab, which enjoyed an overwhelming majority in the assembly, was dismissed by her in February 1980. In the elections to the Punjab assembly that followed, the Congress won a majority and Darbara Singh of the Congress became chief minister.

With both Punjab and Haryana under Congress chief ministers, Indira Gandhi directed the state governments to withdraw their pending suits from the Supreme Court and imposed an agreement on them. On 8 April 1982 she inaugurated the digging work of the SYL canal at Kapoori that was to carry water from Punjab to Haryana. This provided cause to the Akalis to launch a Nehar Roko Morcha from Kapoori.

This was an emotional issue, for it effected the livelihood of agrarian Punjab, and should have been left for adjudication to the Supreme Court, where the matter was pending. Its withdrawal from the Supreme Court and the forced resolution was a mistake. It provoked the Punjab peasantry and projected Indira Gandhi as anti-Punjab.

The Nehar Roko agitation, it may also be mentioned, was preceded by talks, the third in a series, between Prime Minister Indira Gandhi and the Akalis at Parliament House on 5 April 1982.[5]

From all accounts, an agreement was more or less reached but was stymied due to the impending election to the sixth Vidhan Sabha in Haryana due in June 1982. The Congress, at that stage, could not risk an agreement on the water issue that could send a negative signal to Haryana voters. The talks failed and the Akalis went ahead with Nehar Roko.

The Kapoori stir was anchored on an economic issue— the sharing of the river waters of Punjab. Secular leftist parties like the CPI(M) had joined hands with the Akali Dal, though the CPI and other political parties which were also invited by the Akalis to join the stir stayed away. However, once Longowal moved the morcha from Kapoori to the Golden Temple, the CPI(M) left the SYL agitation and joined the CPI and the Bharatiya Janata Party (BJP) to criticize the shift of the agitation to a religious place. Harkishan Singh Surjeet, the CPI(M) leader, called it a 'misconceived morcha'. Locating it in the temple precinct certainly was.

5

The Administrative Collapse

DIG A.S. ATWAL LAY DEAD, HIS BODY STRETCHED OUT ON THE ground at the main entrance to the Golden Temple. In his lifeless hand he clutched the karah prasad he had received as a blessing to carry to his family.

On 25 April 1983 he had gone to the temple to pay obeisance while on an official tour to Amritsar. When he came out, an unidentified terrorist shot him dead in broad daylight. His personal security officer and the driver standing next to his official car parked on the road a few yards away fled. So did a group of policemen deployed at some distance—there were about 100 of them in the area, some armed. The shopkeepers near the temple shut shops in panic as people ran for shelter. The killer strolled back to the Sarai complex at the eastern end of the Golden Temple precinct that consists of a number of guest houses, including Guru Nanak Niwas, and the administrative/office buildings of the SGPC. Hundreds of pilgrims were eyewitnesses to the crime and so was a journalist who saw the killers escape into the complex. The journalist rushed to Longowal and narrated the entire incident to him.

A few minutes later, on receiving the information, Surjit Singh Bains, who had succeeded A.S. Atwal as SSP, Amritsar, on 18 April 1982 rang up Chandigarh, seeking orders on what to do. Chief Minister Darbara Singh, in turn, sought directions from P.C. Alexander, principal secretary to the Prime Minister. That day, Prime Minister Indira Gandhi was on a tour of Rajasthan. For two hours, Atwal lay dead outside the holiest of holy Sikh shrines as Delhi pondered over its options.

Finally, when the order came, it was that the police should not enter the Sarai complex. Darbara Singh fumed and fretted but obediently conveyed Delhi's directive to the district administration. Alexander has stated, 'The entire situation became a highly sensitive one and, eventually, it was decided at a fairly high political level that the police need not enter Guru Nanak Niwas to make the arrests.'[1]

The powerless SP, Surjit Bains, and Sardara Singh, deputy commissioner of Amritsar, approached the temple authorities to hand over the body of Atwal. In Chandigarh, Punjab's police chief C.K. Sawhney decided that the administration should write a formal letter to SGPC authorities to hand over the killers hiding in the complex to the police. The district police on 29 April 1983 complied with the directive by conveying to the SGPC the names of forty persons allegedly hiding in the Sarai complex and involved in various acts of violence.

Union Home Minister P.C. Sethi, while answering L.K. Advani's question in the Rajya Sabha on 27 April 1983, absolved himself of his responsibility by serving an ultimatum to the SGPC to hand over within a week the killers who had allegedly taken cover in the temple complex. His ultimatum went unheeded, and that was the end of the matter. Longowal and Tohra condemned the crime. Even Bhindranwale issued a circumspect condemnation, but blamed the state agencies for committing the crime to tarnish the image of Sikhs.

This tragic incident and the abject surrender of state responsibility mirrored the murky collapse of the politico-administrative structure in Punjab. The district police chief, instead of promptly nabbing the culprits, rang up the chief minister for instructions. He should have been sacked for dereliction of duty. However, he was not. Because the system expected him not to act but instead seek instructions from political bosses. In fact, had he acted on his own, he would have been in trouble.

Law and order is a state subject. The chief minister, however, looked to Delhi for directives. Federalism had faded away and the division of powers between the Centre and the states disappeared because of the way political parties were structured in India, in this case the Indian National Congress. Chief ministers are nominated by the party bigwigs and not elected on their own strength by the party legislators. On sensitive matters, they look to the party high command for directions, who in the present case happened to be the Prime Minister of the country. The Indian Penal Code and the laws of the land proceeded on leave, while she adjudicated in the matter. And when her decision came, the sovereignty of the Sarai complex superseded the sovereignty of the state.

This personified the collapse of the law and order mechanism in India, but things have not changed much since then—only new players have substituted the old ones. The Indian administrative system is yet to internalize that a crime is a crime and is to be dealt with as per the provisions of law, uninfluenced by any extraneous considerations, or worse, twisted to suit political processes.

Atwal's murder and the state's disinclination to pursue the culprits carried a symbolic message for the police force—why put your lives at risk? Stay safe. Punjab Police has enjoyed the reputation of being an effective force since pre-Independence times. In post-Independence India, it crushed the Naxal movement in Punjab in the early 1970s with an iron hand, while other states floundered to contain similar violence. However, over a period of time the police force got politicized, weakening the internal command-and-control structure.

Punjab Police earned the dubious distinction of a revolt when on 8 May 1979 about 200 uniformed men staged a walkout from Police Lines, Patiala, sloganeering against the government for its failure to arrest an Akali Dal member of the Legislative Assembly (MLA) who had allegedly misbehaved with and slapped a constable, Gulab Singh. Agitations are usually infectious, even for disciplined men. In this case, it spread to the other districts of the state and to neighbouring Haryana. Their demands now included a list of better service conditions and recognition of the police union. The Punjab Armed Police joined the agitation on 11 May and the BSF had to be deployed the next day at sensitive points. The army was requisitioned on 13 May to guard the police armouries at Bahadurgarh Fort and at Jalandhar.

In any unrest, politicians see potential for politics. The Congress, then in the Opposition, would not let an opportunity go and lent support to the striking policemen. The police chief, B.S. Danewalia, and the populist chief minister, Badal, quickly yielded, conceding most of the demands. The men were back in their barracks on 17 May. Order was restored, but discipline dived and hierarchy stood enfeebled. This was the beginning of the decline of a great force. Two years later when militancy picked up in the state, it was no wonder that the force was in disarray. It required only a few targeted killings by militants to make it ineffective.

Atwal was SSP in Amritsar at the time of Bhindranwale's arrest at Chowk Mehta on 21 September 1981, when about seven people were killed in police firing. He had joined in Amritsar on 12 September 1981, and Chowk Mehta was part of his jurisdiction. Atwal, therefore, had to be taught a lesson and a strong signal needed to be sent to his fraternity, so strategized the militants.

Terrorist movements invariably target the symbols of state power with the intent to demoralize legitimate authority. In Punjab too, the militants had designed the tactic to pulverize the police and the administration into paralysis. The game plan was to create a chilling effect, benumbing the government system. Atwal's killing was part of this strategic plan, so that the frightened officials would not dare to act against the militants. They specially targeted those officials who had acted boldly against the militants or who were perceived by them as anti-Sikh; they also randomly picked up vulnerable targets and occasionally high-visibility icons to maximize trepidation.

The strategy was put in operation immediately after Bhindranwale's arrest on 20 September 1981 from Chowk Mehta—the same night three motorcycle-borne boys indulged in indiscriminate firing in Jalandhar town, killing four and injuring twelve. The very next day, the market in Tarn Taran saw a shootout, killing one and injuring thirteen.

The first salvo against the state apparatus was fired on 26 September 1981. A bomb exploded in the Central Telegraph Office, Patiala. Bombs are a preferred instrument of terror, easy to make with locally available materials and guaranteed to make an impact. Splinters spread over a large area and cause greater damage, and are comparatively risk-free for militants as they can be thrown or detonated from a distance.

In another retaliatory act, Dal Khalsa activists hijacked an Indian Airlines aircraft on 29 September—the objective was to draw international attention to the emerging Punjab conflict—while setting off bomb explosions in the state. On 6 and 7 October, the militants, in a synchronized move, exploded bombs at the office of the sub-divisional magistrate (SDM), Tarn Taran, and at the residences of the block development officer, Bhatinda, SDM Hoshiarpur and SDM Moga. On 9–10 October two country-made bombs were thrown at the official residence of the general assistant to the deputy commissioner, Amritsar, and at the residence of a police officer at Moga.

The state's ineffectual response emboldened the militants, who now targeted the seat of state power. In a daring attack on 16 October 1981, they shot at Niranjan Singh, an IAS officer and a Nirankari, as he got out of his official car at the civil secretariat, Chandigarh, where the chief minister, chief secretary and DGP preside over state affairs. Niranjan's brother, who was travelling with him, died on the spot, and his bodyguard Khushnasib Singh was injured.

This was followed by an explosion in the office of the DIG of police at Patiala on 1 November. In those days I was serving in the neighbouring district, Sangrur, as additional district magistrate and distinctly recall how these incidents had shaken government officials. They felt that if the well-guarded civil secretariat in Chandigarh and the office of the police DIG were not safe, their unprotected offices were at greater risk.

Then came the Daheru debacle in November 1981. A small group of terrorists hiding in a house at Daheru in Ludhiana forced a twenty-strong police party to retreat, leaving behind the dead bodies of their two colleagues as the terrorists escaped with the weapons of the killed policemen.

In an explosion on the night of 30 November 1981 at Chowk Mehta, a part of the kitchen block of Bhindranwale's HQ blew up, killing three followers. It raised eyebrows, for the police discovered that the remnants found at the blast site tallied with the explosives being used by militants in the state. A case was registered, but as usual, the investigation made slow headway.

Birbal Nath, the then DGP, Punjab, has gone on record to say that the police was demoralized. To quote him, 'the ambivalence on the part of the Govt. had caused demoralisation in police ranks and there was such awe of AISSF that no police officer was prepared to interrogate any of its members or apply to the Court for their remand'.[2]

As if these incidents were not enough to tranquillize the system, Chief Minister Darbara Singh, who had been given the epithet 'Jahangir' by Bhindranwale, was targeted thrice—on 21 January 1982, at village Panchhata near Jalandhar, where he was assaulted with a sharp-edged weapon; on 22–23 July 1982, two country-made bombs were thrown at his house in Jandiala; and on 20 August 1982, two hand grenades were thrown at him in Jalandhar. He had a miraculous escape but his education minister, Harcharan Singh Ajnala, was not so lucky, as splinters of the grenade hit his hand and arm. For a long time, we saw the minister sporting a sling.

I was then serving as the joint secretary, department of education, under Ajnala. His son, Harpartap Singh Ajnala, was my hostel mate at Delhi University's International Students House in the early 1970s. The militants did not leave them in peace—on 22 November 1982, a bomb was thrown at their residence near Amritsar.

On 12 and 13 November, bombs exploded at the police post in Rahon, Jalandhar, at the Canal Rest House in village Athwal near Sri Hargobindpur, and in the office chamber of the SDM, Jalandhar. A few days later, on 26 January 1983, four bomb explosions shook Amritsar and a hand grenade was detected at the Guru Nanak Stadium, the official venue of the Republic Day celebrations. A partially burnt national flag was also thrown in the marketplace.

The police did show some courage. The plucky A.P. Pandey, my IPS batch mate, then serving as SP in Amritsar, laid a *naka* at Mannawala on the Amritsar–Jalandhar road on 16 March 1983. A truck coming from the Beas side was intercepted and an encounter ensued. Pandey was injured and one Hardev Singh, a follower of Bhindranwale, was killed. Bhindranwale called it 'cold-blooded murder'. Three other injured militants, however, escaped and managed to drive all the way to Guru Nanak Niwas in the temple complex. One of the injured later died and his body was handed over to the police by SGPC authorities.

To ward off police entry into the Sarai complex, Tohra declared that Guru Nanak Niwas and the Sarai complex were an integral part of the Golden Temple. Addressing a public gathering at Baghapurana on 22 March 1983, he announced that police entry would not be tolerated and it would be the 'darkest day in the history of Punjab' if the administration attempted it. Bhindranwale made a provocative speech from the Manji Sahib Diwan Hall in the temple complex, calling upon people to take revenge against the police officers. A case under Section 506 of the Indian Penal Code (IPC) was registered on 27 March but, as in other cases, there was no follow-up action.

After the 16 March incident, the police stopped searching the trucks that carried ration for langar, the free community kitchen in the Golden Temple. Some of these trucks were used to sneak in weapons. When a CRPF roadblock near Jallianwala Bagh did search a truck on 12 May 1984, thirty-six hand grenades, 700 cartridges for self-loading rifles, two Sten guns and a revolver were recovered. Tohra, however, on 14 May, telegrammed Union Home Minister Sethi complaining that the temple complex was under siege by the CRPF. Later on, in a press conference, he fulminated that there was 'great resentment and anguish' among the devotees against the CRPF encirclement of the temple. This is an example of how the public posturing of the moderate Sikh leadership lent support to the terrorist movement.

These developments unnerved officials. However, in Chandigarh, we did not realize the level of demoralization that had set in among the district-level officials, but when I visited Amritsar in June 1983, I found the officers and their families leading extremely restricted lives. They feared that anything could happen to them at any time, and the government was incapable of providing protection. The officers had even raised the height of the boundary walls of their official residences. The officers' colony was cordoned off, picketed by police and kept well lit at night to ward off any possible attacks.

But the situation continued to worsen with the militants becoming bolder with each passing day. Audaciously, on 21 September, they fired at D.R. Bhatti, SSP, Ludhiana. The attack was carried out in the well-guarded district administrative complex, which housed the SSP's office. A few days later, on 28 November 1983, K.K. Dhir, IAS, the commissioner of the municipal corporation of Amritsar, was shot at and injured while on his way to his residence from the office.

The institution of the station house officer (SHO) is a lynchpin in police hierarchy. The SHO of Police Station Guru Harsahai in Ferozpur was shot dead in full public view at the area's grain market on 18 December 1983. Earlier, a police post was attacked on 2 July at Baba Bakala and the terrorists took away a rifle. Many more junior officers and the constables faced bullets.

On 14 February, a group of militants confronted a police deployment, not far from the Golden Temple. Six policemen were 'captured' and taken to the complex. Almost twenty-four hours later, a senior police officer was sent as an emissary to Bhindranwale to plead for their release. In the meantime, one of the captured policemen was killed and the remaining five were set free. However, 'their weapons, including three Sten guns and a wireless set, were not returned. No action was ever taken in the case of the murdered policeman.'[3]

By now, paramilitary forces had been extensively deployed in support of the state police. The militants targeted them too. They threw a bomb at the CRPF camp at Dharamkot on 19 March 1984, killing one constable and injuring another. On 24 September 1984, they successfully ambushed a CRPF patrol, killing one constable and injuring two other.

The audacity and organizational capability of the militants was demonstrated when on a single day, 14 April 1984, they burnt thirty-six railway stations in Punjab. Soon, they exported terror to the neighbouring states. On 21 April 1984, Sub-Inspector Shiv Singh and Constable Santokh Singh were killed near Ambala as they tried to intercept a car carrying weapons and terrorists from Jagadhri to Ambala. The inter-state spread of militancy created a greater scare. The militants appeared macho and heroic, and that lured many new recruits to the movement as 'the cause' spread and militancy spilled over to new geographical areas.

Nothing moves without money, including terrorism. To meet their financial needs, the militants targeted banks. In 1983, twenty-one bank branches across Punjab were robbed. Initially, the banks took the stand that cash was insured and therefore needed no security guards. The district administration in the state was hard-pressed to provide police security—Punjab has a very high density of banks, and almost every fifth village has a bank branch or a cash counter.

The militants looted banks and decamped with currency from safe chests. They were bold and did not hesitate to kill when challenged.

The writ of militancy ran deep and wide. Bhindranwale used to hold a daily darbar on the roof of the room serving langar or at the Akal Takht and hear people's grievances. At times, he would summon the person against whom there was a complaint, conduct a kangaroo court and dispense rough and ready justice. No one dared to defy his decisions. It was generally believed that defiance could invite death.

The expressions used by the militants were '*sodh deo*', meaning set right the intransigent, or '*chak deo*' and '*gadee charh deo*', meaning eliminate the person. The range of issues settled in the darbar was sweeping—from matrimonial dissensions, property and patrimony contestations to disaffection against a state government official for non-delivery of services, or bribes, etc. Bhindranwale himself heard the serious squabbles; the contretemps could be resolved at a junior level, say by Bhai Amrik Singh or by a lesser *sewadar*. The government officials would get instructions over the telephone or through a legate and be called to appear in person.

Intelligence agencies were monitoring telephone calls to a few select telephone numbers in the temple complex, and one interesting conversation intercepted was between Sarabjit Singh, the then police chief of Amritsar district, and a frontman of Bhindranwale, demanding the release of a militant arrested by the police in connection with a bomb blast case. Sarabjit declined the 'demand', but settled the matter by giving an assurance that the arrested militant would not be 'bumped off' by police. The 'negotiations' landed the police officer in dismissal proceedings under Article 311 post–Blue Star. However, the matter was finally closed and Sarabjit went on to become DGP, Punjab, in February 1999.

A fear psychosis had gripped the administration, and the public perception was that an official would abide by Bhindranwale's diktat even if the instructions from his official superiors were to the contrary. The parallel command-and-control structure of the militants had rendered the government hors de combat. Many businessmen and shopkeepers, Hindus and Sikhs alike, were subjected to extortion. They would get telephone calls or letters, importuning them to contribute to the cause. Wealthy residents of the city were occasionally summoned by the militants for monetary subscriptions to the cause. The administration had collapsed.

The administrative disarray, in fact, began in 1980, and further deteriorated during the extended period of President's Rule in the state. By 1984, the collapse was total. The police and paramilitary forces, despite odd brave deeds, proved ineffective. Widespread acts of violence made the government look vulnerable and powerless, while the militants came out resilient. The movement also gained foothold among the diaspora; it procured transnational recognition by the hijacking of two aircraft from India. The common man felt terrorized. Something needed to be done.

Possibly, there were two routes to resolve the Punjab problem—either a political solution by accepting the Akali Dal's demands that would isolate the militants and thereafter deal with militancy by co-opting the moderate Akali leadership, or to strong-arm the terrorists. The Central government appeared to be opting for neither of these options.

By then, the Golden Temple had been well fortified as weapons were allowed to accumulate inside the complex. Pritam Singh Bhinder, Punjab Police chief, conceded to *The Statesman*, Delhi (8 July 1984), 'They were not intercepted because there were oral instructions "from the top" until two months ago not to check any of the Kar Sewa trucks.'[4]

Was there a motive in the state's ineffectual response? Governor Pande has disclosed that Indira Gandhi 'did not want a political settlement'.[5] Some scholars allege that the Central government's strategy was to let the situation deteriorate to a point of a national outcry and then strike with a dramatic deterrence to provide the much-needed catharsis and then politically cash in on the national consensus against terrorism.

The delay in addressing the Punjab violence did lead to an outcry. Leaders like C. Rajeswara Rao of the CPI on 20 July 1983 and L.K. Advani on 16 July 1983[6] held the ruling party (Congress) as the principal villain in the dark tragedy that was being enacted in the state, and accused Indira Gandhi of intentionally delaying dealing with the Punjab problem to garner political mileage.[7] By April 1984, all political parties were seeking army intervention in the state. The failure to curb militancy and the apparent ineffectiveness of the administration resulted in the nation demanding military intercession.

Then the time came. The Lok Sabha elections were due in early 1985. The government could ill-afford to appear having failed to ebb the brutal bloodshed of innocent people by terrorists. In June 1984, the army, as always, became the final option and was called in to tackle a situation that was essentially a failure of the political–civil administration. Was it an electoral imperative or were there really no other options? Perceptions will always differ.

6

The Morcha

On a sweltering Wednesday afternoon on 4 August 1982, the spacious compound of the police station at Kotwali reverberated with roars of the morale-boosting Sikh salutation '*Jo bole so nihal, sat sri akal*'. Eleven-hundred Akali workers, which included seventy-one Muslims and five Christians, footslogged from the Golden Temple complex seeking their own arrest. They were led by P.S. Badal, then leader of the Opposition. Their detention marked the beginning of the Dharam Yudh Morcha that continued till the army encircled the temple on 3 June 1984.

From 4 August, Akali volunteers would gather daily at the Manji Sahib in the Golden Temple, recite their prayers and then court arrest. To their credit, the morcha remained by and large peaceful, in the time-honoured tradition of satyagraha. The Akalis believed, in retrospect rather naively, that the Central government would concede their demands if they choked Punjab's jails with people. And their accomplishment was impressive. Between 4 August 1982 till June 1984, over 1,70,000 persons courted arrest. Out of 12,000 odd villages in the state, there were hardly any from where people had not gone to prison.

Their demands were a mixture of religious, economic, political and inter-state issues—forty-five in all—first flagged with the Central government in September 1981. Subsequently, in October of the same year, the demands were shrunk to fifteen. On 3 August 1982, before courting arrest, Badal addressed a letter to all national Opposition parties, conveying the demands—now further reduced to the following ten.

1. To give Punjabi-speaking areas, including Chandigarh, to Punjab.
2. To get due share of Punjab's river waters on the basis of the principles of law, equity and justice.
3. More autonomy and powers for the states of the Union of India in accordance with the real federal set-up.
4. Introducing Punjabi as a second language in Delhi, Haryana, Himachal Pradesh, the Ganganagar area in Rajasthan, etc., in view of the large Punjabi-speaking population in these areas.
5. Stoppage of ejectment of Punjabi settlers in the Terai area of Uttar Pradesh and from Haryana.
6. Release of innocent persons arrested so far and stoppage of police repression in Punjab.
7. Enactment of All India Gurdwaras Act.
8. Setting up broadcasting facilities for gurbani kirtan from the Golden Temple.
9. Grant of holy city status to the city of Amritsar and banning the sale of liquor, tobacco and meat within the walled city.
10. Non-interference in the religious affairs of the Sikhs by the government.

In his letter, Badal emphasized that these demands were for the general interest of Punjabis. Some of the Opposition parties, including the left parties, extended support to the Akali Dal.[1]

The opponents of the Akalis alleged that the charter of demands was just a veneer and the real objective of the agitation was to gain political power in Punjab. It was true—but that is what democracy is all about: a bid to gain power by peaceful politics. The Akali Dal, in any case, was committed to national unity and had unequivocally condemned the demand for Khalistan. It had even sought a public investigation by a high court judge as early as 1981 to expose the minuscule minority demanding Khalistan.

To send a signal to the party cadres, it removed Sukhjinder Singh (formerly of the Talwandi Akali Dal), an otherwise energetic leader, from the membership of the Shiromani Akali Dal as he had espoused the secessionist cause. In August 1983, Longowal, designated the morcha dictator, denounced Dr Jagjit Singh Chauhan, a Khalistani proponent who made a symbolic move to appoint a president of the non-existent Khalistan. Longowal publicly declared that the Akali Dal had nothing to do with the demand for Khalistan.

At this stage, the BJP supported the Akali Dal's demands in a memorandum submitted to Chief Minister Darbara Singh on 23 October 1982. The Rashtriya Swayamsevak Sangh (RSS) also endorsed these—except the Anandpur Sahib Resolution—in a meeting with Swaran Singh, the Central government's interlocutor.[2] Jyoti Basu of the CPI(M), then the chief minister of West Bengal, and the Dravida Munnetra Kazhagam (DMK) lent support to the Akali demand for a review of Centre–state relations, and there appeared to be a broad consensus for a negotiated settlement.

As time passed, the morcha progressed, but the Central government remained unmoved regarding the demands. Discontent and bitterness set in among the Akalis. Movements often fester when allowed to linger for long, and in this case, it was an unfortunate accident that triggered anger. On 11 September 1982, a bus carrying Akali volunteers to jail met with an accident at an unmanned railway crossing near Tarn Taran. Thirty-four Akalis were killed and another twenty were injured. There was spontaneous outrage, and demonstrations followed, culminating in a mourning procession on

11 October all the way from Anandpur Sahib to Delhi, carrying the ashes of those deceased to Parliament.

Then came the Asian Games in November 1982, with India playing the proud host. Swaran Singh, the former Union minister who was in contact with the Akalis, made an earnest effort for rapprochement. An agreement was reached twice, initially in the first week of November and then again with the Cabinet sub-committee on 16 and 17 November 1982.[3] Amarinder Singh, who was inducted into the secret talks by his party's high command, has disclosed that all had been settled but 'the government, an hour before the Home Secretary was to fly to Amritsar, reneged on its commitment'.[4]

How the talks were stalled is a study in political machination. While Amarinder wondered as to who had 'deliberately leaked the proposal'[5] to Haryana Chief Minister Bhajan Lal, who pressured the Prime Minister to scuttle the settlement, it may have been his own innocent chit-chat with not-so-innocent friends that jinxed Punjab and was to blame. Chand Joshi, a veteran journalist who worked with the *Hindustan Times*, describes what happened after the negotiators had dispersed for the day after reaching an understanding:

> The breakdown in negotiations can be directly attributed to the fact that after the negotiations were over, Amarinder Singh had the same evening met some of his friends, including Arun Nehru and Arun Singh. Bhajan Lal was quickly informed of the proposed agreement and he came rushing down to Delhi and aided by the 'take-a-tough stand' lobby convinced the Prime Minister to reverse the decision.[6]

Left leader Harkishan Singh Surjeet, who also played a part in the negotiations at various stages, writes, 'The responsibility for breaking the talks (November 1982) does not lie with the Akalis, they had completely demarcated themselves from the extremists and their slogans.' He goes on to say, 'They [Akalis] took a reasonable position and an agreement was again arrived at on the evening of the 18th. An aircraft was kept ready to fly to Amritsar. Who went back on this agreement? It was again the Government.'[7]

The Central government, it seems, believed in Benjamin Disraeli's dictum that finality is not the language of politics. It was not one or two, but twenty-six futile meetings that took place between 1981 and 1984 in an attempt to come up with a solution. Three of these meetings were chaired by Indira Gandhi, while another four were presided over by members of her Union Cabinet. In the nine secret conferences organized at safe houses that were chaired by Union ministers and included officials and representatives of the Central government, Rajiv Gandhi joined in as well. Ten tripartite conferences involving prominent leaders of the Opposition political parties, the Akalis and Central government representatives were also held.

Starting 24 January 1984, the Central government held five secret parleys, the last of them on 26 May 1984, when they met twice the same day at a safe house in RK Puram, Delhi. The meeting was attended by Tohra, Badal and Surjit Singh Barnala from the Akali side, and the trio of three ministers, R. Venkataraman, Pranab Mukherjee and P. Shiv Shankar, accompanied by three officials, namely P.C. Alexander, T.N. Chaturvedi and C.R. Krishnaswamy Rao, representing the government. Tohra, in a statement before the Delhi High Court, in the suit for damages filed by the SGPC (IPA No.23/86), stated that all the demands were considered at great length and these were:

> Chandigarh be transferred to Punjab, Anandpur Sahib Resolution be referred to Sarkaria Commission and the water issue to Supreme Court through governmental notification, a linguistic commission be established to determine Hindi speaking and Punjabi speaking areas, Punjabi should be declared as a second language in Haryana and Delhi, and to consider framing of All India Gurdwara Act.

In the meeting, Shiv Shankar inquired if Bhindranwale would be satisfied if these demands were accepted, and Tohra, in his statement to the Delhi High Court, disclosed:

> I told him that was the responsibility of the Shiromani Akali Dal, as soon as acceptance of the demands. I also assured him as the President of the SGPC that Mr Bhindranwale shall also accept. The representative of the government had told me that they would be contacting the Prime Minister and would reassemble after lunch. After lunch, the officers did not return, but the Ministers came around at about 4 PM. They told us even without sitting that they were sorry that the Prime Minister was not agreeable to these demands.

Governor Pande has been forthright in confirming, 'It is true that the Prime Minister continued to say that the doors for negotiations were always open. Some clandestine talks were also going on. But mainly the purpose of these was to divert attention.'[8]

Tohra reported the failure of the negotiations of 26 May to Longowal, and a meeting of the Akali Dal was called for 2 June in Amritsar. The same day, Longowal tried to contact the Prime Minister on the telephone, but did not succeed. Tohra further told the court, 'On 2.6.84, I also wrote a letter to the Prime Minister in my capacity of President of SGPC', and the letter was handed over to the deputy commissioner G.S. Brar and, 'he informed me to telephone that my letter had reached the Prime Minister'.

This exercise of negotiations on 26 May, however, appears to be inane camouflage. While the Union ministers were parleying with the Akalis on that day, the Prime Minister on 25 May had summoned the Chief of Army Staff Gen. A.S. Vaidya and mandated him to flush out the terrorists ensconced in the Golden Temple and other gurdwaras. (See Chapter 8, 'Who Moved My Army?'.)

In fact, the government stance had been evasive all along, and at times puckish, as illustrated by Congress MP from Punjab Amrjit Kaur's approach[9] to the renaming of the *Flying Mail* as the *Golden Temple Express*. Her response was, 'They [Akalis] really wanted a "gurdwara-on-wheels".'

A confirmation of the evasive tactics of the Central government comes from a distinguished army officer, Lt Gen. S.K. Sinha, who, in those days, was commanding a corps in Punjab. He had about 80,000 Sikh troops out of about 3,00,000 under his command, and was concerned that if the Punjab turmoil lingered, it might affect the morale and discipline of the troops. Therefore, during the visit of Defence Minister R. Venkataraman to his corps, the general broached the issue, suggesting that 'innocent' demands like renaming the *Flying Mail* as the *Golden Temple Express* 'should not have taken the Government more than a minute to concede'. The minister, who was a member of the sub-committee of the Union Cabinet constituted for a dialogue with the Akalis, however, replied to the general saying, '. . . [I]t was all politics. You give an inch you will have to give a yard. Today they were making these demands but tomorrow they will ask for Amritsar being given the status of Vatican City.'

General Sinha states that he replied to the minister, '. . . [I]n Army we have a saying that you cross a bridge only when you get to it . . . the impression I got after my discussion with Mr Venkataraman was that the Government lacked the political will to resolve the problem quickly. The trauma of Punjab's suffering would continue and would get much worse.'[10]

The general was espousing diplomacy, but the politicians had plans for the army. Indira Gandhi, in fact, had 'lost the art of the politics of accommodation or more likely, has lost interest in it. Therefore, she does not want to or no longer knows how to weave group identities into a national whole. She breaks such identities as she can . . . But what she cannot break, she merely alienates. That is the real cause of the Punjab problem.' So noted the eminent journalist Pran Chopra.[11]

The Prime Minister had earlier conceded three religious demands on 27 February 1983 at Gurdwara Bangla Sahib, Delhi, but the implementation remained tardy. These were: imposing a ban on the sale of cigarettes, liquor and meat in the vicinity of the Golden Temple and Durgiana Mandir; relaying the gurbani via AIR from the Golden Temple; and allowing the kirpan to be carried on Indian Airlines flights. The Akalis were peeved that the Prime Minister had accepted these demands unilaterally at a congregation of pro-Congress Sikhs in Delhi as a gesture of thanks for the support extended by them to Congress (I) in the election to the local bodies in the capital. The Congress lost an opportunity to win over the moderate Akalis and isolate the radicals.

The Turning Point

The turning point in the morcha was the failure of negotiations just before the Asian Games. The indignant Akalis decided to protest at the venue of the Games with the intent to highlight the non-fulfilment of their demands, but little did they realize that it would incur the wrath of the authorities. The police in many states were put on high alert to intercept the agitating Akali workers and stop them from reaching Delhi. The disagreeable Bhajan Lal, chief minister of Haryana, was quick to order a thoughtless blockade of Sikhs travelling through his state to reach Delhi. Without anticipating the repercussion, trains, buses and cars from Punjab to Delhi were indiscriminately searched, including those ferrying retired generals, judges and distinguished individuals. Some were insultingly bodily frisked and a few detained in an attempt to prevent them from reaching Delhi. The Punjab government resorted to preventive mass-scale arrests between 13 and 22 November 1982.

These harsh measures built a crescendo of resentment and the Akali Dal cashed in on the empathy. It used the prevailing angst to enlarge its base among ex-servicemen and Sikh intellectuals. A massive congregation of ex-servicemen at the Golden Temple on 23 December 1982, and another of Sikh intellectuals on 9 January 1983, brought the educated segments of the *panth* on board. Now, retired army generals and officers, writers and authors, professors and professionals, doctors, former civil servants and diplomats, were mobilized, though the peasantry remained the backbone of the movement.

In February 1983, four Akali MPs and thirty-six MLAs submitted their resignations in protest against the Central government's silence over Punjab's demands, but the Speaker rejected the MLA's resignations. In March, the Akali MPs, the MLAs and the presidents of their district units met and decided on a three-pronged programme:

1. To force Congress MLAs to resign from the state assembly in support of the cause;
2. To launch a 'Rasta Roko' agitation; and
3. To enrol 1 lakh *marjiwara*s, that is, sacrificial squads, by administering them an oath at the Akal Takht for the 'supreme sacrifice'.

The government responded on 2 April by arresting fifteen Akali MLAs and nearly 600 mid-level Akali leaders to thwart the agitation but the Akali workers nevertheless blocked traffic in the state on 4 April as part of Rasta Roko. In the resultant scuffle on the roads with the police, about twenty-one workers were killed. The tragedy aggravated public disaffection and the Akali leadership was spurred to broaden the confrontation.

In April 1983, the first group of marjiwaras took an oath at the Akal Takht. In all, a force of 1,00,000 was to be raised. When another group of 20,000 volunteers took the pledge for the panth in May, among them were about 150 Muslims holding Muslim League flags as a gesture of solidarity with the Sikhs. The Shahi Imam of the Jama Masjid, Sayed Abdullah Bukhari, on 10 October 1982 endorsed the morcha as a 'movement against repression' in a display of esprit de corps of the minority communities.

The next steps in the agitation were Rail Roko on 17 June 1983 and Kam Roko on 29 August 1983, which resulted in teargassing agitators at a number of places, including in Amritsar and Gurdaspur, resulting in injuries to about forty-five protesters. But the Central government remained unmoved.

The exasperation of the Akalis was dire; while speaking to a congregation at the Manji Sahib on 13 July 1983, the assiduously moderate Longowal sounded secessionist when he said, 'They have to think whether Sikhs should remain in the country or not.' Prolonged agitation and the non-fulfilment of the morcha demands had frustrated Longowal and that was reflected in the 'existential acceptance' of the radical elements as a tactical ploy when he said, 'He [Bhindranwale] is our danda [stave] with which to beat the government.'[12]

Longowal drew international attention to the struggle by appealing to the Sikh diaspora on 6 September to join the Dharam Yudh Morcha, resulting in the Sikh Council of North America demonstrating in front of the United Nations (UN) headquarters in New York on 28 September while Prime Minister Indira Gandhi addressed the UN General Assembly. Longowal also addressed an open letter to the Commonwealth Heads of Government Meeting (CHOGM) delegates seeking their intervention for the Sikh cause, and thus involved the Commonwealth of Nations in what was essentially a domestic matter. The protests spread to Canada, the UK and the US, where Sikhs demonstrated outside Indian consulates.

These protests, however, had little impact, if any, on the Central government. Longowal, therefore, announced in January 1984 to 'revolutionize' the agitation, and asked the 1,00,000 marjiwaras to be ready to do or die. However, he kept adjourning the dates for the proposed revolutionary action in the hope that the Central government may agree to some of the demands.

The radicals criticized Longowal for inaction and he succumbed. He announced on 23 February an agitation to burn Explanation II to Article 25 of the Constitution. This clause of the Constitution provides that '. . . [T]he reference to Hindus shall be construed as including a reference to persons professing the Sikh, Jain or Buddhist religion . . .' The Akalis interpreted the provision as a threat to Sikh identity; the expression 'Hindus' in the Constitution subsumed 'Sikhs', they argued.

Defiling the Constitution was bound to invite adverse national reaction, but the Akalis went ahead with their plan. On 27 February 1984, P.S. Badal reached Delhi disguised as a driver to avoid preventive arrest, and burnt copies of Explanation II of Article 25 at Gurdwara Bangla Sahib. Tohra did the same in Chandigarh. Both were arrested.

The diaspora abroad burnt copies of the Article in front of Indian embassies; in the UK about 200 Sikhs did it outside India House on 28 February. To keep up the momentum, five Akali workers were instructed to burn more copies every Monday in front of the Parliament. Longowal gave a call on 27 March to 'jail bharo' from 2–7 April and asked volunteers to burn copies at the district headquarters.

To contain criticism and avoid being labelled as anarchists or anti-national, Longowal clarified in a press statement that the Akali Dal stood for the unity and integrity of the nation, but the damage to the Akali image had been done. Most of the Opposition parties were critical of the demand for constitutional severance, and they denounced it.

Many political parties had earlier suggested that in view of the terrorist violence, the Akalis suspend the morcha—the BJP executive in October 1983 at Lucknow, after the selective killing of passengers at Dhillwan, had passed a resolution calling upon them to withdraw the agitation. However, the Central government agreed to the Akali demand to amend Article 25. In Parliament, the Union home minister made a statement on 31 March 1984 to that effect.

The Akali Dal, it seems, had not thought through this demand and was caught unprepared by the Central government's offer of amendment. Union Home Minister Sethi sought a concrete proposal, but the Akali Dal had none. It was only on 1 May that Atma Singh, the acting president of the SGPC, formed an expert group under Gurdarshan Singh Grewal, a former advocate general, to prepare a draft of the proposed amendment to the Constitution and also propose a draft of the Sikh personal law.

The Government of India's positive response on Article 25 resulted in the Akali Dal calling off the proposed mass movement of Panth Liberation Week and the government reciprocated by releasing the detained leaders, including Tohra, Badal and Barnala. The rapprochement, however, was not carried forward as the original long-pending demands were not addressed by the Centre.

Longowal, under constant strain because of the militants and the radicals who would charge him with apathy and inaction, declared on 25 May that they were to launch a non-cooperation movement from 3 June, the martyrdom day of Guru Arjan Dev. It entailed non-payment of government dues such as land revenue and water charges, and blocking all movement of foodgrains from Punjab, the granary of India, to other parts of the country.

The Akali Dal (Talwandi), in competition with the moderate Akalis, went a step further. Expressing disaffection with the proposed non-cooperation call, it instead urged Sikhs to deposit taxes and dues not in the state treasury but at the Akal Takht. It was a direct challenge to state sovereignty—the stage was set for confrontation.

In those days, Punjab was going through an agrarian unrest spearheaded by the Bharatiya Kisan Union (BKU) that had mobilized peasants against low agricultural prices, high costs of inputs, farm indebtedness and demanding the waiver of irrigation and electricity tariffs. In March, the BKU had given a call to farmers not to pay electricity bills. The movement was spreading fast and gaining pan-India support, with farmers from Maharashtra (under the leadership of Sharad Joshi of the Shetkari Sangathan), Madhya Pradesh, Uttar Pradesh and Haryana, and the kisan bodies of the CPI, CPI(M), etc., extending support to the agitation.

On 12 March, 1,00,000 farmers led by the BKU swarmed Chandigarh and laid a weeklong siege to the Raj Bhavan (Punjab was under President's Rule). The governor was confined within his estate, and the northern elite sectors of Chandigarh became an open camping ground, a 'kisan nagar'. Normal day-to-day life in the capital city was completely disrupted.

The governor's gherao was lifted on 18 March, but in April the BKU gave another call, this time not to repay bank loans. In the villages, farmers displayed noticeboards proclaiming a BKU-imposed ban on the entry of loan-recovery officials, and if the officials did dare to ingress, the BKU asked the farmers to confine them to *tooriwala* kothas, that is, rooms to stockpile wheat chaff. During the peak wheat procurement season—from 1–7 May—a call was given not to bring wheat to the mandis; the Kanak Bandh evoked a positive response from farmers and was followed by a repeat of 'Chandigarh Gherao' from 10 May.

These protests were symptomatic of the fast-dwindling prosperity that the Green Revolution had brought to Punjab—the law of diminishing returns had set in. The Akali Dal, a party with a strong support base among peasants and Jat Sikh farmers, could not be seen to lag behind the BKU in pleading the farmer's cause. It seized the opportunity and gave a call for peaceful non-cooperation and blockade of grain movement from Punjab to the rest of India. That provided the justification for the Central government's intervention to address the Punjab problem militarily. What was essentially an agrarian unrest, with the Akali leadership trying to piggyback on an ongoing agitation of the BKU, turned Punjab into a battlefield.[13]

The Last Straw

An intelligence input stated that militants planned to declare Khalistan and set up an interim regime that would be recognized by Pakistan. The President of India was informed that 'extremists had planned to declare the establishment of Khalistan'.[14]

Two unidentified young Sikhs, probably Pakistani agent provocateurs, had approached both Longowal and Bhindranwale on 3 June with an appeal to declare Khalistan. The ISI had not forgotten that on 26 March 1971, India had announced its support to the Bangladeshi freedom movement. The very next day, on 27 March, Bangladesh's freedom fighters had proclaimed independence. It was followed by the recognition of Bangladesh by India in December 1971, after the Bangladesh's government-in-exile had proclaimed independence.

Longowal, subsequent to his release from National Security Act (NSA) detention on 11 March 1985, in an interview to Kuldip Nayar, confirmed that, 'The truth is that two persons I did not know came to me and said they had gone to Bhindranwale and asked him to announce the birth of Khalistan over the loudspeaker.' Bhindranwale directed them to approach Longowal, advising that if Harchand Singh Longowal were to announce it, he would support it. Bhindranwale said to them, 'If you want this to be done, go to the Akali Dal Chief. He is the only one who can do it. If he does it, I shall do so.'[15]

Both of them—Longowal and Bhindranwale—did not fall into the trap. The beguiling allure failed and with that any possible justification for army action on that account. However, the decision to storm the temple had been taken much before 3 June, or even before the Akalis gave the non-cooperation call. Delhi seemed to have made up its mind, and knowledgeable circles in the corridors of power were abuzz with news of the impending army intervention in March–April 1984. In journalistic circles, the pros and cons of such an action were openly commented upon; Pran Chopra, the noted journalist, wrote in the

Indian Express, dated 23 April 1984, about the rumours in New Delhi that the army might be brought in: 'That would be the gravest blunder politically and severely harmful to the army itself.'[16]

The government had used some eminent Punjabis and journalists as a sounding board to gauge the likely reaction to the possible use of the army in the temple. H.K.L. Bhagat, the then minister for information and broadcasting, consulted a few journalists on the proposed military assault; one of them was Kuldip Nayar, the venerated journalist. He wrote, 'Our suspicion was strengthened when H.K.L. Bhagat, the then minister for Information and Broadcasting, came to meet me. He had been sent by Indira Gandhi, as he told me, and asked whether the government should send troops inside the Golden Temple. I replied in the negative.'[17]

In public, however, the government projected the impression that it stood for a political settlement. On 23 March 1984, Rajiv Gandhi, the then All India Congress Committee (AICC) general secretary, in an interview to a journalist said, 'I think we should not enter the Golden Temple.'[18]

Six days later, on 29 March, Rajiv Gandhi's response to certain media queries is revealing:

> Q. Is Bhindranwale an extremist?
> Ans. This is for you to evaluate.
> Q. Do you think he is a political leader?
> Ans. He is a religious leader and has not shown political inclination so far.[19]

The Central government was publicly projecting that they were seeking a settlement through dialogue. The Prime Minister, while addressing a 300-strong conference of the presidents and secretaries of the state and district Congress (I) committee in Delhi on 1 June, reiterated the Central government's approach for a negotiated settlement and to pursue it till the end.

Silently, however, attempts were made to build a national consensus in support of a decisive military solution. This duality of approach sent different signals to different interest groups, and thus sharpened the already divided perceptions of the situation. Four years of ineffectual response since the killing of the Nirankari chief in 1980 had resulted in pent-up anger against the mindless violence of the militants. The government was being blamed for inaction. B.K. Chum wrote in the *Indian Express* on 3 February 1984, 'If the motive behind continuing the stalemate is to secure Hindu votes in the next elections, it is proving to be counter-productive.' The delay in action was unsettling.

By now, some prominent national dailies had begun pressing the government for effective action to curb violence. The *Hindustan Times*, for example, in an editorial on 4 April 1984 titled 'Get the Killers', argued that the situation was turning communal, just as it was in the pre-Partition days. Delegations called on the Central ministers to deploy the army. On 30 May, Ram Gopal Shawlwale of the Arya Samaj League led a delegation to the Prime Minister and sought military intervention and the imposition of emergency in Punjab.

However, this tactic to build a support base for military action was targeting the wrong audience. If anything, opinion should have been built among moderate Sikhs so as to isolate the militants and thereafter decisively act against the terrorists. The calls by non-Sikhs for military action in the temple only furthered malevolence between the two communities.

The Morcha and the Militancy

What was the relation between the Akalis and the militants? The two are often erroneously seen as one. The fact is that both the main political parties, the Akalis and the Congress, were addressing their electoral constituencies—Sikhs and Hindus, respectively. They were competing to capture political power through ballot, and all means to that end were viewed as fair. The militants, however, were not in an electoral race and hence posed no direct challenge to the political aspirations of the traditional political parties and could therefore be 'tolerated'. For this reason, the militants were not persona non grata for the Akalis or the Congress.

In December 1982, Indira Gandhi 'ordered' Amarinder Singh, then a Congress MP, to have a hush-hush tête-à-tête with Bhindranwale. Singh was to later claim 'to be the only person to have slept in Jarnail Singh Bhindranwale's bed other than him'.[20]

Amarinder's endeavour, however, held promise. He succeeded twice to fix in-person meetings between Bhindranwale and Rajiv Gandhi. Once, they even took off from the Safdarjung airport for the rendezvous, but both the times the meetings were aborted at the last minute, apparently for security concerns.

The twice-ditched Bhindranwale was shrewd to foresee the inefficacy of the parleys and cautioned, 'I beg to warn Sikhs to be vigilant against this trick. Keep on having negotiations but also have your preparations complete.'[21] The call for preparation was a call for an armed struggle, and it ran parallel to the peaceful Dharam Yudh Morcha, of which he was an acclaimed leader.

So, while the Akalis filled the jails and held fruitless negotiations, for the militants, '*hakka di hinsa*', or violence for their rights, and police reprisal was a type of dialogue with the state, though by other means. To them, violence was a legitimate means to achieve what they considered a pious objective, and they pursued it unconcerned with the political processes.

Militancy was taken as morally mandated, and since they lacked legitimacy, they fell back on 'the meta-morality that religion provides' and claimed 'a higher degree of loyalty to their sides than parties in a purely political war'.[22] Guns gave them the recognition and power that their moderate counterparts the Akalis could never hope to achieve through political processes or peaceful courting of arrest.

This was best illustrated by the dramatic hijacking of an aircraft by the militants on 4 August 1982 to overshadow the launch of the peaceful morcha by the Akalis. On that day, unknown to the Akalis, one Gurbaksh Singh of the Dal Khalsa, a former sewadar of a gurdwara, boarded the Delhi–Srinagar Indian Airlines flight. Mid-air, he got up from his seat and, using a cloth-wrapped rubber ball which he claimed was a bomb, hijacked the flight to Lahore. The aircraft was not permitted to land there and it came to Amritsar. His demands were akin to those of the morcha, except that he additionally demanded a ransom amount. *India Today* reported that he 'had met Bhindranwale twice'.[23] The hijacking was an act of bravado, and provided publicity to the militants on an international scale.

Commenting on the hijacking, *India Today* noted that, 'The empathy between Punjab Sikh moderates and extremists is there, and is probably growing.' This perception of empathy might not have been correct, but it reflected a delicate fault line of the ethnonational movement. The morcha participants and the militants, in fact, were two different sets of individuals, with fundamental differences in ideology, objectives, approach and methodology. The two sets operated parallel to and independent of each other, one in the constitutional and political domain, and the other strictly underground, covert and beyond the purview of law.

However, unwittingly, the mass mobilization of the people by the political process of the morcha and the expectations it aroused helped create the required favourable religious–social sentiment that provided the militancy the emanation and respectability it needed to thrive. As time passed, the continuous non-resolution of the demands by the Central government spawned discontent, and that lent the required camouflage, if not the justification, to the militancy in its embryonic pre–Blue Star days.

A perilous overlap between militancy and the morcha was the common recruitment base of both among the Sikh peasantry, and this provided a kind of inter se mobility, with individuals graduating from peaceful to radical to militant domains, though many a militant was directly recruited to the gun culture. The morcha and the militancy both claimed to stand for the glory of the panth and the *quam*, and leaned heavily on religion for inspiration.

More critical than these linkages, however, was Bhindranwale as the tactical bridgehead: He was an integral part of the Dharam Yudh Morcha, with the peaceful political struggle as its anchor, but synchronously he also symbolized violence as a legitimate weapon. Thus, the militancy grew surreptitiously and was reared, almost furtively, along with the morcha, in the garb of religious nationalism.

However, the ideological and strategic contradictions between the moderates and the radicals ultimately led to the murder of Longowal, a man of peace, who was sucked in by the incompatible methods and objectives of the militants. Longowal always stood for Hindu–Sikh amity and condemned violence.

And when Bhindranwale's hate speeches turned shriller, Longowal on 19 August 1983 in a strongly worded public statement said, 'Sikh religion does not teach killings or torture of innocents and those who encourage these are the biggest traitors of the panth.' The pro-Bhindranwale Akal Federation took offence to Longowal's stand and called upon the Akal Takht to summon him for distorting Sikh traditions. Jathedar Kirpal Singh of the Akal Takht endorsed Longowal's stand and unequivocally stated that the teachings of the Sikh Gurus were against the killing of innocents.

The Takht's ratification of Longowal's stand, however, did not end violence or resolve his differences with Bhindranwale. The militants became more assertive by the day, and even the non-violent but otherwise radical Akali Dal (T) separated from Longowal to give a call on 13 November 1983 to establish a parallel government in Punjab.

The divide between Bhindranwale and Longowal was no longer about methods and ideology, but had turned personal. They were two distinctly different individuals, incompatible both in thought and action. Longowal was a simple, self-effacing politico-religious soul, who, despite being pushed into the public limelight, shunned power—as exhibited in his retirement to Rishikesh when he was faced with a conflict within the Akali Dal or later when he was pursued to contest for Parliament from the seat vacated by P.S. Badal during the Janata government days. Instead, he preferred a young ballad singer, Balwant Singh Ramoowalia, for the Lok Sabha.

Bhindranwale was equally spartan and puritanical in his personal life, but strikingly aggressive, uncompromisingly iron-willed and not averse to violence. His path had predestined him for a rendezvous with 'martyrdom'. It was just a matter of time.

Privately, Longowal called Bhindranwale 'Prindawallah'—'*prind*' in Punjabi means a wasp. He also called him Chambal, a reference to the Chambal valley dacoits. Bhindranwale would dismiss Longowal as 'Gandhi Ashram', in an obvious reference to his ineffectiveness to deliver. On 1 February 1984, Longowal publicly acknowledged the disagreements, and reasserted that he was committed to communal peace. The divide between the two of them was complete.[24]

Their relations turned hostile when a few people killed Surinder Singh Sodhi, a close associate of Bhindranwale, on 17 April 1984. Sodhi himself was a killer with an impressive score that included H.S. Manchanda, the president of the Delhi Gurdwara Prabandhak Committee, Professor V.N. Tiwari, MP, and Harbans Lal Khanna of the BJP, to name a few.[25]

Gurcharan Singh, an Akali, was suspected to have planned Sodhi's death, though Surinder Singh Chinda and a female accomplice named Baljit Kaur carried out the actual task, not far from the temple complex. Bhindranwale's group retaliated by killing the killers.

The temple complex, in fact, was no more a secure place. On 23 May 1983, a body had been discovered from a gutter behind Guru Nanak Niwas, while another was found on 11 June in a sewer, also close to Guru Nanak Niwas. Still another body was recovered from the sewer behind Guru Ram Das Sarai on 3 September 1983. On 9 January 1984, the body of a Nihang Sikh was discovered on the third floor of Guru Ram Das Sarai. The chain of bodies became unending. The situation worsened by the day as the militants gained the upper hand at the cost and credibility of the moderate Akalis and the morcha.

Longowal now feared for his life, and in April 1984 the *Hindustan Times* quoted him as saying, 'Very soon, even I and my supporters may be on the hit list [of extremists], if we are not already on it.'[26] The words were prophetic. The militants murdered Longowal a year later, on 20 August 1985.

Efforts were made to resolve the differences between the two sants by a five-member committee of jathedars and priests.[27] Bhindranwale and the militants, however, did not honour its findings and recommendations.

Despite these developments, the Akali Dal did not dissociate from or disown Bhindranwale. It could not have done so without alienating its electoral base that had been captured by Bhindranwale, who had acquired the image of an altruistic reformer and crusader for the Sikh cause, while the Akalis were viewed by masses merely as seekers of political power.

Probably for this reason, the Akali Dal considered it inopportune to openly oppose Bhindranwale; they would condemn violence but not Bhindranwale in public. Longowal was characteristically unassertive even after he had received threats to his own life. The Akali Dal was fast becoming marginalized. Its equivocal approach was a political failure and it resulted in the radicals overshadowing the movement and blemishing the party's public image, particularly outside Punjab.

Consequently, by mid-1984, the Akalis, their demands and the morcha itself were no more relevant, but the unmitigated violence that had engulfed the state certainly was. Indira Gandhi in her speech to the nation on 2 June 1984 conveyed this:

> The reality that has emerged is not the adequacy or otherwise of the terms of settlement offered by the Government on the

> various Akali Dal demands, but the fact that the agitation is now in the hands of a few who have scant regard for the unity and integrity of our country or concern for communal peace and harmony or the continued economic progress of Punjab.[28]

She was not wrong, but that was in 1984, years after the peaceful agitation had commenced. The conflict resolution strategy followed by the government was problematic too. By not addressing the regional aspirations at the opportune time or dealing effectively with the ever-worsening law and order situation, the movement was allowed to turn into an ethno-national struggle and it became intractable.

7

The Army Marches On

It was a sticky summer day, with temperatures touching 40 degrees Celsius. In Amritsar, the roads and streets were empty. The curfew had confined people indoors. As the sun set, the eerie silence of an otherwise usually bustling Amritsar was broken by an equally unsettling rumbling sound of heavy trucks and tanks carrying troops from the cantonment. It was 5 June and the army was marching to the Golden Temple. Curious men and women peeped out from behind the closed windows and doors of their homes at the rather bizarre sight of armour-plated vehicles rolling in the bazaars. They were certain, though, that the days of gun-toting militants around them were going to be over.

The rendezvous for the troops was the magnificent Town Hall and Kotwali Complex built in 1870. It was located just a turn away from the Golden Temple. The operation was to commence around 10 p.m. The army had kept the plan a closely guarded secret. The civil administration was not involved and had no prescience of the operational plan. Perhaps the generals did not trust the civil administration. Some of the civilian officers were suspected to be in sympathy, if not in league, with Bhindranwale. That might have been true, but not taking senior civil officers on board at the planning stage or using civilian guides to negotiate the serpentine lanes and meandering alleys around the temple complex proved costly, as we saw. The army had come to aid the civil authority and the normal procedure provided for associating an executive magistrate. This was not done.

With no assigned role to play in the operation, I settled myself for the night at my camp office, converting it into a kind of control room with a police wireless set and a telephone line to the military exchange, just in case we were called upon for the odd contingency. But there was no call from the army. Nor did I get any worthwhile information on the police wireless network. The dead silence of the night, however, was continuously broken by bursts of fire from small arms, with the occasional sound of heavy weapons, which could be heard even in the Civil Lines area, where I was.

I was anxious to get to the scene. As daylight set in on the morning of 6 June, I rushed to the Operation Room of 9 Division, where I found Gen. Sundarji brooding in front of a wall-sized map of the Golden Temple complex. He looked fatigued. Spittle had settled in the corners of his mouth and as he spoke, he frothed. 'Oh hell, how they fought, the desperados,' he said rather disconsolately. On my asking, he briefed me about the operation and thereafter I was escorted to the temple complex.

The Thinking General, as Sundarji was popularly known, had planned a speedy mop-up operation. His strategy was based on overawing Maj. Gen. Shabeg Singh, Bhindranwale's military adviser, and his pack of militants with the spectacle of superior might and the sheer numbers in his legion. The task force had elements from the army, navy and the air force, the last two wings to provide logistical support. The contingent carried an array of weapons—automatic rifles, rockets and light artillery. Armoured personnel carriers, tanks, frogmen, divers and helicopters for reconnaissance reinforced it.

History probably had not seen so many red-ribbon soldiers deployed for such a small arena—the area of the Golden Temple precinct is approximately 35 acres. Led by Sundarji, there were Lt Gen. Ranjit Singh Dayal, Maj. Gen. K.S. Brar, the designated commander of Operation Blue Star, Brig. D.V. Rao, commander, 350 Infantry Brigade, Brig. N.K. Talwar, deputy commandant of 9 Division, Brig. A.K. Dewan, deputy commandant of 15 Division, and, in addition, over a dozen colonels and commandants. Maj. Gen. Jagdish Singh Jamwal, who commanded the Amritsar-based 15 Division, was also on call, though he was not directly involved in the operation. It was a formidable force assembled to confront a band of civilians equipped mainly with small arms.

The foot soldiers were drawn from the BSF, CRPF, SFF (Special Frontier Force), a hush-hush unit under the Cabinet Secretariat, and from eight army infantry battalions, namely 1 Para, 10 Guards, 12 Bihar, 15 Kumaon, 9 Kumaon, 10 Dogra, 26 Madras and 9 Garhwal regiment, the last two having been grafted from 15 Division. Cavalry provided the tanks. There were, in addition, support troops drawn from 60 Engineer Regiment and 8 Mechanized Battalion. The operation was conducted under the command of 350 Infantry Brigade led by Brig. D.V. Rao. The troops were scrambled at short notice from different and far-flung parts of the country. While 9 Division moved from Meerut, some came from as far as the north-east region, Secunderabad, Trivandrum and Pathankot.

The para commandos and the SFF, which constituted the core of the assault group on the Akal Takht, were brought in from the north-east and Sarsawa in Uttar Pradesh, respectively. The troops of 1 Para, under the command of Lt Col. K.C. Padha, were engaged in anti-insurgency operations near the international border with Myanmar in Manipur when on the night of 30 May they were told to drive all the way to Jorhat, Assam, and from there were airlifted to Chandigarh on 2 June. From Chandigarh, they motored to Nahan in Himachal Pradesh, their battalion's base for a briefing. For the first time they were to discover the mystery of their sudden and rather circuitous journey from Manipur to Nahan and then on to Amritsar by road, reaching Guru's Nagri late on the afternoon on 3 June.

Lt Gen. R.S. Dayal, the second senior-most general involved in Operation Blue Star, belonged to this battalion, 1 Para. That seems to me the only reason to pull out troops deployed in active operations thousands of miles away. Dayal had earned the Maha Vir Chakra for capturing the strategic Haji Pir Pass from Pakistan in the 1965 war. Usually, one tends to have greater trust in the prowess of the men you have grown with, more so when they have a proven track record. Dayal was no different in choosing men for the critical leg of Operation Blue Star, even if it meant physically overstretching the troops.

1 Para had sent an advance liaison group to Amritsar on 1 June to coordinate with 9 Division. However, in an interaction with the operational headquarters of 9 Division, all it could get by way of guidance was a layout plan of the temple complex on a tourist map and a few aerial photographs of the buildings. The operational headquarters personnel were new to the area and were unaware of the logistical details required. This, in fact, was the tribulation of the garrison—a total lack of familiarity with the terrain, the layout of the temple complex and the ground conditions.

For air reconnaissance, Jaguar and helicopter sorties were launched but the aerial photographs did not show the interior layout or the location of the weaponry deployed behind the concealed positions. With little operational inputs from 9 Division, 1 Para were forewarned to find their own ground. They launched a foot reconnaissance of the area, moving around the northern and western boundary of the temple on the night of 3 June, the very day they reached Amritsar.

The recce brought them in direct contact with about seventeen outposts set up by the militants on high-rise private buildings surrounding the temple. An exchange of fire followed. Three outposts of the militants on the north-west side were blasted with rocket fire on the night of 3–4 June. This caused the militants to flee and they abandoned most of the outposts in the private buildings around the temple complex.

1 Para also secured a high-rise private building located on the approach lane to the Akal Takht from the Gurdwara Thara Sahib side. The building was a kirpan-manufacturing factory with residences on the upper floors—it was formally requisitioned on 6 June to serve as a temporary base for the commandos. Strangely, however, when the operation was launched on the night of 5 June, this route, which would have given clear and direct access to the right flank of the Akal Takht (as one faces it) was not exploited, not even as a diversionary tactic. Instead, the soldiers entered by the route that the pilgrims take.

The SFF under the command of Lt Col M.P. Choudhary had reached Amritsar on 4 June. It was tasked with carrying out the main assault on the Akal Takht, Bhindranwale's headquarters. The SSF had procured canisters of CS gas, a non-lethal gas, from the BSF facility in Tekanpur near Gwalior. The shells were to be fired into the Akal Takht with the intent to temporarily stun and immobilize the militants. The Special Forces were to seize this opportunity to enter the Akal Takht and overpower the militants, who would be disoriented by CS gas.

However, the gas, like air, does not discriminate between enemies and friends. It could also temporarily befog the troops as much as it would the militants. 1 Para and the SSF were, therefore, to wear gas masks. They were, however, not familiar with the pesky contraption that covered the entire face and made it arduous to speak. There were also not enough masks for all the personnel. I learnt that an SOS was sent to India's military attaché in London, who rushed a consignment of gas masks to Bombay by the first available flight, from where the air force carried it to Amritsar in the afternoon. The SFF and 1 Para troops spent the evening familiarizing themselves with the device and learning how to communicate with each other with their mouths blocked by the masks.

The Objective

The objective of the operation may best be described in Brar's words as 'clearing the Golden Temple complex at Amritsar by a swift and decisive action, and capturing maximum militants, weapons and ammunition.'[1]

The troops were tasked to get Bhindranwale and his gun-toting band, dead or alive. However, they were constrained by a few caveats. They were directed not to fire towards the Harmandir Sahib, the sanctum sanctorum, even if they were fired at from that end. Damage to the sanctum sanctorum would have hurt Sikh sentiments most and was considered an unacceptable option.

Secondly, the operation was to be completed in the shortest time possible. The government apprehended an uprising in rural Punjab if word spread about the army action, which was inevitable with the passage of time. People would march to Amritsar and so any delay could prove costly.

Thirdly, minimum force was to be used. Collateral damage to the Akal Takht and other structures within the Parikrama was to be avoided. This ruled out the use of heavy weapons.

In conventional warfare, the tactic is to pound the target with artillery, an area weapon, so that the opponent keeps his head down, while the infantry advances to close proximity of the target. Annihilation and destruction of the given target is usually an intended objective. The army, in fact, is not trained to fight any other way. Nor were Sundarji's infantry battalions. But this tactic was not possible in the present operation, considering that the army was operating in a sacred space.

The militants were religiously charged, armed to the teeth and well entrenched behind brick-lined battlements and sandbagged foxholes that were not visible from the outside. Their defences had been laid in the basements, at the ground level, escalating to the floors above and on the rooftops. The place had been converted into a fortress.

It was a superhuman mission that Sundarji had undertaken to execute, under a commitment to political leadership to cause negligible tribulation to the temple complex. It was a mortiferous commitment, a catastrophe waiting to happen. But those in charge of the operation failed to anticipate what an officer who requested anonymity said to me in a visibly distressed tone, 'Even a gentleman cadet [trainee] at the Indian Military Academy would have known that the infantry was walking into a death trap in the fortified built-up defences.' The senior officers presumed a quick victory as a certainty and did not plan for contingencies in case things went wrong.

Sundarji had intended Operation Blue Star to be a brisk blitz, and its success largely dependent on elements of speed and surprise. Deception and deflection are strategic tools in any army operation. In open societies, however, it is not easy to achieve these objectives. When troops operate domestically against their own people, it is almost impossible to keep such operations under wraps. Indira Gandhi had addressed the nation on the night of 2 June 1984, and soon after her broadcast, the All India Radio (AIR) had announced that the army had moved in in Punjab to assist the civil authorities.

The movement of troops from Meerut and other far-off places was an indication of the ensuing action. Punjab came under curfew starting 9 p.m. on 3 June (for thirty-six hours). Shabeg Singh was shrewd to sense the impending army action in these developments. In the late evening of 3 June, in an interview with noted journalist Subhash Kirpekar, when asked how soon he expected the army action to start, Shabeg had replied, 'Maybe tonight.'[2] The element of surprise was lost. So, when the troops entered the temple without any diversionary movement from the flanks or the rear, the militants were waiting for them from behind the built-up structures.

Who drafted the operational plan? Brar had conceived it, but after brainstorming and deliberations, it wore the unmistakable print of

Sundarji. The operation was divided into two parts, keeping in mind the layout of the buildings, topography of the temple complex and the location of those in hiding. The complex was marked into two distinct though interconnected zones—the Parikrama complex and the Sarai complex—considering their relative importance. The ultimate target was the Akal Takht at the western end of the Parikrama complex, where Bhindranwale and Shabeg were well entrenched. The place was heavily defended and had the largest concentration of armed men at one place within the complex. Strategically sited automatic weapons with clear lines of fire covered all approaches to the Akal Takht.

The sanctum sanctorum, Harmandir Sahib, which is located in the Amrit Sarowar, or the holy pool, has entry doors from all four directions—east, west, north and south—signifying that all castes are equal and welcome. Muslim saint Mir Mohammad of Lahore had laid its foundation stone in 1588 on an invitation from Guru Arjan Dev, signifying unity of mankind. It is the holiest of Sikh holy shrines. Its safety and sanctity were of paramount consideration for the army while planning the operation. Commando divers were, therefore, detailed to swim across the sarowar and secure the sanctum sanctorum first. It was feared that the militants might have planted underwater dynamites around the temple and might blow them up to give the government a bad name.

1 Para commandos were sent to Patiala and Jalandhar apart from Amritsar to clear the gurdwaras at these stations. The Amritsar group, numbering about 100, was split into three teams. One team was to seize the circumambulatory passage in the west that leads to the Akal Takht from the point where there is a drinking water *piao* on the verandah. The second group under the command of Maj. Prakash Katoch was to capture the Darshani Deori opposite the Akal Takht. The third group under the command of a Sikh officer was to secure the Harmandir Sahib. The divers were part of this group but were separated from the main group so that they could swim across the sarowar from the langar building side in the east to

defuse any underwater explosives. The SFF commandos were tasked with assaulting the core focus of the operation, the Akal Takht, where Bhindranwale with his key aides and about 100 armed men held the defences.

On the ground, the opposing battle commanders were the two generals—one serving, Brar, and one cashiered, Shabeg Singh, Bhindranwale's military strategist. Both of them were from Punjab and were Jat Sikhs. In the 1971 war for the liberation of Bangladesh, they had fought together against the Pakistani Army and distinguished themselves. Brar, then a colonel, had earned a Vir Chakra for bravery. The services of Shabeg, then a brigadier, were applauded for resurrecting, training and leading the guerrilla force, the Mukti Bahini, under an assumed name, Beg Ali. He had then sported a skull cap, worn a Bangladeshi lungi and long kurta—what the Bengalis call '*panjabi*', probably because of its Punjabi origins. The brigadier had earned a well-deserved Ati Vishisht Seva Medal and post the war, he had been elevated to the rank of major general.

What, however, transformed Shabeg from a dedicated bulwark of the Bangladesh war to now battling his own colleagues in olive green is a classic case of perceived deprivation and consequential desire for retribution. He was charged with corruption and cashiered out of the army without a trial a day before the due date of his superannuation by the application of a special clause that empowers the army chief to do so. He lost his pension, the rank and the well-earned battle decorations. Hell hath no fury like a hero humiliated.

Post his dismissal from the service, the CBI nailed him in two cases. He won both in court due to lack of evidence. Convinced of discrimination, he felt he was in disgrace purely because of his religion, and metamorphized to an *amritdhari* (baptized) Sikh, with a flowing beard. He dedicated himself to the cause of the panth, as espoused by Bhindranwale.

The proximity of his ancestral village Khayala to Amritsar facilitated easy access to Bhindranwale, and the traditions in Sikhism sanctifying the use of the sword to avenge injustice (as he perceived) probably helped him overcome the constraints of conscience which surely would have tormented a soldier of his standing—one who had defended his motherland in Jammu and Kashmir in 1948 and China in 1962; who had fought in the Nagaland insurgency; and who had finally dismembered Pakistan in 1971. A month or so before Operation Blue Star, he made the temple complex his home, becoming an in-house consigliere on military affairs to Bhindranwale. Ostensibly, his presence in Amritsar was to hold *akhand paths*, in thanksgiving for winning the criminal cases instituted against him.

Ironically, Shabeg, who was an instructor at the Indian Military Academy, Dehradun, had trained Brar and the two knew each other well. Was it destiny? Here the two were, locked in battle against each other, one under the call of duty and the other under a misplaced commitment to religiosity. I find it a great pity that the two chose not to communicate with each other before the collision. Had they done so, maybe a negotiated surrender of the militants might have been worked out and the devastating outcome of the operation avoided. We'll never know.

The Surrender

On 5 June, we—the civilian officers—were reviewing the situation sitting in the office of Harjit Singh, SP, CID, at the Kotwali complex, which had become our de facto daytime office due to its proximity to the temple, when Col Eustace William Fernandez informed us that the army would launch the assault on the complex that night.

Earlier, Harjit Singh and I had offered to attempt a dialogue with Bhindranwale to persuade him and his men to come out of the temple precinct. In the civil–military liaison conference, Brar had told us that a warning would be sounded to the militants before launching the assault. However, neither the dialogue nor the warning had materialized till then. Brar, in fact, never gave the militants a chance for a negotiated surrender. Perhaps that was not his mandate.

On the afternoon of 5 June, due to the heavy exchange of fire, it had become extremely dangerous to go inside the fortified temple and attempt any negotiation. The only line of communication could have been through the telephones. However, the telephone lines had been disconnected. On our insistence, Col Fernandez sought the approval of his headquarters to facilitate our communication with the Akal Takht, but we were told that the efforts to restore the telephone lines had failed. That ended any attempt to avert the battle.

In the civil–military conferences on 3 and 4 June it was agreed that the civilians living in the immediate vicinity of the temple would be evacuated to avoid collateral damage. However, this was not done till 2.45 p.m. on 5 June. Pilgrims were trapped inside the temple and the civilian population in their homes in the narrow lanes around the temple. Unable to contact the chief secretary or the home secretary, I spoke to Harjit Singh Randhawa, IG, CID, on the police duplex network, urging that the state government intervene.

Randhawa was able to pull the wires, and at about 3.20 p.m., Brig. Talwar, deputy GOC of 9 Division, contacted me and proposed to announce a ceasefire from 4.30 p.m. to 5.30 p.m. He, however, left it to me to make the ceasefire announcement. I entreated that the formal announcement of the ceasefire should be made by the army, and that either Brar or his deputy should be present to supervise a possible surrender by the militants and the evacuation of the civilian population, but he flatly refused, saying, 'You may make an announcement for ceasefire for one and a half hours.'

I fell back on the public relations department, which had stationed a van at the Kotwali complex with a loudspeaker fitted on its hood for proclamation of curfew or its relaxation. The ceasefire announcement was handwritten in chaste Punjabi, deliberately avoiding any use of an expression of surrender. Knowing the Sikh psyche and the deeply embedded tradition of martyrdom in the Khalsa panth, it was considered prudent not to convey a sense of helplessness or capitulation to those inside the temple. Any such suggestion might have inhibited the radicals from surrendering. The announcement, made at 4.30 p.m. in Punjabi, was:

> *Pyari Sadh Sangat Ji,*
>
> *Waheguru Ji Ka Khalsa Waheguru Ji Ki Fateh.*
>
> *App jee nu bentee kiti jandi hai ke hun ton 5.30 vaje dey darmian security forces ney firing bundh ker ditti hai. Iss dauran sari sadh Sangat nu baintee hai ke oh Darshani Deori chowk Ghanta Ghar waley passyon bahar aa key sidhey Kotwali aa jaan. Iss duran jay kissai numaindey ney gal karnee hovey tan wein Kotwali aa jaan. Baintee hai ke sidhey Kotwali aa Jaan, Sujjey khubey jaan wale di jaan nuh khatra ho sakda hai.*

Roughly translated, it was this: 'I entreat you that between 4.30 p.m. and 5.30 p.m. the security forces will cease fire. All are requested to come out from the Ghanta Ghar Deori side, direct to Kotwali. If any representative wants to hold any talks, they should also come to Kotwali and not go to the left or the right side as that could endanger their life.'

The announcement was repeated about eight times, first near Jallianwala Bagh, then at Katra Ahluwalia, and thereafter at Chowk Prag Dass. It yielded limited results. Balwinder Singh, the assistant public relations officer, and Kewal Krishan, the cinema operator, who made the announcements, fearing that the militants might fire at the vehicle, kept a reasonable distance from the temple boundary. The van could not even go all around the temple precinct due to the narrow lanes. Had an armoured vehicle been used by the army to go around the temple to make the announcement, we may have had better results. Secondly, on hearing the ceasefire announcement, the priests started a kirtan recital from the Harmandir Sahib and that muffled the announcements.

Nevertheless, 129 persons, mostly from the Sarai complex, came out by 5.30 p.m. Questioning them convinced us that a large number of devotees were still trapped inside. They could not come out, either because the announcement was not audible or the militants held them back at gunpoint. I requested the army to extend the ceasefire till 6.30 p.m. and thereafter for another half an hour till 7 p.m., each time making fresh announcements. With these extensions, another thirty people came out from the temple complex, taking the total to 159, but none of them were weapon-wielding militants. About 120 of them were later taken to the army camp for interrogation, while a few children, women, septuagenarians and the infirm were let off after initial questioning.

We realized that the militants might come out only if directed to do so by their leaders. Therefore, while the ceasefire was in progress, at the suggestion of the SP, CID, I decided to approach Baldev Singh, the doctor in charge of Sri Guru Ram Das Hospital—the SGPC-owned charitable medical facility—to mediate. Dr Baldev Singh was the personal physician to Tohra, Longowal and Bhindranwale. The doctor–patient relationship fosters mutual confidence—Dr Baldev enjoyed the trust of all of them. I proposed to send him inside the temple to talk to these leaders and persuade them to come out. With this intent, Harjit Singh, SP, CID, M.P.S. Aulakh, who was heading the Intelligence Bureau in Amritsar, and Apar Singh Bajwa, DSP, Amritsar, got into my flag car and we drove towards the SGPC hospital where Dr Baldev Singh lived.[3]

On Circular Road, beyond Burj Baba Phula Singh and near the police station, my car was stopped at the CRPF checkpost. They cautioned us not to proceed further as the tanks had commenced firing. The militants had fortified the high-rise overhead water storage tank near the Teja Singh Samundri Hall and the two high-rise bungas; fortifications on top of these structures dominated the area and the army wanted to neutralize these before launching the operation.

Otherwise, the advancing troops would be easy targets for sniper fire. The army had deployed tanks and 3.7-inch guns to demolish these high battlements. These weapons were located at a reasonable distance from the temple to provide an accessible line of sight and to ensure that the angle of fire was not precipitous. These elevated fortifications were blown up, and with the resultant gaping holes, the water tank located near the Teja Singh Samundri Hall emptied out, leaving the complex waterless.

Ignoring the warning, we drove on, but were stopped again at a little distance, this time by army officers. We saw a tank deployed on Circular Road firing from its main gun towards the temple precincts. It was around 6.45 in the evening, and the ceasefire was still in force. We rushed back to the office at Kotwali and I contacted Chandigarh on the police duplex network. No senior officer was available. I left a message in the office of Randhawa (IG, CID) and sent TPM messages to the chief secretary and the home secretary, pointing out that firing by tanks and other heavy weapons was likely to cause collateral casualties as the areas around the temple had not been evacuated—these were thickly populated narrow lanes, bazaars and residences.

From Kotwali, we dashed to the control room of 9 Division, where both Dayal and Brar were stationed. I shared my apprehensions with Dayal, who brushed aside my concerns. He pulled out a pin from his turban, pointed to its small pinhead and said, 'Tank fire is accurate on targets as tiny as this pinhead. There is no danger to the civilian population or property.' Evacuation of the people from the surrounding areas, he said, in any case was not feasible at this late stage. The troops were ready to launch the assault in a few hours and the electricity supply to the city would be cut off from 9 p.m. To reassure me, the general added, 'It is a small inconvenience. The operation will be over by 1 a.m., after which electricity will be restored.'

The accuracy of the tank fire was, however, exposed by large-scale damage to civilian assets, which I have described in a subsequent chapter. One tank shell, in fact, fell miles away in the cantonment, damaging part of the divisional canteen and injuring an army jawan. A splinter strayed into the official residence of Col O.S. Goraya, Col Admn of 15 Division, but the family escaped harm. Another shell fell in the agricultural fields beyond the grain mandi, on the outskirts of the walled city. Collateral damage to non-combatants is an inevitable adjunct to any battle, and when the battle is in a densely populated area, the losses can be colossal. As they say, when elephants fight, it is the grass that gets trampled, and that is what happened during Blue Star.

8

'Who Moved My Army?'

On 2 June 1984, late in the evening, K.D. Vasudeva, chief secretary, was summoned to Raj Bhavan, Chandigarh. By the time he reached, A.S. Pooni, home secretary, Punjab, had already arrived. The governor, Pande, had an edict for the chief secretary. He had been summoned by the Prime Minister on 28 May and then again a few days later to Delhi. In Delhi, he had been informed about the decision to requisition the army to storm the Golden Temple, but it was to be kept a secret till the last day—he was instructed not to speak about it even to the director of the Intelligence Bureau.[1] This implied that the intelligence agencies were not in the know of the decision to launch Operation Blue Star and this may have deprived the army of valuable intelligence inputs, so crucial for the success of such an operation.

On 2 June, Pande conveyed the decision of the Central government to the chief secretary and Punjab's home secretary. While they conversed over the procedural formalities, the GOC-in-chief,

Western Command, Lt Gen. Sundarji, also arrived at Raj Bhavan. Pande has disclosed that on 6 November 1983, when he had approached Sundarji to deploy the army in Punjab after the terrorists had killed a few Hindu bus passengers, he had 'strongly advised against it', and wanted 'the army to be kept out of the Punjab imbroglio as he feared unpleasant consequences'.[2] Things were different now—they had been instructed by Delhi to do so.

Consequently, a formal requisition letter was issued to Sundarji to deploy the army in Punjab. The subject matter fell within the domain of the home department. Pooni, however, had reservations and had to be persuaded by the chief secretary before he reluctantly complied, affixing his signatures and seal on the DO letter. A few days later, Pooni proceeded on leave.

The operative part of Pooni's letter to Sundarji read, 'I am directed to say that the Government of Punjab considers it necessary to call in the Army in aid to civil power in view of the deteriorating law and order situation in the state. Immediate action may please be taken in this regard.'[3]

Sundarji's chief of staff at Chandimandir, Lt Gen. R.S. Dayal, was appointed security adviser to the Punjab governor on 2 June, and he took over charge the same day, before the formal requisition request was handed to the army. This was probably the first time that a serving general was appointed to an operational civilian post. The army had, in fact, intimated to the government that, '. . . [T]he army officer in charge of aid to Civil Authorities, when the Army is called out, should also be designated as Security Adviser to the Governor and empowered to exercise overall command over the police and paramilitary forces.'[4] Dayal, accordingly, assumed this overarching authority. The objective was to ensure unity of command and coordination between the military, paramilitary forces, police and the civil administration.

Dayal held his first press conference along with Punjab Police chief P.S. Bhinder and the GOC of Punjab, Haryana and Himachal, on the forenoon of 3 June but he did not disclose that the army would storm the Golden Temple. In response to a question, he merely brushed aside the correspondent, saying they should have a 'little more patience and bear with us'.

The Ministry of Defence issued a missive to the army headquarters, and on its strength, the Directorate of Military Operations passed on operational instructions to the Western Command. These were legalities, otherwise so imperative in a democracy, but the forward elements of the Meerut-based 9 Infantry Division tasked with action in the Golden Temple had already arrived in Amritsar on 29 May, covering a distance of about 300 kilometres to assist the civil administration, without the civil administration knowing about it.

The army was formally empowered to act, independent of the executive magistrates and bypassing the provisions of the Criminal Procedure Code (CrPC), 1861, that gave powers to the district magistrate to requisition the army to aid civil power. Section 130 of the CrPC confers powers to the army to arrest and confine persons participating in any unlawful activity 'as the magistrate may direct'. However, with the enactment of the Punjab State Disturbed Areas Act, 1983, and the Armed Forces (Punjab and Chandigarh) Special Powers Act, 1983, the forces, including the air force, were empowered to maintain public order, without any direction from the magistracy. The power to break into any premises, to search, arrest, seize or fire upon or use force that may extend to causing death, etc., was conferred on the forces, and these powers could be exercised without a warrant or magisterial order if reasonable suspicion existed that a person had committed or was about to commit a cognizable offence.

Therefore, no other formal order to requisition the army by the district magistrate was required, nor was any such order issued by any deputy commissioner for the army's operations in forty-three historical gurdwaras in Punjab and Haryana, including the

Golden Temple in Amritsar, the Takht Keshgarh Sahib in Anandpur, the Takht Damdama Sahib in Talwandi, gurdwaras in Fatehgarh, Chamkaur Sahib and Bhatha Sahib in Ropar, gurdwaras at the Muktsar Sahib, Dukhniwaran, Patiala, and in Haryana at the Manji Sahib in Ambala, the Panjokhra Sahib and the Nada Sahib. The law also gave immunity to the army from prosecution, and the legal proceedings for any act done or said to have been done by them in an exercise of power under the 1983 laws.

Hours after Pooni handed over the requisition letter to Sundarji, the Prime Minister addressed the nation, on the night on 2 June. In her speech, there was no indication of the decision to send the army into the temple. She called for further dialogue, 'If any misgivings or doubts on any issue remain, let us sit around the table and find a solution. In a democracy the right and only way to settle problems is through discussion . . . Let us join together to heal wounds . . . To all sections of Punjabis, I appeal: Don't shed blood, shed hatred.'[5]

The next day, a government notification banning media coverage of the ongoing agitation in the state for a period of two months was promulgated. In Amritsar, Deputy Commissioner Gurdev Singh imposed curfew on 3 June, starting from 11 a.m., trapping the pilgrims gathered to commemorate the martyrdom day of Guru Arjan Dev in the Golden Temple complex. On the night of 3 June, electricity and water supply to the temple complex was cut off and telephone lines were snapped.

Gurdev Singh, however, told me that he was not aware of the impending army action. The bureaucracy and the police in Punjab were considered too complicit to confide in. Was it by design or by oversight? In any case, it showed that the Government of India did not want to take the district administration into confidence about the military action.

We, the civil officials, were not the only ignorant ones. Two days later, the supreme commander of the armed forces, President

Zail Singh, was to question: Who moved my army? He had no inkling of the impending Operation Blue Star and learnt about it 'on the morning following the action'.[6]

P.C. Alexander, the principal secretary to Indira Gandhi, gives two reasons why the President was not kept informed. First, because, 'her [Prime Minister's] relations with him by then were strained to the extent of her losing full trust in him.' Secondly, she did not anticipate 'the seriousness of the damage'.[7]

It is, however, in the public domain that the Prime Minister had called on the President at the Rashtrapati Bhavan on 30 May, barely three days before Operation Blue Star. Indira Gandhi spent two hours with him, discussing, according to Rashtrapati Bhavan sources, 'the entire gamut of options'. *India Today* disclosed that Rajiv Gandhi had also met the President twice before the army action. It wrote, 'Perhaps the most significant meeting that Zail Singh had in that spell was with K.P. Singh Deo, the minister of state for defence, on 4 June, the day after the siege had begun.'[8]

The details of what transpired between the President and the Prime Minister and the others are not public knowledge, except the disclosures made by Zail Singh in his memoirs. He writes that he had earnestly advised the Prime Minister against any provocative intervention and to instead resort to subtle strategy to evict the gun-toting men ensconced in the temple.

The President's advice was obviously not accepted, but more serious was the constitutional impropriety that the President was misled to believe that 'police' action was being planned, while the army's advance party of 9 Infantry Division had already reached Amritsar on 29 May. Zail Singh has disclosed in his autobiography that Indira Gandhi had hinted to him 'nonchalantly' that the plan was to flush out the terrorists from the Golden Temple by using 'police force'. Subsequent to Operation Blue Star, the President lamented, 'They could have had a word with me before taking such a drastic step, to which they had no explanation.'[9]

The Cabinet Decision

The decision to deploy the army in Punjab, in fact, had already been taken in May 1984. The Cabinet Committee on Political Affairs met under Prime Minister Indira Gandhi with Home Minister P.V. Narasimha Rao, Defence Minister R. Venkataraman, Energy Minister P. Shiv Shankar and Finance Minister Pranab Mukherjee as members. It resolved to deploy the army and storm the temple in Punjab. Pranab Mukherjee had reservations, but was overruled by the Prime Minister, who said, 'Pranab, I know of the consequences.'[10]

Later on, while releasing a centennial commemorative volume on Indira Gandhi in New Delhi on 13 May 2017, Pranab Mukherjee disclosed, 'I recalled [at the Cabinet Committee meeting] how Ahmad Shah Abdali had to face serious consequences after the Third Battle of Panipat when he did something wrong with the Golden Temple', but Mrs Gandhi replied that, "Sometimes history demands some action to be taken which may not prove correct later on but perhaps is most relevant at that time. This decision cannot be avoided."'[11]

Empowered by the decision of the committee, Indira Gandhi summoned Chief of Army Staff Gen. A.S. Vaidya on 25 May and mandated him to flush out the terrorists ensconced in the Golden Temple and other gurdwaras in Punjab. The army chief proposed a soft option: Encircle the targeted gurdwaras and tire out the militants.

But this strategy was discarded on 29 May. Alexander has disclosed that Gen. Vaidya met Indira Gandhi for a second time after visiting Punjab and brainstorming with the senior commanders and he now recommended a pincer pounce instead of a slow-moving siege. Alexander states that Vaidya bared the blueprint 'so eloquently and with so much confidence about the soundness of his new plan of operation' that Indira Gandhi approved it. The general convinced the Prime Minister to conduct a 'commando operation inside the Golden Temple, which would be conducted with such swiftness and surprise that it would *not result in any damage* to the temple buildings', so states Alexander.[12]

However, this story of Vaidya changing his strategy is not supported by other reliable chronicles. Vaidya, it seems, did not visit Punjab or Chandigarh or meet with Sundarji between 26 and 29 May.[13] Rather, Indira Gandhi was personally and through her inner-circle aides interacting with Sundarji, bypassing the army chief, and it was Sundarji, the strident subordinate, who overruled his boss, the Chief of Army Staff.

Sundarji proposed to conduct a swift blitz—to use present-day terminology, a surgical strike—and the political leadership bought into the idea. Vaidya, it seemed, lacked the grit to discipline his army commander, Sundarji, who secured a carte blanche to conduct the operation, because, as Alexander describes, Indira Gandhi 'respected the professional judgment of the generals'.[14]

On 3 June, Sundarji had a direct one-on-one meeting with the Prime Minister. His wife, Vani, has said in his memoirs, published after Sundarji's death, 'A completely different assignment was Operation Blue Star. Indira Gandhi had summoned him to Delhi from Chandimandir (Chandigarh Cantonment) late at night on 3 June 1984. He met with her alone for over an hour. When he returned home at 2 a.m., all he said to me was: It is a tough one.'

In fact, Sunderji had called on Indira Gandhi more than once, in Delhi. There is independent corroboration from Lt Gen. V.K. Nayar, the then additional director, Military Operations Directorate (MOD), Army Headquarters, who has chronicled that Sundarji and his chief of staff, Dayal, were 'seen coming out of the prime minister's office and Gen. Vaidya was nowhere near the scene'.[15]

If Sundarji alone met the Prime Minister on the night of 3 June, there was at least one more meeting between them, with Dayal in attendance, behind the Chief of Army Staff's back. The political establishment was in direct communication with the operational commanders, bypassing the line of command.

Sundarji committed himself to the Prime Minister for a swift, successful outcome, without realizing what he was headed for. This was the second time in Indian military history that the political leadership ignored the Chief of Army Staff to rely on a junior general, and both times the consequences were disastrous; it happened for the first time in the 1962 war against China when Lt Gen. B.M. Kaul, GOC of the north-east army, was relied upon over the Chief of Army Staff, and then again in 1984 in Operation Blue Star.

The Differences

The Indian Army is a highly disciplined force and operates on the principles of unity of command. However, there are always debates and brainstorming sessions within the stratified hierarchy. An important think tank at the MOD, then headed by Lt Gen. C.N. Somanna, had reservations about the army's involvement in Punjab, purely for professional reasons. Maj. Gen. V.K. Nayar, the then additional director general of military operations, was of the view that Punjab was a religious–political problem that had been allowed to degenerate into terrorism. Military action was no solution.

Gen. Nayar had briefed the army chief, Vaidya, more than once against army involvement in Punjab. One may gauge Nayar's frustration with Vaidya when he writes:

> No response was to become a hallmark of his reaction to any crisis . . . I felt that we had the wrong man to lead the Army at this critical juncture. He had no mind of his own and neither the will nor competence to handle crisis. He would follow the dictates of his political masters and what is worse that he lacked moral courage to restrain his defiant Army Commander, i.e., Lt Gen. K Sundarji.[16]

Vaidya lacked the stature and candidness of Field Marshal Sam Manekshaw, who in April 1971 overruled the Prime Minister by deferring the date of the Bangladesh liberation war from April to December, because in his appraisal the army needed time to prepare. Vaidya, unfortunately, paid the price with his life. Two years after Operation Blue Star and post retirement, he was assassinated in Pune on 10 August 1986 by Khalistan Commando Force militants Harjinder Singh, alias Jinda, and Sukhdev Singh, alias Sukha. Both terrorists were convicted and hanged to death on 9 October 1992.

Vaidya had become the thirteenth Chief of Army Staff after superseding his senior Lt Gen. S.K. Sinha, who had declined the request of the Punjab government in September 1981 for involving the army to arrest Bhindranwale from Chowk Mehta. Sinha was an independent-minded officer with a family link to Lok Nayak Jayaprakash Narayan, who had led the resistance movement against the Emergency in 1975. This, it seems, was Sinha's undoing and the reason for his suppression.

The army headquarters were acutely aware of the downside of engaging with an ethno-religious militant conflict within the precinct of a sacred space. Such interventions invariably leave deep scars, and earlier instances of similar encounters in holy places around the world only confirmed this, if such a corroboration was ever needed.

So, when the army's involvement in Punjab seemed almost a fait accompli, Lt Gen. V.K. Nayar, with the assistance of Col G.S. Ginger Bal and Col S.P. Kapoor, drafted 'an outline plan' in May 1984.[17] As per the plan, the army was to be used more as a psychological weapon rather than an operational force. The strategy was to 'make the public opinion favourable . . . It will put [the] onus of the outcome on the extremists', by strengthening the cordons around the Golden Temple, and to tire out the extremists.[18] Sundarji, however, discarded the MOD strategy and the established chain of command within the army, by going behind their backs directly to the Prime Minister. The MOD was turned into a 'mere spectator', and so was the army chief.

Gen. Nayar has gone on record to state that Sundarji disregarded this plan. Nayar has disclosed:

> Within the Army, consultation with HQ Western Command started in late February or early March 1984 . . . after collecting whatever information I could, I carried out an assessment . . . and held a closed door briefing of then Chief . . . I categorically recommended to him that he should talk to the PM and convey the Army's view . . . The aim was to give PM an honest and uninhibited opinion based on ground level inputs, impose caution on her in hardening the stance and prevent the Army's involvement . . . The main reason for insisting with the then Chief to meet the PM was that Punjab is of vital importance to the army and to prevent a situation when a ring from her or her Secretariat would rush the Army into a situation unprepared.'[19]

Alternative Options

Were alternative options considered to the army intervention? Not much is known about this, but Birbal Nath, the then DG, BSF, has revealed that an 'Israeli-style' attempt to 'deal with Sant Bhindranwale from outside' was debated in government circles. It obviously implied a sharp-shooter picking up Bhindranwale, but the chief of the central agency tasked for the job, while conceding the capability of his organization to execute the plan, pleaded with the Prime Minister an 'inability to carry out the task because of fear of ultimate exposure'.[20] India is a constitutional democracy and extra-legal measures, if exposed, would not only invite criminal prosecution, but also have serious political consequences.

Birbal Nath had proposed a more audacious cloak-and-dagger manoeuvre. He has not disclosed the details of the plan, but it involved hiring the services of 'a man who used to meet Mr Z.A. Bhutto in jail during the black days of General Zia's oppressive rule'. It involved a payout in foreign exchange, but the awaited 'sanction came late'.[21] Consequently, the undercover manoeuvre never unfolded. One can only infer that this option involved using spies under deep cover, those who enjoyed the confidence of the people around Bhindranwale, to 'deal' with him.

Still another indomitable operation code-named Sundown was planned in early 1984 to 'get hold' of Bhindranwale. A select group of commandos of the SFF, the armed wing under the Cabinet Secretariat, conducted mock trials at the Sarsawa Air Force base near Saharanpur. Apparently, all was ready, but as K.P.S. Gill has disclosed, the process was aborted because 'Mrs Gandhi said "no" to Operation Sundown'.[22]

9

The Grand Mosque of Mecca

FIVE YEARS BEFORE OPERATION BLUE STAR AND THOUSANDS OF miles away from the holy city of Amritsar, in another hallowed city, Mecca, a group of about 500 religious acolytes seized the Grand Mosque, the holiest site in Islam, in the sacred month of Muharram in 1979. They were led by Juhayman al Otaybi, an ex–National Guard soldier-turned-religious leader.

Their grouse was against their own state for allegedly having betrayed Islam. They called themselves the Brethren and had been leading a purification movement targeting the Saudi rulers. They picked up guns and turned the mosque into a battlefield.

On 20 November 1979, a group of the Brethren shut the doors of the mosque, held some pilgrims hostage, cut off telephone lines and killed the two unarmed policemen on duty who had attempted to resist. The militants had been stockpiling weapons in the basement of the mosque unnoticed by authorities and they now took up positions at strategic points in the mosque. They set up armed defences inside the sacred space and fortified the minarets that gave them a commanding height to oversee all approaches. Sharpshooters manned these positions.

The State imposed a curfew in Mecca, Medina, and several other places, resorting to large-scale preventive arrests and imposing a complete blackout on domestic and foreign media.

The Saudi Army and National Guard were pressed into action on the night of 20 November, but the frontal assault to secure the mosque failed. The troops suffered heavy casualties. In the operation, the army had used APCs, and the mosque complex suffered damage, inviting public wrath. Another assault by Saudi paratroopers two days later also failed, resulting in casualties. The Saudi forces were joined by Pakistani commandos.

The Saudi rulers faced serious trouble as a section of their forces refused to act against the militants or fire at the mosque; a section of troops called to quell the rebels also rebelled! Religion evoked greater loyalty than the State. Consequently, these men had to be disarmed, but some of them deserted their ranks and joined the rebels. A few were captured and executed for treason to set an example.[1]

To pacify the public and secure a mandate for the assault, the State approached the ulema and secured a fatwa against the rebels and Juhayman al Otaybi, their religious leader. It was made public on 25 November. Stories were planted to discredit the militants, alleging that they had desecrated the holy space by immoral acts. However, instead of securing public support, the fatwa had the opposite effect: The ulema were seen as State agents and they suffered a loss of credibility in the eyes of the faithful.

At this stage, the Saudis sought assistance from the US and France. The French government sent the National Gendarmerie, its elite commandos. However, there was another problem, for non-Muslims are not allowed to enter Mecca and the French commandos were Christians. The entry of the commandos had to be 'legitimized', after which the French could guide the Saudi forces using gas and lethal weapons.

The armed skirmishes lasted about fourteen days. The commander of the militants, Al-Qahtani, was killed, while Juhayman al Otaybi was arrested and later executed. Protests followed. Muslims demonstrated in Jeddah and in front of US embassies in Pakistan, Libya, Bangladesh and many other countries. Several radicals who escaped from the mosque went underground and launched a covert militant movement which lingered for a while.

No two situations are the same and comparisons may be odious. Context, time, locales, people and communities change, but the past always holds wisdom for the future. History has an uncanny habit of repeating itself, and those who do not learn from the past are doomed.

In 1984, did we miss out on the wisdom that the Mecca operations held for the world? The Pakistanis, for sure, did not. Its troops had assisted the Saudis in the Grand Mosque operations and therefore were au fait with the consequences of an armed operation targeting sacred spaces.

The Sikh radicals, who were in touch with the ISI, were guided by it to exploit the sacrosanct space of the Golden Temple complex to gain canonical legitimacy, and amass armaments and build fortifications by exploiting the safety and security of the holy precinct. As per one source, it was the ISI-guided group of militants who had triggered the minor clash between the Babbars and Bhindranwale's men in the Sarai complex of the temple to manoeuvre Bhindranwale's shifting to the Akal Takht from Guru Nanak Niwas. That changed the course of history.

I leave it to readers to draw their conclusions: The similarities in the Mecca and Amritsar situations and the two armed operations are striking. And that leaves one wondering why we did not draw on the lessons from Mecca's past, if the ISI-guided militants did.

10

Operation Blue Star: Part I

Zero hour was 10 p.m. on 5 June. Initially, all went well. The two landmarks identified outside the temple complex, namely Hotel Temple View and Braham Buta Akhara, with a commanding view of the area under militant occupation, were cleared by the BSF and CRPF with little resistance. The easy takeover of these premises was a morale booster for the forces.

Parallel to this action, the infantry battalions led by tanks and APCs moved to their respective launch pads—the open space in front of the main entrance to the temple (Ghanta Ghar Deori) on the northern side and the road leading to the Sarai complex on the eastern side. The assault was to be launched synchronously from these two directions. The Akal Takht, where Bhindranwale was ensconced with his armed men, however, was the prime target.

The Operation in the Parikrama

Militarily, the Akal Takht provides strategic depth. It is located at the western end of the Parikrama and the main entry to it is through the spacious cloister that provides safety against any surprise frontal attack. The Takht itself had been converted into a fortress—its walls and marble slabs had been cut open to make pigeonhole placements for automatic weapons. The militants had mutilated the sacrosanct structure and disfigured its architectural aesthetic.

The troops of 1 Para, SFF, 10 Guards and 26 Madras, all infantry battalions, were tasked with launching the assault in the Parikrama, with the Akal Takht as the main objective. Sundarji, for some inexplicable reason, had planned only a frontal assault on the Akal Takht, eschewing the left and right flanks or a punch from the rear, not even as a diversionary tactic. In hindsight, it was a fatal flaw.

At 10.30 p.m., 1 Para and SFF entered the Parikrama from the northern side, via the Ghanta Ghar Deori, 'with humility in their hearts and prayers on their lips', to quote Brar. Synchronously, 10 Guards, also an infantry battalion, under the command of Lt Col Israr Khan, advanced towards the Parikrama, also from the Ghanta Ghar Deori, to secure the northern side of the circumambulatory passage.

26 Madras was assigned a circuitous route; it was to enter the temple complex via the road that divides Guru Ram Das Sarai from the langar building, and thereafter access the Parikrama from the eastern end, traverse the entire length of the southern part of the Parikrama in front of the Library Deori, and then turn right to the west to link up with 1 Para and SFF in the open space in front of the Darshani Deori that sits directly between the Akal Takht and the Harmandir Sahib. (See map at the end of book.)

The Lull

In the beginning, all was quiet. For some inexplicable reason the usually trigger-happy militants were silent. Maybe it was going to be an easy operation. 1 Para, led by Col Keshav Padha, had reached the launch pad around 8.30 p.m. It was escorted by BSF guides from their camp at Gobindgarh Fort on the outskirts of the walled city to the temple, and positioned outside the Ghanta Ghar Deori. The troops freely moved around in the open space outside the main entrance to the temple; not a single shot was fired at them. The tanks deployed there may have deterred the fortifications of the militants on top of the Ghanta Ghar Deori or it could have been Shabeg Singh's strategy.

The SFF commandos joined 1 Para outside the Ghanta Ghar Deori, and around 10.30 p.m. they entered the temple via the main staircase leading to the Parikrama. On reaching the Parikrama, they turned right towards the Akal Takht—the 1 Para commandos moving through the covered verandah while the SFF troops were on their left, towards the sarowar.

10 Guards, that was tasked with securing the northern Parikrama and the rooms along the verandah in the north, however, was yet to clear these positions of the militants, when SFF and 1 Para, confident and well poised for the final assault, proceeded towards the Akal Takht. They were lucky not to encounter any opposition. From the piao, the stall dispensing drinking water on the verandah at the north-west end, they turned west and were conveniently spread out in front of the Akal Takht. Not a shot had been fired yet.

By now, it was 11 p.m. The SFF launched the CS gas cartridges. The objective was to disorient the militants to provide time to the troops to barge into the Akal Takht. The valiant endeavour, however, failed. Not a single gas canister could penetrate the heavily barricaded and well-blocked doors, windows and other openings of the Akal Takht. Rather, the gas cartridges, on rebound, only aggravated the situation for the troops. Night-vision glasses had not been provided to them, which would have helped them to accurately aim at the pigeonhole openings in the Akal Takht. Some cartridges, in fact, did not even explode when fired. The life-span dates for using these had expired.

The 1 Para team earmarked to capture the Darshani Deori, opposite the Akal Takht, found the main high-rise door of the Deori locked from inside (from the side of the sanctum sanctorum). That grounded them in the open space in front of the Akal Takht.

The 1 Para commandos, unfamiliar with the layout, were not aware that there was a marbled passage around the Deori to bypass its main door. The passage directly connects with the bridge leading to the sanctum sanctorum. This gangway could have been used to access the staircase leading to the top of the Deori that would give the commandos a direct line of fire to target the gun placements at the Akal Takht. Unsure, the troops were pottering around as the team leader, Maj. Prakash Katoch, explored alternatives.

Till then, apart from the ineffectual gas cartridges, neither side had fired a shot. There seemed to be no imminent danger either: The troops had hung around in the open space outside the Ghanta Ghar Deori for quite a while, and thereafter traversed the circumambulatory passage unimpeded. And now they stood in the open space in front of the white-marbled Akal Takht. The militants had maintained complete silence, instilling a false sense of security among the troops. It was a trap.

The Battle

Then, suddenly, the silence was shattered. The machine guns of the militants at the Akal Takht and the buildings on its left and right opened up. All hell broke loose.

The militants had deployed their weapons extremely well behind the fortified structures, leaving only small openings large enough to place the armaments. When fired, the weapons normally radiated a flash, revealing their exact location. Counter-fire or rockets, therefore, could have easily neutralized these battlements. But the barrels of the militants' guns were not jutting out from these openings and the troops could not see any flash when the weapons fired. It was as if bullets were raining down on them from almost all over, but there was not a flash to betray the militant battlements. The militants were so well trained that they were firing from inside the fortified encampments through the small openings, without exposing gun barrels.

The SFF and 1 Para were unable to identify the exact firing positions of the militants and the same could not be neutralized till almost after daylight had set in. The troops suffered heavy casualties. Many lay dead or wounded. Those who managed to escape from the open space in front of the Darshani Deori fell back to the verandah around the Parikrama. But that was not safe either.

The troops had advanced to the Akal Takht without first clearing or occupying the rooms along the verandah. The militants, unknown to the troops, had strategically occupied most of these chambers. Tactically, they had held back fire till then, allowing the troops to advance. However, once the machine guns at the Akal Takht started spewing fire, the militants hiding inside these rooms along the verandah also attacked using guns and grenades. They had set the weapons low, almost at ground level, making it treacherous for the troops to crawl forward or even backward.

By the end of it, seventeen commandos of 1 Para were dead and another thirty-one injured. The junior commissioned officer (JCO) of the company detailed to take over the Darshani Deori was among those killed. Maj. Prakash Katoch, the team leader, sustained a bullet injury in the shoulder. At great personal risk, the surviving men pulled out the casualties from in front of the Akal Takht and evacuated them to the verandah, where they lay, lined up. It was only after the rooms along the verandah were neutralized that the injured could be taken to Military Hospital, Amritsar.

As the number of the injured grew, the Army Medical Depot in Delhi was opened at night and vital supplies were flown to Amritsar.

On the rooftop of the Ghanta Ghar Deori, the militants' battlements swaddled the main access to the temple from the Jallianwala Bagh side. These guns were neutralized by rapid fire from the tank-mounted machine guns deployed outside the Ghanta Ghar

Deori. The militants' guns, now silenced, made the defenceless roof on the Ghanta Ghar side look alluring. These heights should have been seized before entering the temple precinct. The tank machine guns could have provided covering fire if an eventuality arose. It would have been a decisive tactic as it would have provided the troops a wide line of fire, covering the entire Parikrama complex, including the Akal Takht.

There were staircases leading to the upper floors that could have been accessed by entering the rooms with openings towards the Ghanta Ghar market. These would have brought the troops in contact with the militants inside, which in any case was inevitable sooner or later. These options, in fact, could have been exploited right at the beginning of the operation. Commanding heights enable soldiers to dominate an area and are invariably advantageous.

10 Guards, a battle-hardened battalion of mixed troops with a number of Jat Sikhs, mostly from the Majha area of Punjab, suffered heavy casualties. Sundarji was fond of bragging that he knew only two speeds, 'full speed or full stop'.[1] He commanded the battalion down the staircase into the Parikrama of the Golden Temple at full speed, without first clearing the surrounding higher floors or the basements. His bullet speed was met with a hail of fire, bringing the troops to a deadly full stop. He had fulfilled both—full speed and full stop—at a heavy cost.

The main entrance to the temple from the Ghanta Ghar Deori is much higher than the Parikrama. Departing from the Hindu and Islamic traditions of elevated shrines, Guru Arjan Dev had constructed the Harmandir Sahib in a depression. The elevated entry provided a breathtaking view of the majestic Golden Temple, as devotees, with their heads bowed in reverence and walking down a steep slope, negotiated the long staircase to the circumambulatory passage. Some of the rooms along the Parikrama had basements and rose to two storeys. SGPC staff charged with ecclesiastical and ministerial responsibilities had been allotted these accommodations, though some rooms on the ground floor were known to be under unauthorized occupation of the militants. If the cooperation of the resident SGPC employees to enable access to the upper parts of the building had been sought through the civil administration, it could have enabled the troops to employ the rooftop to their advantage, but that was not done.

10 Guards approached the Ghanta Ghar Deori main entrance's staircase assured of their strength. A young Sikh captain by the name of Jasbir Singh Raina had done a reconnaissance of the temple complex three days earlier and he ably guided his men. However, the soldiers were barely halfway through the Parikrama when fury was unleashed. Automatic weapons located in concealed openings in the side rooms played havoc. Twenty soldiers were killed, while Capt. Raina lost his legs. He was conferred the Ashoka Chakra, and continued to serve till his retirement as a colonel.

After a fierce exchange of fire, the bravehearts of 10 Guards finally succeeded in securing a base in the Parikrama, but at a very heavy cost. The bloody room-to-room battles along the left and right flanks of the northern circumambulatory had proved calamitous.

It was past midnight now. The operation had fallen behind schedule. At this stage, the reserve troops of 10 Guards were ordered to climb on to the first floor of the rooms in the Parikrama towards the Akal Takht using makeshift ladders, and later on also on to the second floor, enabling them to give covering fire to the troops in the Parikrama. The initial omission to secure the higher ground was now rectified.

According to the plan, divers would swim across the sarowar to secure the Harmandir Sahib. However, automatic weapons were firing from all directions. Swimming across in the open water, after negotiating a wide, white-marbled Parikrama, was seeking death. The pre-planned plunge across the sarowar by divers to secure the Harmandir Sahib, therefore, had to be abandoned.

The Parikrama and the surrounding white structures accentuated the movement of troops in the moonlit night. To make things worse, the soldiers were wearing black dungarees and olive green. With no camouflage or concealment in the Parikrama or on the open verandah that runs along it, they were conspicuous targets for the militants entrenched behind the embedded battlements. These were death traps. The Black Bhoots, as Brar had called the commandos, were being slaughtered.

1 Para and the SFF, which had been pushed back to the verandah, however, regrouped and launched fresh assaults. Slowly, they trudged towards the Akal Takht and faced direct fire from all directions, including the piao and the manholes in the basement.

Suffering heavy casualties, and having fallen behind schedule, they kept braving the mission to live up to their fabled reputation. They succeeded in securing a foothold near the Akal Takht and a little later on, the first floor of the rooms near the Nishan Sahib—the two saffron Sikh flags mounted on long poles and interconnected towards the top by Sikh insignia, the khanda.

By the early hours of 6 June, 1 Para had discovered a staircase that led to the rooftop of the verandah towards the Nishan Sahib, on the right flank of the Akal Takht. They fought their way to the roof; securing it finally provided them tactical advantage. The SFF too succeeded in getting a foothold in the Parikrama but were unable to penetrate the fortified Akal Takht.

Dayal wanted 1 Para to move to the south-west Parikrama and attempt an assault from that direction. This meant traversing the entire length of the circumambulatory passage around the sarowar; it was risky as militants were firing from the rooms along the verandah. Besides, the gun encampments on top of the langar building and the basements of the two bungas had not been cleared. It was too perilous a promenade. The attempt was rightly abandoned.

Instead, the commanding height of the roof terrace near the Nishan Sahib was exploited; it provided much-needed cover, and also a clear line of fire. The troops rained concentrated direct fire on the Akal Takht and on the fortifications on top of the building opposite the Nishan Sahib. The small arms fire, however, proved ineffective in breaching the Akal Takht's marble-holed defences, though it did provide the SFF, which had also suffered heavy casualties, a breather to make fresh attempts to lodge CS gas cartridges into the Akal Takht.

The Failed Link-Up

All this while the proposed link-up of 26 Madras with 1 Para and the SFF from the south-west side did not materialize. Delayed and lost on the circuitous course, 26 Madras was nowhere to be seen near the Parikrama. Even under normal circumstances the troops could not have kept pace with 1 Para and the SFF, who had only a short foreground to plod. There would have been, in any case, a time lag in reaching the Akal Takht from the northern and southern sides.

However, to make things more arduous for 26 Madras, the huge steel gate at the entry point to the Sarai complex proved impregnable. This obstacle had not been factored in and it took a while before the huge gate could be smashed, for which a tank was deployed. The armed encampments on the brick-lined langar building and the surrounding structures stymied any further advance. Wisely, 26 Madras detoured, eschewing the main entry from the eastern Deori, and entered the Parikrama from near the piao at the south-east end, though running behind the scheduled time.

26 Madras should have, in fact, accessed the southern Parikrama by the direct route, straight from the Library Deori, but it had not planned a foray from this direction. Access to the Library Deori on the Atta Mandi side is through a labyrinth of winding, narrow lanes of the walled city. The troops were not familiar with the pathways, neither could tanks and APC negotiate those serpentine alleys.

The route was also considered risky, as militants had forcibly usurped some of the high-rise private buildings in these streets and set up fortifications. In hindsight, these should not have been considered forbidding constraints. The CRPF had moved in in this area in considerable strength in May and set up parallel fortifications on the rooftops of private buildings around the temple, eyeball to eyeball with the militants. The CRPF had regularly engaged the militants, exposing their locations. Slowly, the militants had thinned out from the area, and these outposts were now more in the nature of modestly manned observation posts, and not fortified battlements. Of course, sniper fire could not be ruled out, but that is a battle risk.

From the night intervening 2 and 3 June 1984, an infantry battalion, 12 Bihar, had reinforced the CRPF in this area and together they covered the periphery of the complex. They had enough time, men and weaponry to clear the remnants of the militants, if any, as was done in Hotel Temple View and Braham Buta Akhara prior to the launch of the operation in the temple complex. This would have given 26 Madras clear access to the southern Parikrama, and also a direct approach to the left flank of the Akal Takht.

In fact, the left and right flanks of the Akal Takht were not exploited by the troops. As we face the Akal Takht, there is a passage on the left side directly opposite the Nishan Sahib and another opening on the right flank from Gurdwara Thara Sahib. These two passages give direct access to the Akal Takht, avoiding the Parikrama. These approaches, however, were not exploited, not even as a tactic to deflect the militants' firepower.

Failure to engage or divert the militants' attention from the southern side or from the left and right flanks of the Akal Takht or from the rear enabled the militants to unleash concentrated firepower on 1 Para and the SFF advancing from the northern Parikrama. This decelerated the operation and caused heavy casualties. Since the planned assault from the south-west by 26 Madras had also got stalled, the generals were left with no option but to requisition the reserve troops.

Fall Back on Reserves

15 Kumaon had arrived from far-off Secunderabad only a day earlier and was initially earmarked as a reserve. With the operation virtually

stalled, the battalion was now requisitioned to the Library Deori for a strike on the Akal Takht from the south-west, under the command of Lt Col N.C. Pant—a task that was otherwise to be undertaken by 26 Madras.

Dayal, who was wary of forsaking the south side, had the foresight to commandeer from 15 Division two companies of 9 Garhwal Rifles as reserves. These men were also pushed in via the back lanes leading to the library entry point that had earlier been ruled out by the seniors. Initially, the 9 Garhwal Rifles troops lost their way in the alleys as they were unfamiliar with the area. They had been deployed on the international border and had moved for this operation at short notice. The battalion was short by sixty men against the sanctioned strength of 240 in the two companies.

To build up their firepower, two APCs and two recoilless guns (RCLs) were detailed with them. The APCs, however, had to be abandoned as these could not negotiate the narrow lanes. There was also a mishap when the troops fired an RCL mounted on a jeep to secure an opening into the temple from the left flank of the Akal Takht (as we stand in front of it), which had been blocked by a wall built by the militants. RCLs have a back blast and need open space at their rear. In the narrow winding lanes, when the gun fired, the back blast flared up, causing casualties. Three jawans manning the gun were burnt to death in the jeep itself, and the fourth was rescued with severe burns. The ammunition in the jeep caught fire, causing extensive damage to civilian properties, igniting a chain of fires in the narrow lane and Bazaar Munarian. To their credit, the situation was quickly salvaged. The troops regrouped and were able to secure the southern side (Library Deori), including the floor above.

It was past 2 a.m. on 6 June but 26 Madras led by Col Panikker was still attempting to link up with the newly inducted reserve troops of the Garhwalis and the Kumaonis. When the battalion's troops finally closed in near the library, an exchange of fire among them and the Garhwalis was averted by the quick intervention of Maj. Gen. A.K. Dewan, then deputy commander of 15 Division in the rank of a brigadier. 26 Madras was not aware of the induction of 9 Garhwal Rifles and mistook these soldiers to be militants. Fortunately, Dewan gave the appropriate signal before any damage occurred.

Dewan, in fact, had no business to be where he was as the operation was the responsibility of 9 Division. An intrepid soldier who earned a Vir Chakra in the 1962 war against China in Leh–Ladakh and fought in the famed tank battle of Longewala in 1971 against Pakistan, he was itching for an opportunity to plunge into the battle of Blue Star. The induction of 9 Garhwal Rifles, a battalion from his 15 Division, gave him the alibi he needed. He joined them at the temple.

After entering the temple complex, Dewan notified his presence over the wireless set to Brar, who first mistook it as interference in his command by 15 Division. However, Brar seized the moment and grafted Dewan to manoeuvre the troops from the south-west. From then onwards, the Akal Takht operation from the south-west was virtually under the command of Dewan. 9 Garhwal Rifles, 15 Kumaon and later 26 Madras—after it made it to the Library Deori—were all put under his command. Together, they launched spirited strikes, suffered heavy casualties and were beaten back each time. The Akal Takht defences proved indestructible.

Sundarji had assured Prime Minister Indira Gandhi that the temple complex would not suffer any serious damage in the army operation. The 'White Paper on the Punjab Agitation', brought out by the Government of India, states, 'Specific orders were given to troops to use the minimum force . . . The use of high trajectory weapons and incendiary ammunition was totally barred.'[2]

However, Dewan, a cavalryman, had seen from ground zero how the foot soldiers were being massacred. Sandbagged battlements were proving impregnable for the infantry. Traversing the white-marbled terra firma on foot meant more casualties. This necessitated a change in the original plan.

The APC

Under the new plan, two decisions were taken. One, permission was sought from Delhi to use Vijayanta Tanks, which had already been positioned within the complex.

Two, it was decided to move soldiers to the base of the Akal Takht in an APC called SKOT because of its Polish–Czechoslovakian origins. The APC could carry a section of troops securely in its fortified steel belly, while its turret-mounted machine gun had the capability to take on militant defences.

APCs, however, have an Achilles heel—their steel frames ride on eight rubber wheels, which lie completely exposed from the sides and partially from the front, rendering them vulnerable. They cannot negotiate staircases, in addition. Therefore, the staircase entry into the Parikrama from the eastern end had to be mowed down to make way for the APC. Once this was done, the APC had an easy run on the eastern and southern sides, but as it negotiated the turn towards the Akal Takht, near the point where devotees take the karah prasad, the militants immobilized it by rupturing its right front tyres.

The giant vehicle tilted rightwards under its own 15 metric tons of weight. A few soldiers could have stayed on inside the APC and used the turret-mounted machine gun to target the militants' fortifications. However, it was feared that the militants would use Molotov cocktails—a crude grenade made by filling a bottle with flammable liquid and a wick—to set the stationary vehicle on fire. The men, therefore, evacuated the APC, and were now no better placed than the foot soldiers. This robust effort, thus, failed around 5 a.m. on 6 June.

If it was a tracked APC which ran on a metal conveyer chain instead of the rubber-tyred SKOT, the operation may have had a better chance of success. This was not done, apparently to avoid damage to the Parikrama, though by then three tracked tanks had already been driven into the circumambulatory passage. The damage to the marbled floor had been caused.

What went wrong in the APC operation? There are different versions. Brar in his account[3] has stated that an anti-tank RPG-7 (rifle propel grenade) hit the APC. Two Chinese-made RPGs were recovered, among other weapons, from the rubble of the Akal Takht.

However, when I visited the temple complex on the morning of 7 June, I did not notice any damage to the main body of the APC, which would have occurred when hit by an anti-armour weapon. The APC only had two flat front right rubber tyres, with no visible collateral damage to its steel frame. In fact, even the tyres had not been blasted or blown up, but merely punctured.

I learnt from the troops that a militant had managed to crawl close to the APC and fired, targeting the tyres. He was crushed to death when the driver manoeuvred the APC, but the flattened tyres immobilized the carrier. The commanding officer (CO) of the APC, Maj. Hardev Singh, was injured as he abandoned the immobilized vehicle. A bullet hit him in the belly and he lay on the ground in the open Parikrama. The APC driver protected him by providing cover till he was evacuated by the advancing Kumaon and Garhwal battalions.

In the meantime, Dewan attempted a fresh direct strike on the Akal Takht by 15 Kumaon. The battalion was supported by small arms fire from the tanks that had already been brought into the Parikrama. The Kumaon battalion did succeed in reaching the base of the Akal Takht, but seven soldiers were killed and twenty-three wounded.

Till then, the 26 Madras contingent was lucky to have not suffered any major casualty. Dewan grafted them to launch another frontal attack from the south-west under the command of young Lt Jyoti Dang. Some of them managed to reach up to the staircase leading to the first floor of the Akal Takht. However, they were massacred by machine-gun fire that rained from six locations, including the basement of the Akal Takht. Fourteen soldiers were killed and another forty-nine wounded—all from 26 Madras. Operation Blue Star was as good as stalled.

Brar now tasked Dewan to regroup the men of the Garhwal, Kumaon and Madras regiments to make it to battalion strength and launch another frontal assault on the Akal Takht. Dewan refused point-blank. He bluntly told Brar, 'Why re-enact failure?'

He felt that the infantry did not match the fortified militants in the built-up area and any assault on the Akal Takht would only result in more deaths. When Brar insisted, he countered, 'Why don't you come here [Library Point] and see for yourself? You are only a little distance away.' Later on, Dewan told me, 'The infantry was not equipped to face the heavily fortified positions.' So he suggested that they employ the cavalry instead.

The Tanks

Twilight had set in by the time the Government of India's acquiescence to use tanks was conveyed to 16 Armoured Regiment. Originally raised in 1776 by the East India Company, it was one of the oldest cavalry units in the Indian Army. In 1984, the indigenously built Vijayanta Tanks were added to its arsenal—three of these stood in a single-line formation in the southern Parikrama.

One by one, they opened fire. One of them, however, mistook the Darshani Deori as the intended target; the shell left a gaping hole in its wall. The 1 Para commandos, who were witnessing the operation from the rooftop near the Nishan Sahib, sent a frantic signal to redirect the tank fire to the Akal Takht, saving the Deori from further damage.

Armour-piercing squash-head shells were discharged from a close range of about 100–150 metres, first targeting the top cupola of the Akal Takht and thereafter the floors below. The Darshani Deori lay in the line of fire and blocked a substantial part of the Akal Takht, therefore the dome and the higher floors were targeted. Within minutes, the front façade of the Akal Takht was gone. A portion of the dome and the roof fell in. A fire began.

The guns in the Akal Takht fell silent by 9 a.m. on 6 June. The soldiers, however, held back from entering the battered structure, lest surviving militants caused more casualties.

The SGPC employees buttoned up in the sanctum sanctorum later recalled that they had counted over seventy-six shells being fired from the main guns of the three tanks. The record, however, showed a lower number. I later learnt that Col Chakraborty, the CO of 16 Cavalry, was directed within days of Operation Blue Star to move the tanks to the Naraingarh field firing range for practice with live ammunition.

Eyebrows were raised, for 15 Division, to which the cavalry belonged, was deployed on the international border to guard against any misadventure by Pakistan. To move the tanks for firing practice during that delicate time was rather unusual. The grapevine attributed this untimely movement of the tanks as a venture to take care of the discrepancy in the official account of the ammunition fired at the temple complex.

Lt Gen. P.N. Hoon, who succeeded Sundarji as GOC-in-chief of the Western Command, Chandimandir, in 1986–87 was to question the veracity of the official record regarding the number of shells fired. He wrote:

> Even after the inquiry the official version is that one tank was used, and only a few rounds were fired. In reality three tanks were used and over sixty rounds were fired. After taking control of near mutiny in my Corps, I visited the Golden Temple to assess the situation for myself. I was later told that some of the ammunition fired there was shown as practice ammunition fired on a range. I question Sundarji's role in the falsification of even official records. 'Why could it not be said that three tanks had been used and over 60 rounds fired?[4]

Sundarji, in fact, wanted to deny the use of tanks in the operation. Dewan told me that he was asked to brief the media that no tanks were involved in the operation and only Howitzers were used. Dewan politely refused to do so. His simple explanation: 'Why tell a lie that will be detected?' Knowledgeable media, he said, would easily discern the truth as Howitzers fire on high trajectories at low velocities.

Howitzers and light mountain guns were used too. These were deployed in and around Jallianwala Bagh to target specific high-rise structures. One gun was laboriously taken to the roof of a private building adjoining Jallianwala Bagh as that offered a clearer line of sight to the complex. However, it was the tanks that proved decisive and clinched the bitterly fought battle of the Akal Takht.

11

Operation Blue Star: Part II

ON THE MORNING OF 7 JUNE, AS I CLIMBED THE STEEP STAIRS from the Parikrama to the Ghanta Ghar Deori, there Bhindranwale was—his tall, slender body lifeless on the floor. Bhindranwale's long, patrician face, with its aquiline nose and flowing beard, had a grim and rigid expression. The trademark steel arrow which he always carried was gone—it probably lay twisted under the debris of the Akal Takht. To keep him company even in death were his confidants Baba Thara Singh and Bhai Amrik Singh, also stowed on the floor a few steps away. The army had brought them there.

The dead need identification. Harjit Singh, superintendent of police, CID, and Apar Singh Bajwa, DSP, had personally known Bhindranwale and his dead companions. Both were called in to confirm their identities, which they did. The army brought in Bhindranwale's brother, a serving army JCO, who unhesitatingly confirmed his death.

But how did he die? I was told that it was only around noon on 6 June that the bodies of Bhindranwale and five or six others, including Bhai Amrik Singh, were found dead in the open on the right side of the Akal Takht, and they had later been shifted to the Ghanta Ghar Deori, the main entrance to the temple.

Shabeg's body was in the basement of the Akal Takht; it was also located on 6 June. Lying on a heap of thousands of empty cartridges of the expended ammunition, the body was marked with burns and blisters, caused due to intense heat. The basement was burning hot. The militants had tried to cool the place by drawing water from the well at the back of the Akal Takht, causing the floor to be flooded.

On 6 June, in the operation room at the divisional headquarters, around 5 p.m., there was frenetic communication. The officer manning the controls did not want to be disrupted. 'The temple is communicating with Delhi regarding an important decision,' he said. I speculated: Could it be that one of the key figures had been caught?

Bhindranwale was last seen alive around 6.30 a.m. on the morning of 6 June. Giani Pritam Singh, the head priest of the Akal Takht, among the few eyewitnesses who survived Blue Star, told me what he saw. He, along with some granthis (reciters of the Guru Granth Sahib) and a few others, had stayed back at the Akal Takht on the evening of 5 June to ensure that the religious *maryada* (ceremony) was not interrupted.

When the battle began in the night, Giani Pritam Singh and the granthis took cover in the residential rooms in the north-west, located at the back of the Akal Takht, as they considered these to be comparatively more secure.

On the morning of 6 June, around 6.30 a.m., Giani Pritam Singh saw Bhindranwale climb up from the basement of the Takht and use the washroom next to his room. He remembers Bhindranwale looking calm and composed.

A little while later, Bhai Amrik Singh too came up and used the same washroom. Amrik Singh and Giani Pritam Singh ended up speaking to each other. In the brief interaction they had, Amrik Singh told him of Bhindranwale's resolve to fight to the death and attain shaheedi—he had timed it for 9.30 a.m.—and he advised Giani Pritam Singh to move out of the Akal Takht to a safer place.

Pritam Singh and his companions escaped from the Akal Takht to the adjoining house of SGPC employee Bhai Balbir Singh via Boharwali street towards Gurdwara Thara Sahib. They were arrested from there on the morning of 8 June by the BSF and taken to an army detention camp.

Giani Pritam Singh's narrative was corroborated by his companions. The tanks were ordered to fire their main guns around 7–7.30 a.m. on the morning of 6 June, and in all likelihood the death of Bhindranwale and his key companions occurred thereafter. They may have charged out and got killed near the Nishan Sahib, where their bodies were said to have been found by the army. If Bhindranwale wanted, he could have also escaped via the route taken by Pritam Singh, though he would have been quickly arrested as the entire area was cordoned off.

Harmandir Sahib

The army kept its distance from the Harmandir Sahib. It hadn't marched beyond the Darshani Deori, from where a bridge led to the sanctum sanctorum. They had no knowledge about the goings-on there, or the number of people inside, even though the guns had been quiet for a while.

The Harmandir Sahib stands tall at the centre of the sarowar, the only way to reach it is via the bridge from the Darshani Deori. Guru Arjan Dev had designed the temple and it was constructed with the labour of love, kar sewa. Its upper portion was plated with gold during the reign of Ranjit Singh, the Sikh ruler of Lahore. Hence its name: Swaran Mandir.

Inside the temple, under the elaborately embellished gold and silver zari canopy, the Guru Granth Sahib is installed on a palanquin, enfolded with embroidered clothes called *rumalas*. The Guru Granth Sahib propagates the unity of God and truthful living; it is an inclusive granth, incorporating hymns of the Sikh Gurus, Muslim fakirs and Hindu sadhus. Sikhs revere the Granth Sahib as a living guru. The only rite allowed inside the sanctum sanctorum is the recitation of Guru Granth Sahib hymns, composed to conform to traditional ragas. Ragis (singers) recite kirtans (hymns) to the accompaniment of musical instruments, chiefly the harmonium and tabla.

On 5 June, when army units started moving towards the walled city, evening prayers were being performed at the sanctum sanctorum—bedtime hymns called kirtan *sohila* were being recited. However, the Guru Granth Sahib, which is carried every night in a palki to the Kotha Sahib located in the Akal Takht, could not be taken to its resting place that day as the intense firing made it unsafe to move out of the Harmandir Sahib. Sukhasan (retiring the Granth for the night) was therefore done within the Harmandir Sahib by carrying the palki to the upper storey of the Golden Temple.

About twenty-four or twenty-five ragis, granthis and sewadars (attendants) who were inside the sanctum sanctorum stayed back for the night, considering it too perilous to step out. They were to become witnesses to Operation Blue Star.

Bullets were flying from all directions and in the exchange of fire between the troops and the militants the Golden Temple received, by one count, nearly 300 bullet marks—even its gold dome was not spared. Fortuitously, it did not suffer any major damage. History records that Muslim invaders had razed it to the ground thrice, and each time it was restored by devotees with steely determination. Chroniclers have recorded that when its foundation was being laid in 1589, the mason displaced the foundation bricks, and noticing that, Guru Arjan is said to have prophesied that it would be rebuilt.[1]

When the troops finally did enter the sanctum sanctorum on the evening of 6 June, no weapons were recovered from inside it. The militants had not planted any dynamite around the Golden Temple, as was initially feared by the army. Nor were there any fortifications or battlements built inside the Harmandir Sahib.

Brar has stated in his book *Operation Blue Star: The True Story* that militants were firing from the Harmandir Sahib. However, from whatever I witnessed and according to what the granthis told me, there were no armed militants inside the sanctum sanctorum, therefore neither were any armed militants arrested from inside the sanctum sanctorum, nor any weapons recovered.[2]

Giani Kirpal Singh, jathedar of the Akal Takht, in fact, had issued an edict banning firearms inside the Harmandir Sahib. Towards the end of 1983, he proposed to enforce an embargo on carrying firearms inside the Parikrama, but had to restrict the ban to only the sanctum sanctorum as even Akali leaders did not support the move. Kirpal Singh's good-intentioned injunction was partly scuttled by quoting historical traditions from Guru Hargobind Singh's time, who in his struggle against Mughal tyranny had asked followers of the faith to bring arms as an offering at the Akal Takht. The issues and concerns faced by Sikhs in 1984 were deliberated and decided under the aegis of history, ignoring the fact that times had changed.

Though Bhindranwale carried a weapon in a holster hung across his shoulder and was invariably accompanied by armed men, he and his men obeyed the ban. They would pay obeisance from outside, from near the Darshani Deori, and not enter the Harmandir Sahib with weapons. Bhindranwale's obedience of Kirpal's edict prevented the militants from raising fortifications inside the Harmandir Sahib, which must have been tempting given its strategic location and the commanding view it afforded of the entire precinct—a clear line of fire in all directions.

But the absence of firearms inside the Harmandir Sahib did not save it from the shadow of tragedy. A stray bullet hit Avtar Singh, a ragi. No medical aid was available to him and he slowly bled to death inside the sanctum sanctorum. A bullet also went through the Guru Granth Sahib up to about Ang 296.

On 6 June, in the morning, the granthis holed up in the sanctum sanctorum resumed religious rites inside the temple. However, they still did not dare to step out, even though the Akal Takht defences had crumbled and the weapons had fallen silent. Dewan sought approval to seek the surrender of the militants and others who may still be holed up in the other parts of the Parikrama complex, but was ordered to hold back. The troops in the meantime consolidated their position and cleared the bodies of their colleagues.

Around 4 p.m. the approval for initiating surrender was received and Lt Col Tejinder Singh, CO of the Garhwalis, using a loudspeaker, announced in chaste Punjabi, 'Leave your weapons, and walk out with your hands raised over heads, from wherever you are.' More than 200 people emerged from different parts of the Parikrama complex, including from the residences around the promenade surrounding the Sarowar.

From among them, SGPC employees were identified and segregated. The remaining men were put to a litmus test—checking for circumcision. Only seven or eight of them were found to be circumcised. Two of them sported false beards, which during the physical search peeled off their faces.

Years later, I learnt from the SGPC employees that these men were put to 'sleep' on 7 June morning at about 4 a.m., outside the complex on the west, beyond the Udasi Akhara near the kirpan factory. They were suspected to be Pakistanis or possibly illegal Bangladeshis who often took shelter in the complex and waited for an opportune time to cross over into Pakistan.

On hearing the announcement, the twenty-two plucky granthis and ragis, who in the face of combat had maintained the sacred ritual of recitation of the Guru Granth Sahib, came out of the Harmandir Sahib, leaving two others inside to continue with the religious rites. Subsequently, the army evacuated them as well and the religious rites were temporarily interrupted.

The senior-most granthi, Giani Puran Singh, was deputed to fetch Giani Sahib Singh, head priest of the Golden Temple, from his residence nearby, and together they identified and verified the antecedents of ragis and granthis. They all were released from army custody and deputed to restore religious rites in the temple. A copy of the Guru Granth Sahib was brought from Gurdwara Laachi Beri (a tree so named because of the diminutive size of its berries) located in the Parikrama, and installed in the Harmandir Sahib.

The tragedy of Indian federalism was on full display. For years, the government had stubbornly eschewed even the religious demands of the Akalis, which included the innocuous demand for a live relay of the kirtan from the Golden Temple. Those were the days of socialism, when the state had complete monopoly over radio and television. Those seeking entrepreneurial elbow room to start a radio station or a TV channel had to wait. As a mark of protest, on 1 December 1979, the revolutionary Akali Dal founded by Dr Jagjit Singh Chauhan handed over a small transmitter to the SGPC. The transmitter was installed, but without legal approval. It could hardly be heard beyond the boundary of the precinct, but it was a symbolic expression of an unfulfilled wish.

In a unilateral announcement on 27 February 1983, the Prime Minister had finally conceded the four religious demands of the Akalis, but the actual broadcast of the gurbani never commenced. Now, after all the death and destruction of Operation Blue Star, AIR was directed, post-haste, to start the morning and evening relay of the kirtan from the sanctum sanctorum.

The first broadcast was on 8 June 1984. The government was eager to commence it because it wanted to convey to the public that normalcy had returned to the temple and its religious rites had been restored. There was no better medium than the radio to convey this, particularly since the temple was still out of bounds for the public.

The Akal Takht

Unlike the sanctum sanctorum, it was not possible to resume the usual religious rituals at the badly battered Akal Takht. On the evening of 7 June, Giani Kirpal Singh, jathedar of the Akal Takht, was escorted there for the first time since Operation Blue Star, with the intent to involve him in the normalization process. When he entered the complex, he could hardly speak. There were tears in his eyes. The Akal Takht lay dilapidated. There was a stench of blood, death and destruction all around. In a choked voice, he said, '*Eh ke ho gaya* [What has happened]?' It was his responsibility to preserve the sanctity of the Akal Takht but he had been too timid to stop Bhindranwale from converting a portion of it into his billet. The consequences were for him to see.

I asked him, 'Giani ji, why did you allow them to occupy the Akal Takht?' His reply summed up his plight, 'Who listened? They pointed guns at me. Pardhan ji [Tohra] had spoken to Bhindranwale, but then he [Tohra] also kept quiet.'

The violence had numbed the clergy into silence. Their fears were not unfounded—on 10 May 1984, the terrorists had killed the octogenarian Giani Pratap Singh, the former scholarly jathedar of the Akal Takht. He had dared to raise his voice against the senseless violence and occupation of the Akal Takht by Bhindranwale. Other religious personalities who had raised their voices against the militants were also murdered, including Niranjan Singh, granthi of Gurdwara Toot Sahib, Granthi Surat Singh of Majauli and Granthi Jarnail Singh of Valtoha, to name a few.

Jathedar Kirpal Singh's turn came on 16 January 1985. He was waylaid while travelling near Ludhiana and shot. His sin was to have unwittingly become party to the publicity blitz of the government—an exercise in dissemination of fact and some fiction in an effort to modulate public sentiments regarding the army action.

The army had asked Kirpal Singh to make a well-drafted, factually correct statement regarding the damage to the complex. To downplay the destruction of the Akal Takht, a line was added in the statement: '*Kotha Sahib theek thaak hai* [Kotha Sahib is intact].'

In a televised statement, probably made on 11 June, the government's spin doctors made Kirpal Singh repeat the sentence, '*Kotha Sahib theek thaak hai.*' Little did they realize that the Sikhs were enraged, and when religious equipoise is in turmoil, publicity and propaganda prove counterproductive. To focus on the Kotha Sahib, a room within the Akal Takht where the Guru Granth Sahib is kept for the night, when the Akal Takht itself was in ruins made Kirpal Singh an object of ridicule. For months, referring to Giani Kirpal Singh, Sikhs would snigger, '*Kotha Sahib theek thaak hai.*' It took a while for the self-effacing Kirpal Singh to recover his creditability, if indeed at all.

Historically, the Akal Takht is an assertion of the sovereignty of the Sikh faith. Its foundation stone was laid by Guru Hargobind in 1606, and its base was kept at a level higher than the Mughal throne in the Red Fort as a statement of supremacy against the ruling powers. It was built by Bhai Gurdas and Baba Budha, by kar sewa. Guru Hargobind had resolved to raise a Sikh army to fight the tyranny of the Mughal rulers and would sit at the Akal Takht to receive horses, weapons and volunteers.

Bhindranwale had shifted to the Akal Takht, the second-most sacred space within the temple precincts, on 15 December 1983. The Akal Takht is not a residential quarter—it is the holy seat of Miri Piri (spiritual and temporal authority), a Sikh symbol of resistance against Mughal atrocities. Bhindranwale's occupying the few rooms at the back of this hallowed place as his living quarters was questionable. Earlier, Sant Fateh Singh had camped at the Akal Takht in 1965 and built an *agni kund* to immolate himself during the Punjabi Suba agitation and had come under criticism.

Bhindranwale's move to the Akal Takht elevated him from a mere head of the religious seminary at Chowk Mehta to a leader of the Sikh quam. Symbolically, it positioned him in higher public standing than the Akalis and SGPC leaders, who were confined to the peripheral residential quarters. Bhindranwale had, in any case, left these leaders far behind in terms of mass appeal.

The migration to the Akal Takht lent historical legitimacy to Bhindranwale's heady mix of religion and politics in the tradition of Miri Piri. In Sikh perception, this situated him beyond the pale of the law. Who would dare to breach the Akal Takht, the abode of the timeless? ('Akal' means timeless and 'takht' means throne.) That was the real objective behind this manoeuvre; it was triggered, allegedly, by a stage-managed clash with the Babbar Khalsa in Guru Nanak Niwas to justify the migration to the Akal Takht with the objective to secure personal safety and security.

Militarily, however, it was suicidal for Bhindranwale and his men to quarantine themselves within a small space with little leverage for mobility or manoeuvrability. Till date, it foxes military strategists why Shabeg, a veteran of guerrilla warfare in Bangladesh, would allow the entire leadership and bulk of the militant cadre to hole up in one place. They all could be eliminated in one go. That is what finally happened.

This strategic blunder can be explained only in terms of Bhindranwale's excessive reliance on the expectation of a mass Sikh uprising if the army ever attacked the temple. He planned to appeal to people to reach Amritsar en masse to defend the temple against the invading Indian Army. Shabeg had strategized that his fortifications would hold security forces at bay for a day or two, and in the meantime, Sikhs would march to Amritsar to protect the temple.

There was also a misplaced expectation of support from Pakistan. The militants had been made to believe by their contacts that Pakistan would mobilize its military along the international border as a diversionary tactic, if not directly intervene in Indian territory. But the Pakistani Army did not stir. To deter them, 15 Infantry Division had already been deployed on the international border, behind BSF lines, starting 30 May.

Shabeg had misjudged the scenario. Punjab was no Bangladesh; the mass insurrection of the kind that had erupted in Bangladesh did not happen in Amritsar because the militants lacked a mass base. A few isolated groups did attempt to march towards Amritsar but they were intercepted and detained. The statewide curfew had, in any case, confined the population indoors.

In the end, Shabeg relied on the tenacity sustained by the religiosity of his boys to fight till the finish. He did start with an advantage—the well-fortified encampments protected them, while the troops had to move in the open. The militants had intimate knowledge of the inner layout of the rooms, their interconnectivity; the staircases and the basements provided them point-to-point mobility within the walls of the built-up structures. No number of sand-model exercises, which the SSF had conducted at Chakrata near Dehradun, could possibly have given the army similar familiarity with the inner layout and interconnectivity of the rooms, corridors and basements.

Had Bhindranwale, however, stepped out from behind the walled fortifications and allowed the law to take its normal course, it would have saved the Akal Takht from destruction and desecration by both sides.

The Library

The Sikhs have a long-established tradition of maintaining libraries. Starting with Guru Arjan's reign, Sikh Gurus have laid great emphasis on scribal tradition and on creating a designated space called the Pothi Mahal, which housed holy scriptures. In this historical tradition, a Sikh reference library was maintained near the southern Deori, within the Parikrama complex. During Blue Star it was gutted.

On 7 June, when I visited the temple early in the morning, the inside of the library had been reduced to ashes. The holy books, historical chronicles, rare manuscripts and copies of the Adi Guru Granth, Dasam Granth, hukamnamas and valuable parchments now reduced to ashes rested on the burnt shelves, some still smouldering.

How and when these got charred remains unknown, as the accounts and versions vary. The SGPC and some others have accused the forces of deliberately destroying Sikh heritage, and compared it with the burning of the library of Alexandria by Julius Caesar. The subject is still raised from time to time, inculpating the army and the CBI of a deliberate destruction of Sikh religious–cultural endowments and causing irreparable loss to Punjabi history.

I do not subscribe to the view that the library was intentionally set on fire. It was an accidental consequence of the exchange of fire between the militants and the troops. As per eyewitness accounts of the soldiers deployed inside the Parikrama, smoke was seen billowing from the upper floor of the library around 7–7.30 a.m. on 6 June. This is corroborated by Lt Col Adarsh Sharma, the intelligence officer of 15 Division, who had reached the Sarai complex around 10 a.m. on the day to escort the moderate Akali leaders to safety.

Col Sharma had climbed to the top of the Teja Singh Samundri Hall and found that the Akal Takht was still on fire, with flames leaping into the sky—the library building was engulfed. It would have caught fire before that time. By then, though, the battle was almost over, but intermittent firing could still be heard. The delay in extinguishing the fire resulted in the destruction of valuable manuscripts. The fire brigade could have accessed the library only from the Parikrama, and that was perilous at that hour.

General K.S. Brar, while describing this incident, has put the time as 'sometime on the afternoon of 6 June'. His version: The militants had opened fired and thrown grenades at the soldiers sitting on the verandah below the library. The troops retaliated and, within minutes, the library was on fire. The general writes, 'By the time the militants were finally overpowered or killed, the library had been gutted.'[3] However, later, the general presented a conflicting story to a chronicler. In reply to a question, he was quoted as saying, 'It got burnt by accident on the night between 5 and 6 June.'[4] The 'White Paper on the Punjab Agitation' published by the government gives different details still.

Vikram Jit Singh, of the *Times of India* (16 January 2014) has provided another version, quoting Jamwal. He reported, 'Maj. Gen. Jamwal reveals that he [Brar] ordered his troops to fire an anti-tank shell into a wall of the Akal Takth but the misdirected shell hit the Sikh reference library and it burst into flames.'

There are inconsistencies in this version. First, there was no hole in the walls of the library, which would have been an inevitable consequence if an anti-tank shell had hit it. Secondly, the library was not in the line of fire of the tanks deployed in the Parikrama. It is improbable that a tank would misfire its gun towards the south when it was aimed to the west. The *Times of India* reported that Jamwal was critical of Brar for a 'badly planned' Blue Star. Brar, in turn, retorted that Jamwal 'is a bitter, jealous man'. The newspaper goes on to write, 'Asked about the specific instances of failure detailed by Maj. Gen. Jamwal, Lt Gen. Brar said: "I don't want to comment beyond that. There is obviously something lacking in Maj. Gen. Jamwal that he did not make it beyond Maj. Gen. rank."' The two of them, obviously, were settling personal scores in public.

The library in-charge, Devinder Singh Duggal, lived with his family in the rooms next to it. He disclosed that the library was intact till the afternoon of 6 June. However, from what I learnt, Devinder Singh had shifted out from his quarters to a house on the periphery of the temple complex on 5 June. For this reason, I hesitate to accept his account regarding the time of fire, particularly as the soldiers inside the Parikrama put the time around early morning on 6 June.

If one were to believe yet another version, there was the one given to me by Gen. Dewan, stating that the unfortunate destruction of the library was an accident. Invaluable Sikh heritage was lost because the general chose to have his puris! Dewan told me that he had not eaten since 5 June, and after the guns fell silent in the Akal Takht, he and a few senior officers, around the afternoon of 6 June, sat down at the southern Darshani Deori near the library to satiate their hunger with dry puris, a type of fried Indian bread. Suddenly, a bullet whizzed past his ear and they all ducked. It was traced as coming from the direction of the library, and in the retaliatory firing an incendiary bomb set the historical parchments on flame.

The army had constituted a board under the chairmanship of Brig. Sawhney with an executive magistrate as my nominee and two representatives of the SGPC as its members to inspect the library. It met for the first time on 3 July, but disbursed without investigating the genesis of the fire. Its terms of reference were confined to take stock of the state of the library and make an inventory of the articles.

The magistrate reported to me in writing, 'It is further added that the board has not gone into the cause, date and time of fire.' Why the army did not want this aspect to be investigated, was, however, not mentioned by him in the report. He had recorded that in the big hall 100 closets, wooden and steel, and seven racks were completely gutted and that 'when we entered this hall, there was nothing. Even ash was removed.' Obviously, by then the place had been cleared by the army.

The report further stated that in the two rooms on the ground floor, Granth Sahibs were lying safe, as also were daily newspapers since 1934 that had escaped any damage. Significantly, he also disclosed that four live cartridges of revolvers and three or four used cartridges of some heavy weapons were found under one almirah on the ground floor, an indication that firing had taken place inside the library.

These multiple accounts and the glaring differences among them have resulted in people propagating the version that suits their purpose or perception. It has led to avoidable diverse interpretations of the unfortunate occurrence and the consequential accusations. The issue could have been settled by the army once and for all by instituting a court of inquiry. However, none was conducted. Alternatively, the war history of the concerned regiments could be made public. Each unit, post an operation, writes its own war story and its disclosure could put all speculation to rest.

12

Operation Blue Star: Part III

THE WORST CATACLYSM OF OPERATION BLUE STAR WAS IN THE Sarai complex, where a large number of innocents who had come to pay obeisance on their Guru's martyrdom day, perished. Those who survived—and their number is large—have given uninhibited eyewitness accounts. Their stories are gut-wrenching. Some of these have been published and are in the public domain.

When I visited the complex on the morning of 7 June, it presented a gruesome sight. More than 150 people had died in the Sarai complex, another 200 suffered varying degrees of wounds and over 1,000 had been detained. The ground was awash with blood, and the walls bore obvious marks of violence. A nauseating stench permeated the environment. It was sickening. Many rooms had been blackened with smoke, while localized fires were still smouldering in a few rooms of the Teja Singh Samundri Hall and Guru Nanak Niwas. In some of the rooms the combustible articles, clothes, bedsheets, etc., were said to have caught fire. In some cases, I was told that these had been set up to flush out the militants who may still be hiding inside.

I asked the army officer on the spot to extinguish the fires as these could prove fatal for any wounded yet to be evacuated. Also, the fires could get out of control. Instructions were given to the commissioner of the municipal corporation to dispatch the fire brigade—two water tenders reached the complex a little later.

However, when I visited the complex again on 8 June (I was escorting the chief secretary, Punjab, and some others), to my horror I found smoke still rising from a few places. The dead, the wounded and those detained had already been moved out but mopping operations were on. The fire brigade was standing idle. My reprimand was deflected by the fire brigade in-charge, 'We are not being allowed by the army to put these off.' The brigade commander who was accompanying us immediately intervened and the firemen moved in to dowse the fires.

I considered this to be a serious misdemeanour and addressed a DO letter to Kanwar Gulwant Singh, municipal commissioner, who had accompanied us to the temple and was witness to the entire episode, to hold an inquiry and record the statements of the firemen so that the matter could be pursued further for appropriate action. After a reminder and gap of more than a month, I got an evasive reply dated 12 July from the municipal commissioner saying that the matter had been discussed with the chief secretary in Chandigarh and he had not sought 'any such information'. It is unfortunate that responsibility for the alleged igniting of some of the fires, for not allowing the fire brigade to operate and the consequent loss it caused was not fixed. This lent weight to the allegations that the Sikh reference library was purposefully set on fire.

The Sarai Complex

The Sarai complex is a conglomerate of residential and administrative blocks, such as the Guru Ram Das Sarai, Teja Singh Samundri Hall (the SGPC office), Guru Nanak Niwas and the office building of the Akali Dal. Pilgrims and devotees visiting the temple are accommodated in some of these buildings.

3 June is the martyrdom day of Guru Arjan Dev, and a large number of pilgrims had to stay back in the sarai due to the sudden curfew. The sarai complex also anchored Akali workers and volunteers who would travel in batches daily to Amritsar from all over the state to court arrest as part of the ongoing Akali agitation. On 3 June, a jatha of about 300 volunteers belonging to Sangrur district under the leadership of Nachhatar Singh had arrived to court arrest on 4 June. Nachhatar Singh and many of his companions were killed on the night intervening 5 and 6 June.

Longowal was also headquartered here, and so was Tohra, who had his office and residence in the Teja Singh Samundri Hall. Babbar Khalsa, a zealot militant group not on good terms with Bhindranwale, had a dominating presence in this area, though some elements of the All India Sikh Students Federation and Bhindranwale's loyalists also lived there.

The buildings in the sarai complex, however, were not heavily fortified, and the number of militants ensconced in this part was comparatively lower. Strategically, the sarai complex, therefore, was of a lesser priority to the objectives of Operation Blue Star than the rooms around the Parikrama and the Akal Takht.

The Military Operation

9 Kumaon, an infantry battalion under the command of Lt Col K. Bhaumik, was detailed to clear the militants from the Sarai area. Drawing its troops from the Kumaon hills and the plains around it, the regiment has distinguished itself in the various wars, bringing glory to the nation. However, the Kumaonis had little experience of operating in built-up areas that sheltered more innocent citizens than the militants—as it turned out, it executed a badly planned operation to a tragic end.

On 5 June, 9 Kumaon was led into the complex by cavalry; four Vijayanta Tanks and columns of APCs launched the foot soldiers into the Sarai complex around the same time as 1 Para, the SFF and 10 Guards entered the Parikrama from the Ghanta Ghar Deori.

The cavalry did a quick job to silence the fortifications on the rooftops of some of the Sarai buildings, with the tank-mounted guns blazing. Thereafter, 9 Kumaon entered these buildings and eliminated the remaining militants hiding inside.

The topography and inner layout of the buildings in the complex made the operation onerous. There are a few hundred residential rooms and eight halls in the Guru Ram Das Sarai alone. The adjoining Teja Singh Samundri Hall and Guru Nanak Niwas, similarly, are multistorey edifices.

In the darkness, how do you clear so many rooms housing both militants and innocents? Built-up areas are tricky to handle. These require not just grit and valour but also restraint, equanimity and compassion. The job of the 9 Kumaon regiment was cut out. In the dead of night, it is not easy to identify a militant or a pilgrim. And if you do not get the militant first, he will get you. It was a perilously delicate task.

Appropriately, therefore, after the tanks had silenced the rooftop fortifications, the troops should have waited for daybreak. Tanks and APCs had been lined up outside these buildings on the road, and they acted as a deterrent for any misadventure by the militants, whose number in any case was small. These armoured vehicles segregated the sarai complex from the rest of the temple.

Therefore, the troops could have—in fact, they should have—waited till dawn and then made announcements over loudspeaker seeking surrender. This would have encouraged at least the innocent pilgrims to emerge. I strongly feel that even the militants would have capitulated. After all, by then, they would have seen the fate of their leaders in the Parikrama complex. The Sarai structures are high enough to give a wide view of what was happening in the Parikrama area and at the Akal Takht.

However, the Kumaonis were directed to secure the Sarai complex by 1.30–2 a.m. on 6 June. Sundarji wanted the entire operation to be over before daylight. So, 9 Kumaon did what infantry is best trained for: room-to-room mopping-up operations in the darkness of the night. The troops began with Guru Ram Das Sarai, and thereafter swooped in on the Teja Singh Samundri Hall and Guru Nanak Niwas.

Brig. Onkar Singh Goraya, then a colonel with 15 Division, was the first person from outside the operational troops of 9 Division to reach the sarai complex on the morning of 6 June. His eyewitness account is revealing:

> The compound in the centre was littered with dead and wounded, all civilians. The army causalities had been lifted away. There were many more dead, wounded and survivors in the verandahs and the rooms. Each of the few rooms that I checked had two or three dead bodies, some of [them] old men and women and a few survivors, dazed due to shock and heat, barely alive. Many more were bleeding and awaiting death, begging for their last drink of water. The sight of one young man with his entrails spilling out is still fresh in my mind.

He adds:

> The casualties were obviously caused when the Jawans went from room to room clearing them of suspected militants. It would be unfair to blame them. They must have acted in accordance with the 'room clearing drill' as taught to them—approach the room from a side, kick the door open, lob a grenade and wait, then enter and spray the room with sten fire; repeat the drill for the next room. It would be suicidal to presume those inside to be all innocent civilians. There was no

> time to call the roll and identity . . . No one was tending to the wounded or even offering water.[1]

The water supply to the complex was disconnected on 4 June when tank shells smashed the overhead water storage facility—where the militants had set up fortifications. Langar services were also halted that night, there was no food or water since then. Electricity supply was also cut off. In the intense heat of June, people were packed like sardines inside rooms, with doors and windows shut. Casualties started occurring from the evening of 5 June, but it was only on the afternoon of 6 June that the injured were attended to. Many bled to death writhing in pain and agony, deprived of medical aid and even water.

In hindsight, I think the delicacy of the operation had not sunk into the psyche of the troops. Kumaonis are brave soldiers, but they were not trained to execute a delicate task as the one that faced them in the Golden Temple that day. The topography of the sarai complex and handling its myriad occupants required skilled commandos trained to operate in built-up areas—the ones who know when to fire and when to hold it.

The heartless terrorists functioning at their worst unleashed unmitigated misery upon the innocent people. Going by the accounts of Brar, there were three ill-fated incidents. In the first, the victims were about fifty persons who had come out of the rooms and collected together in the compound of the building in the middle of the night.[2] Reportedly, the terrorists threw a grenade from the upper storey of the building, and the resultant chaos drove people in all directions. Panicking, the Kumaonis opened fire. Some survivors later recounted that it was indiscriminate firing—killing many innocent men, women and children.

Another grenade was lobbed by a militant around 4.30 a.m., and in the resultant panic firing by the troops, more innocent people perished.

The third time was in broad daylight. Around 9 a.m., a group of about 250 devotees who had taken shelter in the basement of Guru Ram Das Sarai and spent the night in comparative ease thought it would be safe to surrender. As they climbed up from the cellar, there was firing, resulting in more deaths. As per Brar's version, in these three gruesome incidents the devotees suffered eighty-five casualties. The eyewitnesses, however, put the figure at a few hundred.

More disturbing, however, are the allegations of the eyewitnesses who saw and, in some cases, suffered violence at the hands of the soldiers. Balwant Singh Ramoowalia, a former Union minister who was trapped inside the complex with Longowal and rescued on 6 June by Goraya, said, soon after his rescue, that unarmed people were killed by the troops after being lined up against a wall. Ramoowalia has repeated the charge many times over, including on camera. Bhan Singh, secretary of the SGPC, who was also inside the sarai complex, corroborated Ramoowalia's allegation. Many pilgrims had similar harrowing tales to tell. Goraya has recorded:

> A little later in the morning, according to Balwant Singh Ramoowalia, a Major of the same unit lined up about 20 Sikh youth against a wall and had them massacred with machine gun fire. A few days later Bhan Singh repeated the same episode to me. This was not the only incident of its kind. In the subsequent weeks a few cases of similar nature, though not many, came to my notice from different sources. Unarmed Sikh youth were allegedly murdered in cold blood after apprehension by soldiers, as if they were members of an enemy force and not own countrymen. The Government and army tend to dismiss such allegations as cooked up. I believe not all, but some of them were true.[3]

The army dismisses these charges, but the gravity of the accusation calls for a public inquiry, a 'truth commission'. It is such incidents, or the perception thereof, that have produced more militants post Operation Blue Star, more than the number the army may have eliminated in the operation. The wound still festers.

Surrender of Tohra and Longowal

Another controversy involving Blue Star is whether Longowal and Tohra surrendered to the troops. Or were they rescued and taken into protective custody?

On that fateful night, Longowal was in his room in the Sarai complex, which he had occupied since the Akali Dal's agitation shifted to Amritsar on 4 August 1982 from Kapoori in Patiala district. He was the dictator of the Dharam Yudh Morcha, and that tied him down to Amritsar, the hub of the agitation. On the night of 5 June, as bullets started flying, his room was deemed unsafe and he, along with Ramoowalia, moved to Tohra's ground-floor office-cum-residence in the Teja Singh Samundri Hall. Tohra stayed there whenever he was in Amritsar—he had reached Amritsar on the evening of 1 June.

By the time Longowal moved to Tohra's room, Darshan Singh Issapur; Bhan Singh, secretary, SGPC; Avinashi Singh, assistant secretary, SGPC; and Gurmeet Singh, press secretary, SGPC, were already there, while a few others like Bibi Amarjit Kaur of the Akhand Kirtani Jatha, Harminder Singh Sandhu, Ramoowalia and a few others joined them later, taking the total to ten.

It was well known that Longowal and Bhindranwale had fallen out and it was feared that pro-Bhindranwale militants would try to eliminate the moderate leadership. Surjit Singh Sokhey, the then press secretary of the Akali Dal, in fact, has disclosed that two armed Sikhs did make an attempt to kill Longowal and a grenade was thrown towards him that killed two Akali workers, Gurcharan Singh and Bagga Singh.[4]

9 Kumaon, deployed in the Sarai complex, had instructions to handle the Akali leaders solicitously. After securing a foothold in the Ram Das Sarai, the troops moved to the Samundri Hall and isolated

all the key Akali leaders in a room on the ground floor by 4 a.m. on 6 June. The Akali leaders were now under protected confinement.

Instructions had also gone to 15 Division to shift these leaders to safety in the cantonment. Lt Col Adarsh Sharma, the intelligence officer of 15 Division who belonged to Khanna and was fluent in Punjabi, was the first to reach the sarai complex at about 10 a.m. on 6 June. He was soon joined by his senior colleague Goraya who had been assigned the rescue of moderate Akali leaders in an APC.

Plodding through blood, the dead and the wounded, the two colonels escorted the Akali leaders around 1 p.m. to an APC parked outside on the road dividing the Sarai complex from the langar building. The leaders walked under the cover of army guards and that gave the erroneous impression that they were under arrest or had surrendered. Legally speaking, they did not surrender and nor were they under arrest, for there was no criminal charge against Longowal and Tohra and they had not committed any offence. Therefore, until their detention under the National Security Act, they were under protective custody of the army. Had they been released immediately, it was likely they would have suffered a loss of credibility among the Sikh masses. Emotions were running high and the moderate leadership had lost their cachet. Their detention was in their own interest.

These Akali leaders, in fact, did face public disapproval. They had shifted to the safety of the Military Engineering Services (MES) inspection bungalow, the army guest house, while the devotees and party workers lay dead, wounded or detained without water or food. This, certainly, was not leader-like comportment, though in the spirit of fairness it must be stated that Longowal asked Adarsh Sharma to ensure that all the injured were attended to quickly, and he, in turn, passed on the instructions to a captain from the local formation.

Pointing discreetly to a cot on which a group of young boys were sitting, Longowal told Adarsh Sharma about an attempt on his life by these very men on the night intervening 5 and 6 June. Adarsh Sharma was alarmed when he recognized one of them—he was the younger brother of Bhai Amrik Singh.

Tohra and Longowal were lodged together in the only air-conditioned room of the guest house, and on 8 June were flown to Rajasthan. Tohra was detained in Jodhpur, while Longowal was moved to the Udaipur jail.

From Adarsh Sharma and Goraya's accounts, it appears that Tohra was worried about securing his licensed weapons, the money in his room that belonged to the SGPC and other belongings he had left behind in the Teja Singh Samundri Hall. Let history judge these men.

Langar and Manji Sahib

The imposing brick-lined langar building stands on the right side of the road leading to the Sarai complex if one is travelling from the Jallianwala Bagh end. The road goes to Baba Atal, located at the south-eastern end of the temple complex, and links up with the lanes leading to private localities near Kaul Sar and Atta Mandi. (See map.)

In official records, this road is a public thoroughfare and its ownership vests in the Municipal Corporation of Amritsar. However, the SGPC had built a huge high-rise iron gate at the entry point to the road and controlled all access to it. It even claimed ownership by possession over the years. The writ of civil administration did not run over this road as the state's political hierarchy had acceded, de facto, to its status as an integral part of the temple complex.

The militants used this route to smuggle weapons, mostly in trucks carrying construction material or rations. Large numbers of trucks and tractors would cart eatables daily to the langar, which catered free food to over 50,000 pilgrims in those days (now the number is over 1 lakh every day). It is the largest free community kitchen in the world. This made it easy for militants to smuggle weapons into the complex.

Post Operation Blue Star, on instructions from the state government, the district administration reclaimed possession of the road and police-patrolled it regularly, while the municipal corporation took care of its upkeep. However, it has again slipped under the control of the SGPC, which objects to police presence on the road, asserting that the passage is an innate part of the sacred space of the temple precincts.

Langar is an intrinsic part of Sikh temples, and is a great leveller. Devotees sit on the ground, in rows, without any distinction of sex, class or religion, and partake in langar. The practice was started by Guru Nanak and institutionalized by Guru Amar Das, who declared that no devotee was to see him without eating a langar meal. Emperor Akbar, who was blessed by Guru Arjan on one of his expeditions, after his victory, detoured to the Goindwal Sahib on his way to Lahore from Delhi and ate at a langar. Akbar was so impressed by the tradition that he offered a jagir to the Guru, who declined it. Thereupon, Akbar conferred the jagir of a few villages to Bibi Bhani, the Guru's daughter. In his heyday, Bhindranwale would hold darbar almost daily on the rooftop of the langar building.

However, after the army surrounded the complex, the kitchen was shut from 4 June. When troops entered the langar building on the night of 5 June, the spacious dining halls were empty, with a few militants manning the fortifications, mostly on the roof. They had not spared even this great institution of munificence, and established machine-gun battlements on top of the langar building. The guns overlooked not only the road dividing the sarai from the langar building, but dominated the approach to the Parikrama complex from the eastern side.

On 5 June, the militant battlements on the langar building tormented the troops of 26 Madras. Targeted firing by the militants was effective in halting the advancing troops, who were detailed to enter the Parikrama from the langar end.

In the exchange of fire, foodgrains, cooking oil and other inflammables stored in the langar caught fire. Gas cylinders stored inside burst as well. Finally, the militants made their way into the basement of the adjoining Bunga Ramgarhia and played havoc. Some of them continued to hide in the basement and were finally cleared by SFF commandos on the morning of 9 June.

The militants had also occupied the Dewan Hall, a large hall used for religious congregations situated next to the langar in the south-east. The hall overlooks the approach to the Parikrama from the eastern end and is, like the langar building, of great strategic importance. The militants put up dogged resistance from the Dewan Hall on the night intervening 5 and 6 June. They held back the 26 Madras troops for quite a while; they were able to make their way to the Parikrama only around 2 a.m. on 6 June. Thereafter, they linked up with 1 Para and the SFF near the Akal Takht from the left end.

On 6 June, by the time the operation was over, the temple precincts were in a battered state, some said reminiscent of Ahmad Shah Abdali's invasion in 1764. It was littered with bodies, some of them afloat in the holy pond. The Akal Takht was in ruins and all the structures in the complex were pockmarked with holes caused by bullets and shells. The library had burnt, the upper levels of the historical bungas were crumbling and the administrative complex, including the Teja Singh Samundri Hall and Guru Nanak Niwas, were bullet-riddled.

There were demands for a judicial inquiry but none was held; even Akali leaders who had earlier sought a public inquiry when they came to power in 1977 abandoned the idea on the grounds that it would reopen old wounds. Perhaps there is logic in it.

13

The Desertions and the Demurral

THE TEMPLE COMPLEX WAS FAST RETURNING TO ITS NORMAL religious routine. However, on 9 June, the usually calm Jamwal was visibly under strain. When we met for the daily civil–military liaison, I casually inquired, 'Is everything fine, you look tense.' He replied, 'You don't know what is happening.'

Indeed, a lot was afoot. He had every reason to be worried. In protest against the army's assault on the Golden Temple, soldiers had deserted their units at about eight places in various parts of the country.

For the first time since Independence, Amritsar's boundary with the other districts of the state had to be sealed. At the three main access points to the district—the Beas, Goindwal Sahib and Harike—tanks and machine guns were deployed. Their barrels pointed not towards neighbour Pakistan, but India. A battle could ensue should the deserters manage to reach the Beas river that divides Amritsar from the rest of the country. The instructions were clear and firm—the deserters were not to be allowed to enter the district, come what may.

In a tradition harking back to the days of the British Raj, Indian soldiers continue to fight in the name of their faith. The new recruits to the Sikh regiment pledge allegiance to the country on the Guru Granth Sahib and the holy Granth accompanies them to the battlefield. Their battle cry, the Sikh jaikara—'*Bole so nihal, sat sri akal*'—has been the historical war cry from the days of the tenth Guru, Guru Gobind Singh. With the regimental motto '*Nischay kar apni jeet karon* [With determination I shall be triumphant]', they have distinguished themselves in every battle they have fought, starting with Saragarhi in 1897, when the British Parliament rose in a standing ovation to the twenty-two Sikhs (of the 4 Battalion of the Sikh regiment of the British Indian Army) who fought till the last man standing.

In independent India, 1 Sikh fought the country's first battle in 1947. They were the lead troops airlifted to Srinagar when the Pakistanis invaded Jammu and Kashmir and successfully managed to drive them back. The first Maha Vir Chakra of independent India was posthumously conferred upon the CO of this battalion. The regiment later fought with distinction in 1962 against the Chinese, and against Pakistan in 1965, 1971 and in the Kargil war. It earned two Param Vir Chakras, twenty-four Maha Vir Chakras and sixty-seven Vir Chakras, apart from seventy-five battle honours and many citations, including the 'bravest of the brave'.

However, in 1984, they killed their own Centre Commandant Brig. S.C. Puri and his Sikh driver, and injured Deputy Commandant Col Jagdev Singh, also a Sikh. They looted the armoury and more than 1,400 of them, mostly fresh recruits, fully armed, proceeded from Ramgarh near Ranchi towards Amritsar to avenge—what rumours had led them to believe—the destruction and defilement of their holiest of holy shrines, the Harmandir Sahib.

Prime Minister Indira Gandhi had visited Ranchi on 1 May 1984 and addressed the troops in the local cantonment. Meaningfully, she inquired of the local general how good the communication between Ranchi and Amritsar was. Not knowing the background to her query, the general replied, 'Madam, we have a direct train to Amritsar.' The general was later to lament to S.S. Dhanoa, the then home secretary, Bihar, that only if she had hinted at what was coming, they would have psychologically prepared the troops and modulated their response.

The excessive secrecy surrounding Operation Blue Star resulted in wild rumours. No one knew what was happening—the commandants were as ignorant as their men. The gagging of the media did not quieten the murmurs, but instead aggravated them. Rumours, I have learnt by experience, have a disquieting manner of gathering greater distortion and twists each time they travel from one mouth to the next. Physical distance from the scene of an incident often lends a multiplier effect. That is what happened at Ramgarh, tucked away in remote rural Bihar. Exaggerated hearsay about the desecration of the sanctum sanctorum reached the soldiers and triggered both religiosity and revolt.

On hearing about the assault on the temple, the young soldiers at Ramgarh sought permission to proceed to Amritsar. Permission was denied. They spontaneously protested, abjuring dinner that night. However, that went unnoticed by the seniors, who failed to address and pacify the heightened sensibilities. In regular military practice, the officers would have held a darbar and pacified the new recruits. But this was not done.

In the dead of night, in their barracks, the recruits sat planning their next move. The next morning, which was a Sunday, they gathered at the regimental gurdwara and, after offering prayers, proceeded on the long journey to Amritsar in whatever transport they could manage. They were intercepted at various places in Bihar and Uttar Pradesh en route to Punjab and disarmed. The mutiny was an abject failure of the command-and-control structure and the commandant paid with his life. The regiment was blemished and the nation suffered an avertable rebellion.

Far away from Ranchi, in Rajasthan, another 387 soldiers of the 9 Sikh battalion abandoned their barracks on the night intervening 7 and 8 June. Raised on 1 April 1964, 9 Sikh was a young battalion, only twenty years old. Within a short time, it had made its mark and earned a good name. In the 1971 war, it changed the map of India by adding 46 square kilometres of territory to India in Nowgaon sector of Jammu and Kashmir. The area was captured by the battalion from Pakistan and retained after the war, unlike the other territories on the international border between the two countries that had to be returned. The battalion invariably won the various in-service competitions with the other units, including the General Chaudhuri Trophy (named after Gen. J.N. Chaudhuri, Chief of Army Staff, 1962–66), from the very first year of its formation.

The year 1984, however, proved calamitous. The battalion was out on exercise near Bikaner; upon returning to its location (headquarters) at Lalgarh Jattan in Rajasthan on 6 June, the soldiers heard Mark Tully on the BBC reporting that the Akal Takht had suffered extensive damage and Bhindranwale and his men had been killed. They also heard about Operation Woodrose active in Punjab.

Some of the soldiers were deeply religious. One of them was young Tarlochan Singh Manochahal, brother of Gurbachan Singh Manochahal, an aide of Bhindranwale. A taunt by a fellow soldier set him to mobilize men. Hav. Gian Singh 'Runner' (so called because he was the Asian champion in the 400–800-metre race) threw a jibe at Tarlochan, '*Sara karah prasad kha janeo, hun kucch karo* [You eat away all the prasad, now do something].' This provoked Tarlochan, who, assisted by Nb Sub. (religious teacher) Karnail Singh, motivated men and manoeuvred duties at quarter guard and the magazine where arms and ammunition were kept.

They managed to procure light machine guns (LMGs), eighteen rockets, four RCL jeep-mounted anti-tank guns and small weapons, a total of about 500 firearms of different kinds; vehicles included jeeps, and 1-ton and 5-ton trucks. A total of 387 soldiers (no officer or JCO joined them) out of more than 800 combat personnel of the battalion left the barracks on the night intervening 7 and 8 June for Amritsar, raising the *jaikara*—*'Bole so nihal, sat sri akal.'*

Their departure was not furtive: They fired in the air to announce their exit from the headquarters. A burst was also fired at the mess room that housed CO Lt Col Iqbal Singh Sabharwal. The bullets pierced through the backrest of his bed. Earlier, the mutinying soldiers had beaten up Nb Sub. Satnam Singh, Hav. Major Karam Singh and a few others who tried to persuade and calm the men down. The two adjoining battalions—Madras and Rajput—did not attempt to stop them either, and it was only near Sri Ganganagar that they encountered a blockade by the Rajasthan police. They ran over it, firing LMG shots. The next encounter was on Abohar–Malout road, where soldiers of 94 Field Regiment were waiting in ambush. While most of the convoy passed, the final three vehicles faced the brunt of the gunners, which resulted in the death of thirteen deserters and injury to another twenty.

The main group of vehicles, on reaching Muktsar, took to link roads along the canal via village Assa Bhuttar to avoid ambush or blockades. On reaching Kot Sukhia near Moga, their way was blocked by tanks, led by a Sikh general, who persuaded them to surrender. The battle at the Golden Temple was over, he told them—Operation Woodrose had been called off and they would not be achieving anything by going to Amritsar. He diverted them to Suratgarh, where they were disarmed, detained and tried. Tarlochan Singh and three others were sentenced to fourteen years of imprisonment while others got lesser punishments. However, they were all released after about six years in a goodwill gesture during V.P. Singh's premiership. The CO was demoted to the rank of major and retired. The brigade commander, Brig. Paul Singh, did not earn further promotion.

On 1 September 1985, the battalion was disbanded. It was a touching moment for Lt Col Karam Singh Virk, who had taken over as CO on 31 October 1984. He had joined the battalion as a lieutenant and led his men in two wars. Later, on promotion, he was shifted to

26 Sikh as commandant but was brought back to the parent battalion after the desertions to sort out the mess. As the battalion flag was lowered for the last time, tears rolled down the battalion officers' eyes. Akhand Path was performed at the regimental gurdwara and the embroidered *rumala* the soldiers offered had '*Tera Bhana Meetha Lage*'—everything happens as per His will—inscribed on it.

3 Sikh, whose soldiers were on internal security duty in the north-east, heard the news of the operation on 11 June and a few hundred men deserted and proceeded in groups towards Amritsar. Col J.S. Kahlon, the commandant, tried to persuade them otherwise, but he was pushed aside. However, most of the deserters were arrested in Assam. Another eighty soldiers of 18 Sikh at Miran Sahib near Jammu abandoned their barracks and were intercepted in Gurdaspur district, on their way to Amritsar. Another 127 of the 14 Sikh battalion left for Amritsar with arms and ammunition but were intercepted in Maharashtra. Similar news came from Thane, Pune, Alwar and from some stations in Jammu and Kashmir.

In all, approximately 2,900 troops deserted their barracks. It was an abject breakdown of army discipline and a failure to sensitize the soldiers—otherwise, desertions would not have happened as late as 11 June, five days after Blue Star. The army brass was caught by surprise. It had underestimated the situation. Birbal Nath was then heading the BSF, which was monitoring the flurry of army messages exchanged about desertions and mutinous acts of soldiers in Rajasthan and Jammu and Kashmir. He later disclosed that the army brass did not suitably alert the political leaders in Delhi. 'When the BSF placed those messages before the Government, there was a gasp of horrified disbelief.'[1]

However, at the places where the army leadership displayed foresight, either there was no backlash from the soldiers, or if there was any, it was nipped in the bud. Illustratively, 2 Sikh Light Infantry commanded by Col D.D. Singh was headquartered in Amritsar, and there was no adverse fallout among its men, who, in fact, were deployed inside the Golden Temple from the night of 6 June, directly opposite the battered Akal Takht.

Another example is of the two units under 15 Corps located in a sensitive area close to the Line of Control (LoC) in Kashmir, whose men had shown resentment and some of them had even protested. In a bold move, Lt Gen. P.N. Hoon, the corps commander, flew to Uri and landed his helicopter on the very football ground where the armed deserters had gathered. He addressed them firmly and dispelled their doubts regarding the alleged destruction of the sanctum sanctorum. He offered to send them in batches to Amritsar so that they could see for themselves that the news they had heard on Radio Pakistan was false.

Hoon told the men that 'if you believe what you have heard, then I do not have anything further to say' and reminded them that the border to Pakistan was only two miles from Uri. 'How many amongst you are prepared to go to Pakistan? If you believe what was said on Radio Pakistan and if you wish to go, you are most welcome.' He asked them to raise their hands, but not a single soldier protested.[2] The heart-to-heart approach yielded dividends. The men were pacified and dispatched back to duty on the border.

None of the groups of armed deserters reached Amritsar as they were all intercepted and disarmed on the way. A few individual solders did manage to arrive at the Golden Temple, but without any weapons. Dafadar Gurjant Singh of 4 Horse, who had deserted in an army jeep, was apprehended on 4 September 1984 from the temple complex. Naik Gurmej Singh, posted at CVD Delhi Cantt, reached his village, Deo, and was caught while involved in a bank robbery at Malian. Still another deserter, Grenadier Gurpreet Singh of 193 Field Regiment, was arrested on 2 July, when he joined a jatha protesting Blue Star.

During the course of the road blockades set up to intercept deserters, and the exchange of fire that ensued at different places en route to Amritsar, about forty-nine deserters were killed and another nineteen were reported untraced. The surviving deserters were arrested and dealt with firmly, including being discharged from service. The 365 deserters who played leading roles were dismissed from service. Out of these, 277 were sent to civil prisons and were released on completion of their prison terms.[3]

Once things settled down, the government took a sympathetic approach, treating their desertion as an act of emotional outburst. Their rehabilitation was part of the Rajiv–Longowal Accord. The next of kin of those killed or missing were given an ex-gratia grant of Rs 1 lakh each. Employment in civilian jobs, interest-free loans for self-employment, education grants for children, widow-subsistence grants and self-subsistence grants were some of the financial rehabilitation measures.

As per data from the Punjab government's Defence Services Welfare Department in 2018, about 116 deserters and twenty-five widows were receiving monthly subsistence grants from it. Even the SGPC has, at its level, extended employment and financial assistance to '*dharmi* faujis', as they are called.

Demurral of Civil Servants

Protests against Operation Blue Star by a few civilian Sikh officers began with A.S. Pooni, the then home secretary, Punjab. In that capacity, he had issued a formal letter to requisition the army in Punjab, but was among the first to proceed on leave. Remorse probably overtook him after knowing what happened in Amritsar.

Four of his other colleagues, namely Rajinder Singh, secretary, transport; G.P.S. Sahi, secretary, rural development; Hardial Singh, secretary, education; and S.S. Boparai, secretary, industries, also applied for leave on 8 June, ostensibly to participate in kar sewa to reconstruct the Akal Takht. However, the government viewed the move as a message for other Sikh officers to follow. The governor was anxious that it might set a trend. These officers, therefore, were advised not to press for acceptance of their leave requests and wait till kar sewa commenced, the date for which had not been finalized till then.

Surreptitiously, news was planted in the local media (it appeared on 15–16 June) that the Centre was considering amending the cadre allocation rules for All India Services to enable it to transfer serving All India Services personnel from one state to another without their consent. It was a subtle signal to the officers not to go on leave—or face consequences. They were advised to seek leave only as and when kar sewa work commenced, on an indeterminate future date.

Harinder Singh Khalsa, my batchmate from the foreign service, was serving as first secretary in the Indian embassy in Oslo, Norway. He defected in protest against Blue Star and to survive ran a restaurant and worked as a postman in Norway for a few years, returning to India in 1990 with the intervention of friends who had interceded with the government for his rehabilitation. The charges against Khalsa were dropped, and though he was not re-inducted in the foreign service, he entered politics, and has been successfully elected twice to the Lok Sabha.

The attitude towards our colleague in the police, Simranjit Singh Mann, was more unforgiving. He was posted at Bombay in the Central Industrial Security Force when Blue Star took place. He resigned on 18 July 1984, addressing a provocatively worded letter to President Zail Singh, by name. Simranjit Singh concluded his resignation letter by an appeal to all Sikhs to march to the residence of the Prime Minister and 'offer their heads, so that she may quench her thirst for Sikh blood'.[4]

The government's response was dismissal from service without inquiry or opportunity to explain his conduct by applying a malevolent proviso of the Constitution that empowers the President to dismiss an employee without inquiry 'in the interest of security of the State'. Unwisely, he went underground and tried to escape to Nepal. He was arrested at the border checkpost on the Bihar–Nepal border, which had been alerted and provided with his photograph for identification. He was jailed under the National Security Act and charged with sedition. His dismissal and detention gave Simranjit Singh the eminence he needed; Sikh sentiment swayed in his favour, and so did human rights activists and the diaspora. Projected as a victim and hence a hero, he won the Tarn Taran seat with a staggering margin when he contested the Lok Sabha elections in 1989. However, he has frittered away the goodwill he had earned and is now living on the fringes of separatist Sikh politics.

IAS officer Chiranjeev Singh, indignant at the army action, led a protest through the streets of Bangalore to Raj Bhawan. In the memorandum submitted to the governor on 10 June, the protesters demanded the resignation of Zail Singh, the commander-in-chief of the armed forces. The Karnataka government was more astute than Simranjit Singh's police bosses. Chiranjeev's misconduct was ignored as a passing paroxysm of passion and he was let off. He went on to become India's ambassador to UNESCO in Paris.

Many public Sikh figures felt indignant at the army action and protested by returning state awards and recognitions. Prominent Sikh journalist and author–historian Khushwant Singh, a self-proclaimed agonistic who had on different occasions publicly called Bhindranwale 'evil', 'a menace', 'a mad monk', 'a hate monger' and 'an evil man undeserving of the title sant attached to him', now felt grievously hurt at the assault on the temple.

A Rajya Sabha member (1980–86), he had told the government to take timely action against the militants, and strongly condemned the demand for Khalistan. He had also denounced the Anandpur Sahib Resolution, which he felt 'had seeds of separatism in it'.

This secular scholar, however, disapproved of Operation Blue Star and, in protest, surrendered the national honour of the Padma Bhushan that had been conferred on him by Indira Gandhi's government in 1974. He became a hero and a villain at the same time. In an interview he said, 'I am appalled at the reaction at my turning in my Padma Bhushan: every one of the hundreds of telegrams

I have received from Sikhs have lauded my action. Every one of the hundreds of letters from Hindus have been condemning and abusive. To be at the receiving end of communal prejudice is a very unpleasant experience. I feel I am not facing a secular India but a Hindu India.'[5] The polarization of communities was at its worst. However, in 2007 Khushwant Singh was conferred a higher recognition—the Padma Vibhushan, the second-highest national award.

Two MPs from the Congress—Capt. Amarinder Singh and Devinder Singh Garcha—resigned from the Lok Sabha to mark their protest. Bishan Singh Bedi, the iconic cricketer, publicly stated, 'Mrs Gandhi is living on the strength of bullets like Bhindranwale did. But two wrongs do not make a right.'[6]

Anger and anguish were palpable on the streets of the state. Punjab turned saffron all the way—with men and women sporting bright orange turbans, chunnis and dupattas as a mark of protest. The anger and the hurt has lingered for decades, and every year in the month of June these are revived by bhog ceremonies and memorials.

14

Blue Star: A Blunder?

'Indira Gandhi did not consider Operation Blue Star a mistake,' disclosed P.C. Alexander, her principal secretary.[1] In an interview to the BBC, when asked if she had any regrets about how her government had handled the situation, Indira Gandhi replied, 'Well, perhaps we should have acted earlier. On the other hand, it was difficult to act earlier until you could prove to them that you had no other option.' On being asked if there was nothing else she could have done, she answered: 'I do not think in this particular situation we could have done much.'[2]

The perception among Sikhs is different. I have often asked people about how they perceive Operation Blue Star—was it an assault on the Golden Temple or was it an operation to clear the temple of the armed radicals who had laid siege to the hallowed space and posed a challenge to the legitimacy of a constitutionally established polity?

Not surprisingly, most Sikhs viewed Blue Star as a premeditated, sacrilegious invasion of their holy shrine. And that explains the backlash that followed the operation; it synthesized the sentiments of the quam against the state as a collective voice. In the battle of public perception, the state had miserably failed to carry the community along. That was, more than any other factor, the cause of the fatal consequences that followed Blue Star, and it continues to haunt the community even today.

In matters of faith, they say, reason usually is the first casualty. Sacrosanct spaces require empathetic handling; the holier a hallowed place, the greater the sensitivity of the faithful, and still stronger their reaction if in their eyes its sanctity is violated. The state ignored this sentiment and the consequences were catastrophic.

Still worse was the way Blue Star was carried out. It was a disaster—ill conceived, poorly planned, terribly executed. Consequently, for the troops it was a pyrrhic victory. A few hundred militants were killed. But their death sowed the seeds for ethno-religious nationalism to proliferate and generate a violence far worse than what the operation had eliminated. Blue Star was not the epilogue, but a prelude to the violent struggle for Khalistan. The army won the battle, but at the cost of peace in Punjab.

As the events unfolded, it became obvious that the Central leadership and the key military advisers were not conscious of the public sentiment or the political consequences of launching a direct assault on the sacred space. The troops deployed in the operation were oblivious to Sikh sentiments. Hurriedly inducted without familiarization with the area or the layout of the temple precincts, a frontal assault on a well-fortified built-up area without cover or camouflage against religiously motivated militants was suicidal. There could only be one kind of outcome—death and destruction. The holy space was desecrated, soldiers were massacred, a large number of innocent civilians were killed and the collateral damage was prohibitive.

Anticipating a situation where the army may be summoned to aid the civil administration, Lt Gen. S.K. Sinha, the then GOC-in-chief,

Western Command, had issued instructions in 1982 on the 'procedure for conducting such an operation'. To maintain absolute transparency and build favourable public opinion, he had proposed that the operation be videotaped and two prominent but non-political Sikhs be invited to witness the operation. The troops were to cordon the temple and make repeated announcements on the loudspeaker asking the militants to surrender. He has stated, 'They [militants] were to be told that they were violating the sanctity of the holy place by remaining inside. If the troops were forced to enter, the blame for this would rest on them. Extremists should be given maximum possible time and psychological pressure put on them.'[3]

The general wanted Akhand Path to be performed outside the temple with the help of a regimental granthi to pray for peace, so that the troops do not have to enter the complex—all part of psychological warfare. 'If in spite of all this,' he had planned, 'the extremists did not come out, then the troops would be ordered to enter the gurdwara and flush them out using minimum force. Prior to doing so, it should be ensured that all personnel take off their shoes and cover their heads, and they should seek the blessings of Guru Granth Sahib where Akhand Path was being offered. Thereafter, they should go into the operation shouting "*Bole So Nihal, Sat Siri Akal*".'

He had emphasized the need to execute the operation in a manner that would cause minimum alienation, and later regretted that the psychological aspect was not factored in and the mistake 'cost us dearly as a nation'.

Those in command of Blue Star—and two of them were Sikhs—did not pay heed to what had been proposed earlier by the other generals, erroneously presuming that the operation would be swift; or rather they suffered from the illusion that the mere sight and rumbling of the heavy armaments, tanks and APCs, the flying choppers, and the numerical superiority and might of the army garrison would scare the militants out of their pigeonholes and they would not put up a fight. It was a fatal miscalculation.

It was a flawed strategy to presume that the militants would give up on their own. Consequently, at no stage did the troops appeal to the militants to surrender. The army commanders made no attempt to hold a dialogue or negotiate with the militants to forestall the armed confrontation. The troops launched the attack suo moto. 'The extremists under Bhindranwale, Bhai Amrik Singh and ex-Maj. Gen. Shabeg Singh fought because they were given no option,' observed Lt Gen. V.K. Nayar, who had succeeded Sundarji as GOC-in-chief, Western Command, in 1987–89.[4]

When the militants repulsed the attack, the top army brass responded by deploying more troops and weapons of higher calibre. When repeated frontal assaults failed, the APCs and tanks were employed, with catastrophic consequences. Perhaps Brar did not apprise his superior, Sundarji, of what Sir Lepil Griffin had written about the Sikh character in his book *Maharaja Ranjit Singh and the Sikhs*, which Brar has so approvingly quoted in his book on Blue Star:

> When aroused, he [the Sikh] has the fury of ten elephants. It is difficult to check him. He becomes excited, loses his mental equilibrium, and does not care for the consequences of his action. You may have to break him, but you cannot bend him. When he is in a desperate mood, he responds only to tactful handling, sympathetic treatment and persuasion. Handled in tactful measure, he easily forgives and forgets, and is ready to side with erstwhile enemies.[5]

How true. The braves of the army of Ranjit Singh who had fought the British bitterly in the two Anglo-Sikh wars, within a few years, were won over and became proud soldiers of the British Indian Army, the very enemy that had vanquished them and liquidated their Khalsa Raj!

What Was Bhindranwale Fighting for?

Bhindranwale had never openly sought a separate Sikh state of Khalistan. What was he fighting for then? The answer lies in the Sikh history and tradition that shaped the militant's mental disposition. The tradition of shaheedi is intensely ingrained in the Sikh ethos, and this gives them the tenacity to defend their faith. The Khalsa is not known for desertions, but for ferocious fights and deaths on the battlefield when confronted.

The Akal Takht symbolizes the historical Sikh assertion of sovereignty and their resistance to Mughal and Afghan tyranny. The militants appropriated the legacy of this Sikh struggle and juxtaposed it with the perceived denial of ethno-religious rights of the panth by the Delhi durbar. They merely substituted the Mughals and the Afghans that had invaded the Golden Temple with the present-day 'invaders' and put up a fight.

Sikhism evolved in resistance to religious persecution by Mughal and Afghan invaders, and its tradition is studded with endless sacrifices for the freedom of the faith. Sikhs revere martyrdom, eulogize martyrs and avow their sacrifices every day in *ardas* (prayer) and on socio-cultural occasions through *vaar*s (heroic odes) of the *dhadhis* (ballad singers) and folklore. They idolize what scholars call 'martyr art',[6] portrayed graphically in paintings and print posters or the yearly annual calendars that show Sikh heroes being bodily torn apart, broken on wheels or scalped alive or sawn asunder, all in defence of their faith. These visuals serve as a daily reminder of the resistance, courage and sacrifice of the generations gone by. No wonder the historian Louis E. Fenech concluded that martyrdom has evolved into the symbol 'of corporate Sikh identity par excellence'. Shaheedi is a 'community-sealant', a binding force that inspires future generations to emulate the tradition of sacrifice.[7]

Bhindranwale played up this tradition of sacrifices, transporting history into the present day, constructing the perception of a systematic denial of Sikh rights by the Delhi darbar and 'Brahminical imperialism'. He would highlight the *zabar janah* (injustice) Sikhs had suffered in the past, casting the Indira Gandhi–led Central government as invading Mughals and Afghans, but conveniently diminishing the fact that times had changed and India had a democratically elected government with a robust constitutional mechanism to redress injustice.

He envisioned himself as a modern-day saviour of the faith and thereby a defender of the Golden Temple. He would remind his boys that Muslim invaders had razed the Golden Temple to the ground thrice, and they, the present generation, had to keep the tradition of shaheedi of countless martyrs—including the iconic Mani Singh, the manager of the temple who was executed by Mughals in 1734—alive. In keeping with the faith's noble tradition, the temple had to be defended against invading troops, even though the very reason the army invaded it in 1984 was due to its occupation by him and his band of merry militia. The call, coming as it did from a religious crusader, provided unparalleled motivational stimulus to the faithful to fight till the finish.

Bhindranwale would often mock the Delhi sarkar as topiwallas, incapable of a fight. In interactions with journalists, he would pronounce that Sikhs would rise and march to the Golden Temple to protect it from any desecration by the State. In aggressive lingo and public bravado, he would dismiss the army's superiority. His general refrain is well captured in what he told Subhash Kirpekar, a distinguished journalist, who met the sant on 3 June 1984. Kirpekar asked him, 'Will you not be outnumbered by the army, which has superior weapons too?' He replied, 'Sheep always outnumber the lions. But one lion can take care of a thousand sheep. When the lion sleeps, the birds chirp. When it awakes, the birds fly away.'[8]

His bravado was key to keeping up the morale of his boys. He would address them, 'If the authorities enter the Temple, we will teach them such a lesson that the throne of Indira will crumble.'[9] Doublespeak and parables were used to create the myth of Bhindranwale, the bold and the brave, which sustained the esprit de corps of the men surrounding him. They would nod and guffaw at such rhetoric, much to the embarrassment, if not utter sheepishness, of the visiting pilgrims and pressmen.

As it often plays out with men who become living myths, Bhindranwale became a victim of his own delusive utterances. He failed to oversee the fatality of army action, or perhaps chose to ignore it in the tradition of shaheedi. When the tanks finally fired from the main guns and the end seemed close, to surrender would have been cowardice. It would have been living death for Bhindranwale—he and his boys choose shaheedi, in the tradition of Baba Deep Singh, the first head of the Damdami Taksal, of which Bhindranwale himself was the fourteenth successor, triggering an ethno-national struggle for Khalistan.[10]

Operation Blue Star decimated him, but in his shaheedi he got back at the State, fomenting more militancy in his death than when he was alive.

The Generals Speak

Some of the highly acerbic criticism regarding Operation Blue Star came from the army, with a few army generals even going on record to castigate it. The strongest condemnation came from Lt Gen. P.N. Hoon, hero of the Meghdoot operation that led to the capture of the Siachen heights in 1984. He had succeeded Sundarji as GOC-in-chief of the Western Command in 1986–87. In a book published after his retirement, Lt Gen. Hoon described Blue Star as 'ill-planned, ill-conceived and ill-implemented', 'a black-chapter' in the 'history of Armed Forces'.

In rather harsh words Hoon writes, 'It was as brutal as General Dyer's firing at Jallianwalla Bagh.' He even imputed motives to Sundarji and accused him of over-enthusiasm and personal ambition. 'Sundarji continued to be a "Yes, Prime Minister" general only so as to become a Field Marshal. And if revelations can be relied on, then he even went beyond the decisions of the Prime Minister.'[11]

Gen. V.K. Singh, who retired as Chief of Army Staff, and is currently a minister in the Union Cabinet of Prime Minister Modi, is equally severe in his criticism of the operation:

> The plans for the attack were ad hoc, and virtually all basic tenets of fighting in a built-up area were ignored . . . The most obvious lesson was: never bypass the chain of command. The genesis of the entire problem lay in the Prime Minister inviting the Western Army Commander to her residence when the decision to involve the army was taken. The events that were set in motion that day eventually cost the Prime Minister her own life.

He further writes:

> The moment General Sundarji pulled the carpet out from under the feet of the COAS [Chief of Army Staff], the military logic had been compromised and each subsequent decision was guided by political rather than operational logic. It is also underlined the fact that someone somewhere along the line had to have the gumption to point out that the situation was being handled wrongly. This never happened and Army HQ effectively became a spectator.[12]

Lt Gen. Jagjit Singh Aurora, hero of the Pakistani surrender at Dhaka in 1971 that resulted in the creation of Bangladesh, felt that the operation was neither necessary nor the only solution. He criticized the cloak of secrecy surrounding Blue Star, and the great rush in which the operation was launched. He said, 'The fault mainly lies in not permitting them [Army] enough time which was required for proper planning and preparation.'[13]

The operation also invited censure from two other iconic warriors, Lt Gen. Harbaksh Singh, who saved the overrunning of Punjab by Pakistan in 1965, and the only marshal of the Indian Air Force, Arjan Singh—particularly the way it was executed.

The list of critics is long. Suffice it to say that the armed solution in the absence of a political narrative to address the ethno-religious

Gordian knot was rife with problems. Before launching the assault, attempts to seek a surrender from the militants could have delegitimized them in the public eye—if they did not surrender, the blame would lie squarely on the militants and not on the security forces for the operation's consequences. But no effort was made to build public opinion among the moderate Sikhs, nor were the SGPC or the high priests taken on board or co-opted. Rather, they all, including the moderate leadership, were viewed as part of the Punjab problem.

The media blackout further led to the otherwise avoidable rumours of alleged excesses; it resulted in a loss of credibility for the State, as the press and public only saw the death and destruction in the aftermath of the military action and not the bloody attack the militants had unleashed on the army. The inappropriate choice of a day sacred to the Sikhs to launch the operation, the excessive use of force that killed a large number of innocent pilgrims and extensive damage to the sacred shrine alienated the Sikh community; that helped the radicals multiply their ranks, aided by Pakistan, post–Blue Star.

A black chapter in our history, Blue Star continues and probably will continue to cause pain for a long time to come.

15

The President and the Prime Minister Arrive

On 8 June, we were in a meeting at the headquarters of 15 Division with Chief Secretary K.D. Vasudeva, IGP Bhinder, Maj. Gen. J.S. Jamwal and Maj. Gen. K.S. Brar, among others. Around 11 a.m. an urgent message was conveyed to me that the supreme commander of the armed forces, the President of India, would land in Raja Sansi at 4 p.m. The President was to visit the Golden Temple.

The communiqué was like setting a cat among the pigeons. The chief secretary was apprehensive—why was the President coming at such short notice? Would he resign? There were rumours that Zail Singh was deeply distressed at the destruction in the temple and that he was contemplating quitting office after paying obeisance there.

A tour by the head of State entails an onerous security drill and strict adherence to protocol. We had only four and a half hours; we rushed to make the required arrangements in our respective administrative domains. Brar dashed to the Golden Temple to clean up—it still had bloodstains, and the nauseating stench of putrefied bodies hung in the air, even after the corpses had been removed and the Parikrama had been washed with sarowar water several times over. I hurried to check the security and transportation arrangements and to ensure availability of the high priests for a meeting with the President.

In the meantime, another message was received that Governor Pande would be arriving half an hour before the President. However, the two aircraft—of the governor and the President—arrived together. The President naturally had precedence over Pande to land first. So, when Zail Singh deplaned at about 4.15 p.m., the governor was not among those lined up to receive him.[1]

Vasudeva had served as deputy commissioner, Bhatinda, when Zail Singh was the chief minister of Punjab. Since those days, he was not very comfortable with Zail Singh and therefore wanted to avoid travelling with him, which he would have to do as the senior-most state official at the airport. Under the pretext of receiving the governor, Vasudeva stayed back.

I.S. Bindra, an IAS officer of the Punjab cadre, who was then posted with the President, travelled in my car from the airport to the temple. I briefed him about the operation. Known to be outspoken, he, however, listened to every detail, but did not comment.

Zail Singh, wearing a white Nehru-style achkan, with a red rose broached on the button, looked cool and composed. As he alighted from the car outside the Ghanta Ghar Deori to the Golden Temple, his *darban* pulled out a multicoloured canopy to shelter him from the heat. In June, the sun in Punjab is piercingly sharp, even in the evenings. However, the President himself waved away Sikhawat Khan, the liveried bearer of the Rashtrapati Bhavan. This was enough to land the President in trouble and became one of the three charges levelled against him, when the high priests pronounced him *tankhaiya*, culpable of religious misconduct.

Brar escorted the President inside the complex, explaining the sequence of events, pointing out the fortifications, the pigeonhole firing positions of the militants. As we neared Ber Baba Budha Ji in the Parikrama, there was a sudden burst of fire. The sound came from the east, from the direction of Dukh Bhanjani Beri. The President has written in his memoirs, 'The bullet fell just a few feet away from where I was standing. It was followed by another shot, which hit one Col MP Choudhary in his shoulder. He was one of the officers surrounding me for security.'[2]

Zail Singh has stated that the bullets were aimed at him. Even Brar has averred, '. . . There was a sudden, unexpected, lone burst of fire towards Zail Singh . . .'[3]

The fact is that no bullet fell or hit anyone near the President. I was with him. Col. Choudhary was not part of the President's immediate security ring. He was positioned at a considerable distance, on the eastern side of the Parikrama. We heard the firing sound at a distance and understandably there was commotion and concern, but no panic. The commandos tightened the ring around the President, and we moved forward in the Parikrama towards the Akal Takht.

Near the piao at the north-western verandah, Brar stopped and pointed towards a manhole in the ground covered with an iron grill on top. He explained to the President how the militants would appear from the basement, launch a grenade and disappear underneath. Tarlochan Singh, who was then the public relations official attached with the President, quizzically whispered, 'But there are no craters on the floor or the walls.' His pertinent observation, however, remained unanswered.

The President stopped for a few minutes in front of the dilapidated Akal Takht. Silently, he observed the surroundings. Brar tried to give details, but Zail Singh indicated little interest. There were no outward signs of distress or emotion. He paid obeisance at the Harmandir Sahib and sat inside for a few minutes. Thereafter, in the Parikrama, he put his arm around the head priest, Giani Sahib Singh, and took him aside—Sahib Singh availed this opportunity to tell the President their grievances and complaints against the army. Arun Singh and R.K. Dhawan, special assistant to Indira Gandhi, who had accompanied Zail Singh from Delhi, tailed the President inside the Golden Temple, staying within listening range of the conversation. The murmurs were that they were the Prime Minister's spies.

From the temple, the President and his entourage drove to Gobindgarh Fort located in the north-west, outside the walled city. The fort was set up by the Sikh Bhangi Misl. They are called *bhangis* because they were addicted to marijuana; they are also known for wresting away the dreaded Zamzama canon of Ahmad Shah Abdali in 1762, which thereafter defended their fort. The fort, however, soon fell to Maharaja Ranjit Singh, who renamed it Gobindgarh. Then came the British, with General Dyer setting up a torture chamber and a Phansi Ghar to hang freedom fighters within the fort. The fort is now a tourist site. In 1984 it housed a small army garrison.

The weapons recovered from the militants had been displayed at the fort for the President's visit. There were about 850 weapons—thirty-eight LMGs, forty-eight assault rifles, two anti-armour launchers and about 780 guns, rifles and small arms like pistols and revolvers. (Gen. Brar in his book has put the number of weapons recovered at 927.) That the militants had managed to smuggle these into the temple was evidence of the total collapse of the civil administration and the firepower the army had encountered from the militants.

But what intrigued many was the fact that barring a few weapons of Chinese origin, most of the arms were of the same make as used by the Indian Army. The ISI had shrewdly supplied the militants Indian armaments that its army had captured during the two wars with India. That was a clever smokescreen to cover Pakistan's involvement in the supply of weapons from across the porous border.

Displayed among the weapons were a few traditional arms like swords. N.S. Rattan, the commissioner, given his childhood association with the temple, was quick to point out that these were holy relics. The Akal Takht housed some weapons belonging to the Gurus and a few Sikh icons. These were kept in safe custody but were open to the public for darshan during select times and on religious occasions. Some more relics were later recovered from the debris of the Akal Takht. All these were restored to the SGPC and are now safely lodged in the temple.

The President left for Delhi around 6.45 p.m. Before boarding the aircraft, he expressed his displeasure to Governor Pande regarding the state government's failure to stop accumulation of the weapons and the fortification of the Golden Temple by the terrorists. Only a few minutes earlier, he had, in his characteristic congenial manner, called us aside one by one—me, the SSP, the DIG and the commissioner—and exchanged pleasantries, but had pointedly ignored the chief secretary and the governor. His conduct was calculated to convey a message. If Pande was upset, he did not show it. Rattan and I agreed that changes at the top were in the wings.

The President's impromptu dash to Amritsar had left many disappointed. The generals were disenchanted at Zail Singh's lack of concern for the dead and the injured soldiers. Many of them were struggling for survival in the Military Hospital. He was the supreme commander of the armed forces but had made no inquiries about their well-being nor visited them in the hospital, which is customary on such occasions. The civil officers were also downcast at the public rap the governor got from the President. Such grave issues are not matters of casual comments in public. The priests at the temple were despondent because apart from making promises, the President had done little to redress their grievances. Zail Singh himself would be disheartened because the visit provided the grounds to the priests to declare him tankhaiya. VVIP visits to sensitive religious places when emotions are surcharged require deeper thought than had gone into this instance.

Before flying back to Chandigarh, the governor and the chief secretary took a quick review meeting at the airport lounge and laid out priorities for us. These were: care of injured civilians, strict enforcement of law and order, supply of essential commodities to curfew-bound areas, concerted efforts to restore day-to-day life for the common man and repair work at the temple—this being on top of the list.

As I returned to the Circuit House, waiting there for me were M.S. Bains, chief engineer, PWD, Building & Roads, and chief architect J. Malhotra. They had been sent from Chandigarh for the repair and restoration work at the temple. I noticed they were out of depth and a little shaken. They had witnessed a tragic happening and had not fully regained their composure.

Around 6 p.m., after the President had left, they were near the Akal Takht, when a boy crawled out of the debris from an upper floor of the Takht and threw a slab, targeting a soldier below. Another soldier yelled asking him to watch out, enabling the targeted soldier to duck and save himself. The slab fell on the soldier's feet. The second soldier fired a volley and the boy came tumbling down. The first soldier, blinded by rage and pain, threw that very stone slab on the fallen boy's chest. The boy had, in any case, collapsed before that.

I wondered what the consequences would have been if the incident had occurred while the President was at the Akal Takht or if the boy had chosen to target him. The President had, in any case, seen a firing incident—a burst of machine-gun fire from the Bunga Ramgarhia in the east. Lt Col Choudhary, the CO of the SFF, who was covering that area during the President's visit, was hit on the shoulder and another bullet got imbedded in his helmet, just above the temple region. It was a stroke of good luck for Choudhary that it was a lesser muzzle velocity bullet, and so it had failed to penetrate the helmet. Choudhary, I am told, has preserved the helmet—it adorns his home as a souvenir.

Bunga Ramgarhia is a Nanak Shahi brick structure with basements from the Misl period. A few terrorists were hiding there and had escaped the extensive search conducted by the army on 6 and 7 June.

After the President's departure, the troops were detailed to clear the bunga of the militants. In this operation, four soldiers were wounded.

Captain Rampal, the doctor of 10 Dogra, was tending to the injured when the militants in a swift move dragged him and two of his nursing staff into the basement of the bunga. Appeals to them did not yield any results. The militants were adamant that Giani Sahib Singh, the head priest, be sent to the basement to negotiate with them. We, however, could not trust the militants, nor was Giani Sahib Singh willing. As darkness had set in, it was risky to execute an assault on the multi-floored edifice. The operation was rescheduled for the wee hours of the next day and 1 Para and the SFF were assigned to rid it of the militants.

On the morning of 9 June, 1 Para blasted a wall of the bunga with shaped charges. This made gaping holes in the wall, providing access to the basement. The SFF commandos rushed down to the basement but it was too late for Rampal and his men, who had been brutally murdered the night before; their bodies bore marks of torture. The blast had blown up the militants holed up in the basement. This was the last military action of Operation Blue Star.

The Prime Minister Arrives

On 23 June, Prime Minister Indira Gandhi paid obeisance at the Golden Temple. Like the President's visit, it was a cursory trip. She arrived in Amritsar at 9.30 a.m. and departed for Delhi at 1.30 p.m.

The visit was shrouded in secrecy. The army had assumed all responsibility for the arrangements, and the civil administration was not involved. Brar, however, alerted me on the evening of 22 June about her schedule and cautioned me not to share the information or speak about it over the telephone or wireless for security considerations. Therefore, I did not inform my commissioner, Dinesh Chandra, who had returned from his leave, about the visit.

On 23 June, when the Prime Minister arrived, Chandra hadn't been informed despite protocol demanding that the commissioner be present to receive her. His absence was not noticed, but Chandra was unhappy and called for me for an explanation, holding me accountable for the slip-up. I explained my position, holding the state home department responsible for not keeping him in the loop, bluntly pointing out that if the governor and his two advisers could come from Chandigarh, surely the commissioner could have been conveyed to join the protocol cavalcade if the state government wanted.

I never heard back from the commissioner, but the incident underscored the ceremonial tamasha that is enacted each time a VVIP visits a place, requiring the highest to the lowest official to be part of the ceremony. It also highlighted the ever-increasing redundancy of the institution of divisional commissioner in Punjab.

Equally peeved was the local press. Blacked out from the visit, they had had no intimation of the Prime Minister's visit, and neither were they allowed access to the temple. How could the Prime Minister's first visit to the Golden Temple after Blue Star go unreported by the local media! They lodged a protest with me and I had to pacify them with all the ingenuity at my command.

The top-rung political leaders of the SGPC were under detention. The high priests, however, stepped in to fill the void. I had sent a confidential messenger to Giani Kirpal Singh, jathedar of the Akal Takht, and Giani Sahib Singh, head priest of the Golden Temple, and they both assured us of their availability to meet the Prime Minister.

However, on the morning of 23 June, the jathedar of the Akal Takht and a few priests surprised us when they held a conclave at Guru Ram Das Hospital and resolved to boycott the Prime Minister's visit. Giani Sahib Singh was not party to the decision and was therefore present at the temple during the Prime Minister's visit. His presence turned out to be crucial as the Prime Minister was able to get a first-hand account of Blue Star from a bona fide Sikh representative. Giani Sahib Singh showed her around, narrated the happenings of the operation, and pointed out the destruction of the sacred space and the large number of deaths due to Operation Blue Star. He urged her to withdraw the army, but the Prime Minister did not commit. On her return to Delhi, she decided that the army should stay put till the damaged structures were reconstructed.

By the end of her visit, the Prime Minister looked visibly disconsolate—her glum face and her body language betrayed deep discomfort. Visibly stiff throughout her visit, she had wrapped her sari around her head and pulled it down to her chin, where she held it tightly by hand, exposing only the front of her face. It made her look as if she was wearing a balaclava. She spoke little and her stern silence displayed her despondency at the destruction in the complex, as if saying to the generals, 'This is not the plan you had projected to me.'

On her return to Delhi, she directed P.C. Alexander: '[R]eplacements should be immediately found for the governor, the chief of police and the advisers.'[4] They were all shifted within days.

Traditionally, a siropa—scarf—is bestowed on visiting dignitaries at the temple as a symbol of sacred benefaction. However, none was presented to the President or the Prime Minister during their visits. But, despite the palpable tension and anger against the government and the boycott declared by the jathedar of the Akal Takht, due courtesies were observed by the priests.

But soon thereafter, the priests started expressing disdain for government dignitaries visiting the temple, though diplomatically. The gurbani is full of hymns that are critical of inhuman and cruel rulers in history, and the moment a government dignitary stepped inside the temple, the ragis would sing these hymns. It was too much of a coincidence for it to happen each time a VIP visited, and therefore I made a discreet inquiry of Giani Sahib Singh, who was forthright enough to confirm that it was a conscious collective decision by the high priests to convey the anguish of the Sikhs.

A frequently sung hymn was '*Kutta Raj Bahaliye Phir Chakki Chatte*'—a dog, even when crowned on a throne, bowing to his nature, will lick the flour grinder; a snake, even if fed on milk, will spout poison. Another hymn frequently recited can be translated as: 'Kings are like bloodthirsty tigers and their officials like bloodhounds.'

These hymns of Guru Nanak Dev Ji, called Babur Bani, were an expression of anguish against the atrocities perpetrated by Babur during his invasions of India. These hymns were now an expression of outrage and dissent against the death and destruction caused by the two operations, Blue Star and Woodrose, and, later, the carnage that followed the Prime Minister's assassination—these manifested as a symbolic catharsis of the crisis that the panth faced.

16

The Treasure Trove: Toshakhana

On the morning of 7 June as I reached the southern end of the Parikrama in the Golden Temple, a round hole in the upper-storey wall of the Darshani Deori facing the sanctum sanctorum caught my eye. From outside, it appeared to be a neat orifice, as if it was a man-made perforation. There was no marked blackening of the wall around the opening. I would have ignored it had I not known that the floor was the treasury chest of the prized valuables preserved over centuries by the temple authorities.

The culprit was a mis-aimed 105-mm squash-head shell fired from a Vijayanta tank that had penetrated the wall. We did not know what damage it had caused to the valuables inside as the outer locked doors were intact. Access to the valuables is through numerous shutters and doors, and different custodians hold the keys to the many locks so that no one individual may open it alone. The multiple wardens of the keys had to be summoned together to access the *toshakhana*—the treasury of the valuable articles presented to the Golden Temple.

Fortuitously, Goraya of 15 Division had deployed men on sentry duty drawn from 2 Sikh Light Infantry, starting from the night of 6 June, to ward off any pilferage.

The issue needed to be addressed urgently—Sikhs have a deep memory when it comes to their history and the toshakhana is part of India's history of struggle for self-rule. 'First battle of India's freedom won. Congratulations.' That was the telegram Mahatma Gandhi had sent in January 1922 to Baba Kharak Singh, president of the SGPC, then a non-statutory voluntary institution. The Sikhs had launched a non-violent agitation to wrest the management rights of the Golden Temple and other historical gurdwaras, which were then being administered by the British through *sarbrah*s (managers) and mahants.

The Sikhs were particularly perturbed when in 1920 the local Amritsar administration forced Arur Singh, the British sarbrah of the Golden Temple, to honour General Dyer of Jallianwala Bagh notoriety with a siropa in front of the Akal Takht. The Sikhs forced Arur Singh to resign and apologize to the sangat (community). The agitation launched by the Sikhs to free the gurdwaras from the control of sarbrahs and mahants gained momentum, and to avoid confrontation, J.M. Dunnett, the then deputy commissioner of Amritsar, ordered a handing over of the keys of the toshakhana to Baba Kharak Singh in 1922. That is when Gandhi sent his congratulatory telegram.

It was a hard-won victory for Indians—who were fighting for the right to manage their own religious shrines—and was celebrated by all, including Mahatma Gandhi, the Indian National Congress and the Muslim leaders of the ongoing Khilafat movement.

The British were keen to retain their hold over the Sikh shrines. For one, the Sikh regiments in the British Indian Army were driven deeply by religious fervour. The British, as a policy, encouraged strict adherence to religious rituals and Sikh symbols by soldiers. The Sikh regiments had granthis on their rolls, drawn from Sikh temples. The British even permitted Sikh soldiers to participate in singh sabhas, the voluntary civilian organizations formed to promote Sikh community interests, particularly religious reforms, and a few Sikh army battalions even formed their own Singh Sabhas.

The army '. . . became a life line for Tat Khalsa thinking, finances and institutions'.[1] Secondly, the abortive attempt in the late 1880s to restore the Lahore kingdom to Duleep Singh, the deposed Sikh ruler, had the tacit support of Sikh religious elites and the clergy. Thirdly, Punjab had become the garrison province of the British empire and therefore the hold over the religious affairs of Sikhs became a governance imperative—a conscious strategy for the British.

Given this historical past, the army was quick to constitute a joint civil–military Board of Officers on 7 June to open the locks of the damaged toshakhana and take stock of the valuables. The board was presided over by Col M.M. Malik, deputy commandant of 54 Infantry Brigade. The board members opened the toshakhana on 10 June and found bullet marks on the walls. The main door bore signs of damage, but it had not been broken down. Providentially, all the valuables were intact, except a chandova (roof covering) that was completely burnt, its ashes spread on the ground. A sehra made by Maharaja Ranjit Singh for his grandson was partially damaged.

The chandova has a fascinating history. In 1826, the Nizam of Hyderabad was facing internal uncertainty in his empire when he sent Darvesh Mohiuddin as his ambassador to the Lahore court. He carried expensive gifts for Maharaja Ranjit Singh, which included the chandova. In 1832, the maharaja reciprocated by dispatching a small contingent of Sikh soldiers under 14 Risaldars to assist the nizam to discipline the unbridled jagirdars in his empire. The Sikh soldiers accomplished the assignment and were encouraged by the nizam to settle down in Hyderabad. Their next generations were mostly absorbed in the service of the nizams and are known as Deccani Sikhs. They have forgotten their language, but their appearance and religious fervour has not changed.

Maharaja Ranjit Singh was so impressed by the opulence and grandeur of the chandova that he donated it to the Golden Temple. The priests, however, are said to have reprimanded the maharaja for donating a hand-me-down—it had passed two hands, the nizam and the maharaja, and may have been used by them. The priests, therefore, did not use it in the Harmandir Sahib and instead consigned it to the temple treasury, where it lay for 158 years before it got burnt in Blue Star. In 1930, the SGPC had got the value of the chandova assessed, and one gem was valued at Rs 35,000. There were 200 such gems studded in it. The SGPC claimed that the value of the total loss in the toshakhana was Rs 200 crore in 1984.

The ash of the chandova was collected in bags and sealed by the Board of Officers, so that it may not be misused to instigate or provoke people against the army or the government. The sealed bags were kept in the toshakhana. Its custody remained with the army till 29 September 1984, when the keys were handed over to the high priests and SGPC Secretary Bhan Singh by R.V. Subramaniam, the senior adviser to the Governor. The historical weapons of the Akal Takht, the reference library and the museum were also handed over to the SGPC. The temple was opened to the public. The sarai complex, however, continued to be under army occupation.

The chandova ash remained in the custody of the SGPC at the toshakhana. Two years later, the Board of Officers reassembled on 3 September 1986—it was assumed that with the lapse of time the flared Sikh tempers would have cooled, and it would be time to dispose of the ash. However, the SGPC president, in compliance with the decision of the executive committee of the SGPC, desired to get the ash examined by experts of their choice. The seal on the bags, therefore, was not broken and the Board of Officers dispersed.

A controversy was created by the Punjabi daily *Akali Patrika* on 13 April 1986 when it carried a story by S.S. Bajwa with the title '*Toshakhana Da Lutya Hoya Mal Kathe Giya*', alleging that members of the board took away historical valuables from the toshakhana and the SGPC was party to it. The libelous story had no base, but mirrored the downturn in vernacular journalism.

The board, headed by Col Malik, also made an inventory of the valuables recovered from other places within the temple, except the Akal Takht Sahib and the museum, for which two separate boards were constituted. Interestingly, the well behind the Akal Takht Sahib yielded gold, gold ornaments, precious stones and Indian currency. In all, 114 earrings, fifty-three tikas, 197 rings, nineteen necklaces, ninety-five karas, twenty-three pendant chains, gold bars and currency notes valued at Rs 30,93,926, etc., were recovered.

In Sikhism, there is no tradition to offer gold ornaments at gurdwaras. The presumption, therefore, is that these valuables were thrown into the well by the militants occupying the Akal Takht. How they had acquired this treasure or why they had stockpiled it at a religious place remains an unanswered question.

The board, for tabulating the valuables recovered from the Akal Takht, was presided over by Brig. L. Venkatachalam from the headquarters of 11 Corps. Historical weapons, gold-plated copper sheets and six *birs* of Sri Guru Granth Sahib Ji were among the articles restored to the SGPC.

Still another board to secure the belongings of the Sikh museum was constituted with the deputy commander of 350 Infantry Brigade as the presiding officer. A few artefacts and paintings in the museum had been blemished and were subsequently restored by the SGPC.

Were Narcotics Recovered?

On 14 June, Doordarshan and AIR ran a news item, and some newspapers carried a similar story the next morning that heroin, charas, hashish, foreign currency, etc., had been seized from inside the temple complex. The news also referred to the involvement of senior government officials in trafficking of the contraband items. The rumour mills went wild. Besides narcotics and foreign currency, objectionable objects such as condoms, soiled women's clothing, etc., were added to the list of items discovered. The rumour had gotten so out of hand that when S.S. Dhanoa, who was sent on deputation to Punjab as chief secretary in August, reached Delhi on his way to Chandigarh, he was briefed by the Punjab resident commissioner that the security forces had 'found in one of the rooms, a few young girls who had been kept confined there by the extremists'.[2]

While a few thousand rupees in Pakistani currency were seized from the lockers in Teja Singh Samundri Hall and subsequently during the kar sewa recovered from the sarowar, packed in neat plastic sheets, there was no truth in the news about the recovery of stocks of narcotics, condoms or girls. It was infelicitous propaganda. Obviously, the story was a plant; overenthusiastic spin masters were deftly executing psychological warfare to defame the terrorists.

The false news and the tittle-tattle that stemmed from it piqued the Sikhs. Organizations like the Chief Khalsa Dewan protested to me. The matter was taken up in the joint civil–military conference, where Jamwal confirmed that the news was baseless. I wrote to the two generals —Jamwal and Brar—and to the home secretary, Punjab, stating that such inaccurate news plants served no purpose other than hurting the already-frayed sensibilities of the Sikhs. These also tarnished the image of the administration as involvement of senior officers in trafficking of the contraband items had been alleged.

I asked the home department to deny the news and hold an inquiry to figure out how the news had appeared in government-controlled media. I never heard back, but Brar responded in writing: 'At no stage have I contradicted the news item on TV and newspapers that narcotics were seized from Golden Temple Complex. All that I stated was that "I have no further comment to offer".'

The general not denying or confirming the facts was a failure to stand by the truth. Who gained, and what, by this canard, I still wonder.

17

Death and Destruction

Bhindranwale's Cremation

THE BODIES OF BHINDRANWALE, AMRIK SINGH AND THARA SINGH were handed over by the army to the civil administration late on the afternoon of 7 June. I, along with Harjit Singh, SP, CID, escorted the bodies to the mortuary. Despite the city being under curfew, there had been a few incidents of mob violence and burning of private properties by people who were furious at the military action. The bodies of the dead could become a powerful provocation for further mob violence. I did not, therefore, want to take any chances.

We sat by the roadside opposite the mortuary at the medical college with a contingent of the police force as the doctors performed the post-mortems. Suddenly. a voice called out, 'Sir, please come inside. I live here.' It was a clerk who worked in my office, peeping out of a window above the road. He escorted us to his living room.

We had no shroud to cover the dead. As I instructed an officer to get a shop opened and procure the same, the clerk's wife overheard my predicament. She was extremely gracious and pulled out two new, white, cotton sheets from her trunk, and a shawl, which we spread over the bodies of Bhindranwale, Baba Thara Singh and Bhai Amrik Singh. They were cremated as per Sikh rituals. Ardas was performed and individual pyres were lit.

S.S. Dhillon, executive magistrate, was deputed to carry the last remains of the dead to Gurdwara Patalpuri, Kiratpur Sahib, in Ropar district, under army escort. After ardas, the remains of Bhindranwale and the others were immersed in the Sutlej on the morning of 14 June. An entry to that effect exists in the records of the gurdwara. It was the end of an epoch in Punjab's history.

Bhindranwale's cremation at the Chatiwind Shaheedan cremation ground stoked a controversy. 'Shaheed' in Punjabi means a martyr. A few senior army officers, not familiar with Amritsar, interpreted the cremations at Shaheedan to mean that the civilian administration had bestowed the status of martyrs on the dead! The cremation ground is called Shaheedan because of its vicinity to Gurdwara Shaheed Baba Deep Singh, named after the great martyr who had laid down his life fighting Ahmad Shah Abdali's forces in 1762 when the Afghan invaders attacked and flattened the Golden Temple. It did not mean that martyrs alone were cremated on this ground. Later, the Golden Temple was rebuilt, and a gurdwara, popularly called Gurdwara Shaheed Baba Deep Singh, was raised to commemorate his martyrdom. Sikhs living in and around Amritsar cremate their dead at the Shaheedan cremation ground, while families from other communities usually carry their dead to the Shiv Puri cremation ground near Durgiana Mandir, though there is no rigid division on religious lines. Cremation at Shaheedan, by itself, confers no martyr status.

The SGPC, however, has built a gurdwara within the temple complex in memory of Bhindranwale and those who died in the army action in 1984. They are regarded as martyrs of the quam.

Counting the Dead

Even after thirty-eight years, the number of the dead in Operation Blue Star remains a contentious issue.

As per the official version given by Brar, soon after the operation, eighty-three soldiers (four officers, four JCOs and seventy-five from other ranks) died, and another 249 (thirteen officers, sixteen JCOs and 220 from other ranks) were wounded. However, P.N. Hoon, who succeeded Sundarji as commander-in-chief, Western Command (1986–87), and therefore would know the facts, has put the number of security personnel killed at 336. He has written, 'Over 1,000 persons were killed in Operation Blue Star. Some 336 of this number were men from the Indian Army and security forces.'[1]

There is also no unanimity on the number of civilian deaths in the operation. Some Sikh organizations have alleged that a few thousand perished over 3–9 June. For example, Simranjit Singh Mann has asserted that '25,000 innocents were martyred'.[2] These claims are highly exaggerated and factually incorrect. The official figure given by the Government of India in the 'White Paper on the Punjab Agitation' published in July 1984 has put the number of civilian deaths, both innocent and terrorist, at 493. B.D. Pande, the then governor of Punjab, in his memoir published in 2021 has put the number of casualties at 1,200. However, he admits that his account is not 'based on documents and records made at that time. It is based on memory only and memory is, very often, deceptive and of course, forgetful'.[3]

However, the fact is that 717 civilians perished inside the temple complex, starting the night of 3 June. The DSP (City), who monitored the task of transporting the dead and injured from the temple, had counted 717 bodies of civilians in the precinct. This figure is confirmed by Hoon, who has stated, 'There were 717 bodies lying there, not including that of the Army.'[4]

The total number of dead, however, is even higher as some people were killed outside the temple by stray bullets and shells hitting the buildings adjoining the complex. Some of the injured who were evacuated to hospitals from the temple succumbed to injures on later dates. People also died in the mob violence that erupted in the city following the operation.

Therefore, I looked at the number of people cremated during those days at the two cremation grounds—Chatiwind Shaheedan and Shiv Puri. According to Chatiwind Shaheedan's records, 763 bodies were cremated there. Another twenty bodies were cremated on the Shiv Puri ground.

To complicate the figures further, from 7–18 June, post-mortems were performed only on 536 bodies, out of which 495 were male, thirty-three female and the rest children. There was a discrepancy in the number of bodies cremated at the two grounds and the number of post-mortems performed, as some were cremated without post-mortems. The municipal workforce, exhausted and nauseated by handling the emetic bodies, took a number of the dead directly to the cremation grounds. The police later conducted an inquiry into the matter.

Still another way to determine the number of deaths is to look at the figure of the families of innocent persons killed that availed relief from the government at the rate of Rs 20,000 per death in 1984. Relief was claimed for only 594 dead persons.

In June 1990, however, the compensation amount was scaled up to Rs 50,000 by the then governor, Nirmal Mukarji. Wide publicity was given to the decision and fresh claims were invited from those who may have failed to avail it in 1984. By then, I had moved to Chandigarh as the managing director of Markfed, and the government appointed me the chairman of the state-level committee to deal with these fresh claims. Sarabjit Singh and S.S. Channy, the deputy commissioners of Amritsar and Gurdaspur, respectively, and I.D. Kanwar, director, relief and resettlement, were made members of the committee.

The matter remained under process till 1992, when it was decided that relief should be given even in cases where death certificates could not be issued due to lack of identification, provided the person had not been heard of since 1984. Seven years had passed and such persons were legally presumed dead. In all, eighty-two new claims were received. I do not recall how many out of these were accepted after verification of the antecedents of the applicants, but assuming this figure of eighty-two, it would take the total number of deaths of innocent people to 675.

The SGPC also gave financial grants to the next of kin of those who had died in the operation, and published a list of beneficiaries. Its figure of the legatees is 741.[5] These figures are closer to the number of the cremations at the Shaheedan cremation ground.

Considering these facts, I would put the final number of Blue Star deaths at around 783. This includes twenty-six innocent persons who died outside the temple precinct, due to stray bullets, and the wounded who succumbed to injuries on later dates in hospitals. Eight persons detained in the army prison camp were killed on the night intervening 7 and 8 June as the guards opened fire on a group of detainees. These prisoners were suspected to be hardcore extremists and confined in a secure room. Some of them, it was reported, tried to escape by snatching weapons from the guards, who then opened fire.

On 8 June, there was another unfortunate incident at Dera Baba Sham Singh in Bazar Atta Mandi, where fourteen persons were shot. The venerated Baba Kharak Singh of kar sewa fame (not to be confused with the legendary figure Kharak Singh of the 1920 Akali movement) was head of the dera. The matter was reported to the home department but I never heard back. In those days silence was the standard response of the government.

Dhanoa, the late chief secretary, Punjab, in his autobiography, however, unravelled the mystery of the government's silence.[6] Dhanoa has written that the deputy commissioner, Amritsar, 'had mentioned in his confidential report about a case where a section of the Army had indulged in the looting of money from a kar sewa dera, and in order to cover their trail they had killed a Sikh Baba and some of his associates in cold blood. The concerned file never came back from the Governor. I am still not sure if I should have done something more in this case.' Dhanoa, however, has erroneously mentioned that the army was involved in this incident. It was, in fact, a few BSF men who were involved.

Differences also persist on the contentious issue of the number of bodies brought to the mortuary with their hands tied behind their backs. The issue is relevant, as often it has been alleged that some people were killed while in the custody of the forces. Since the rumours persisted despite denials, to put the record straight I wrote to Dr Dalbir Singh, the chief medical officer in Amritsar, for a report in the matter. He confirmed that eight bodies were brought to the mortuary with hands tied behind their backs. Post-mortems were performed on three of these bodies on 8 June and on the remaining five on 10 June.

There was also a miraculous survival among the 'deceased'—one young boy soaked in blood was presumed dead and brought from the temple complex to the mortuary. But as the surgeon forced his knife into the body during post-mortem, he showed signs of life and was saved—*jisko rakhe saiyan*—God has his ways!

But others were not so lucky. There were heart-rending scenes as the survivors discovered that their companions had perished. Surinder Kaur from far-off Bhurkunda near Hazaribagh in Bihar (now Jharkhand) had come to the temple with her four children, a nephew and two friends on the martyrdom day of Guru Arjan Dev. She lost all of them and was inconsolable. I bought her a ticket for the return journey and she boarded the train, wailing, alone. There were many such ill-fated people; it seemed like even God had abandoned them.

The Injured

In all, 178 civilians were admitted to Sri Guru Tegh Bahadur Hospital. After verification by the state CID, 102 of them were found innocent and eligible for compensation, depending upon the degree of disability at the time of discharge from the hospital. Most of these were pilgrims and Akali workers who had come to court arrest in the morcha launched by the Akali Dal.

Among the injured were also Hindus; fourteen of them were admitted to Guru Tegh Bahadur Hospital on 4 June. Out of these, six were brought from the Chheharta and Sultanwind areas of the city, with injuries caused by sharp-edged weapons wielded by unruly crowds protesting the operation. It took time for the police force, who were stretched beyond capacity, to control the mob. Sporadic violence continued for a few days. Eight injured persons were admitted to the hospital on 5 June, eleven on 6 June, four on 7 June and two on 8 June, taking the total number of wounded Hindus to thirty-eight.

Amritsar is well equipped to deal with medical emergencies, but the influx of the injured, and the dead for post-mortems was beyond local capabilities. On my request, teams of doctors were rushed to Amritsar from the adjoining districts of Gurdaspur, Jalandhar and Kapurthala, with ambulances. Director, health service, Dr D.S. Kang, who was then touring in the adjoining district of Gurdaspur, was directed by the state government to station himself at Amritsar and supervise the medical services. The doctors worked round the clock and rendered yeoman service.

Handling the Dead

A sensitive issue that often evokes criticism is the way the bodies were managed. Deaths in the temple complex had started occurring from the evening of 3 June, most of them due to bleeding from bullet wounds. In the intense heat of June, the blood-soaked bodies had putrefied by the afternoon of 6 June (when the battle ended), filling the entire area with a nauseating stench. About ten to fifteen bloated bodies were found floating in the sarowar. The policemen, who were tasked to move the dead to the mortuary, could not cope and withdrew after shifting the injured to hospital.

Given the large number of bodies—it required at least four persons to lift one body—there was not enough manpower to cope with the miasmic task. The municipal corporation staff was, therefore, deployed with a fleet of tractors and trucks. They, too, however, slumped, and finally the *safai karamcharis* were summoned, under the overall supervision of Dr Raj Pal Bhatia, health officer, to lift the dead into the trucks, offload them at the morgue and thereafter further transport the bodies to the cremation ground.

The festered skin of the dead was melting away when lifted. That made the task not only delicate but also problematic. The nauseating malodour made many safai karamcharis sick; they were supplied fresh cloth to cover their noses and faces, and some later alleged that the scene haunted them for days together and they could go to sleep only after consuming alcohol.

The administration was berated for using safai karamcharis and municipal trucks to transport the dead. Some chroniclers have provided heart-churning accounts of the way the dead were 'carted' in garbage trucks, mass-cremated and their last remains disposed.

The entire state was under curfew, all services and facilities had been shut and communication channels were cut off. To handle the large number of decomposed bodies, there was no option but to requisition the available municipal resources with the approval of the state government.

The municipal corporation, in fact, did not have any budget provision to meet the exigency. The district Red Cross, of which I was the chairman, stepped in to cover the costs. The municipal staff had to be incentivized for the highly unpleasant and disagreeable job. The cremation charges, including the cost of the fast-dwindling firewood stock, was also met by the Red Cross. Subsequently, the state government reimbursed the expenditure to the corporation for disposal of unclaimed bodies, removal of the debris of the damaged properties from public streets and for restoring electricity supply in and around the temple.

Collateral Loss, Relief and Resettlement

The temple complex is situated in the middle of the thickly populated walled city, and the deployment of heavy-calibre weapons like tanks and artillery, which are area weapons, resulted in the death of many innocents and led to colossal collateral damage to buildings that left 475 families homeless or shopless.

A touching case was of Gurdeep Singh, an employee of the office of the assistant excise and taxation commissioner, Amritsar. He considered himself blessed because for five generations his family had been living in the vicinity of the holy temple, in Bazar Muniaran.

On 3 June 1984, he was home when curfew was imposed in the area. The family was used to the sudden imposition of curfew due to the disturbed conditions and took it lightly until the next day, when the sound of rapid fire woke them up as security forces engaged the terrorists. The firing intensified on the evening on 5 June. Then heavy shelling started. An adjoining house, hit by a shell, caught fire. Stray shells and bullets perforated the upper portions of his four-storey house and a wall collapsed. In panic, he ran out into the street with his two toddlers, his aged parents and his wife. Screaming, they ran for their lives.

Many people from the adjoining houses were already out on the street, which had got partially blocked by the falling debris. By the time Gurdeep reached Bazar Kathian, he got separated from his wife and his mother. The security forces did not permit him to go back to trace them. His mother was injured by a stray splinter from a shell and died. He believed that his wife, struck by falling debris, was lying unconscious on the streets. For days we searched for her—under debris, in hospitals, in the army camp and even in prison—but she was nowhere to be found. Gurdeep finally reconciled himself to the possibility that she may have died and her body disposed of as one of the many unidentified victims.

Gurdeep was not the only one to suffer such a tragedy. The first innocent death outside the temple complex had occurred on 1 June before the operation had even commenced. The CRPF had set up a picket at the five-storey building of Shahzada Nand Girls' College. In the exchange of fire, a stray bullet wounded Balwinder, an employee of the Punjab and Sind Bank at Chowk Paragdas. He had just returned home from the bank and as he opened his fridge to take out some water, a bullet pierced the window and got him. He later died in hospital.

Freak shell splinters, bullets and falling debris killed twenty-six innocent civilians in the areas around the temple, most of them from 4 to 7 June. Ad-hoc relief at the rate of Rs 20,000 was disbursed to their legal heirs.

However, the magnitude of the tragedy went unnoticed till 13 June because of the prevailing curfew and suspended telephone communication. On that day I flew over the walled city in a helicopter with Jamwal and Rattan. We were shocked to see the badly battered bazaars and homes in the area around the temple. Building after building had collapsed and the lanes were blocked with debris. The same evening, Rattan and I surveyed the entire area on foot. The narrow lanes around the temple bore the look of dilapidated towns like we often see in war movies.

The area beyond the Akal Takht on the western end of the temple complex had accidentally become part of the battle zone. Stray shells overshooting the intended targets hit a large number of private buildings, both commercial and residential, and that caused extensive collateral destruction in the thickly populated lanes around the temple.

The worst affected were Bazar Muniaran, Bazar Kathian, Chowk Darbar Sahib, Katra Dal Singh, Bazar Papran, Gali Tarkhana, Bazar Thara Sahib and Katra Mohar Singh. Nearly the entire premises of Bazar Kathian, located at the back of the Akal Takht, caught fire on the early morning of 6 June. Firemen were not able to reach the spot due to the ongoing exchange of fire, resulting in substantial loss to these properties.

The affected persons later formed an association, the Chowk Darbar Sahib Area Sufferers Association. They launched a vigorous campaign, seeking relief.

Verifying the damage and monetizing the loss to buildings, merchandise and household goods and thereafter disbursing compensation in a time-bound fashion became a challenging task. It was completed successfully without any complaints, though many were despondent at the scale of compensation. Their businesses had been wrecked and took years to resuscitate. The Improvement Trust, Amritsar, then headed by IAS officer R.P.S. Pawar, built temporary tin sheds in the parking area of the nearby Dharam Singh market, where the sufferers were allotted makeshift shops.

To identify the private structures that had suffered damage, a committee under the chairmanship of the executive officer of the municipal corporation with the naib tehsildar, Amritsar, and superintendent, house tax, municipal corporation, as its members was constituted. The committee verified that in eighty-two commercial building units, 162 shops were wholly destroyed and another forty-eight partially damaged. In forty commercial-cum-residential units, seventy-eight shops and residences were wholly destroyed. Similarly, in twenty-three exclusively residential property units, fifteen residences were wholly destroyed while another eight suffered partial damage. The extent of damage to the structures was monetized by another committee and relief was disbursed at the rate of 50 per cent of the assessed loss, subject to a maximum of Rs 50,000.

In the case of loss of household goods, compensation was awarded in 125 cases. The committee constituted to assess the loss of merchandise in commercial establishments recommended compensation in 334 cases. The shopkeepers were suitably indemnified, after adjusting insurance claims. Insurance companies were unwilling to honour the claims as the losses were caused by the state, a situation not covered by most insurance policies. They had to be persuaded to pay, but not many got compensated by the insurance companies.

Still another category of affected persons were the employees of the SGPC, including twelve blind ragis living in the residential areas within the complex. They had suffered the loss of household goods. Initially, the government did not admit their claims but later the loss of household articles suffered by innocent SGPC employees was allowed at the same scale as for private citizens outside the complex.

The SGPC also lodged a claim of 1,000 crore rupees for damage to the various buildings and structures that included studded jewels and gold-plated domes and the museum, loss of cash and valuables, historical scriptures and manuscripts, artwork and other items. Subsequently, it filed a suit for recovery of these damages, which is still pending for adjudication.

Akal Takht Parikrama

The rear boundary of the temple complex was very close to the Akal Takht and that left little open space between the Takht and the outer boundary wall of the temple complex. For reasons of security and to create a circumambulatory passage, a decision was taken to merge some of the private buildings around the Akal Takht and a part of the street at its rear within the temple complex.

In all, twenty-three buildings were assimilated with in the Golden Temple complex. Seven of these belonged to the SGPC, four to another religious institution and twelve to private persons, and another 2,250 sq. ft area under a municipal street; as with the merger of private properties into the temple complex, the lane became redundant. Compensation was paid to non-SGPC owners, both for the land and the structures on it.

An exigent case was of the Dera Udasian, the followers of Baba Sri Chand, elder son of Guru Nanak Dev, the first Sikh Guru.

Baba Sri Chand had founded the ascetic sect Udasian; its 100-year-old dera building managed by the Sindhi Trust fell within the zone of the proposed circumambulatory passage around the Akal Takht. The dera followers worshipped idols of Lord Krishna, Baba Sri Chand and the Guru Granth Sahib.

The Nihang followers of Baba Santa Singh, who had undertaken kar sewa of the Akal Takht, forcibly removed the idols from the Udasian Dera and commenced the demolition of the dera building. We had an agitation on our hands, as the indignant followers of the dera protested. The trustees were pacified by the restoration of idols and termination of the demolition work. Subsequently, prolonged negotiations were held with the trustees of the dera and they willingly handed over possession of the structure on payment of compensation of Rs 3 lakh, funds for which were arranged by Union Minister Buta Singh. A historical landmark was thus amalgamated within the temple precincts.

Managing the Prisoners

By the morning of 7 June, the army had mopped up the entire complex and rounded up every person within the precincts. They were all taken to the Central School in the cantonment; the army did not want to part with these prisoners until they had been identified, screened and their innocence established.

The Central School, thus, became a jail without being one. The number of detainees was 1,782, but the tally rose as more were apprehended after 7 June, including those by 54 Infantry Division from the Patti area. There were about 260 women and over thirty children.

The living arrangements for these people needed to be addressed, but there was no budgetary provision for it. The army provided all rations except milk, which was catered to by the district administration. The detainees had no clothes or essentials like toiletries—the Red Cross stepped in to provide these. The cloth shops in the curfew-bound city were opened and cotton cloth procured in bulk. More than a dozen tailors were deployed to stitch togas, long underwear and ladies' dresses.

Joint teams of officers drawn from the army, intelligence agencies and the CBI were constituted to interrogate the prisoners and verify their credentials. It was a laborious process and took days to complete. Post the inquisition, these prisoners were classified into three categories. Category A consisted of those identified as innocent—they constituted the bulk of the detainees, about 896. Category B, those in the grey area, numbered about 556; and Category C, or the 'blacks', numbered about 330.

These people had been in custody of the army, but our legal advisers were not unanimous about the procedure to be followed or the substantive charge to be levelled against them. There was a jurisprudential discord between the civil administration and the army, and the adviser to Governor Surendra Nath air-dashed to Amritsar to intervene. Marathon meetings followed and ultimately the ubiquitous provisions of Sections 107/51 CrPC that have stood the test of pragmatism—though not always of the law—were applied ex-post facto to all the detainees, even against those belonging to Category C who had 'waged war against the state'. They were, however, subsequently charged with criminal offences. The wise SSP Sube Singh became a scapegoat and was posted out of Amritsar on 16 June, to be succeeded by IPS Bua Singh of the Uttar Pradesh cadre.

A detainee under Section 107/51 of the CrPC is entitled to release on a bond of good conduct which leaves a magistrate with little discretion in the matter but to bail out the prisoner. Dhillon, the executive magistrate to whom I had assigned CrPC cases within the jurisdiction of police stations in the city, was disinclined to extend the period of detentions under 107/51. His judicial patience was wearing thin. The interrogation of prisoners at the army camp jail was intense and time-consuming. Surendra Nath again intervened to persuade Dhillon to cooperate and, finally, after interrogation by the joint teams was over, the first group of 494 Category A prisoners belonging to Amritsar district were discharged on 15 June—eight days after they had been taken into custody. The second group of 182 innocents, which included eleven children, was released the next day and the third batch of 192 on 29 June.

However, the innocent prisoners not belonging to Amritsar were transferred to the district concerned and these included fourteen children sent to Ludhiana jail on 6 July. Another 114 prisoners (104 women and ten teenagers) and thirty infants were transferred to Sangrur on 21 July.

Much later, the consequences of Surendra Nath's tweaking of the law were to meet judicial disapproval. In a judgment delivered on 12 April 2017, Amritsar District Judge Gurbir Singh granted compensation of Rs 4 lakh each to forty plaintiffs who were detained on 6 June 1984 from the Golden Temple and kept for eight days—in what the court held as 'illegal custody'—in the army camp and later shifted to Jodhpur. The court held it to be a case of 'malicious prosecution and illegal detention' and that 'No evidence is there on record that plaintiff had fired towards Army personnel during Operation Blue Star. Inference cannot take the place of proof.'[7]

Was it due to administrative apathy or the then prevailing environment of trepidation that the release of even innocents was delayed? Every right has a remedy, but it seems that the resilient Punjabis had lost the will to seek justice. It needed the Mangalore-born intrepid Kamaladevi Chattopadhyay, a social activist of long standing, to move the Supreme Court under Article 32 of the Constitution to plead for the plight of the innocent children and their mothers detained in jails after they had been transferred from Amritsar to their respective districts. The court restored their freedom, but by then they had been interned for four months simply for being at the Golden Temple at the wrong time. The court observed, 'Neither the affidavit of the Superintendent of the Central Jail nor the report of the learned District Judge indicates any reasons for the detention of any of these persons.'[8]

All twenty-six of them were released. They were in the age group of one year to seventy-two years. However, those who had been identified in Category B or C after the investigation were detained under the National Security Act. Some of them were transferred to jails at Jaipur, Jodhpur, and a few to Ladda Kothi at Sangrur, Nabha and Patiala. Among the detained were Longowal and Tohra.

Ramoowalia, Bhan Singh and Avinashi Singh were discharged on 23 June. Others, however, were not so lucky or high-profile and remained under detention. We had to issue hundreds of detention orders within a short time and that put our legal skills to the test; the concerned branch of my office wore the appearance of a law firm on a fire-fighting mission. The district attorney and all of us worked round the clock. The detention orders were subject to judicial review and there was no room for solecism.

Years later, the Jodhpur detainees were also considered 'innocent' and the first batch of forty such prisoners was released in March 1988. More releases followed later. Realization now dawned that some of them had suffered for years and the young among them had lost prime years and crossed the employable age. Therefore, they deserved to be compensated. Tejinder Khanna, financial commissioner (revenue), worked out a relief package. It was opposed by Julio Ribeiro, then serving as adviser to the governor, and finally a truncated package of case-to-case assistance from the governor's discretionary fund was approved by S.S. Ray, the governor in 1988.

Some of the prisoners were so traumatized that they refused to be released—one high-profile case, often quoted, was of a female relative of Harbans Singh, who was adviser to the Punjab governor. The middle-aged lady was arrested from inside the temple, where she had apparently gone for obeisance, but when interrogated said she would take to the gun to avenge the desecration of the temple. She was categorized 'Black' and detained. It needed the governor's intervention and Harbans Singh's persuasion before she walked free.

18

Thefts, Violence and Shortages

Thefts

WITHIN DAYS OF OPERATION BLUE STAR, WE WERE INUNDATED with complaints from the residents of the lanes and bazars around the Golden Temple complex regarding theft and pillage of private property. When the operation started, people scurried out of their homes to safer places, and when they returned, many found cash and expensive goods missing.

It may have been easy for the thieves to access the buildings that had been damaged in the shelling, but strangely even the structures that were intact—and their number was more than 100—had their locks broken. All this happened while the town was still under curfew. In all, 607 complaints of theft were filed in the police stations of the walled city, including by SGPC employees living within the temple complex and around it.

The security forces had cordoned off the entire area from 3 June. Civilians were not allowed to enter the zone for about two weeks. The thefts, therefore, could not be an outside job. The needle of suspicion naturally pointed towards the security personnel—the guardians themselves were suspect. Men belonging to 26 Madras, 12 Bihar and 58 Battalion of the BSF had manned the area.

I took up the matter with the home secretary, Punjab, and with Maj. Gen. J.S. Jamwal, who, to his credit, was prompt to act. Initially, the local army units denied any involvement but the authorities ordered extensive searches by a team of officers not involved in the operation. The doubt was confirmed when some of the pillaged goods were recovered from the barracks. These were restored to the owners. Liquid cash, however, was lost in almost all the instances of theft.

It was a serious failure of the command-and-control structure of these units. The army authorities instituted inquiries to identify and punish the guilty. A few officers, JCOs and men were penalized. The CO, Lt Col K.M.G. Panikker of 26 Madras, and others were held responsible for not exercising proper command and control over their men, resulting in their 'picking up various items wantonly'.

58 Battalion of the BSF detained some of its own men involved in these incidents. Jewellery, cash, electronic items and other valuables were recovered. One BSF man, in fact, had posted the stolen valuables to his ancestral home. By an accident of fate, the particulars of the addressee on the parcel got wiped out by rain and the parcel was returned to the sender. On return, BSF officials intercepted it and the culprit was suitably chastised.

The valuables of the SGPC employees living in the temple complex, however, had been taken into protective custody by the army. Lt Col Govinder Singh, assistant quartermaster general of 15 Division, the custodian of the property, handed these items over to the police as case property for restoring these to the rightful owners through legal process.

The action taken by the army and paramilitary forces against their own guilty men was kept confidential on the fallacious logic that disclosures would dampen the morale and image of the forces. The people who had lost their property thus remained unaware of the action instituted after the findings of the inquiries. Suppression of information only impaired the image of the forces. It would have been advisable to come clean and help the forces gain public goodwill.

The issue, nevertheless, keeps on surfacing in the public domain. Some army officers who were proceeded against moved courts, and their cases have lingered. Maj. K.A. Singh of 26 Madras was one of those who fought it out till the level of the Supreme Court. His case was finally decided in 2018, thirty-three years after Blue Star. A court of inquiry had held five officers responsible for 'illegal detention' (a euphemism for possessing stolen goods) of household electronic items. Maj. Singh contested the charge and was finally exonerated by the Supreme Court, restoring his honour and substantive rank of Lt Colonel. His defence plea was that on 8 June 1984, the troops of the battalion had brought a few electronic items to the headquarters 'in the presence of Lt Col Panikker', the CO of the regiment, who allowed retention of the same as battle 'souvenirs'.[1]

Mob Violence

Despite the media blackout, news of the army assault spread fast—sections of Sikhs hit the streets. A curfew was in force, but that did not deter the mobs. They were in anguish and their anger poured out in spasmodic violence that kept us on the run.

It started on 4 June, as about 1,500 people gathered at the Majitha Road Gurdwara and resolved to march to the Golden Temple to confront the forces. They were, however, persuaded to disperse. The residents of Gohalwar, Kazi Kot Tharu, Pandori, Nagoke and some other villages of Tarn Taran sub-division were up in arms, again on 4 June, and had to be contained.

From 4–6 June, ten innocent persons, mostly Hindus, were murdered in Amritsar district, another seventeen were injured and sixteen cases of arson targeting government buildings, school and banks took place in the areas of Sarhali, Chabhal, Verowal and Tarn Taran. Militants at Chawinda Devi killed five members of a minority community, again on 4 June.

In Amritsar, a large mob breached curfew and set fire to commercial, industrial and residential properties in the Sultanwind area—sixty-six premises were damaged and many persons injured. There were stray incidents of violence in Putligarh and confrontation between Sikhs and Hindus was averted by prompt preventive deployment of the forces.

People would gather in gurdwaras, make inflammatory speeches against the army action and attempt to march towards Amritsar. On 5 June, a mob of more than 500 gathered at Kukranwala in Ajnala. Carrying kirpans, spears, etc., they advanced towards Amritsar but were intercepted near Raja Sansi. Force had to be used and in the resultant firing five people died and more were injured.

Around 200 people gathered at village Chhina Karam Singh in Ajnala sub-division and footslogged towards Amritsar but were intercepted and physically stopped. On 6 June, three persons of the minority Hindu community were wounded with sharp-edged weapons at Muradabad and another was wounded at Amritsar. On 7 June, three banks in Jalalabad and another one at Chak Kare Khan in the Tarn Taran area were set on fire.

On 11 June, a determined mob of 5,000 people marched from Tarn Taran; some of them had trudged all the way from far-off villages like Moga. They were intercepted at the Sangrana Sahib and persuaded to return.

The extremists were active in areas like Sultanwind, Kot Baba Deep Singh, Kot Karnail Singh and East Mohan Nagar at one end of the city, and Kot Khalsa, Putligarh, Pipli Sahib, Chheharta and surrounding villages at the other end.

The Bhakra main line canal was breached in Ropar, which triggered a spate of canal cuts in other districts. In Amritsar, the water channels were breached at Saidpur Harni village, flooding it, and at Malakwala, near Fatehgarh; and a 7-ft-wide cut was caused in the Amritsar distributary on 6 August near village Mule Chak. Intensive patrolling, tactful handling and in a few cases the use of force prevented more untoward incidents.

There were some instances of defiance too, as in the case of a Nihang, who, while travelling in a bus that was stopped for a routine check at UBDC bridge on 28 June at the police station in Ajnala, reportedly refused to be body-searched. The CRPF insisted that he step out of the bus and hand over the kirpan. In the ensuing altercation, he allegedly assaulted a constable and was shot dead.

Unsavoury scenes such as sections of jubilant Hindu groups celebrating and distributing sweets to the soldiers were also witnessed in the walled city. People had lived under the shadow of terror for years and now felt reassured by the presence of the army. They extended hospitality to the soldiers, even while a curfew was in force. When there were stray instances of celebrations despite firm instructions, the issue was raised in the army–civilian conference, and this distasteful conduct came to an end.

In fact, there was an inter-divisional tiff too. On 8 June, an agitated Brar walked into the conference room while Vasudeva, Bhinder, Rattan and I were in a meeting with Jamwal at the headquarters of 15 Division. Jamwal's men, along with the paramilitary, had been deployed in the town. Brar, the GOC of 9 Division, was upset that despite clear orders, some of the army men were still allowing people to come out to the streets and distribute sweets. Addressing Jamwal, Brar said, 'I will not accept this situation. Either you control your boys or I will have to take action. I will not accept this *ladoo baatna* [distribution of sweets].' He added, 'I have ordered that any jawan accepting anything will be court-martialed.'

Sant Jarnail Singh Bhindranwale (left) and Sant Harchand Singh Longowal—the conviviality that did not last long.

Photo credit: Satpal Singh

Bhindranwale (with his trademark arrow) and Longowal at the Golden Temple.

Photo credit: Satpal Singh

Longowal (left), P.S. Badal (with a garland) and Bhindranwale (standing) at the launch of Dharam Yudh Morcha, Golden Temple.

Photo credit: Satpal Singh

4 August 1982: P.S. Badal leading 1,100 Akali workers to court arrest. Courting of arrests by Akali workers became a daily feature of the Dharam Yudh Morcha until the Army encircled the temple on 3 June 1984.

Photo credit: Satpal Singh

The Akal Takht before Operation Blue Star.

Photo credit: Satpal Singh

The badly damaged Akal Takht after Operation Blue Star.

Photo credit: Satpal Singh

Baba Santa Singh, the Budha Dal chief, at Nihangan di Chawoni, Amritsar, before the commencing of the government-sponsored kar sewa at the Akal Takht.

Photo credit: Satpal Singh

The massive response to Sarbat Khalsa, the community congregation at the Golden Temple after Operation Blue Star.

Photo credit: Satpal Singh

'My services may be accepted in this house of God,' prayed Arjun Singh at the Golden Temple on 16 March 1985, after taking over as governor of Punjab. Also seen in the image is his wife (on the right) and the author, beside him.

Photo © The Indian Express (P) Ltd

Photo © The Indian Express (P) Ltd

S.S. Barnala, chief minister of Punjab, cleaning shoes of devotees at Gurdwara Anandpur Sahib, with a placard hung around his neck declaring that he is a 'sinner', to atone for the 'Tankha' imposed by the Akal Takht.

The Blue Star commanders—Lieutenant General R.S. Dayal (left) and Lieutenant General K. Sundarji—addressing a press conference.

Photo © The Tribune

Indira Gandhi at the Golden Temple after Operation Blue Star. On her right is Giani Sahib Singh, the head priest.

Photo © The Tribune, Chandigarh

Photo © The Tribune, Chandigarh

Kar sewa of the sarowar, Golden Temple.

29 September 1984: The historic day the possession of the Golden Temple was handed back to Shiromani Gurdwara Parbandhak Committee (SGPC) after Operation Blue Star. From left: SGPC secretary Bhan Singh and jathedar Akal Takht Giani Kirpal Singh receive the keys of the Toshakana from R.V. Subramaniam, senior adviser to the governor of Punjab (with a cap), as Chief Secretary of Punjab S.S. Dhanoa looks on.

The healing touch: (From left) Mufti Mohammad Sayeed, the then Union home minister, Devi Lal, the then deputy prime minister, Inder Kumar Gujral, the then minister of external affairs, and Prime Minister V.P. Singh, after paying obeisance at the Golden Temple.

The author with President Giani Zail Singh at the Rashtrapati Bhavan, after the Padma award investiture ceremony, in 1986. The author (extreme right) was conferred the Padma Shree.

Photo credit: Google Maps

Amritsar was built around the Golden Temple. The high collateral damage to the civilian population and property in Operation Blue Star was due to the density of the built-up area around the temple. Image From Google Maps.

The author (extreme right) with Governor of Punjab K.T. Satarawala, in 1984. On the left is Dinesh Chandra, the then commissioner, Jalandhar division.

From left: Chief Minister P.S. Badal, the author, D.S. Guru, principal secretary to the CM, and N.P.S. Aulakh, DGP of Punjab, in Amritsar, 2008.

The author receiving the National Citizen's Award from President of India Ramaswamy Venkataraman, at Vigyan Bhavan, Delhi.

President Zail Singh at the Golden Temple on 27 September 1984, after he had been exonerated by the high priests of the Tankhaiya charges. Behind him (on the right) is the author.

The APC disabled by the militants in Operation Blue Star at the Golden Temple. On the extreme right are Lieutenant General K. Sundarji, Lieutenant General R.S. Dayal and Major General K.S. Brar.

Celebrating Punjab's agrarian prosperity with a return of normalcy in 1995, with the author seen at the steering wheel of a tractor.

How different it was from the 1965 and 1971 war days. It was the same army but in a different situation. During the wars, Punjabis had risked their lives to supply food to the troops right up to the firing lines on the border and beyond. However, now the same population resented the distribution of sweets to security personnel. The communal schism was deepening and the possibility of inter-community clashes could not be ruled out. That kept us on high alert.

These occurrences ratified—if such an attestation was needed—the rationale to bring the entire state under curfew and the exigency to conclude the operation in the shortest possible time.

Shortages

The town was under continuous curfew for three days, starting 3 June. Relaxation was given for the first time on 6 June for two hours, from 3–5 p.m., and it resulted in a sea of humanity storming general stores, vegetable shops and eateries as people were not sure when the curfew would be relaxed again. The shops sold out stocks in the very first hour and supplies ran out quick. There had been no replenishment of essential commodities from outside the city due to the statewide curfew. Within days, the town faced a dire paucity of vegetables, fruits, milk, sugar, wheat flour, pulses, etc. Cooking gas, petrol and kerosene were rationed. The paddy-sowing season had commenced but there was acute shortage of fertilizers, gypsum and other agricultural inputs.

Not just people, animals suffered too. Amritsar had a large population of cattle, particularly buffaloes, and a few died due to hunger and heat over 3–6 June. Regular inflow of processed cattle feed from the Markfed plant at Kapurthala and supply of green fodder from rural areas was marshalled from 7 June onwards to save the cattle population.

It became my daily routine, and an important one, to review the availability of essential commodities with the officers of the departments of civil supplies, transport, the Food Corporation of India and PUNSUP, and indent the required commodities from outside. It was a major endeavour as the working hours were limited due to daytime curfew.

Curfew Lifted

Post–Blue Star, the daytime curfew was finally lifted in Amritsar from 8 a.m. to 5.30 p.m. daily with effect from 11 June, except in the areas around the Golden Temple, which continued to reel under a clampdown for many more days. A semblance of normalcy was restored as banks and offices opened for the first time on 11 June, though school and colleges remained closed for a few more days.

The disconnected telephone lines were restored on 11 June, and for the first time three buses each were allowed to ply in convoys from Amritsar to the sub-divisional towns of the district and to Jalandhar to evacuate people who had been grounded since 3 June.

107 Pakistanis on visitor visas to India were held up in Amritsar, and on 12 June a special train was organized from Wagah to Lahore to evacuate them. A similar train carrying 1,875 stranded Indian passengers reached from Pakistan on 20 June. Cinema houses, a sure sign of normalcy, started daytime shows from 20 June. Factories and industrial units were also allowed to operate from that date. Regular train and air services, however, commenced only by the end of June. The night curfew was lifted from 7 July, but given the tense situation it was reimposed on the night of 15 July. It continued on and off, depending upon the local situation. Amritsar city remained under curfews of varying duration for 109 days in 1984.

There were some unexpected fallouts of the curfew relaxation on 6 June. A group of militants, mostly from the Babbar Khalsa, escaped from the temple precincts via the Bagha Wali Gali on the rear end of the Teja Singh Samundri Hall. The gali ends near Guru Nanak Niwas with a high wall that blocks and partitions the temple complex from the street. The armed forces were not deployed at this point as it was a dead end. The militants, however, punctured the wall and disappeared through the neighbouring houses during the curfew relaxation period. Superintending the periphery of the temple complex was not an easy assignment, given that in 1984, it had about fourteen entrances and exit routes, in addition to many more small inlets.[2]

19

The Purge

In the aftermath of Operation Blue Star, there was palpable disquiet in official circles. The government had launched a weeding-out exercise that caused much consternation among the civil servants. We were directed that the administration be purged of the quislings before the army marched back to the barracks. Terrorism could not have proliferated without the active abetment of perfidious policemen and double-dealing *sarkari mulazams* (government servants).

An elaborate scrutiny was launched on priority, and by the end of June in Amritsar district, twenty-two police officials were compulsorily retired, including two sub-inspectors and ten ASIs, and one head constable, Karnail Singh, was detained under the National Security Act. Ajay Pal Singh Mann, IPS, who was the SSP of Amritsar from 3 October 1983 to 28 March 1984, was dismissed from service as he was perceived to be close to Bhindranwale. It was during his tenure as district police chief that a sizeable number of weapons had been smuggled into the temple. IPS Simranjit Singh Mann, then serving as DIG with the CISF, was also dismissed. Throughout the state, about 200 policemen were sent home. A few revenue officials were also discharged from service, though mostly at the lower end of the administrative chain.

The Government of India constituted a committee under the chairmanship of R.V. Subramaniam, a retired secretary to the Government of India. His committee was tasked with identifying men of doubtful credentials among the upper echelons of the administration with the objective to shear the system. More importantly, the committee was to recommend measures to tone up the administration and the security set-up for the future.

The committee toured the state and arrived in Amritsar on 18 July and held extensive deliberations with local officials at the Circuit House. We were called in, one by one, and quizzed on the how and why of what had happened. Honest opinions, particularly if they are censorious of the powers that be, are rarely welcome. At the end of my session, I felt I had spoken out of turn, but was pleasantly surprised when, before leaving Amritsar, Subramaniam complimented me for an 'insightful' analysis. This was encouraging, and I expected that the committee would undertake a systemic refit of the state administration.

The committee, in fact, did give elaborate recommendations, but it only resulted in the usual musical chairs—postings and transfers of deputy commissioners and senior superintendents of police, which was projected as a great administrative toning-up of the state apparatus. Illustratively, the deputy commissioner of Jalandhar was posted out, apparently for failure to control the retaliatory mob violence that engulfed the town following the daylight killing of Ramesh Chandra, the managing editor of *Punjab Kesari*, by terrorists at a busy market intersection of Jalandhar. There were similar changes in some other districts, of both civil and police officers, but no real overhaul or review of the way the state operates.

There was a shake-up at the top too. Indira Gandhi's hand-picked governor of Punjab, B.D. Pande, was asked to put in his papers. The distinguished former civil servant was blamed for turning Punjab into terrorist territory in the nine months he had governed it. It did not matter that the man was never given a free hand to run Punjab—his strategies to handle terrorism and address Akali political aspirations were never taken on board. Pande was clear that a policy of reconciliation rather than confrontation would prove rewarding.

But now the entire blame was put on him and he was asked to resign, which he did gracefully, leaving the Raj Bhavan on 3 July 1984. K.T. Satarawala was shifted from Goa to Punjab. An affable and well-intentioned but worn-out gentleman, I found him rather senile and unsure of himself. It was a surprise that he lasted as long as he did—about eight months—till 14 March 1985.

The sagacious chief secretary, Vasudeva, proceeded on leave on 15 August and was later moved to Delhi as secretary to the Government of India. Pooni, the ambivalent home secretary who had gone on leave, was shifted from the home department.

Gone also was Pritam Singh Bhinder, the police chief of Punjab, shifted in the first week of July 1984. He was the Gandhi family's trusted officer and the whispers in the corridors of power were that he had been hand-picked for Punjab to strike a deal with Bhindranwale. The veteran leftist leader Harkishan Singh Surjeet in his address in the Rajya Sabha on 15 November 1983 said:

> For, suddenly and without the knowledge of the state government, P.S. Bhinder was dispatched to Punjab as the police official in charge. He was sent—and I say this with authority, and want to bring the facts before you—he was sent to make up with Bhindranwale, on the understanding that without involving him no settlement was possible.[1]

It was then speculated that on the basis of acceptance of the religious demands of the Dharam Yudh Morcha on 27 February 1983, a deal could be struck with Bhindranwale and that would 'teach a lesson to the Akali leaders'.[2] Bhinder's wife, Mrs Sukhbans Kaur Bhinder, was a Congress MP. She had won from Gurdaspur in 1980 with a thumping majority, intriguingly with the tacit support of Bhindranwale, whose Chowk Mehta headquarters is not far from Gurdaspur, her parliamentary constituency.

With Bhinder gone, Kirpal Singh Dhillon, then serving as a joint director in the CBI, was inducted as the police chief. Dhillon was my course director during the foundational course at the IAS academy, Mussoorie, when the 1974 batch joined the service. He and Dhanoa were personally interviewed by Prime Minister Indira Gandhi and their credentials were vetted at the highest level.

Soon, however, Indira Gandhi found Dhillon '*bahut shareef*'.[3] Dhanoa and Dhillon were gentlemen officers—sincere, suave and upright. However, these qualities were not considered enough. Both of them were shifted out; Dhillon rather unceremoniously, after the assassination of Longowal in September 1985. Dhanoa was made the adviser once Arjun Singh joined as governor. P.H. Vaishnav of the Punjab cadre was elevated to chief secretary on 8 May 1985.

M.C. Trikha, a Madhya Pradesh-cadre IPS officer, replaced intelligence chief H.S. Randhawa. K.P.S. Gill, of the Assam cadre, was brought in as IG, Punjab Armed Police and law and order in September 1984, and he turned out to be the longest-lasting among all. Two DIG-rank officers were also inducted, but did not survive long and were repatriated to their parent cadres. S.S. Virk of the Maharashtra cadre, however, like K.P.S. Gill, had a long tenure, serving as the police chief at Jalandhar and Amritsar, and thereafter as DIG, on deputation and then as DGP, Punjab, from February 2005 to January 2007. Bua Singh, an IPS officer of the Uttar Pradesh cadre, was brought in as SSP, Amritsar, but left the state after serving for a short while. The first set of advisers to the governor appointed in October 1983 were also moved out.[4]

The frequent shifting of governors, their advisers and key functionaries of the state became the Central government's solution to the Punjab problem. It was not a one-time administrative purge but a running conveyer belt of governors, advisers, chief secretaries, DGPs and lower functionaries. They came and moved on, leaving faint footprints, if at all.

Between 1984 and 1991, Punjab saw ten governors, five chief secretaries and eight DGPs.[5] Transfers were proffered as a solution, but the transferred officials were mere scapegoats; the changes were marketed as a shake-up of the system, while there was, at best, only a nugatory shift in the quality of the administrative ethos, the citizen–state interface and the delivery of state services. Meanwhile, terrorist violence was accelerating by the day.

However, the frequent transfers served a purpose. The constant shuffling of governors and civil and police officials deflected the blame to the bureaucracy, allowing the political leadership to escape its responsibility for the bloodshed and the mess Punjab was in. Change sustains hope, and that seemed to be the policy of the government.

20

The Politics of Kar Sewa

The Akal Takht was in ruins. A few other structures in the complex had also suffered extensive damage. The army had planned to quick-fix any damage that the precinct may have suffered during the operation, but the Army Engineering Unit found the mission beyond its capacity. It had commenced repairs on 19 June, post-haste, but soon sought civil help to finish the job.

To assist the army, N.N. Vohra, secretary, Public Works Department (PWD), Punjab, who went on to become the governor of Jammu and Kashmir, inducted the Punjab PWD for the repair works, under the overall command of the army. Specifically, the PWD was assigned to repair the staircase near the langar building leading to the Parikrama (these had been crushed by tanks), the walkways, and the pillars and rooms on the verandah around the circumambulatory passage. The PWD commenced the restoration work from 26 June under the overall supervision of S. Bains, chief engineer, assisted by two XENs (executive engineers) T.S. Gill and K.S. Brar, but the civil engineers soon panicked as the militants threatened them.

The chief engineer conveyed in writing that his officers were reluctant to continue with the assignment. On 26 July, he repeated his request to withdraw them from the complex. Thereafter, Satinder Singh, SE (superintending engineer), National Highway, at Amritsar, who was a follower of Baba Kharak Singh, a respected sant of the area, was inducted. The work now progressed smoothly and Satinder Singh even procured Nanakshahi small bricks for the Akal Takht repairs, but I intervened and stopped him. These were second-hand bricks removed from a decrepit private property, and their utilization in a sacred structure was bound to invite objections.

Meanwhile, a rumour spread that the militant groups were pressuring the SGPC to preserve the battered Akal Takht by erecting a glass case around it as a perpetual reminder of the destruction caused by the army. Alarmed, Union Minister Buta Singh was dispatched by the Prime Minister to mediate with the high priests who, however, pronounced that the reconstruction work could be undertaken only as per the Sikh tradition through kar sewa, selfless service and voluntary labour under the leadership of a respected Sikh sant.

Induction of the government agencies in the reconstruction of the takht went against Sikh tradition. Illustratively, the relations between Emperor Jahangir and Guru Hargobind Singh became cordial after the Guru's release from Gwalior fort, where he had been detained for over a year allegedly for non-payment of a fine imposed on his father, and the emperor, on a visit to Amritsar offered to fund the construction of the Akal Takht. The Guru declined the offer, saying that it had to be built by kar sewa, as a gesture of service and sacrifice, and not as a monument of imperial munificence.

In keeping with the tradition of service in the construction of the sacred space, Buta Singh persuaded Baba Harbans Singh and Sant Karnail Singh of Delhi to lead the kar sewa. The priests agreed but laid down fifteen stipulations, the primary condition being that the army be withdrawn from the temple and its control transferred to the SGPC. Kar sewa, they declared, cannot be conducted under the shadow of guns—it requires free movement and voluntary participation of the *sangat* (devotees).

Buta Singh conceded to these caveats on 19 June and on the same evening made a formal announcement to this effect to the media. He did not realize that his assurance would not go down well with the powers in Delhi. When he returned to the capital, he was told to rescind his public announcement, which he did. The government was not willing to withdraw troops from the temple till the time the Akal Takht was reconstructed, under the apprehension that the militants would work to preserve the battered structure. This caused a crisis of confidence between the Central government and the Sikh leadership.

Fresh efforts were initiated, and this time Buta Singh involved Gurdial Singh, a former Union minister and later Speaker, Lok Sabha, who belonged to Amritsar, to persuade Baba Kharak Singh to lead the kar sewa. Baba Kharak Singh, had been vocal against the mindless violence of the militants even during the height of Bhindranwale's reign.

On 8 July, in a tripartite meeting between the government representatives, Buta Singh and Gurdial Singh, the high priests and SGPC officials and Baba Kharak Singh, an agreement was reached. But similar to the caveat issued by the high priests, Kharak Singh, too, demanded the withdrawal of the army from the temple complex. Buta Singh and Gurdial Singh consented to the condition. The SGPC executive committee was scheduled to meet on 10 July and it was decided that it would approve and formally announce the commencement of kar sewa by Kharak Singh on that day.

As a gesture of goodwill, on 10 July security forces were withdrawn from the Bunga Ramgarhia, a part of which used to be in the possession of Baba Kharak Singh before Blue Star. His men were allowed to fix their locks on the doors of the bunga. Buta Singh, however, again failed to persuade the Centre to endorse the withdrawal of the troops. Apparently, the Prime Minister reprimanded Buta Singh for transferring the possession of the bunga to Kharak Singh, and on 11 July the army took the keys back. The possession of the langar building had also been transferred earlier, but when the SGPC wanted to commence community cooking on 11 July, it was disallowed.

This was the second time the State authorities had let down the high priests. They issued a hukamnama (edict) on 11 July that anyone engaged in the reconstruction of the Akal Takht on behalf of the government would be treated as an adversary of the Sikh panth and would invite stringent action. The same day, the executive committee of the SGPC resolved to launch daily shaheedi jathas to 'liberate' the temple from army control. The first jatha, an all-women's group led by the firebrand Rajinder Kaur, former MP, courted arrest on 16 July. Thereafter, jathas from different districts would arrive at Amritsar and court arrest every day. This continued till 30 September. Men wore black turbans and women sported black dupattas as a mark of protest.

The government and the Sikhs were back on a collision course. What was worse was that the militants became active again. The details of negotiations with Baba Kharak Singh had leaked and he received threats from radical elements warning him against taking up kar sewa. Posters appeared at Gurdwara Shaheedan opposite the dera of Baba Kharak Singh, listing seven names on the hit list, including that of the President of India, the Prime Minister, Rajiv Gandhi, R.S. Dayal and Baba Kharak Singh.

Parallel to the efforts of Buta Singh, in a quiet move unknown to the civil administration, the army had been directed to initiate negotiations with the Sikh religious leadership. Jamwal, Brar and Dayal conducted a conciliatory dialogue with the high priests and kar sewa babas through the good offices of Prakash Singh Majithia, acting president of the Akali Dal; R.S. Dhaliwal, acting chief of the SGPC; and Dalbir Singh, a respectable Sikh representing the chief, Khalsa Dewan.

After preliminary discussions that spanned several days, the officiating Chief of Army Staff, Gen. Tirath Singh Oberoi (Vaidya, regular army chief, was out of the country), reached Amritsar and that was when I got a whiff of these back-door mediations. The ostensible objective of the chief's visit to Amritsar was to review the prevailing situation, but he was primarily engaged in the politics of kar sewa.

For two days—14 and 15 July—they were in arbitration with the Sikh leaders, cajoling them to commence kar sewa; they even succeeded in hammering out a compromise. The army chief agreed to withdraw the uniformed troops from the temple precincts and retain only a small contingent of Sikh troops in civilian clothes and without arms to deal with any untoward exigency. In turn, the Sikh leaders agreed to commence kar sewa under the leadership of Baba Kharak Singh.

An understanding had been reached, and it was to be formalized by the civilian officials—to keep the army's role out of the public gaze. The success was celebrated with the usual *chotta* (small) peg. Their happiness, however, was not to last beyond the night. Little did they know of the games that politicians play.

Late on the night of 15 July, the DC, Bhatinda, rang up to alert me that Baba Santa Singh, the Nihang leader, had left Bhatinda with about 250 armed followers to undertake kar sewa. They arrived at Amritsar the next day, the same day K.C. Pant and Arun Nehru landed at the Raja Sansi airport. I was intimated about the arrival of Pant and Nehru only after they had concluded their meeting with the generals in the cantonment. The two of them wanted to visit the temple and curiously also Burj Baba Phula Singh, known as Nihangan di Chawoni or the cantonment of the Nihang Sikhs, the headquarters of Baba Sant Singh.

I escorted them from the cantonment and found Arun Nehru up front. Pant, however, was vexatious. He blamed the army and the Sikh leadership for frustrating every attempt to settle kar sewa squabbles and with mischievous levity announced that they had found a solution for it—the political leadership had surreptitiously brought in the 96 Karori Panth's Rattan Baba Santa Singh, head of the Budha Dal.

Outmanoeuvred by the political leadership, Oberoi found himself in a fix. He had to wriggle out of the commitments the army had made to the high priests and others. Therefore, they conveniently blamed the priests for their belligerence and insistence on the withdrawal of troops from the complex as a precondition. Maintaining a stoic face, the mild-mannered Dayal announced that the dialogue had failed. On 18 July, both Oberoi and Brar departed from Amritsar.[1]

Baba Santa Singh and his men were Buta Singh's guests at Amritsar. While leaving the Raja Sansi airport late in the evening for Delhi on 16 July, Buta Singh took me aside and said he wanted to hand over a large sum of money to meet the cost of their rations, which was to include bhang (marijuana). I politely refused and suggested that another senior officer, also present at the airport, handle the supplies. Some revenue and police officers were assigned to the job. On 25 July, Buta Singh got an account opened in Punjab National Bank in the name of Baba Ranjodh Singh, deputy chief of the Budha Dal, by donating Rs 5 lakh. Henceforth, the Budha Dal was to take care of its needs from the account, which would be replenished from time to time.

The Budha Dal traces its history from the days of Guru Gobind Singh; it styles itself as the '*chalda vaheer panjwan takht of the Khalsa* (the mobile fifth throne of the Khalsa)'. The dal has a glorious history. Two of its legendary heads, Nawab Kapoor Singh (1697–1753) and his aide, Jassa Singh Ahluwalia (1718–83), had played key roles in kar sewa after Muslim invaders had ransacked the Harmandir Sahib. Jassa Singh Ahluwalia was the founder of the princely state of Kapurthala and he had facilitated Baghel Singh's conquest of Delhi in 1783—they mounted the kesari flag over the Red Fort.

Taking over Delhi, however, was not for a political objective; the dal voluntarily withdrew to Punjab after imposing a levy on the Mughal emperor and securing from him lands where the present-day historic gurdwaras in Delhi were built. Two latter-day Nihang chiefs—Akali Phula Singh (1761–1823) and Baba Hanuman Singh (1756–1846)—were contemporaries of Maharaja Ranjit Singh (1780–1839) and played heroic roles in wars to consolidate the Sikh empire. With this history of the Nihang Budha Dal, it was inexplicable why Santa Singh should get into a head-on collision with the institutional Sikh leadership that had opposed his involvement in the Akal Takht's reconstruction as it was viewed as 'sarkar sewa', or construction by the government.

Unmindful of the Sikh opposition, on 17 July at 7 a.m., Santa Singh commenced removing the debris of the damaged Akal Takht in the presence of Buta Singh. The granthis and priests of the temple objected to it. A scuffle ensued between the followers of Santa Singh and the priests and SGPC employees. Santa Singh's followers assaulted two granthis and chased away a few female pilgrims who had also raised objections.

The same evening, the five high priests issued a show-cause notice to Baba Santa Singh to explain his defiance of the hukamnama dated 11 July. Santa Singh did not respond; he instead challenged the authority of the high priests to issue the directive to him. Therefore, on 19 July, the high priests declared Santa Singh guilty of religious misconduct and summoned him on 21 July for sentencing. Santa Singh did not respond and was excommunicated from the Sikh panth on 22 July.

The work at the Akal Takht progressed at a slow pace. It was obvious that the Budha Dal lacked both technical knowledge and skilled manpower to execute the delicate restoration task. Therefore, on 19 July, Buta Singh and K.P. Singh Deo, the deputy defence minister, accompanied by Arun Singh and Jagdish Tytler, MPs, visited Amritsar and reviewed the construction work with the chief engineer of the Punjab PWD and officers of the Central PWD, who had also reached from Delhi. The presence of K.S. Bains, IAS, then a joint secretary with the Government of India at Delhi, was a surprise. He was perceived to be close to Buta Singh, who had brought him along.

In the meeting it was decided to constitute a committee to coordinate kar sewa and Bains was made its chairman. In that capacity, he was to later make a few trips to Amritsar. The involvement of a joint secretary of the Union Ministry of Heavy Industries in a supervisory capacity in kar sewa without any formal order of the government was rather odd and mocked the age-old neutrality of the civil services. Contrary to the induction of Delhi-based Bains, the senior IAS officers at Chandigarh such as S.S. Boparai, G.P.S. Sahi, Hardial Singh and some others who had earlier applied for leave to undertake kar sewa had not been sanctioned the same.

Bains's involvement affirmed the criticism that the restoration work was not kar sewa but sarkar sewa. However, the physical distance between Delhi and Amritsar constrained him. He soon withdrew from the assigned role, and to give the façade of voluntary community construction, an advisory committee of eight public men was formed on 25 July.

It was decided that the dilapidated Akal Takht would not be demolished; the ramshackle structure was to be restored to its original condition by extensive repair and restoration. Santa Singh formally commenced the masonry work on 1 August by laying two bricks at the Akal Takht in the presence of Buta Singh and a few other religious personalities.

Services of three agencies—two of the government and one private company—were requisitioned for the restoration work; separate areas of responsibility were assigned to each one of them. The National Buildings Construction Corporation (NBCC), a Government of India unit, was tasked with repairing the basement and the first floor of the Akal Takht. The Central Public Works Department (CPWD) was assigned the task of restoring the dome. The second and third floors were allocated to Skipper Builders, a private company owned by Tejwant Singh from Delhi.

Kar sewa of the gold work at the Harmandir Sahib commenced on 5 August and was carried out at night to avoid publicity. Restoration of the Darshani Deori was done by the CPWD under chief engineer A. Shankaran, who was later replaced by K.D. Bali, a retired CPWD chief engineer, re-employed for kar sewa and stationed at Amritsar. His assignment to restore the virtually extinct dome of the Akal Takht was most challenging. Experts felt that ordinary cement may not be strong enough to hold up the ramshackle structure. Therefore, binding chemical agents used to plug cracks in dams were procured from Bhakra dam and abroad and liberally used. The work at the Akal Takht progressed in two shifts to meet the deadline of end September.

Sarbat Khalsa

The SGPC was not happy with these developments and in a parallel move, on 21 July, to counter the government's construction work, it formally assigned kar sewa of the Akal Takht to Baba Kharak Singh. To seek wider support in favour of its decision, a *sant samaj* (congregation of prominent Sikh sants) was called on 28 July which endorsed the decision.

In view of this development, Santa Singh stood completely isolated. Buta Singh felt that the situation needed to be countered. On 29 July, he met Baba Santa Singh and together they worked out a strategy to seek Sikh support by holding a public rally on 11 August. To lend the rally a religious hue, the congregation was labelled '*Sarbat Khalsa*', meaning an assembly of the entire Khalsa panth. The entire Sikh community, obviously, cannot meet at one physical place. The Sarbat Khalsa merely denoted a representative theological–political congregation of the panth.

Buta Singh's decision to summon the Sarbat Khalsa congregation resurrected an obsolete and historically dead practice. The first congregation was called in 1723 by Bhai Mani Singh to settle the differences between the Tat Khalsa and Bandais over who would manage the affairs of the Golden Temple. The Sarbat Khalsa resolved to settle the issue by a physical duel between Niri Singh, the nominee wrestler of Tat Khalsa, and Sangat Singh, representing the Bandais. The Tat Khalsa wrestler won and that clinched the issue in their favour.

The last time a Sarbat Khalsa was convened was in 1760 when the Sikh Misl chiefs decided to capture Lahore from the Mughals, following which the Dal Khalsa—the unified Sikh forces—under the command of Jassa Singh Ahluwalia, captured Lahore in 1761. However, once Ranjit Singh ascended the Lahore throne, the tradition of the Sarbat Khalsa congregations fell in obsolescence. He was not comfortable with a parallel political–ecclesiastical centre of authority.

Now, 224 years later, the political spin masters dabbled in the religious affairs of Sikhs and resuscitated an institution that had gone defunct. By naming the political rally as the Sarbat Khalsa, they revived the extinct tradition and set a modern-day precedent that was replicated by militants who held the next Sarbat Khalsa congregation on 26 January 1986.[2] Since then, numerous Sarbat Khalsas have been held, helping resolve some issues but also triggering fresh religious conflicts in the state.

The formal invite for the government-sponsored Sarbat Khalsa was issued in the name of Santa Singh and a host of other sects and sants. However, Buta Singh and R.L. Bhatia, the local MP, were the main organizers and met at Amritsar on 6 August to strategize.

The jathedar of the Akal Takht, Giani Kirpal Singh, criticized the move, dubbing it an attempt to divide the Sikhs. Pamphlets and posters appeared opposing the proposed congregation, while the posters circulated by the sponsors appealed to people to attend in large numbers. The media described it as a war of posters for and against the convention.

On 9 August, Lt Gen. Gowri Shankar, accompanied by DGP, Punjab, landed in Amritsar and reviewed the arrangements for the Sarbat Khalsa. I had banned the assembly of five or more persons under Section 144 of the CrPC, but it was conveyed to me that the government had decided to permit the congregation, and accordingly a formal approval to hold it was granted. As an added incentive, the decision was taken to permit all those who came for the Sarbat Khalsa to visit the Golden Temple to pay obeisance. In those days, the entry of the general public to the temple was not free, but was regulated by the administration.

Buta Singh reached Amritsar on 10 August and brought with him Man Singh, jathedar of the Takht Patna Sahib. It was a prized participation; Buta Singh had succeeded in dividing the jathedars of the five takhts, the supreme centres of Sikh authority. But the scales were heavily tilted against Santa Singh, as it was a single jathedar of the Takht Patna Sahib against the four other takhts, who opposed the convention.

On the day of the rally, we were on our toes. The jittery governor, Satarawala, was not satisfied with the police and intelligence inputs given to him and wanted me to personally report to him about the goings-on in the congregation—he was concerned about the size of the crowd. I was near the site of the congregation and it had no telephone connectivity. Ultimately, the governor was quite happy to receive half-hourly briefings from my steno who manned the telephone in my office—the governor personally received his calls!

The estimates of the crowd varied. The organizers claimed a gathering of over 1.5 lakh people, while my own eyewitness estimate was not more than 30,000. I conveyed this figure to the government and that, of course, did not please the governor. Whatever the exact number, it was chiefly a Congress congregation and the who's who of the Punjab Congress had turned up.

The Sarbat Khalsa passed several resolutions. It endorsed and ratified the kar sewa of the Akal Takht by Baba Santa Singh, presented him with a siropa and conferred the exalted honorific of Singh Sahib—an expression usually used to address high priests—on him. Thus, the primary objective of convening the gathering to legitimize kar sewa was achieved; it was now presumed to have the sanction of the panth, the Sikh community.

However, the congregation went on to ex-communicate Tohra, SGPC president, for his alleged anti-Sikh pursuits, and for permitting the sacred Sikh shrines to be misused by the militants. The Akali Dal was criticized for launching the Dharam Yudh agitation and for setting the Sikhs on an anti-national path.

More problematic, however, was a resolution that brought forth a fundamental theological issue: Who is a Sikh and who should control their sacred spaces? The congregation resolved that sects such as Nirmalas, Udasis, Nanak Panthis, Bidhi Chandias, Sewa Panthis, Satnamis and other Darbars, etc., are to be retained as 'pearls of the same string of the Samuchi Sangat or commonwealth'. Many of these sects, in contravention of Guru Gobind Singh's edict, do not maintain *sabat surat*, or unshorn hair, or some of the external symbols of Khalsa, and some even practise idolatry. The resolution of the Sarbat Khalsa thus posed a challenge to the boundaries of the Khalsa religion and had the potential of reviving the historical struggle between the Tat Khalsa on the one hand and the Sahajdharis and Sanatan Sikhs who have a liberal or polysemous perspective of the religion on the other.[3]

The public meeting, in any case, was not a Sarbat Khalsa because by tradition a Sarbat Khalsa congregation is held only in front of the Akal Takht; secondly, this congregation had a sprinkling of non-Sikhs in the audience; even Muslims such as Sajida Begum, Congress MLA from Malerkotla, had attended with her followers. They all were party to the Gurmatas, the decisions of the Sikh panth.

In another contentious resolution, the government-ordained Sarbat Khalsa proposed to make changes in the SGPC law pertaining to the administration of gurdwaras to ensure that the high priests on the payroll of the SGPC—hence, employees—become independent. To crystallize these Gurmatas, Santa Singh was authorized by the Sarbat Khalsa to secure the services of suitable religious personalities and pursue the matter. This was seen by others as a direct attempt to capture and control the SGPC.

What created still greater resentment, however, was a bit of news surreptitiously planted in the media that the Central government proposed to replace the existing SGPC structure with a new managing board. This was a teaser to test the public response to amend the SGPC Act as there was no formal resolution of the Sarbat Khalsa to this effect. The SGPC law was enacted by the British following a long agitation by Sikhs to acquire the right to administer gurdwaras through their elected bodies. The rumour to instal a government-controlled board to manage Sikh affairs, therefore, generated avoidable tension. It magnified the ongoing conflict between the SGPC–Akali combine and the Central government.

Attempts had been made earlier to amend the SGPC law that provides an institutional and organized base to the Sikh religion. In April 1959, Master Tara Singh had threatened to undertake a fast unto death 'to protest against Government interference in Gurdwara affairs'. He was persuaded not to do so, and the Nehru–Tara Singh Pact was signed on 11 April 1959 with the government agreeing, 'No amendment in the Gurdwara Act will be made except with the consent of the general house of the Shiromani Gurdwara Parbandhak Committee expressed through a resolution passed by two-third majority of the members of the SGPC.'[4] Therefore, the ill-conceived move to form a board of prominent Sikhs as an alternative to the SGPC was allowed to die a natural death.

21

'The President Is Guilty'

'GAINI ZAIL SINGH IS GUILTY.' THUS PRONOUNCED THE HIGH priests on 2 September 1984 at the World Sikh Convention. The head of the secular republic was held culpable by the ecclesiastical authority for personal misdemeanour and for his conduct as the supreme commander of the armed forces.

The confrontation between the State and the theological authorities had been simmering ever since the government assigned kar sewa of the Akal Takht to Baba Santa Singh, against the wishes of the high priests and the SGPC. The Sarbat Khalsa organized by the government served as provocation to the high priests and the SGPC.

Therefore, as a counter measure, on 13 August the jathedars decided to hold a World Sikh Convention on 2 September 1984 at Gurdwara Shaheedan. This convention was not labelled a Sarbat Khalsa because the high priests were conscious of the historical precedents of holding such congregations only at the Akal Takht. The army was still present inside the temple complex and a public conclave, the priests knew, would not be permitted.

On the appointed day of the convention, the priests issued two hukamnamas, pronouncing Zail Singh and Union Minister Buta Singh as tankhaiyas. Sikhs were directed not to associate with them in any manner until they appeared before the Akal Takht, sought forgiveness and were exonerated of the charges.

The term 'tankha', literally means remuneration. In the Sikh lexicon, however, it has acquired an additional connotation of punishment. Tankha is imposed on a Sikh who commits an act of *kurahit*, a misdemeanour of a religious or moral nature. The objective is to retrieve the delinquent back to the faith after they wash off their sins by undergoing the punishment, which is usually in the nature of performing humble services like scrubbing utensils at community kitchens or buffing the shoes of devotees, recital of scriptures, offering karah prasad and small amounts of money at a gurdwara.

A trial proceeding against those pronounced guilty is conducted before a five-member bench of high priests of the ecclesiastical court of the Akal Takht, and the procedure is essentially democratic in nature. The delinquent is given due opportunity to defend himself and if the explanation is found satisfactory the offender is exonerated. Or the punishment is decided and the person is declared guilty. If the tankha order is defied, the offender may invite excommunication from the Sikh community, resulting in the termination of all ties of roti and beti (social relations) with him.

In the case of Zail Singh and Buta Singh, however, the due procedure was short-circuited. No notice to show cause was issued, nor were they afforded an opportunity to explain their conduct before they were declared tankhaiya. Their offences, the high priests claimed, were too conspicuous and in the public domain and hence the due procedure was dispensable.

The specific charge against the President was two-fold. First, as supreme commander of the armed forces he had ordered the military to invade the temple and he was therefore responsible for the resultant deaths and destruction; secondly, he was guilty of religious insolence—when he visited the temple on 8 June, a regal canopy was carried over his head and he wore shoes inside the temple.

Unlike in churches, Sikhs remove shoes before entering gurdwaras. For this reason, during the Khalsa Raj, Europeans were not allowed into the Golden Temple, for they would not remove their shoes. H.M. Lawrence, resident, Lahore, had to issue a direction, '. . . [B]y order of the Governor General, British subjects are forbidden to the temple . . . with their shoes'.[1] Historian Dr Madanjit Kaur has narrated an interesting incident—in 1838, when Lord Auckland and the commander-in-chief, Sir Henry Fane, visited the Darbar Sahib, 'there arose an argument about the propriety of his covering his shoes with a pair of dark stockings instead of removing them. But eventually he was admitted.'[2] Zail Singh, however, was no foreigner to be ignorant of the Sikh traditions and was, therefore, held liable for the breach of conduct.

Buta Singh also faced two charges—he was culpable for inducting Baba Santa Singh, a 'henchman' of the government, to reconstruct the Akal Takht. Second, he had betrayed Sikhs and challenged the authority of the Akal Takht by going against the well-established convention of voluntary kar sewa.

World Sikh Convention

To hold the World Sikh Convention, the high priests were required to take approval of the district magistrate, as the assembly of five or more persons had been banned in Amritsar under Section 144. To avoid prohibitory orders, the priests had decided to hold the convention at Gurdwara Shaheedan, but anticipating a large crowd, they shifted the venue to Sakatari Bagh and sought permission for this site. It was denied, as the police considered the location unsuitable to house a large congregation. I proposed an alternative to the priests, but they rejected the offer, accusing the government of attempts to thwart the convention.

Permission to hold the convention was never denied; only the venue of Sakatari Bagh was not agreed to, but the jathedar of the Akal Takht, Kirpal Singh, publicly stated, 'Due to the Delhi ruler's negative reply he [Ramesh Inder Singh] expressed his inability to accede to our demand.' I stuck to my stand and ultimately the congregation was held at Gurdwara Shaheedan, which was the original venue proposed by the high priests.

Until then, the actions of the high priests had been reasonably restrained. However, on 25 August, officers at an army checkpost near the Central Jail seized a stock of posters and pamphlets from an SGPC vehicle. These were in the form of an open letter from the high priests that bore their printed signatures and carried the seal of the Akal Takht. The posters implored Sikhs to congregate at the proposed convention and accused the Central government of deliberate destruction of the Akal Takht, riddling Harmandir Sahib with bullets, killing unaccounted innocent Sikhs, detaining many more and planning the liquidation of the Sikh panth. The Central government was compared with the Mughals for its atrocities, and parallels were drawn with the British for its dishonesty and deceit. Sikhs were called upon to sacrifice their lives to save their religion and stated that the government would not be content with the sacrifices of only a few Sikhs, in an obvious reference to those killed in the operation.

The district attorney opined that the posters were calculated to excite feelings of hatred and ill-will and prima facie an offence under Section 124 A of the IPC was made against the publishers and the printers, that is, the high priests and the SGPC. The home department, however, decided not to take any action in the matter. Probably, the high status of the priests and the apprehension that any action against them could ignite public protests and create law and order problems weighed on the department. Consequently, the legal opinion was ignored.

Non-enforcement of law rarely pays or at least it did not in this case. Some mischievous elements took their cue from these placards and brought out fresh, pictorially provocative posters which did not disclose the name of the printer or publisher. One poster showed Indira Gandhi asking for the blood of Sikhs with Zail Singh holding a bucketful of blood, stating that he had enough for her to bathe with. Another showed Indira Gandhi dressed in the army uniform and Zail Singh, Darbara Singh and Buta Singh standing in attendance before her dressed as women. A third poster depicted the army squashing Sikhs in a lemon squeezer with Indira Gandhi saying, 'Crush them to their bones.'

These developments brought Dhanoa, the chief secretary, to Amritsar. He held a meeting with the high priests at the Darshani Deori and later reviewed the prevailing charged environment with us. The government was concerned that a large number of people would descend on Amritsar on 2 September, and it could become impossible to control the crowd. Therefore, it was decided to make preventive arrests of key figures at the convention throughout the state. Bus services to and from Amritsar were suspended on 1 September to prevent people from reaching the city.

Despite the inhibitory measures, on 2 September, people started gathering early in the morning and the enthusiastic crowd spilled on to the roads, crossing the boundary of the venue. The high priests and some others, in a smart move, had shifted the night before to the gurdwara, the adjoining buildings of Guru Ram Das Hospital and two nearby schools under SGPC management, apprehending preventive detention by the government to foil the convention.

My estimate was that about 15,000 people attended the congregation. A media correspondent quoted me, and three days later I received the first threat letter—out of the many I received during my tenure in Amritsar. It was a handwritten postal note from a militant organization, accusing me of deliberately misleading the Sikhs by quoting a low figure of the attendees. The letter put the number of people at over 1 lakh and warned me to behave myself in the future or face the consequences.

Jathedar Kirpal Singh, in his inaugural remarks, equated the Indian Army with the Mughal agent Massa Ranghar, who had desecrated the Golden Temple in 1740 by converting the Harmandir Sahib into a drinking and dancing hall. Massa Ranghar's real name was Mir Musalul Khan, but he was nicknamed Ranghar, which meant mixed blood of Hindu and Muslim parentage. Two Sikhs posing as Muslims gained access to the Harmandir Sahib and slaughtered Ranghar while he was indulging in general debauchery and thereafter made a daring escape. The jathedar accused the Central government, the excommunicated Baba Santa Singh and the 'slave of Delhi Darbar Buta Singh' for dividing the Sikh community and appealed for unity of the Khalsa panth under one banner. Implicit in the comparison was a poignant recall of historical tradition, the kind that impels the like-minded to martyrdom.

In an emotive peroration, the jathedars served an ultimatum to the government to withdraw the army from the temple and hand over possession of the complex to the SGPC by 30 September, failing which an appeal was made to the Sikhs to peacefully march under the leadership of the high priests to liberate the temple on 1 October. The radicals, however, were unhappy with this announcement. They demanded that the gathering straight away march to the Golden Temple and liberate it from army control. When the jathedars did not yield, the activists raised pro-Khalistan slogans. Kirpal Singh had to remind the congregation that it was a religious conference and the participants should refrain from raising political slogans. The radicals, however, continued and even hoisted a kesari flag outside the gurdwara, which they proclaimed to be the Khalistan flag.

I had intentionally informed Giani Kirpal Singh that kar sewa by Santa Singh and the basic repair work of the complex was scheduled to finish by 29 September. The troops were likely to be withdrawn from the temple thereafter. Aware of these facts, the jathedar was eager to avoid confrontation with the government by marching to the temple complex and therefore deliberately postponed the Liberation March to 1 October.

Evidently, there were sharp differences in the approach of the moderates and the radicals. The high priests had a difficult task at hand and to carry the radicals with them, apart from declaring the President and Buta Singh tankhaiyas, they proposed ten resolutions which were passed by the World Sikh Convention, amidst shouts of '*Bole so nihal, sat sri akal*', and the occasional pro-Khalistan slogan by the radicals. Some of these resolutions were: The congregation condemned the army's 'invasion' of the temple and sought a probe into the 'barbaric atrocities' committed by it; it condemned the government's intervention in Sikh religious affairs by inducting Santa Singh under army tutelage to do kar sewa; it denounced the illegal detentions and killings of Sikh youth in 'fake encounters'; it censured the move to dissolve the SGPC; and it applauded the 'courageous' role of the Sikh soldiers who had abandoned barracks and sought a general amnesty for army deserters.

A Pardon for the President

The head priests, as a strategy, while pronouncing Zail Singh and Buta Singh tankhaiyas, had not fixed a date for their personal appearance before the ecclesiastical court to seek pardon. That left the window open for the government to withdraw the army from the temple before 1 October, in which case the priests could consider pardoning the President. Otherwise, it was certain that Zail Singh and Buta Singh would be ex-communicated from the Sikh panth.

I sent a report to the government on 9 September, firmly pleading to transfer possession of the temple to the SGPC before 30 September or be ready to resort to large-scale preventive arrests, including of the high priests, Akali leaders and SGPC members. I was certain that people from all over the state would descend on Amritsar in large numbers, and therefore, public entry into the district would have to be banned; if required, a curfew would have to be imposed. It would necessitate the statewide deployment of troops.

In the meantime, Zail Singh initiated a back-door manoeuvre. Rawail Singh, a former minister, was the key interlocutor. Rawail Singh had an onerous assignment—he had to intercede not only with the priests, but also with Prime Minister Indira Gandhi, who was not sanguine about the President appearing before the high priests. The constitutional luminaries had opined that the priests had 'no authority to indict the President of the Republic' and the President 'could seek heavy damages for defamation'.[3] But for Zail Singh it was not the constitutionality or the legality of the action instituted against him that mattered but his image as a devout Sikh—he could not go down in history as the Sikh who defied the Akal Takht.

Rawail Singh, therefore, met the Prime Minister 'a couple of times'[4] and also visited Amritsar accompanied by officials of the Rashtrapati Bhavan on at least three occasions. Being a sensitive subject, it was also discussed in the Political Affairs Committee of the Central Cabinet and some ministers even proposed that the President also help Buta Singh get acquittal, but 'I [Zail Singh] told Mrs Gandhi that I would be in no position to take the responsibility of getting Buta Singh exonerated'.[5]

During those days, the senior-most SGPC functionary available at Amritsar was Senior Vice-President Atma Singh. He had been detained under the National Security Act on 28 June, but was transferred to Guru Nanak Dev Hospital, Amritsar, apparently for a heart condition, and his presence in Amritsar facilitated negotiations with him. A.C. Bandyopadhyay, secretary to the President of India, rang up in mid-September to convey that Atma Singh might not be shifted back to jail as parleys were going on.

On 23 September, Tarlochan Singh, press secretary to the President, accompanied by Rawail Singh, met Atma Singh in the presence of

Jathedar Kirpal Singh, Giani Sahib Singh and Jathedar Lakha Singh of the Damdama Sahib. It was agreed that the army would be withdrawn from the temple as a precondition to grant pardon to the President. Zail Singh, in turn, was to write a letter to the high priests, explaining his position, who would thereafter consider pardoning him.

In the entente, both sides made compromises. The President agreed to submit to the authority of the high priests and explain his alleged misconduct. The priests, in turn, conceded not to insist on the personal appearance of the President before them to seek pardon. Instead, he was to send his written reply through an emissary. By tradition, an 'accused' has to submit before the five head priests in person. The priests faced flak from zealots for this concession, and Jathedar Kirpal Singh had to clarify that in cases where facts for acquittal of an 'accused' were, on the face of it, obvious, personal appearance was not mandatory to seek exoneration.

As per the understanding that had been arrived at, Rawail Singh carried a handwritten letter in Punjabi from Zail Singh to Jathedar Giani Kirpal Singh. In the letter, Zail Singh explained his position and denied that he had entered the Parikrama wearing shoes or with a canopy over his head. This was factually true. I was an eyewitness to it.

His reply to the second charge, however, was equivocal. He explained that the army action was a matter of the Constitution and law of the country and that he had already conveyed 'painful expression of my feelings' in the address to the nation on 17 June. He did not clarify if he had given approval for the army operation as supreme commander of the armed forces, nor did he refute that charge. Later, however, in his autobiography, he denied any knowledge of the operation. Probably, the constraints of his constitutional position justified an inconclusive narrative to the priests at that sensitive time. He concluded the letter by expressing his eternal veneration for the supreme religious authority of the Akal Takht and Darbar Sahib.

The high priests, after considering the written explanation, the evidence on record and the submissions of Rawail Singh and Kulwant Singh, personal assistant to the President, ruled on 26 September that Zail Singh's 'explanation is satisfactory. No further action is required.'

The President had been exonerated. He was now an 'honourable Sikh' and in that capacity called on the five high priests at the Darshani Deori, the Golden Temple, on 27 September, while we waited outside. Later, he addressed a small crowd in front of the Akal Takht. His speech was followed by a rather scathing oration by Jathedar Kirpal Singh in an attempt—though in vain—to placate the radicals who had gathered in large numbers and had been held back outside the temple by the security forces. They were shouting pro-Khalistan and anti–Zail Singh slogans, a reminder that they were a relevant force to reckon with.

Army Withdrawal

Before departing from the temple, the President instructed us to ensure that the troops were withdrawn from the complex without delay. His statement was splashed in the media. This angered Rajiv Gandhi, the general secretary of the Congress (I),[6] who was prompt to issue a contrary public statement to the effect that the army would be withdrawn only if the priests and the Akalis agreed to a few preconditions in writing. The differences between the President and Indira Gandhi were now public.

As it turned out, the real issue at stake was not the withdrawal of the army or transfer of possession of the temple to SGPC, but who got credit for it. Unknown to Zail Singh or us in Punjab, Alexander, the principal secretary to the Prime Minister, had opened a parallel channel of negotiations with the then acting president of the Akali Dal, Prakash Singh Majithia, using the good offices of Ashwani Kumar, a prominent former IPS officer of the Punjab cadre.

Majithia, in a meeting held in Delhi on 20 September with Alexander and Union minister P.V. Narasimha Rao, had agreed to certain preconditions for the withdrawal of the army, one being that the priests would ensure that the militants were not allowed to recapture the temple. The Prime Minister and Rao met Zail Singh to apprise him of the developments and she tried to dissuade him from visiting the Golden Temple on 27 September, but Zail Singh remained firm on his plan.[7] To forestall him from appropriating the credit for the army's withdrawal, the Prime Minister had pre-empted him by making an announcement on the night of 25 September that the army would be withdrawn.

Multiple intermediaries and many channels of negotiations, often operating unknown to each other, were a manifestation of the competing stakeholders in a race to claim credit. This often resulted in one group stalling or attempting to block the other from reaching a settlement. This kept the Punjab cauldron on the boil.

So, when on 29 September, pursuant to Zail Singh's assurance to withdraw the army, the senior adviser to Governor R.V. Subramaniam and Chief Secretary Dhanoa reached the temple and were engaged in the process of handing over its charge to the high priests, I received an urgent message from my office that Subramaniam should speak to Alexander. Those were not the days of mobile phones and there was no landline telephone in our immediate vicinity. Subramaniam, therefore, first handed over the keys of the toshakhana to the priests in a simple and quick ceremony, and then proceeded to make a call to Alexander.

Earlier in the day, around 10 a.m., Baba Santa Singh and about 300 Nihangs had held a valedictory congregation at the Akal Takht—now fully repaired and restored to its original form. The job assigned to them was over. They paid their obeisance for the last time at the Akal Takht and bid adieu. Thereafter, the high priests moved in and commenced the akhand path at the Akal Takht. The temple complex was now under their de facto control and the priests withdrew their call for the Liberation March scheduled for 1 October—there was no need for it now. The day was observed as a thanksgiving day instead.

But when Subramaniam reached Alexander on the telephone, he had a shock waiting for him. Alexander directed Subramaniam to immediately return to Chandigarh and not transfer possession of the temple to the priests, nor withdraw the army. The high priests, said Alexander, had not signed the ten-point charter that had been negotiated with Prakash Singh Majithia and until that was done, the army was to stay on. The possession of the temple should not be given to the SGPC.

It was too late to set the clock back. The lack of telecommunication technology and the time gap in connecting with Alexander had already determined the course of history. Subramaniam, however, had to save his job. He resorted to a face-saving alternative to extricate himself from the situation and ordered that the army stay put in the Sarai complex of the temple, around the residential and office buildings of the Guru Ram Das Sarai, Guru Nanak Niwas and Teja Singh Samundri Hall.

For the high priests, it was an inexplicable partial reversal of the stated stand of the government. Embarrassed, the trio of Subramaniam, Dhanoa and Gen. Gowri Shankar, with us in toe, made a hasty departure from the temple. Later, Subramaniam was summoned to Delhi—he was never to recover the prime position at Chandigarh, his senior adviser nomenclature notwithstanding.

22

The Garrison State

On 8 June 1984, in the wee hours of the day, an Ambassador car was halted at the Beas bridge by the army. The flag post on the bonnet of the car read 'Divisional Commissioner'. The commissioner, N.S. Rattan, was travelling to Amritsar from Jalandhar under government orders to meet the chief secretary—who was expected at the Golden Temple along with the police chief to take stock of the situation. The red beacon atop the vehicle now emitted no red signals. Within his own territorial domain, under the instructions of the major in charge of the roadblock on the Jalandhar end of the bridge over the Beas river that divides Amritsar from Kapurthala district, the commissioner sat distraught in his car, parked by the roadside.

In a polite but firm voice the major said, 'Sir, I have orders not to let anyone cross the river.' Only after the local deputy superintendent of police identified Rattan did the major signal his superiors for instructions. After he received clearance, the car was allowed to approach the bridge. The commissioner was again stopped on the Amritsar side of the bridge, which came under the jurisdiction of 15 Division. The officer in charge insisted on seeking approval from his chain of command; the fact that the car had been allowed to proceed from the other end of the bridge served no relevance. The commissioner, within his own jurisdiction, could move only as allowed by the army. For the first few weeks of the operation, not a soul stirred in Punjab without the permission of the army.

When Rattan finally made it to the Circuit House in Amritsar, the chief secretary, Vasudeva, and the police chief, Bhinder, had already arrived. No army officer came to receive the two chiefs or confabulate with them. They had to drive to Jamwal's office at 15 Infantry Division and Rattan did not miss reminding them that under protocol the general was a rank junior to a chief secretary. But then, those were no times to abide by protocol.

The decision to summon the military to aid civilian affairs is the prerogative of the civilian executive. However, once the army arrives, it takes over. And that is what happened in Amritsar during June 1984. Starting on 3 June evening, the civil administration was in a state of suspended animation. De jure, it was aid to the civil authority but de facto it was a total eclipse of the civil set-up. Punjab was now a garrison state.

Interestingly, that is how the army itself perceived the situation. Brig. O.S. Goraya, post-retirement, in his account of those days has titled a chapter in his book as 'Period of Army Rule'. He says:

> Starting from 3 June 1984, for about two and a half months Punjab was virtually ruled by the army without a Martial Law being proclaimed. Our neighbouring country, Pakistan, has tasted Martial Law on many occasions and for fairly long durations, but in India this was the first and only occasion when the Army controlled almost all aspects of civil

administration for any length of time over the geographical jurisdiction of a state.[1]

The capitulation of the civilian administration started from the top. With a serving lieutenant general who retained his army post presiding over the key government departments in his capacity as adviser to the governor, Punjab, the governor was ineffectual. The principal secretary, home, the police chief and all other civilian officials were under the general's line of command. The police and paramilitary forces in the state were placed under the operational control of the army. The district magistrates were directed to attend meetings at the headquarters of their respective area army commanders and cooperate, implying they should carry out the decisions taken by the army. This arrangement institutionalized the army–civilian working equations.

At the risk of repetition, I may mention that in Amritsar the army had seized the telephone exchange on the night of 3 June, and it controlled all communications. Telephones went dead and, consequently, the district police chief, the additional district magistrate, the magistrates and other district officials were without any telephone links with each other. Outstation calls, including my calls to the Punjab chief secretary and the home secretary, were not put through by the exchange.

The second instance, also mentioned earlier, was of the Chief of Army Staff actively engaging himself in the politics of kar sewa, essentially a non-military function. An otherwise apolitical army pursued religious–political negotiations with Sikh babas and sants. It is for the army brass to consider whether it should have engaged in these negotiations and that too at the level of the Chief of Army Staff. Obviously, no lessons had been learnt from the pre-Independence fiasco when, in 1924, Gen. William Birdwood, the commander of the Northern Command, on directions of the viceroy, had entangled the army in the protracted but futile dialogue with the agitating

Akali Dal and the SGPC on the issue of enactment of an All India Gurdwara Act.[2]

Operation Woodrose

The civil administration had laboured under the impression that once Operation Blue Star was over, they would have the run of the administration again. But that was not to be. Operation Woodrose, launched alongside Blue Star, was a military scan of the district and its people. Its objectives were two-fold: to seal the border with Pakistan and to comb the district for militants and eliminate them. The operation was planned to forestall any possible outbreak of unrest or mob protests against Blue Star.

At the senior level, the army officers were mostly congenial and just. They were good-intentioned and resolute, driven to achieve the given objectives—but that could not always be said about some of the civilian officers.

The problem, however, was at the field unit level. There was no sharing of any operational information by the army with the civil administration, nor did it involve civil officers in its search, seizure and arrest operations. The entire state was under curfew. Legally, it was imposed under the orders of the district magistrates. However, the military and the paramilitary, and not the police, enforced it. Curfew passes issued by the additional district magistrate (ADM) and the sub-divisional magistrates (SDM) were not being honoured by the army unless they were countersigned by the designated army representative. The SDMs bemoaned that they were not being allowed to move around.

Troops were positioned everywhere in the district. With the movement of the public restricted, absence of the media from the scene and a receding civil administration, the news of any digression by local army units would reach us only in driblets, and that too after a lot of delay. We met daily at the headquarters of 15 Division, with Jamwal in the chair, reviewed the day's happenings and discussing issues of common coordination. The general was eager to address any grievance, but the problem was that complaints against local units would take time to travel to the headquarters at Amritsar, and still longer to redress.

The SDM at Ajnala, an ex-army officer, Capt. Narinder Singh, PCS, was ordered in writing by 96 Brigade, which was deployed in Ajnala, to report to its field headquarters daily in the morning and not to leave without the permission of Brig. M.S. Bains. The brigade commander, otherwise a fine officer, was acting as if he was the overall in-charge of the sub-division, even in civil affairs, and treated the SDM as a subordinate officer under his command.

I visited Ajnala with Jamwal to sort out the matter and took up the issue with the government. The written direction to report daily to the brigade commander issued to the SDM and DSP by 96 Brigade was withdrawn, but to my surprise Narinder was posted out of Ajnala on 22 June and shifted to Amritsar. The entire episode was dubbed as a personality clash between the SDM and the DSP on the one side and the brigade commander on the other.

The differences in the modus operandi of the civil administration and the army often triggered coordination conflicts. B.S. Sudan, SDM, Tarn Taran, spoke to Lt Col D.S. Bajwa, the commanding officer of 10 Dogra, to conduct extensive patrolling of villages where, from 4 to 6 June, nine Hindus were murdered, seventeen were injured and sixteen cases of arson were reported by unidentified terrorists. Sudan followed up his request with a DO letter, which is the normal channel of communication in civil administration. He, however, was surprised to receive a quick response from Col Bajwa reminding the SDM that the needful was already being done and that 'we have no time to carry out any such correspondence. You are advised not to write such letters in future.' Col N.C. Pant succeeded Bajwa, and by then an amiable working relationship had evolved.

The SHOs, who used to rule the roost in rural areas, were miffed. They complained that the local army commanders had directed them not to step out of the police stations without their prior approval. In a rather comical episode, unfortunate as it was, a high-handed army battalion commander made an SHO run in circles around the courtyard of his police station carrying a bicycle in his arms as the police constabulary watched in disbelief. This was an improvised 'pithu parade' for the cop, as if he was an erring jawan under the colonel's command.

On 22 June, an army unit issued written directions to the SSP, Amritsar, that his men should not conduct any raids or searches without the prior approval of the commander. During my joint visit with Jamwal to Chowk Mehta, the SHO complained that the local battalion commander had given written instructions to him that police personnel should not come out of police stations after 6 p.m. without his approval. The matter was subsequently sorted out in a tripartite meeting between the IGP, Jamwal and me.

K.S. Janjua, then secretary to the Punjab government, rang up one day to seek help for a friend from Valtoha, a prominent person in the area. A major had picked him up allegedly for illegal possession of a plot of land belonging to a widow, and ordered him to restore the possession of the disputed land to the lady if he wanted to be released. This was, however, not the only instance of this kind. Many complaints were received about the army intervening in personal and property disputes. They conducted kangaroo courts and delivered rough and ready justice. On one level, this reflected the people's faith in the army, and on another it was mocking the rule of law.

Rattan wrote to the state government that the army had increasingly started exercising powers that legitimately belonged to the civil administration and consequently it led to the creation of a parallel centre of authority. It encouraged vested interests to play one centre of authority against the other. This was true not only of the Jalandhar division under Rattan, but similar interference in civil matters was reported from other parts of the state.

S.V. Singh, the police chief of Faridkot district in 1984, reported, 'But the Brigadier at Moga created problems. He started sorting out civil disputes in villages. Little did he realize that the calling of the army in "aid to civil authorities" did not visualize any such course of action. When we tried to reason with him, he refused to listen. Some other officers in other districts also started treading on the same path.'[3]

Jamwal issued strict instructions to troops to exercise restraint, not to entertain private disputes and to forward all civilian complaints to the district magistrate. However, odd instances of such happenings continued.

During June and July, Jamwal and I started joint tours of the district to get first-hand feedback, to interact with people in rural areas and address their grievances. Almost daily, two of us would fly in his chopper from the helipad of 15 Division and cover a specific area, after issuing an advance notice so that people could assemble at one point.

On our joint trip to Baba Bakala sub-division, where 11 Guards under the command of Col Mehra was deployed, we learnt about an unpleasant incident. On 22 June, the army checkpost at Beas had stopped a tractor carrying a few Nihangs in their traditional vibrant blue dress for a routine check. Nihangs are nomadic warriors—they carry traditional weapons like swords and spears, and wear quoits of steel around imposing conical turbans that rise high, in some cases a few feet high. The Nihang group was body-searched, de-robed and left standing on the Grand Trunk Road to Delhi in their *kacheras* (undershorts). It was an instance of extreme callousness and a gross failure on the part of the soldiers to display basic civility.

Jamwal decided to make amends by a public gesture of offering new robes to the Nihangs. A congregation was organized at Rayya Government School and the Nihangs were invited to the podium one by one to receive them. One of them, in a display of acerbic wit, walked to the rostrum in his undershorts and told the General,

'*Ek vaar lah diti, pher ki pani e* [Once I have unrobed, why bear the burden of dressing up again]?'

This gesture earnt Jamwal considerable goodwill, with the media carrying complimentary stories. Perhaps his experience of serving as a colonel in Bangladesh in 1971, where he had assisted the local administration, motivated the general in grappling with civilian issues in Amritsar. He launched a drive to streamline city traffic, deployed military police to tow away wrongly parked cars, supervised cleanliness drives that included 'removal of cow-dung cakes' from the walls of houses in Putligarh and even planned the shifting of buffaloes from the walled city of Amritsar.

These well-intentioned decisions were lauded by the people of Amritsar, but these were misplaced priorities for the army, which had been called in to aid the civil administration to deal with terrorism. I had to remind Jamwal that Amritsar was not Bangladesh, but that did not dampen his drive.

More serious, however, was the situation in the mufassil, where the local army units operated independently, made their own plans, chose their own targets and carried out their own operations, unmindful of the fact that they had been called in to assist the civil set-up and not replace it. The police faced redundancy. The army had gained a statutory mandate to act independently, but my experience is that except for anti-insurgency operations or sudden exigencies and situations that may develop on the spot, it is always advantageous and in the interest of the army to take a magistrate and the police along while conducting any operation. That lends a civil face to any search and seizure or arrest operations carried out by the armed forces. Though some magistrates, I am sure, were happy to stay away from these arguably dangerous situations, their comfort doesn't take precedence over good governance and maintaining the rule of law.

In the border belt of Amritsar and its adjoining districts, in village after village, the army units would encircle the habitations, get the menfolk out from their homes, collect them at one point and thereafter carry out search and seizure operations. Such exercises, by the very nature of the task, were time-consuming and irksome. While the objective to unearth illegal weapons and arrest underground terrorists was timely and laudable, the methods employed alienated the people. I may clarify that no planned or deliberate excesses were committed, but the Sikh psyche was so frayed by this time that deviation from normal legal procedures—and there were too many of these—evoked strong disapproval and even the occasional face-off.

Illustratively, on 10 July 1984, the men of 10 Bihar Regiment cordoned off village Kot Hirde Ram in the Amritsar sub-division. In the search operations that followed, an altercation ensued between the village sarpanch, Mohan Singh, and a few jawans. Mohan Singh fired from his licensed weapon, killing 2nd Lt Salesh Kumar and injuring Sub. Sher Bahadur and a jawan. The sarpanch and his son Major Singh were killed in the exchange of fire. Satyapal Dang, the well-intentioned CPI leader who led the fight against militancy, reported in writing the case of retired subedar Mohinder Singh of village Kathanian, who 'had not even the remotest connection with extremists or terrorists' but was killed on 12 July in similar circumstances by a search and seizure party of the army.

These were odd cases, but were enough to inflame discontent among the local population and even among ex-servicemen, who were often mistreated by the security forces as suspect civilians and that continued even after the formal withdrawal of the army. Consequently, in June 1985, the Indian Ex-services League under Lt Gen. G.S. Buch (retd) passed a resolution against the harassment and humiliation of ex-servicemen by the security forces and appealed to the government to respect their dignity and honour.

The army men's domineering attitude, coupled with the harsh language employed at times by them, hurt people the most. Hastily inducted forces, often brought from far-off places, were neither aware of the land's cultural milieu nor the sensibilities of the local population. The worst example, often quoted by almost every chronicler on Punjab, is the July issue of *Batchit*, an in-house army publication that described amritdharis—baptized Sikhs—as dangerous men, committed to arson and terrorism. It displayed ignorance about Sikhs, their traditions and the rural areas of Punjab that the army was operating in.

In July 1984, the army did not allow baptized Sikh students to carry a kirpan to exam halls. At the Polytechnic College, Batala, on 20 July, the students boycotted the exam in protest and only nine out of seventy-four examinees wrote their paper. Interestingly, in pre-Independence days, the British Army regulations stipulated, 'The pahul or religious pledge of the Sikh fraternity should on no account be interfered with.'[4]

Civilian officers—the SDM and revenue officials—who could have played a mollifying role, were not asked to participate in these search and seizure operations. Often, the civilian officers were not even aware of the venue or timing of these operations. The soldiers would pick up anyone they suspected of having links with militants for interrogation. The army intel was not always reliable—at times they went by inputs given by locals; village communities are a highly fragmented lot and often inter-personal rivalries led to motivated complaints and occasional excesses.

The genuine *kharkoos*, as the militants called themselves, had, in any case, vanished from their homes. Many had gone into hiding or crossed over to Pakistan through the porous border to avoid army searches or detention under the Terrorist and Disruptive Activities (Prevention) Act (TADA). By one account, a few thousand had crossed the Ravi into Pakistan. They returned hardened, indoctrinated and vengeful. And they did not take long to announce their return; late on the evening of 12 September, an armed group of nine men commandeered a bus to a secluded spot near Naushera Majha Singh village, close to the international border in the district of Gurdaspur. They selected eight Hindu passengers, mercilessly shot them dead and cycled away in the dark. The army was still on the ground and so were the terrorists, back from Pakistan. The two operations—Blue Star and Woodrose—had succeeded in killing some militants but not militancy.

The nadir of civil–military relations was reached in January 1985. The BSF, CRPF and other paramilitary forces had been placed under the operational command of the army on 3 June 1984, and now, as a prelude to the withdrawal of the army, Home Secretary M.M. Vohra issued instructions that the responsibility for maintenance of law and order would rest on the civil administration with effect from 11 January 1985. Consequently, the BSF, CRPF and other paramilitary were to operate 'subject to the control and command of senior superintendents of police of Amritsar and Gurdaspur districts respectively, who shall take all decisions regarding the maintenance of law and order in consultation with their district magistrates'. These instructions required the district magistrates to settle the modalities for the reversion of responsibility of law and order to the civil administration.

However, the local army command refused to relieve the paramilitary forces and when the matter was raised in the joint civil–military conference on 21 January, Dewan, the then GOC, ruled that 'no change will take place till ordered by this Div. HQ'. The situation was reported to the state government and settled with the intervention of the adviser to the governor (security), who was none other than a serving Lt. Gen.

Corrective Steps

It was much later, in the late 1980s, with the wisdom of hindsight, that the army took corrective measures. Steps were taken to soothe the frayed feelings of the rural population. The people-centric welfare measures taken by the army, such as deputing army doctors for healthcare or lending a helping hand in building an embankment or two, and deputing its education corps to temporarily teach in the schools where the teachers had gone missing due to militancy, earned the army goodwill and the confidence of the Punjabis.

The army worked in tandem with the civil administration, which extended its resources, including funds for minor public works or finances from the district Red Cross to dispense free medicines. Civil–military coordination was institutionalized at the state and district levels. The chief secretary chaired review meetings with civil and army officers in Chandigarh while the district magistrates did so in their respective jurisdictions.

During the two Rakshak operations in 1990–92, the army operated only on specific information and intelligence inputs, in close coordination with the police. The troops were not allowed to conduct a 'general scan' of the civilian population or search private homes, a task left to the police, which was the public face of these operations. In these operations now the policemen formed the inner cordon, with the army providing the outer cordon. The troops had been sensitized to the religious sensibilities of the local population and briefed on the manner in which to interact with them. They were issued instructions that barred them from entering religious places or damaging crops while establishing field camps. The success of these measures in the 1990s was owed to the synchronized and integrated approach of the civil–military authorities.

During the tenure of Chief of Army Staff Gen. J.J. Singh (2005–07), a doctrine of 'sub-conventional operations/low-intensity conflict' based on the philosophy of 'an iron fist and a velvet glove' was evolved. The army, while deployed to provide a secure and safe environment, also worked to ensure that people were not alienated and human rights were observed—'wanton kicking of innocent civilians is terrorist [sic], not a war against terrorism,' declared Gen. Singh, quoting Noam Chomsky.

The ten commandments of the chief of the army staff first issued in 1993 by Gen. B.P. Joshi, the then chief, which included 'no meddling in civil administration', were further strengthened by Gen. Singh with the directive to win people's hearts and minds and to 'employ all resources under your command to improve their living conditions'. It called for synergizing army actions with the civil administration and not conducting operations without police representatives. A counter-insurgency specialized force, Rashtriya Rifles, composed of infantry men, was formed in 1990, and it has observed these directives and served well in disturbed areas.

Nevertheless, there is now a greater realization for the need to evolve a civil–military maxim beyond the traditional coordination mechanisms—a counter-insurgency civil–military administrative model. This is due to the changed role of the armed forces in the civil domain. During the early years, post-Independence, the army's aid to the civil administration was limited to deal with catastrophic conditions like floods and earthquakes or occasionally to deal with mob violence or riots. Army operations were limited both in time and by the nature of the specific tasks it undertook.

However, as insurgency and terrorism reared their ugly heads in different parts of the country, longer involvement of the armed forces—a stay-in role stretched over protracted periods of time—has become inescapable. Such circumstances have made the military a stakeholder in these situations and given it a role in policymaking to deal with militancy. Consequently, military and civil domains overlap and sometimes lines get blurred.

Often, the strategy and tactics that the military adopts to deal with civilian situations has far-reaching national consequences. Illustratively, the use of tanks in the Golden Temple and the resultant extensive structural devastation to the temple complex had dangerous social and political outcomes. Therefore, there is a need to evolve a civil–military maxim, a doctrine that deals with terrorism and counter-insurgency situations, and to establish an institutional structure with well-defined procedures for civil oversight of military operations undertaken in the civil domain. A systemic mechanism would help contain socio-political fallouts of civil–military operations that often have had roller-coaster effects on the Indian polity.

The world over it is now well recognized that the military is an interest group, like any other. The Indian Army, to its credit, has remained professional and apolitical but one cannot rule out the possibility that it may not be able to buck the trend for long, particularly in the current highly politicized environment it operates in. In fact, the tell-tale signs are already there. Institutionalized civil–military responses in situations of extended army deployment, therefore, need to be systematized and a civil–military maxim established, rather than relying upon the present joint command concept, which often gets reduced to mere 'meet and greet' conferences.

23

Indira's Assassination

IN PUNJAB'S TURMOIL, WEDNESDAYS WENT ON TO BECOME somewhat of a fatal juncture—31 October 1984 was a Wednesday, just like 6 June 1984 was, when the army conducted Operation Blue Star in the Golden Temple.

The governor, Satarawala, rang me up around 10.30 a.m. on 31 October, a Wednesday. In a feeble voice, while fumbling for words, he whispered, 'The Prime Minister has been shot. She is critical.' He added, 'Take all precautions. Do not share the information with anyone.'

Indira Gandhi had been cautioned by the intelligence agencies not to retain Sikhs in her security—not that there were too many of them—but the two she did not remove proved fatal. It was a security blunder. The intelligence agencies, after alerting Indira Gandhi of the risk of retaining Sikhs in her security staff, seemed to have absolved themselves of the responsibility; there was no follow-up vigilance on the few Sikhs in her security set-up that could have easily forewarned of the designs of her killers. Consequently, when Beant Singh and Satwant Singh pumped bullets into her frail frame, it was left for the investigating team to assiduously establish the missing links that led to her death.

After hearing from the governor, I called up Bua Singh, SSP, and we got together to plan the precautions to be taken, just in case there was public reaction to the tragedy. The local CID unit was alerted, police parties were dispatched to patrol the city, checkposts were set up in sensitive localities and a meeting of the peace committee, a district-level body of prominent persons, opinion-makers and political leaders, was convened in the evening without disclosing what had prompted me to suddenly summon it. However, within hours of her being shot, the news spread like wildfire. Her death was yet to be formally announced, but almost everyone seemed to know that she was no more.

We were concerned about the reaction of the high priests to the tragedy as any public statement they made could influence the Sikh response to her death. Bua Singh and I rushed to the Golden Temple. On my request, the three priests—Giani Kirpal Singh, jathedar of the Akal Takht, Giani Sahib Singh, head priest of the Golden Temple, and Giani Pritam Singh, head priest of the Akal Takht—gathered at the upper-storey dwelling of Giani Sahib Singh on the Ghanta Ghar end of the Parikrama. They had guessed the purpose of our visit and without any prodding agreed to both condole the death and condemn the killers.

Gurmit Singh Cheema, the press officer of the SGPC, released a signed joint press statement on behalf of the priests. It was drafted by him there, in our presence. The three priests, in the joint statement, expressed grief and described her death as a loss to the nation. They also censured the killers and appealed to the 'people to maintain peace, communal harmony and amity'. I took a copy of the joint press statement and read it out at the peace committee meeting held in the evening at the Red Cross Bhavan.

However, as the press statement of the high priests appeared on the ticker of the news agencies and became public, some of the radicals and militants became active. The priests started receiving death threats. Even the Jagdev Singh Talwandi faction of the Akali Dal criticized the priests for condemning the assassins. For the militants, those assassins were '*panth rattan*'—jewels of the community—who had avenged the desecration of the holiest Sikh shrine.

Under duress, the priests rang up local correspondents denying that they had issued any statement condemning the killers. Kirpal Singh, who spoke to the press, said that the priests had never condemned the killers, though he owned up to the part of the statement relating to the appeal to the panth to maintain communal harmony and peace. The next day, the newspapers carried both the joint press statement of the priests and their partial denial.

This was yet another instance of the militancy-induced fear that often caused the clergy to crumble. The priests had reasons to panic, for the state had repeatedly floundered to protect those who were known to be on the hit list of the militants. In fact, all the three priests were later assaulted, their partial retraction of the joint press statement notwithstanding. Kirpal Singh was shot at on 16 January 1985, a Wednesday, near Ludhiana, but was lucky to escape death. Giani Pritam Singh was boxed inside the temple at the Akal Takht, on 12 February 1985, by one Gurmit Singh Majitha, who was arrested. During his interrogation Gurmit said that he had acted on a divine direction to *sodho* (set right) the priest.

Giani Sahib Singh was shot at and seriously wounded inside the temple on 27 November 1985, a Wednesday, and the birthday of Guru Nanak Dev. His bodyguard, a police constable, was killed. In all, ten shots were fired as Giani Sahib Singh negotiated the stairs to the Parikrama via the Ghanta Ghar entry to the temple. The killers escaped towards the Dukh Bhanjani Beri and disappeared in the crowd of devotees. I reached the spot almost immediately and Sahib

Singh bemoaned, 'DC Sahib, we had told you.' I had no answer to offer for our failure to protect him.

As Indira Gandhi's death became public, violence engulfed Delhi and many other parts of the country. In Delhi, in seventy-two hours starting 1 November 1984, official figures put the death toll of Sikhs at 2,733. It was a massacre. The State machinery was defunct, while armed mobs butchered Sikhs and looted or burnt their properties. Well-intentioned persons like I.K. Gujral, who went on to become the Prime Minister, personally approached the home minister to intervene, but without any result. Home Minister P.V. Narasimha Rao, so claims his biographer,[1] was made redundant and told that 'all information [on violence] should be sent to the PMO', apparently to 'coordinate a single response to the violence'.

K.C. Singh, my foreign service batchmate, who was then serving at the Rashtrapati Bhavan, was to later disclose that the Union home minister was so helpless that he rang up Zail Singh to seek his help to deploy the President's Bodyguard, a ceremonial army formation, to rescue a Sikh friend of Narasimha Rao's from his farmhouse that came under mob attack. The law and order handling had been usurped by Rajiv Gandhi's close circle of political friends, superseding the law agencies' systemic response to violence.

A delegation of prominent Sikhs also approached President Zail Singh to put an end to the violence. The President, however, was non-functional. Air Chief Marshal Arjan Singh and Lt Gen. J.S. Aurora, heroes of the 1965 and 1971 wars, respectively, and a few others met Zail Singh on 1 November 1984, 'emphatically spelling out for him the violence overtaking the Sikhs throughout the city', but, Zail Singh replied, 'I do not have powers to intervene.'[2] I.K. Gujral later deposed before the Nanavati Commission that he had contacted the President on the telephone, but 'he advised me to visit some of the affected areas and contact the government. I considered it very odd that the President of India had asked me to do such a thing.'

The scale of one-sided violence against Sikhs has been described by many an author as genocide and the account of violence has been well documented by independent chroniclers, as also the failure of successive governments to punish the perpetrators. Consequently, echoes of injustice resonate till date, not only in India but also abroad—even in the legislative forums of a few foreign countries.

We, in Amritsar, were worried about the possible backlash of Delhi's anti-Sikh carnage in our district. The danger lay in the mufassil, the villages, where Hindus are in a woeful minority. Every village had a few Hindu households and even a small trigger could descend into a massacre. Fortunately, the historical umbilical cord that binds the two communities made our task easy. There was no attack on any Hindu. It is not that there was no reaction—in Amritsar one shop belonging to a Hindu was set on fire by a protesting mob, but that was the only stray act of violence. Attempts to take out processions were nipped in the bud and the law enforced rigorously. Effective patrolling, holding of peace committee meetings at the grass-roots level and appeals through local Sikh sants, gurdwaras and deras helped to maintain calm.

There was, however, a strong undercurrent of anger as news of what had happened in Delhi and other parts of the country trickled in. A sort of censorship on news had been enforced for a few days in Amritsar, and even aircraft coming from Delhi on landing in Amritsar were searched and cleared of all Delhi newspapers so that people would not know the gory details of the carnage. But through word of mouth and channels like the BBC, the details of the horror enacted on the streets of Delhi spread like wildfire.

On 2 November 1984, the head priests announced their intent to visit Delhi on 7 November, to meet the victims of violence. It took all our persuasion to convince them to postpone the visit, as the situation was still charged. They only agreed to reschedule the visit to 13 November, and therefore it had to be conveyed point-blank that they would be detained at the airport if they defied our appeal. They saw reason and the visit never came to fruition.

Then came the unwise utterance of Rajiv Gandhi on 19 November 1984. In his first public rally at the Boat Club in Delhi, after assuming office as Prime Minister, he rationalized the killings of Sikhs by saying that when a mighty tree falls, the earth around it shakes. He said: *'Jab Indira Ji ki hatya hui thi, to hamare desh mein kucch dange-phasaad hue the . . . Lekin jab bhi koi bada per girta hai, to dharti thodi hilti hai.'*

It was an unfortunate response to the pogrom against Sikhs. While intellectuals like Prof. D.S. Maini of Punjabi University reminded Rajiv that one does not taunt people while they are still grieving their dead, jathedar Giani Kirpal Singh was more direct: Rajiv should not forget that when a tree falls, its root and branches are uprooted with it.

The Sikh genocide achieved what Bhindranwale had not succeeded in doing: It transformed jingoistic religious militancy into a full-blown, bloody ethno-national movement. The carnage provided both reason and resolve to radical Sikhs to take up arms. The dormant terrorist modules became active and there was a spontaneous surge in new recruitment to the militancy.

'*Khoon ka badla khoon*', words that had resonated on the streets of Delhi, now became the catchphrase of militancy in Punjab. Violence accelerated, and the terrorists targeted Hindus in rural areas. For the first time, Hindu migration from Punjab began. The communal violence distorted the age-old peaceful Hindu–Sikh narrative, even though there were many glowing examples of neighbours helping each other during the carnage.

It was left to Prime Minister Manmohan Singh, a Sikh, to admit on the floor of Parliament on 11 August 2005, twenty-one years after the carnage, that there were lapses on the part of the State in 1984. He apologized, 'On behalf of our government, on behalf of the entire people of this country, I bow in shame that such a thing happened.'

This was a welcome apology but it failed to assuage the Sikh psyche, for the guilty had not been brought to book, some not even till date. The CBI in its written submission to Justice Muralidhar and Justice Vinod Goel of the Delhi High Court in an appeal against the acquittal of Sajjan Kumar said, '. . . Delhi Police personnel in uniform were either silent spectators to the crime or abettors or even the perpetrators.'[3] Despite the investigations, reinvestigations, countless inquiry commissions and SITs that have been formed over the last thirty-seven years, justice eludes the victims of violence.

As the saying goes, 'There can be no revolution unless there is a festering wound and a villain.' The wound and the villain continued to provide justification to radical elements for the resurgence of the ethno-national movement. The tragedy of Punjab remained unending.

24

The Accord and Longowal's Assassination

Rajiv Gandhi was sworn in as Prime Minister on 31 October, but he visited his South Block office for the first time only after the twelve-day State mourning period was over. His immediate concern were the elections to the eighth Lok Sabha. He had to secure office for the next five years and there could not be a better time, with the entire nation behind him in sympathy. He directed his principal secretary, P.C. Alexander, to approach R.K. Trivedi, chief election commissioner, for holding elections early, which in any case were due. The Election Commission scheduled them for December 1984.

The Punjab problem became a central issue in the elections. In a visible departure from the politics of ideology, the appeal was to emotions, and it polarized communities by underpinning the fear of terrorism. 'Will the country's border finally be moved to your doorsteps?' That was a public advertisement carried in the

Indian Express on 27 November 1984, suggestively reminding voters of the militancy in Punjab. Another advertisement showed a Sikh taxi driver, with a question addressed to the reader—do you feel safe in the taxi? The strategy paid dividends and the Congress romped in with a thumping majority, winning 414 seats in the Lok Sabha and securing 49.1 per cent of the total votes polled.

Once in power, Rajiv Gandhi showed statesmanship. He initiated a politics of accords and the outcome was two settlements, one each for Punjab and Assam. For Punjab, it certainly was a felicitous step. The Punjabis were sulking and that showed up in the ever-increasing number of saffron turbans and black dupattas—marks of protest. The militants had also started regrouping. The top Akali leaders were still in jails, but the middle-rung leadership worked to regain Sikh support. In early March 1985, in an impressive congregation amidst fiery speeches and sloganeering, they announced the intent to re-commence the morcha that was suspended since Blue Star. They were spoiling for a fight.

The Union government had two options: Continue with President's Rule and face both the militants and the Akalis, or strategically rehabilitate the Akalis, assuage their feelings and leave them to deal with the Sikh alienation and the militancy. Rajiv picked the second option. In any case, constitutionally, Central rule could not be continued in the state forever.

In a well-considered move, the detained Akali leaders, therefore, were discharged from jails in batches. Longowal, Barnala and a host of amenable leaders were released first, on 11 March 1985. R.V. Subramaniam, senior adviser to the governor, had, in fact, met Longowal in jail on 14 February 1985 at Udaipur and probed his response to a settlement. Longowal was non-committal, but the adviser had set the ball rolling. Tohra and Badal, known for their apathetic approach towards the Congress and considered comparatively arduous to deal with, were released later in April.

The Central government viewed them as strategic reserves for a future contingency should the amenable ones fail to deliver.

The day Longowal was released, Arjun Singh was sworn in as chief minister for a second term in Bhopal. He had led his party to victory in Madhya Pradesh in the February 1985 elections to the state assembly. Arjun Singh had earned the goodwill of some of the Akali leaders detained at Pachmarhi, a small hill resort in Madhya Pradesh. Politically astute, he was considered the best bet for talks with the Akalis and was chosen for the seemingly intractable negotiations.

Rajiv Gandhi summoned Arjun Singh to Delhi; he went under the impression that it was to discuss the expansion of his Cabinet in Madhya Pradesh; instead, he was asked to proceed to Punjab. That ended his two-day tenure as chief minister. But he had a more onerous responsibility waiting for him—a job he took over on 14 March—as governor of Punjab. He took his oath of office in chaste Punjabi, sending a signal that the media did not miss to highlight.

On 16 March, Arjun Singh arrived in Amritsar. I escorted him to the Golden Temple, where he prayed for peace and recorded in the visitor's book at the SGPC office, 'It is my prayer that my services may be accepted in this house of God.' And God acknowledged his intent, for, a few days later, he clinched a deal with Longowal.

Weeks after his visit to Amritsar, I received a call from the Raj Bhavan, conveying that the state aircraft was being dispatched to ferry me to Chandigarh for an audience with the governor. I was asked to bring along Harjit Singh, SP, CID. Such sudden summons were repeated at least two more times and on one occasion we also picked up Inderjit Singh, DC from Ferozepur, landing at the abandoned World War II airstrip at Ferozepur that had to be cleared of cattle and stray dogs by deploying a contingent of policemen. It was rather unusual for junior officials to be called by the governor directly, bypassing administrative hierarchy.

Arjun Singh did not meet us together. We were called in one by one, in turns, while the others waited in the ADC's room. The governor was a man of few words, he spoke in a low voice often interspersed with silence, giving one the impression that he was formulating his thoughts. His queries, however, were insightful and primarily centred on the law and order situation and the political scenario in the state. He also made inquiries about certain individuals, and the kind of influence they wielded among the Akalis, and their acceptability to radicals and militants. We realized later that he was scrutinizing the possible interlocutors suggested to him for covertly negotiating with Longowal to prepare the ground for a political settlement.

Given the highly charged atmosphere and the divisive nature of Akali politics, this was the correct course as any move made under a public gaze could stymie the negotiations even before they began. Arjun Singh's building blocks, therefore, by their very nature were exclusionary—his initiative ignored not only the likes of Badal and Tohra, but also the radical political elements like the United Akali Dal led by Joginder Singh. For this reason, there was a discord within Sikh circles over the accord.

Once the interlocutors assured Arjun Singh of a positive response from Longowal, he wrote a personal letter to him, hand-delivered by an intermediary. It resulted in their first meeting on 13 April 1985 at the Jalandhar residence of Barjinder Singh Hamdard of the Ajit group of newspapers. The governor travelled without the usual paraphernalia, accompanied by Shiv Mohan Singh, DIG, CRPF.

Longowal was impressed by Arjun Singh's sincerity, and the two agreed to work out a deal. Subsequently, Longowal took the senior Akali leadership on board and shared the outline of the terms of the proposed accord. Badal and Tohra had reservations and cautioned him about a possible betrayal by the Central government, but Longowal went ahead.

Both the government and the Akalis initiated baby steps to create public opinion in favour of a settlement. The government released around 2,000 prisoners who were not facing any serious criminal charges. The ban on the AISSF was lifted. Longowal toured Punjab, met the victims of anti-Sikh violence in Delhi and addressed public gatherings. He, at times, even adopted a radical stance to neutralize the hotheads.

The Central government appointed Justice Ranganath Misra on 26 April 1985 to inquire into the November 1984 violence in Delhi, almost six months after the bloodbath—even an investigation into the carnage became conditional to a rapprochement strategy, rather than an issue of justice and enforcement of law and order. Earlier, Rajiv had inducted H.K.L. Bhagat and Jagdish Tytler as ministers in his Cabinet, despite these men being perceived to have instigated the mobs in Delhi.

Arjun Singh was conscious of the militants' ability to scuttle the peace process by creating mayhem in the state. In the past, they had sabotaged Akali–Centre dialogue by committing heinous mass crimes. In fact, B.D. Pande, the governor of Punjab, even feared that there was a mole in the PMO; the militants had managed to derail the negotiations by accelerating violence each time these neared a conclusion. The Intelligence Bureau zeroed in on the suspects in the PMO and on 17 January 1985, the private secretary to Alexander and three personal assistants in his office were arrested and charged with leaking official information. Who they were working for is not information in the public domain.

Arjun Singh, therefore, deemed it vital to neutralize the radicals and at least a section of the militants so that they did not create hurdles. He held secret meetings with AISSF leaders, led by Harminder Singh, at a safe house in Delhi. He also met a Babbar Khalsa militant. Arjun Singh described him as one who 'did not think twice before killing anyone, if the need arose'[1] and he was allowed to carry his weapon on him when he met the governor.

Arjun Singh, however, ignored Jagdev Singh Talwandi and Baba Joginder Singh, father of Bhindranwale, the two Akali factions opposed to the Akali Dal (Longowal). To usurp power, the Baba in a surprise move had announced the merger of all Akali Dals to form a United Akali Dal in May 1985. Simranjit Singh Mann was made its president and since he was under detention, Baba Joginder Singh became its convener. The Akali Dal (Longowal), however, rejected the unification. Jagdev Singh Talwandi and Baba Joginder Singh were, thus, the only leaders left in the United Dal. Their political base was insignificant, though Baba Joginder Singh wielded influence over some of the militant groups. They both were opposed to the accord.[2]

In July 1985, Rajiv Gandhi wrote a letter to Longowal inviting him to Delhi. The opposition of the United Akali Dal, of Badal and Tohra within the Akali Dal, had made Longowal ambivalent about the move. He, therefore, resorted to what most devout Sikhs do—taking *vaak* or hukamnama from the Guru Granth Sahib at the Chandigarh residence of Balwant Singh. The Guru ordained, 'Whichever way I looked I saw His presence as far as I could see, He is everything that exists; ever meditate Him.'[3]

The vaak was interpreted to have given a go-ahead, and on 23 July, Longowal proceeded to Delhi accompanied by Barnala and Balwant Singh. In Delhi, to maintain secrecy they were accommodated at the Kapurthala House, the state guest house. The deal was so hush-hush that neither the Union home secretary nor the chief secretary, Punjab, or the political leadership of the Congress, knew about it till the morning of 24 July, when the accord was signed in Rajiv Gandhi's office in Parliament, in the presence of Arjun Singh and Vishwanath Pratap Singh. Even the Congress's fix-all man for Punjab, Buta Singh, was oblivious of it till he reached Parliament House in the morning of that day after he had flown in from Chandigarh with Dhanoa, the chief secretary. They pleasantly discovered Longowal, Barnala and Balwant, the three architects of the accord, in the corridors of Parliament House.

The accord was signed by both Rajiv and Longowal—for the first time a Prime Minister formally entered into a settlement on public affairs with an individual. The accord addressed the original demands of the Akalis and the new issues that had arisen during the prolonged period of agitation and Operation Blue Star. The Akalis hailed it as a victory for Sikhs, and projected the accord as an agreement between the panth and the State, drawing a comparison with the covenant Maharaja Ranjit Singh and Lord William Bentinck, the then governor general of India, had concluded in 1831, on the banks of the Sutlej at Ropar.

But all was not well with the accord. Its language, in any case, left most of the issues indeterminate. Irresolute expressions such as the Central government 'may' consider to take measures to promote Punjabi, or to 'consider' formulation of an All India Gurdwara Act, 'in consultation with all concerned', or refer the Anandpur Sahib Resolution to the Sarkaria Commission to 'consider' federal relations, etc., rendered its outcomes uncertain, dependent upon uncertain variables and future contingencies. Haryana and Rajasthan, the two vital stakeholders in the issue of sharing of river waters and division of territory, were not party to the accord; that was a serious failure in a federal set-up. Bhajan Lal was the first to raise the banner of revolt against his own high command at the All India Congress Committee session in Bombay and threatened that 'if Chandigarh was given to Punjab, he would not allow any Sikh to cross his state to reach Delhi'.[4]

The radicals, including the United Akali Dal, perceived the accord as a surrender to the Central government and a betrayal of the panth. Within the Akali Dal (Longowal), given the selective way in which a section of the leadership had been picked for dialogue, bypassing key leaders like Badal and Tohar, created an in-house and not-so-silent opposition to the settlement.

Still worse, the sincerity of the Central government to honour the accord was doubted by the very person who had piloted the agreement. To quote Arjun Singh, 'I had become aware of the fact that, in New Delhi, a powerful nexus of politicians and bureaucrats was dead set against establishing peace and stability in Punjab and they considered the accord their main hurdle.'[5] Shrewd Arjun Singh requested Rajiv Gandhi to permit him to quit the governorship, and he exited Punjab four months after the accord had been signed. He achieved the given objective and felt that someone else should handle the blame for the inevitable fiasco it would eventually turn into. We weren't aware of these developments, but on 14 November, Arjun Singh landed in Amritsar at 8.30 a.m. and went to pay obeisance at the Golden Temple. We guessed it could be a goodbye visit and so it turned out to be—he was inducted as a Union Cabinet minister on 15 November 1985.

Dr Shankar Dayal Sharma was appointed the new governor on 26 November, which was a rather insensitive development—militants had killed Sharma's son-in-law and his daughter Gitanjali Makin only four months earlier for their alleged role in engineering the anti-Sikh carnage in Delhi. Killing Makin soon after the Longowal–Rajiv Accord was a signal. Sharma's appointment as governor was seen by radicals as a counter-signal. Sikh circles viewed his appointment as a move to scuttle the accord, though Sharma was too gentle a person to hold grudges. I found him withdrawn and understandably grieving when he came to Amritsar on 10 December 1985.

The accord, in any case, had not addressed the bruised Sikh psyche and the issue of panthic honour. A visit to the Golden Temple and an expression of penitence by the Prime Minister may have served to settle the Punjab problem better than the signing of an irresolute accord.

Assassination of Longowal

The radical elements viewed the accord as a cop-out and Longowal a sell-out for signing it. He came to Amritsar on 30 July 1985, and about 500 agitated workers of the United Akali Dal, AISSF and other radicals, carrying kirpans and sticks, came close to assaulting him. His car was surrounded by the agitators near Guru Nanak Niwas in the temple complex and they shouted the slogan, '*Congress de tin dalal, Balwant, Barnala te Longowal* [There are three agents of

Congress: Balwant, Barnala and Longowal].' If it weren't for the timely intervention of plain-clothes policemen, Longowal's life could have been in danger. S.S. Virk, SSP, and I were present at the scene and intervened to prevent a possible clash between the radicals and the Akali Dal workers, who had gathered to welcome Longowal and were chanting pro-Longowal slogans like '*Sardar-a-azim Longowal, saree quam tere naal* [The entire community is with you]'.

However, Longowal's luck ran out on 20 August 1985, incidentally also Rajiv Gandhi's birthday. He was shot dead by three Sikh youth at Gurdwara Sherpur, Sangrur district, while on a visit to address the sangat. Two persons from the crowd opened fire, killing a youth and injuring two others. People around Longowal provided cover and he seemed to have escaped the bid on his life, but as he was being shifted to the safety of a hall in the gurdwara, a third assailant pumped in bullets from a close range and Longowal collapsed. His security personnel, who had left to eat a meal, leaving him unguarded, rushed back but it was too late. Paramjit Singh Sandhu, SSP, Sangrur, who manned the outer corridor of the venue, led his men to chase the assailants. Two of them were caught on the spot while the third one was arrested later.

The state ordered an inquiry by Gowri Shankar, the then adviser (security) to the governor, and another judicial inquiry was conducted later by Justice Gurnam Singh, my maternal uncle. It was, to say the least, a security lapse far more severe than in Indira Gandhi's case—all the security guards had left Longowal unguarded to have lunch.

Longowal was initially too diffident to accept police protection but was eventually persuaded by Governor Arjun Singh to agree. Gurbachan Singh Mann, SP, was deputed with a contingent of policemen to protect him, but inexplicably, K.P.S. Gill, IG, PAP, replaced him with Jit Singh, another SP who was facing proceedings for removal from service on the charge of having links with the militants. The file for Jit Singh's dismissal was then pending with the Raj Bhavan. Jit Singh had served with me in Faridkot district in

1979–80, when he was DSP, Muktsar, and I was additional deputy commissioner. I had found him honest and committed. His failing, however, was his fundamental predilection. He was close to Simranjit Singh Mann, then SSP, and together they used to facilitate Amrit Parchar camps in the district. After Longowal's killing, Jit Singh was dismissed from service and he joined Mann's political party.

The police chief, Kirpal Dhillon, was unceremoniously repatriated to his parent cadre of IPS, Madhya Pradesh—the transfer order was served to him while he was travelling to Phillaur on 22 August by stopping his cavalcade on the highway. Arjun Singh was that annoyed over the failure of the police to protect Longowal.

Longowal was given a state funeral. The general house of the SGPC in November 1985 conferred the honorific Panth Rattan on Longowal. The Central government in December 1991 opened the Sant Longowal Institute of Engineering and Technology in his village to commemorate him. I had the opportunity to serve on its governing body for a few years. The institute has earned a name in technical education in the state.

25

The Protocol Blues

R.L. Bhatia, MP from Amritsar and AICC (I) general secretary, who later served as Union minister of state for external affairs and governor of Kerala and Bihar, had his ancestral house on the elite Mall Road, not far from my official residence. On the morning of 17 April 1985, he was meeting his constituents on the lawns of his residence when two young men posing as petitioners walked in and fired from a 455 bore pistol, killing a visitor. Bhatia ran inside the house but was chased and shot at thrice. The assailants coolly walked out of the house, snatched a scooter at gunpoint and drove away. This was the usual modus operandi of the terrorists to strike unguarded targets. Bhatia, in fact, had been extended security cover, but in December 1984 he declined to retain the gunman, trusting that he was safe.

I rushed to the spot. Bhatia was shifted to the Guru Tegh Bahadur Hospital, where the doctors succeeded in saving him. Governor Arjun Singh and a stream of senior officials and political dignitaries from Delhi and Punjab reached Amritsar to call on Bhatia and that kept us occupied throughout the day.

By the evening, we received information that the assailants had escaped to the Guru Ram Das Sarai, which the SGPC had claimed as an integral part of the Golden Temple. Given the atmosphere, police entry into the Sarai was a sensitive issue but there was no other alternative. The police swooped in on the Sarai complex at about 1 a.m. on 20 April. The unearthly hour was chosen to maintain an element of surprise. It also gave enough time to the police and the paramilitary forces to search the few hundred rooms in the sarai and other residential and administrative buildings before sunrise. The operation was over by 4 a.m. Bua Singh, SSP, and I returned to our homes around 5 a.m. for a much-needed nap before office hours. 20 April was *amavas* and the temple would attract a large number of devotees for darshan *ishnan*. We had to be alert during the day, should there be any public reaction to the raid on the sarai.

The SGPC, as expected, condemned the police entry in the sarai and accused the administration of an 'unprovoked and deplorable attack on Sri Darbar Sahib complex'. Bhan Singh, secretary, SGPC, wrote demanding me 'to hold a thorough inquiry and tender a written apology'; he sought an 'assurance for stopping once and for all such attacks on the complex in the future to assuage the hurt feelings of the Sikhs'. But the police had not crossed the road that separates the sarai complex from the langar building to ensure that the sanctity of the temple was not violated. In the search, unlicensed weapons, including one improvised hand grenade, a 315-bore rifle with live ammunition and one 12-bore pistol, were recovered and three suspects were arrested. Therefore, it was the SGPC that had failed to preserve the sanctity of the complex.

Two days later, Chief Secretary P.H. Vaishnav rang me up. In his indomitable style, he said, '*Sardar Ji pher hun tussi fuss hi gaye*. Give your explanation within two days.' I thought the government had taken an adverse note of our entry into the complex without its prior approval. However, the chief secretary was referring to the slip-up in protocol during the visit of Lok Sabha Speaker Balram Jakhar on the morning of 20 April. The Lok Sabha Secretariat had intimated that the Speaker would reach Amritsar at 7 a.m., call on the convalescing Bhatia and thereafter head straight to Delhi.

Bua Singh and I were not sure of how the operation in the Guru Ram Das Sarai would go and had, therefore, deputed Additional Deputy Commissioner Manmohan Kalia and Inderjit Singh Sidhu, SP City, Amritsar, to receive him and take him around. The Speaker was unhappy that neither the deputy commissioner nor the SSP had received him at the airport. To add to his annoyance, when he reached the hospital the patient was missing from the designated room. The nurse on duty had no clue where Bhatia was. Early that morning, he had been shifted to another wing, but the pilot car did not know the way around and went around in circles to locate the new ward. Finally, when they did reach the right room, there was no doctor to receive him or brief him about Bhatia's health. These were protocol lapses.

The Lok Sabha Secretariat wrote to the chief secretary that the Speaker 'had taken a serious view of the lapses'. The news leaked, the *Indian Express,* Chandigarh, on 1 May carried a story: 'DC, SSP Face Action on Protocol Issue.' The *Tribune* followed it up the next day with the headline, 'Action against DC, SSP Initiated.' Bua Singh and I were left red-faced. N.N. Vohra, the home secretary, sagacious as he is, advised me not to send a reply and suggested that we sleep over the matter for a few days to let the issue cool down. And that is what happened. By the end of May, the matter had died down. Our explanation was accepted. But we learnt a lesson—protocol is paramount, even in a conflict zone.

26

Barnala Becomes Chief Minister

Elections to the state assembly and the Lok Sabha from Punjab had already been announced, but after Longowal's murder, the dates for these were rescheduled to 25 September 1985.

Governor Arjun Singh, the architect of the peace accord, now worked behind the scenes to help Barnala, who had taken over as the acting president of the Akali Dal (Longowal) on 25 August. The governor also had to 'manage' the militants to ensure that the poll process passed off peacefully. The militants and radicals were a divided house but some of them were won over by 'other means'. Just before the elections to the state assembly, an aircraft made two sorties to Delhi. On one of these trips, four large suitcases were ferried from the Delhi residence of a political leader. As the bags were being loaded into the aircraft, one of the suitcases fell, and its lock opened. The officials were left sweeping the aisle, collecting the currency notes that had spilled out. Such happenings are difficult to corroborate, but I learnt that the money was used to 'silence' some of the weapon-wielding militant set-ups.

The Akali Dal won the elections with a thumping majority. It won seventy-three seats out of 117 in the Vidhan Sabha and seven out of thirteen seats in the Lok Sabha, with a voter turnout of about 66.5 per cent. The Akalis had also given tickets to a few Muslims, Hindus and Christians to rebuild its image as an inclusive political party. In the election campaign, the candidates refrained from raising divisive issues and its manifesto skipped any reference to the entry of the army into the Golden Temple. The focus was to glorify the Punjab accord, highlight Hindu–Sikh amity and tend a healing touch to the victims of the past turmoil.

Barnala became chief minister on 29 September 1985, and offered Badal the post of deputy chief minister—he declined. Amarinder Singh, who had quit the Congress in protest against Blue Star, joined the Akali Dal in August and was inducted into the Cabinet as agriculture minister.

The Barnala government initiated several policy initiatives to sooth frayed Sikh sentiments. Justice Ajit Singh Bains, a retired judge of the Punjab and Haryana High Court, was commissioned to review the cases of the detainees and nearly 3,800 jailed people were released. The government offered financial help to the victims of terrorism and anti-Sikh riots, proposed employment and rehabilitation measures for army deserters and conferred the honorific of dharmi faujis on them. But these measures earned him little favour—they were considered inadequate by the radicals, while the non-Sikhs looked at these measures as appeasement.

To make things difficult, the militants became active again and violence resurfaced. Targeted killings of Hindus created alarm—Ram Labhaya, president of the municipal committee, Tarn Taran, was shot dead on 16 October 1985; Raj Kumar, Congress president at Fatehgarh Churian, was killed on 19 October 1985; and Vijay Kumar, president of the Hindu Shiv Sena, Phillaur, was murdered on

11 November 1985. Some attributed the resurgence of violence to the Barnala government's soft approach—but militant organizations like the Babbar Khalsa claimed these violent acts as retribution for the 1984 Sikh massacre in Delhi. After the anti-Sikh violence in Delhi, there were a series of blasts in Delhi and adjoining areas that had killed about sixty-nine people and injured 127.

There was still another challenge facing Barnala: the issue of the demolition of the Akal Takht repaired by Santa Singh. The militants wanted to demolish it because they perceived Santa Singh and the construction he had executed as 'sarkar sewa'. On 31 October 1985, the Damdami Taksal lent support to a Shaheedi Samagam at Manji Sahib. It was organized by radical elements and they resolved to demolish the Akal Takht and rebuild it by kar sewa. In the melee, some of the radicals damaged the marble facade of the Akal Takht to symbolically commence the demolition work. They announced kar sewa from 26 January 1986.

To checkmate these radical elements, Akali Dal (L) workers, some of them armed with licensed weapons, reached Amritsar in large numbers on 19 January 1986. Most of them were from Sangrur district and led by Gagandeep Singh, Barnala's son. Supported by SGPC workers, they chased out the radicals of the Damdami Taksal and the AISSF from inside the complex. Tohra played a conciliatory role and after negotiations with the Damdami Taksal and Baba Kharak Singh, it was decided that Baba Kharak Singh would lead the kar sewa to demolish and rebuild the Akal Takht. Seemingly, the conflict was resolved but in fact the power struggle intensified.

The Coup: The Militants Dissolve SGPC

Within days of the settlement of the kar sewa issue, the militants staged a coup against the SGPC and Akali Dal. On 26 January 1986, as India celebrated its Republic Day, the Baba Thakur Singh–led Damdami Taksal and the AISSF gathered in front of the Akal Takht and organized a Sarbat Khalsa. They declared dissolution of the statutory SGPC, ex-communicated and removed from office the SGPC-appointed jathedar of the Akal Takht, Giani Kirpal Singh, and the head priest, Giani Sahib Singh. The jathedars of the other three Sikh takhts were directed to resign.

In place of the democratically elected statutory SGPC, the Sarbat Khalsa constituted a five-member panthic committee to manage Sikh religious affairs. From the composition of the panthic committee, the imprint of the Damdami Taksal was evident. Its five members were Bhai Wassan Singh, Bhai Dhanna Singh, Bhai Gurbachan Singh Manochahal, Bhai Gurdev Singh and Bhai Arur Singh, all associated with the Taksal. Jasbir Singh Rode, a nephew of the late Bhindranwale, was appointed jathedar of the Akal Takht in place of the 'removed' Giani Kirpal Singh. Since he was under detention at that time, Gurdev Singh Kaunke was appointed to officiate as jathedar.

By another resolution, President Zail Singh and Buta Singh were excommunicated, the Akali Dal was pronounced as a 'traitor' party and the Longowal–Rajiv Accord was rejected. Bhindranwale, Bhai Amrik Singh and Shabeg Singh were eulogized and honoured as martyrs. Though the gathering refrained from use of the word 'Khalistan', it declared that 'Sikhs are slaves', and appealed to Sikhs living outside Punjab to migrate to Punjab.

Since the militants had usurped control, the employees of the SGPC either abandoned their offices or complied with the dictates of the militants. It was an absolute takeover of the temple precincts by the panthic committee. The SGPC-appointed high priests could no longer even enter the temple complex to pay obeisance, forget discharging their duties. Tohra publicly acknowledged the de facto control of the AISSF and Damdami Taksal over the temple complex. Barnala's cabinet met on 27 January at Chandigarh and 'strongly' condemned the Sarbat Khalsa and its resolutions, and appealed to Punjabis to isolate these anti-national forces.

Well-meaning intermediaries made earnest attempts to resolve the conflict by mediation. Jathedar Onkar Singh Matenangal, an

SGPC member, risked his life to build bridges between the Taksal and Tohra, but in retaliation the terrorists killed his son, Surinderpal Singh, on 8 February 1986. Another member of the SGPC, Jathedar Dalip Singh, president of the Gurdwara Bazidpur, was also killed.

In abject capitulation to the militants, the SGPC and the Akali Dal, which had their head offices within the temple precincts, shifted their operations to Anandpur Sahib. The General House of the SGPC, which normally meets at its headquarters in the Golden Temple complex, held its meeting at Anandpur Sahib on 28 January 1986.

To counter the militants, SGPC's five high priests called a Sarbat Khalsa on 16 February 1986. Its venue, however, was not the Akal Takht where such congregations were usually held, but at Anandpur Sahib. The same day, the Taksal and AISSF held an ardas divas in the Golden Temple for Chardi Kala (well-being) of Indira Gandhi's assassins. The Sarbat Khalsa at Anandpur Sahib was massive—over 2 lakh Sikhs gathered there, compared to the 20,000 that had attended the January Sarbat Khalsa organized by the militants. It was proof that the moderate political leadership, when united, enjoyed the confidence of the masses.

The Sarbat Khalsa at Anandpur Sahib condemned the killings and the acts of violence and rejected all the resolutions adopted by the 26 January Sarbat Khalsa. It criticized the militants for lawlessness and their attempts to create a fratricidal war within the panth. The congregation highlighted the statutory status of the SGPC to manage the affairs of the panth and authorized the SGPC and Akali Dal to evict these undesirable groups from the Golden Temple complex, end their illegal activities and restore *maryada*.

However, Parkash Singh Badal, in his speech, laid down a caveat: no use of force to evict these elements from the complex. This caution, as we will see in the following chapter, caused a split in the Akali Dal, after Operation Black Thunder I. For the first time since the launch of the morcha in August 1982, the Akali Dal and the moderate

Sikh leadership had shown the courage to publicly challenge the militants. This was an appropriate time for the Central government to strengthen the hands of the moderate Akali leadership for the fight against the radicals and the militants. Public opinion was with the moderates.

But political interests prevailed over the peace imperatives in Punjab. The Congress had lost elections in West Bengal and Kerala in March 1987 and now the elections to the Haryana assembly were due. The Congress needed to win Haryana. The Central government, therefore, was hesitant to project a pro-Punjab image by according concessions to the Barnala government. Result: The Longowal–Rajiv Accord was given a go-by. The first breach had already occurred on 26 January 1986, when Chandigarh was not transferred to Punjab on the appointed day.

The Central government thought Barnala's dismissal could send a positive signal to the Haryanvi voter that they had no reason to worry about the river-water share, the territorial readjustments and other pending interstate disputes with Punjab. The Barnala government was, therefore, unexpectedly dismissed on 11 June 1987, despite the fact that Barnala had taken on the militants and executed Operation Black Thunder I at Rajiv Gandhi's bidding.

Significantly, the announcement regarding the imposition of President's Rule in Punjab was made on the last working day of the then ongoing session of Parliament and just a few days before the electoral process was to start for electing the seventh Vidhan Sabha of Haryana. Darshan Singh, jathedar of the Akal Takht, the radicals and the militants publicly welcomed Barnala's removal. But Barnala's dismissal failed to woo Haryanvi voters—the Congress lost the election.

27

The Hindu Exodus

About fifty Hindu families from Tarn Taran village moved out to Karnal, without the civil administration knowing about it—we had been caught napping. There had been no intelligence alerts, nor had the grass-roots revenue officials sent any report. It was a collective administrative dereliction. The news of mass migration in the media set alarm bells ringing and I rushed to Haryana to persuade the Hindus to return to their homes in Punjab.

The migration had started from Batala, the industrial town in Gurdaspur district. On 20 February 1986, the terrorists targeted innocent civilians in this town. The situation assumed a communal colour when the supply of essential commodities to the town was stopped, by provoking the people of surrounding villages to lay blockades on all entry points to the city. Nearly thirty shops were damaged or looted and about seven factories were set on fire by the mobs. Curfew was imposed. The administration did succeed in controlling the situation, but the ineffectiveness of the system to protect the innocents got ingrained in the minds of the common man. Faith in the ability of the administration was further eroded when on 24 February, in a daring raid on the armoury of the Government Railway Police at Tarn Taran, terrorists looted sixteen rifles and over 400 cartridges, and escaped.

In Amritsar district, the migration began as a trickle in early 1986, first from the hotbed of terrorism, Fatehabad, and its adjoining villages, and slowly spread to other parts of the district. Suddenly, posters appeared in the villages asking Hindus to leave. In a few cases, prominent Hindus received threat letters. It was a chilling affair. In village after village, the militants would come, usually at midnight, mercilessly slaughter the targeted men and even women and children, fire warning shots in the air, occasionally raise slogans and disappear. They did not even spare the old and the infirm. Our sector scheme under which paramilitary forces were deployed to cover villages with Hindu habitations had not worked. Nor had the liberal grant of arms licences to Hindus or the setting up of village defence committees and *thikri pehra*, where all able-bodied men and those holding licensed weapons were voluntarily inducted to keep vigil.

It was a well-planned strategy of the ISI to sharpen communal polarization in Punjab. Pakistan-sponsored agents had started working on it in the early 1980s by planting cigarettes in gurdwaras and severed parts of cows in temples, but at that time, passions were modulated by saner elements in both the communities.

However, 1984 provided militants with the opportunity to trigger an exodus from Punjab, when victims of the anti-Sikh violence, after the assassination of Indira Gandhi, started converging from all over India to Punjab. By the second week of November 1984, some 50,000 of them had reached the state. Over 1,814 of them arrived in Amritsar in the first few days of November, hoping for help from the SGPC. They narrated horrendous stories of killings and that added to the prevailing social tension in the city. In December 1984, another 275 persons arrived from other parts of the country due to rumours that there could be fresh violence targeting Sikhs during the elections to Parliament. Some of them returned to their homes later. We were still struggling to settle those who had stayed back when the Hindu migration started.

When the violence increased, Hindus in remote villages, unable to dispose of their properties for there were no buyers, locked their homes, handed over the keys to their Sikh neighbours, who were equally helpless, and quietly slipped away with as much luggage as they could transport. Sikhs too lived under the fear of the terrorists, and many among them migrated too. By one estimate, Sikhs accounted for about 25 per cent of the total migration from rural areas to cities within Punjab.

On 7 May, in a targeted killing, terrorists pulled out six Hindus from a private bus near Hothian village in Tarn Taran and another three from a tonga and shot them dead. The sectarian violence was calculated to provoke a communal response. The Shiv Sena called for a bandh and I had to impose curfew in Tarn Taran to control the situation. On 30 May, night curfew was imposed in Jandiala, following the killing of two Hindus outside Balmiki Mandir where a Ramayana path was in progress. Rajinder Singh, then SP at Amritsar, and I faced a hostile Hindu mob at Jandiala that was protesting against the killings. Someone threw at us two petrol bombs from an upper storey of a building. We escaped by a whisker.

Then, in an audacious attempt that mocked the state authority, six armed terrorists leisurely walked through Krishna Nagar colony of Amritsar city on 21 May, spraying bullets. Eleven people were killed. An inquiry was ordered and the DIG of Jalandhar range, P.C. Dogra, found it difficult to fix responsibility—both the CRPF and the Punjab Police denied that it was their beat jurisdiction.

The regrettable outcome was that the two main communities looked at the two forces as pro or anti them. Hindus tended to regard the Punjab Police as derelict and deficient, if not conniving; the Sikhs looked at the CRPF as obtrusive and unfriendly. Given the terrible scenario the forces found themselves in, both were, in fact, performing an arduous and high-risk job reasonably well, but partisan public perception about them became another one of our problems.

By the end of May 1986, the wheat procurement operation was over. Many Hindu *arthias* (commission agents) in the small towns, once free from their professional grain-procurement commitments, just vanished overnight. In some cases, they left without paying the farmers for their crops and I would receive representations seeking criminal cases against them. It further aggravated tensions.

We saw polarization of the population at its worst in Amritsar when eight Hindus were killed by terrorists in a nearby village on 20 June. Other Hindus took to the streets. The police had to fire in the air and one person, unfortunately a Hindu, was killed. That triggered mob violence and arson, with six stabbing incidents. Sikhs became the target in the bandh call given by the Rashtriya Suraksha Samiti, the Hindu Shiv Sena, Brahmin Sabha and a few trade and business associations. Durgiana Mandir became the hub of their activities.

Our predicament was compounded by an unhealthy competition amongst Hindu organizations; each adopted a more strident stance than the other to garner a greater following and mass base among the community. At times they clashed among themselves and on one occasion, the president of the Hindu Rashtriya Sangathan, Surinder Kumar Billa, shot at the local Shiv Sena chief and the president of the Brahmin Sabha, Kishore Chand, after a heated argument. The bullet missed Kishore Chand, but an innocent bystander, Kapoor Chand, who had come to the Durgiana Mandir, was hit.

In Patiala, a radical Hindu, Pawan Kumar Sharma, who was later detained, vitiated the environment, resulting in communal clashes. Strangely, a few Congress leaders, including the chief minister of Haryana, Bhajan Lal, and P.C. Sethi, Union home minister, approached the then governor, Pande, to 'release Pawan Kumar'. Pande has recorded, '. . . [T]hese extreme Hindu communalists were being helped by the highest Congress (I) circles in Delhi and elsewhere.'[1]

The bellicose posture of these new-fangled Hindu organizations was making the BJP and RSS look not only moderate but also redundant. A.B. Vajpayee, the BJP president, in fact, as early as 23 March 1984 at Kolhapur, while addressing the media, had accused the Congress of being responsible for the emergence of the Hindu Raksha Dal and the Hindu Party. He charged Indira Gandhi, the then Prime Minister, of 'deliberate' delay in addressing the Punjab problem to garner Hindu support for her party.[2] On his visit to Amritsar on 19 August 1984, Vajpayee repeated the charge, while addressing a public meeting at the Arya Samaj Mandir, that the then ruling party was creating conditions to divide Hindus and Sikhs.

The BJP, RSS, Congress and Akalis all had endured violence in Punjab—the BJP lost its state president, Hit Abhilashi, who was killed in 1988, and the RSS lost twenty-seven of its *swayamsevak*s in one go in June 1989 in a shooting at Moga's Nehru Park, where they had gathered for the daily shakha. These tragedies caused social tensions, but the BJP stuck to the slogan: '*Hindu–Sikh nu ladan nahin dena; san santali hon ni dena* [We will not let Hindu–Sikh combat, nor allow 1947 to repeat itself].'

Years later, I accompanied Chief Minister Badal when he called on the then Union human resource development minister in the Vajpayee government, to seek his help to celebrate the tercentenary of the birth of the Khalsa as a national event in 1999. The minister, while promptly consenting to Badal's entreaty, added, 'Badal Sahib, had there been no Guru Gobind Singh, today you would not know me as Murli Manohar Joshi, but as Murli Mohammad Khan.' However, in the 1980s, the shared heritage and history of the Hindus and the Sikhs had faded into oblivion.

In May 1986, I ordered a survey of the district to quantify the migration numbers. The survey reported negligible outward movement from Ajnala and Baba Bakala sub-divisions, and some migration from Patti. However, the figures from the Tarn Taran sub-division were alarming. Small towns and villages like Fatehabad,

Chola Sahib, Dera Sahib, Goindwal and Khadoor Sahib were the worst affected. At Fatehabad, out of about 100 Hindu families, only a handful were left behind. By the end of August 1986, about 548 Hindu families had abandoned their homes in Amritsar district. It was estimated that out of these, a little over 200 migrated for good. Some, unable to adjust to the alien environment of the new places, came back.

By November 1986, it was estimated that nearly 1,253 Hindu families had left the state, settling mostly in Haryana, and some in Delhi, Himachal Pradesh and Uttar Pradesh. By May 1987, the number swelled to 2,149 families consisting of 9,720 members who had migrated to Delhi alone. They were provided temporary tenements with basic facilities like free medical care, water and electricity, in addition to a fixed monthly financial assistance.[3] It was not even 0.1 per cent of the state's Hindu population, but then it was not a question of numbers or ratios. The notion of cross-migration was sinister; it reminded one of 1947.

I made two visits to Karnal, which had the largest concentration of migrants from my district, to persuade them to return. On the second visit, led by Tara Singh Layalpuri, a minister in the Barnala government, and accompanied by S.L. Kapoor, the financial commissioner (revenue) in charge of relief and rehabilitation, we faced a hostile crowd at the brahmin dharamshala. Our persuasion failed to bring them back, except for four families of government employees. The people did not feel secure enough to return.

To infuse a sense of security, Julio Ribeiro, then DGP, Punjab, revamped the sector scheme in May 1986, with each sub-division coming under the charge of a CRPF battalion. The commandants of the battalion were made personally accountable within their respective jurisdictions, and day and night patrolling was augmented. But the killings continued. It was suspected that the terrorists had made the marshy Mand their hideout. The riverine Mand area in Amritsar district stretches along three sub-divisions—Baba Bakala, Tarn Taran and Patti. The militants, camouflaged in inaccessible reaches covered by thick, stubborn elephant grass during the daytime, would appear mostly at night and, after committing crimes, disappear into the wetlands.

Most of the Mand area is inaccessible by land, and approachable only by boats, making the task daunting for the security forces. The area is formed by the confluence of the Sutlej and Beas rivers, and spreads over many districts—Amritsar, Kapurthala and Ferozepur. In this complicated curbing of crime, inter-district coordination issues would come up, making it easy for the militants to slip from one district into the other.

The international border with Pakistan is not far from Harike, the barrage over the Sutlej river. The army had combed the area as part of Operation Woodrose in 1984. Paramilitary forces again scanned it in May 1986 without any significant outcome. However, in July 1986, based on specific intelligence inputs that two terrorist groups (one led by Avtar Singh and the other by Bhor Singh) had made Mand their base, an operation was launched under the command of S.S. Virk, then DIG, CRPF, and Izhar Alam, SSP, Amritsar. Helicopters provided logistical support, while the troops combed the riverine Mand area with boats and on foot through the narrow pathways. However, no militant was nabbed.

The failure of the operation emboldened the militants. They ambushed a Punjab Police party at Chola Sahib on 31 August 1986. Thereafter, supported by a massive contingent of the Punjab Police, a joint operation by the CRPF and BSF was launched on 9 September. A permanent CRPF picket was established in Mand to deter terrorists—but it didn't lead to cessation of the militants' violent machinates or an end to the Hindus' torment. In fact, the terrorists retaliated by waylaying a CRPF petrol party near village Siru in Tarn Taran on 19 November. Four jawans were massacred, and the terrorists escaped with their weapons.

Sadly, the year 1986 ended in a string of killings. I received an anonymous call on 17 December. The caller conveyed an ultimatum: Stop fake encounters or we will kill officers' children. The first thought that crossed my mind was the safety of my own family. I had two nursery-going toddlers and they travelled without guards. Only a few days earlier, terrorists had gunned down the SP of Amritsar H.S. Kahlon's nineteen-year-old son on the Guru Nanak Dev University campus. I cautioned my batchmate Izhar Alam, SSP, to take precautions and alert police officers who had school- and college-going children.

Two days later, they struck in the heart of Amritsar city. Arun Kumar, son of police inspector Brahmdev Sharma, was shot dead as he cycled to school. The killers escaped on a scooter. A caller, claiming to be Sukhdev Singh Babbar, then a notorious militant, rang up soon after to claim credit for the killing. He had the temerity to demand that the police stop the killing and torture of 'innocent' Sikh youth, as he put it, failing which they would face more murders of their kin.

Sharma was a god-fearing policeman, and was not involved in any encounters, fake or otherwise. People reacted to the killing of his son and the Hindu Shiv Sena, Arya Samaj, Brahmin Sabha, Rashtriya Suraksha Samiti and the Durgiana Temple Committee enforced a bandh in the city, resulting in stray incidents of mob violence. Educational institutions were closed and curfew imposed in parts of the town. Noticeably, when Kahlon's son Ravneet Singh was killed by militants only a few days earlier, there was no public outcry. Polarization, it seemed, had divided the people even on the matter of children's deaths.

On 14 December, terrorists had killed Dr Kewal Kishan Bhatia, a BJP leader, and three others in Vijay Nagar, Amritsar. Curfew had to be imposed in parts of the town following mob fury. It became a pattern—killings, mob outrage, curfew and then the next killing. It went on.

All these unfortunate occurrences, however, had only one consequence: They caused deep insecurity among the people, particularly Hindus, who felt that terrorists could kill at will and the state was utterly ineffective. Barnala, when he was chief minister, and thereafter Governor S.S. Ray and his wife, Maya, would invariably air-dash to Amritsar after each major incident to console the bereaved families, carrying compensation cheques, but that was all they could offer. They would spend time comforting the grieved, but that was of little help to frightened families who would nevertheless abandon villages for towns, at times beyond Punjab.

However, by 1987, there was a perceptible shift. It wasn't that the killings stopped—Hindus were still being targeted by the militants—but there was now a jump in the number of Sikhs being murdered by the terrorists—196 Sikhs were killed in 1987, as against sixty-six the previous year. There were two main reasons for this. Criminals, outlaws and malefactors had swelled in the militant ranks. For them, extortion, lootings and money outweighed religion or any ideological commitment—as a matter of fact they had no ideology or doctrine to go by.

Secondly, wanton killings, brutal excesses, forced stays at homes in villages for food and shelter had alienated the rural population. Fed up with violence, people started sharing information with the police about militants' movements and hideouts. For these reasons, the Sikhs, who in any case outnumbered Hindus in the villages, were now outrageously targeted. At times, after killing the innocent, the terrorists would set their victim's homes and property on fire to convey a message to perceived police informers.

The Sikh killings got so bad that the self-appointed Council of Khalistan in March 1988 issued an advisory to the different militant establishments to stop violence against Sikhs and mercifully also against women, children and the innocent. Even the three militant groups—Khalistan Commando Force (KCF), Khalistan Liberation Force (KLF) and the Babbars—denied involvement in the killings of innocent people. Instead, they all conveniently blamed the government for engineering these incidents. The panthic committee on 8 March censured the Black Cats Commando Force of Khalistan, a militant outfit, for violence, calling it a government front organization. It even 'authorized' the killing of the self-appointed chief of the Black Cats, one General Jagrup Singh.

The senseless violence unleashed by the militants had cost them support in rural areas. That explained the new public posture adopted by militant outfits. However, killings and murders of innocents, regardless of religion, did not stop, but a subtle shift in strategy was discernible. Illustratively, at Chogawan, a small town not far from Amritsar city, a well-respected and dedicated Hindu headmaster of a government school was not killed or threatened but instead issued a handwritten missive, a kind of demarche, graciously acknowledging his good services and counselling him that it was time he left Punjab! Public image, it seemed, now mattered to the militants, for they were losing people's sympathy—essential to survive and operate in the flat terrain of Punjab, with no jungles or mountains to hide in.

The people were also becoming bolder. In April, at the Jastarwal village near the international border with Pakistan, a group of armed militants killed eight Hindus, but had to face stiff retaliatory fire from the thikri pehra contingent, the voluntary group of armed villagers. The villagers engaged the militants for almost an hour till the CRPF party reached the site. This was unheard of earlier.

Similarly, when, on the intervening night of 31 March and 1 April, eighteen Hindus were gunned down at Theh Rajba village in Patti sub-division, and another six at Shahid, some of the militant organizations, including Pakistan's ISI-supported Gurjit Singh's faction of the AISSF, denied their involvement in the crime and blamed 'government agencies'. Earlier, they would take the credit for such killings.

The Hindu migration, worrying as it was, was a passing phase. It ended with the end of militancy and most of the Hindu families returning to their ancestral bases. The historic Hindu–Sikh bond continues to flourish and the percentage of the Hindu population in the state has increased since then. When extremism began in 1981, Sikhs were 60.75 per cent of Punjab's population and Hindus 36.93 per cent (as per the 1981 census figures). In 2011, the census figures show that Sikhs were 57.69 per cent and Hindus 38.49 per cent. The Sikhs were able to bring down their population growth rate from 11.8 per cent in the period 1991–2001 to 8.4 per cent during 2001–11, and that primarily accounts for the decline in their numbers, though immigration abroad and migratory labour coming to Punjab from other states have also contributed to the Sikh population's percentage going down. The harmonious environment and tranquillity that characterized the state from the 1990s has helped all communities reap the benefits of peace and proliferate.

28

The Hindu Terrorists

TERRORISM HAS NO RELIGION. THE WORDS 'HINDU TERRORISTS' may conjure up in your mind images of gun-wielding Hindu groups daring Sikh militant outfits as a counter force. Far from it. The Hindu terrorists were in fact the Hindus who joined the Sikh cause to wield weapons and slaughter Hindus and Sikhs alike. They were as secular (read indiscreet) in picking their targets as their Sikh comrades.

The Punjab militancy was not a monolithic movement, nor did the terrorists have a common background. Diverse elements and individuals with equally diverse motivations constituted this amorphous movement, commonly described as an ethno-national struggle. The only factor common among them was violence camouflaged as '*haki hinsa*', or violence for their rights. Otherwise, their social roots, origin, ancestry, motivation, objectives and even religion were not always the same.

The number of Hindus who joined the militancy was not too large but they were projected as 'dharmi soormas' (religious warriors), who had converted to Sikhism out of conviction and taken to arms for the cause of the panth. This may have been true in few cases, but what motivated most of them was either unemployment, the lure of easy money or the thrill and adventure of 'gun power' that added some value to their commonplace, colourless existence. In a few cases they just got sucked in when their Sikh friends joined militant groups; they merely strode along with them into militancy or were coerced into it.

In those days, it was not uncommon for young Hindu boys in interior rural areas to grow beards and sport turbans to disguise their identity. Slipping into terrorism was but a few steps forward. The sociological realities of rural Punjab aided matters—socio-economically cohesive, here the cause of one community easily becomes a concern of the other. Many Hindus were hurt by Blue Star just as much as Sikhs and that made their emotional, if not physical, involvement easy.

Their engagement with guns would usually start in their days as overground workers, acting as guides or couriers of messages and material, including weapons, or to recce routes to check police deployment, etc. Once they were entangled in such seemingly innocuous tasks, there was no going back. The only way forward was to do bigger things either because of fear of their militant peers, indoctrination, easy money or a desire to settle personal scores.

The life span of these squaddies, like their Sikh comrades, was rarely more than a few years. And when they died, it would usually be in bloody gun battles with the forces or in rare cases by consuming cyanide. As their last rites, their comrades would organize a bhog ceremony just as they would for the Sikh terrorists.

Towards the end of the 1980s, the practice of inserting advertisements in newspapers to eulogize militants as shaheeds of the quam became common. The objective was to attract people to bhog functions, build goodwill for the cause and create an aura of martyrdom around the kharkoos. The 'martyrs' and their services to the panth were recognized by conferring siropas on their next of kin, and in some cases extending financial assistance. In the case of prominent militants, calls for bandhs and hartals were also given.

What is baffling is why so many Brahmins became fighters for the Sikh cause. Brahmins in Punjab, unlike some other parts of the country, had long been marginalized from their exalted status under the varna system. In the social stratification of rural Punjab, the peasant–proprietor had dislodged the Brahmin and usurped their dominant position. Was this the reason that the Brahmins emulated the Jat peasantry, which provided the bulk of terrorists? Probably. Sociologists and anthropologists may have a more detailed explanation.

However, a few life stories of these combatants would illustrate their individual motivation in taking to arms. Among the seemingly genuine conversions was Roshan Lal Bairagi, a Brahmin from Varpal village in Amritsar. His was one of the earliest instances of a proselyte. Under the influence of a Sikh seminary, he converted to Sikhism and was soon sucked in by militancy. Later, he married Nirpreet Kaur, a young Sikh girl from Delhi, a victim of the 1984 riots whose father was killed in the Delhi carnage against Sikhs. Roshan Lal, enraged by the tragedy she had undergone, got more and more involved in violent acts. While on a visit to Delhi, he was arrested and in late December 1986 is said to have 'escaped' near the Beas from police custody, a euphemism for those who have not been traced since then.

Similar is the narrative of two Brahmin brothers, Vishnu and Prem Kumar. They belonged to Jamalpur village near Chowk Mehta, Bhindranwale's headquarters. They were swayed by the ideological indoctrination of the seminary, partook amrit and became devout Sikhs. Vishnu joined the dreaded KCF, and Prem Kumar, who became Panthjit Singh, joined the Khalistan Armed Force (KAF). Both met the end terrorists are destined to meet—death.

The list of Brahmin converts to terrorism is long but there were many non-Brahmin Hindus too who swelled the terrorist ranks.

Rakesh Kumar, a well-employed salesman near the Beas, became Ranjit Singh. His life story shows how your surroundings often suck you in, instinctively, almost unnoticed. He was leading a normal life with no apparent reason to prompt him into the militancy. However, his job had stationed him in a rural area, where the militants operated at will. That brought him in contact with the kharkoos. Once, he was waylaid and mugged of his hard-earned money. The next time he decided to do it himself and joined the KCF. He was accused of over a dozen murders, and eventually met the same fate himself. Penury, unemployment and living on the fringe turned some others towards the alien cause.

Such stories are many. Suffice it to say that most of them were arrested or killed by 1993, when Punjab turned peaceful and fresh induction into militancy stopped.

29

Declaration of Khalistan

We had no intimation of the visit of Chief Minister Surjit Singh Barnala. It was unscheduled and sudden. At 11 p.m. on 29 April 1986, the local IB unit alerted S.S. Virk, the SSP, Amritsar, that the chief minister and a few VVIPs were reaching the Raja Sansi airport at 12.30 a.m. on 30 April. It was a confidential mission and due to this reason the usual protocol arrangements were to be dispensed with.

I got in touch with the principal secretary to the chief minister to get the details, but he had none except that the chief minister was in Delhi for a meeting of the National Development Council. In those days, though technically an international airport, Raja Sansi had very few civilian flights and these too were confined to the daytime. The only international flight was operated twice a week or so by Ariana, the Afghan airlines, carrying cargo and some passengers travelling on cheap tickets to Europe via Kabul. The airport would close early in the day and the place would go dead by sunset.

Virk and I, therefore, hurried to Raja Sansi, 11 kilometres out of Amritsar, unaccompanied by the usual paraphernalia, and got the airport functional. The airport officer had been informed that a BSF plane from Delhi would land, but was unaware of its occupants. As the aircraft taxied to a stop, Virk and I stood at the tarmac waiting for the VVIPs to alight. But instead, we were summoned inside the aircraft. Arun Singh, minister of state for defence, and Arjun Singh, vice-president of the Congress, were accompanying the chief minister. With them was R.T. Nagrani, director general of the National Security Guard (NSG).

J.F. Ribeiro, who had joined in March 1986 as DGP, Punjab, was touring the neighbouring district of Gurdaspur that day. Late in the night, a message had directly gone to him from Delhi regarding the chief minister's visit and he reached Raja Sansi at about 2.30 a.m. on 30 April.

The declaration of Khalistan by the panthic committee on 29 April in a press conference held in the Golden Temple complex was what had brought the chief minister and his companions at this unearthly hour to Amritsar. That day, in the afternoon, the DIG (security), Punjab, had contacted me, seeking confirmation and details of the developments in the temple. The IB had alerted the police headquarters about the panthic committee's press conference.

I had no information and, as usual, the district administration was not in the IB loop. The district police control room too was oblivious of the goings-on. The office of the SP, CID, was walking distance from the temple complex, but these plainclothesmen were marked by extremists and they rarely risked going inside the complex.

In 1984, the army action had cleared the temple precincts of militants, but since then they had reoccupied some of the rooms. They moved in and out of the complex unhindered, and as it was risky for policemen to be seen inside the temple, Harjit Singh, SP, CID, had to largely depend on his sources among SGPC employees and a few press correspondents for information. So, when I called him for details, he gave me his standard reply, 'Sir, the press people are still inside the temple. I will brief you once they come out.'

Singh was true to his word and soon I had the details. The panthic committee, the militant's executive body created to parallel the statutory SGPC, lead the ethno-religious struggle and provide it with an institutional framework, had declared the formation of the sovereign state of Khalistan.

The committee did not delineate the geographical limits of Khalistan, nor did it name its president or prime minister. However, it notified the formation of its armed force, the KCF under General Hari Singh, an assumed name after Maharaja Ranjit Singh's famous Sikh General Hari Singh Nalwa, to confer historical legitimacy on the new force. Manvir Singh, a proclaimed offender, was designated as 'General' Hari Singh.

In an act of bravado typical of terrorists, the committee proclaimed war against India and pronounced that the kesari flag would flutter atop the Red Fort. To sweeten the announcement, it was declared that the state policy of Khalistan would conform to the philosophy of the Sikh Gurus '*sarbat da bhala*', universal brotherhood and well-being of all.

The committee circulated a ten-page signed statement to the media appealing to the United Nations and foreign countries, including Pakistan, to recognize the new state. At the end of the press conference, the correspondents were not permitted to leave the room till the members of the panthic committee slipped out of the temple precincts, disappearing into the narrow, serpentine lanes of the old city. Years later, two members of the panthic committee 'managed' to migrate abroad and at least one of them, Dhanna Singh, has freely given interviews to journalists and researchers.

Bhindranwale, during his lifetime, had refrained from preconizing Khalistan. He was conscious of the fact that it had no popular base among Sikhs and therefore would never forthrightly demand it, but would play with words—'I do not seek Khalistan,' he would say, 'but if the Government of India wants to give it to Sikhs that is its choice.'

In what turned out to be his last interview before his death on 3 June 1984, the noted journalist Subhash Kirpekar asked him, 'Do you support the creation of Khalistan?' The sant replied, 'I never opposed it; nor have I supported it.'[1]

Bhindranwale, however, had unequivocally declared that the foundation of Khalistan would be laid the day security forces defiled the sanctity of the Golden Temple. The sacred space of the temple, thus intertwined to the ethno-national movement, lent the movement its 'holy' credentials. Blue Star provided the militants with the opportunity to pursue the cause of Khalistan and a section among them pressed the leadership to formally pronounce its formation. It was argued that the Sikh cause would proliferate only if it had a perceptible political objective: Khalistan.

However, there was no unanimity among them as a section opposed the move, more as a strategy than an ideology. They argued that Sikhs had no resources to secure Khalistan—wanton killings of innocent people or terrorizing the civilian population would not achieve anything. This group also apprehended that a formal declaration of a sovereign state would provide an alibi to the government to suppress the militants with an iron hand and that would push the movement underground, whereas it would serve the Sikh cause better to remain political and overground.

It was Dr Sohan Singh, a retired director of the Health Service, Punjab, who ultimately tilted the decision in favour of the declaration. He had organized several brainstorming sessions at Chowk Mehta, and influenced the Damdami Taksal and the panthic committee to make the formal proclamation of sovereignty. He is said to have drafted the ten-page Khalistan statement released to the media on 29 April. The panthic committee chose the venue of the temple to make the announcement for reasons of security and to lend religious affirmation to the declaration.

After the declaration of Khalistan, Dr Sohan Singh crossed over to Pakistan, and was arrested in 1992 from Nepal, though the record shows that the formal arrest was made at Mohali. He was jailed but later released in 1995, after observing due process of law. He died in 2012 at the ripe age of about ninety-eight. His son, Swaran Singh Boparai, a decorated IAS officer (Padma Shri, Kirti Chakar), was my immediate neighbour at the secretariat in 1982. I was serving as joint secretary in the Department of Education in those days.

With the formation of the panthic committee and the declaration of Khalistan, a facile unity had been achieved among the factionalized extremist elements. They now had a common objective and an unswerving cause. That, for the time being, brought them together under the banner of one organizational structure and posed a direct challenge not only to the Indian state, but also to the statutory SGPC and the traditional Sikh leadership. It also provided legitimacy to the separatist cause and its accompanying violence.

The martyrdom of stalwarts like Bhindranwale and Amrik Singh lent a certain charisma to the cause, but it also created a vacuum in leadership. Unlike them, the panthic committee members lacked credibility. They also lacked ideological moorings and were neither preachers like Bhindranwale nor political ideologues. Mere religious zealots who had taken to the gun, and operating only within their respective localized geographical areas, none of them could provide pan-Punjab leadership. Owing to these reasons, soon, parallel panthic committees and many militant organizations emerged. The Khalistan movement, which lacked popular support, was doomed to die due to its internal conflicts even before it really took off.

Entry Allowed

In those days, Amritsar was never without anxious movements. While we were grappling with the Khalistan declaration, Virk was chasing terrorists in Tarn Taran. Some unidentified militants had snatched a Fiat car at gunpoint near Bharowal village and killed three persons at about 12.45 p.m. on 29 April. Virk was informed of the developments in Amritsar and he was quick to return to the headquarters. In the meantime, executive magistrates and the forces were alerted to guard against any possible reaction from the Hindu community, particularly the volatile elements of the Shiv Sena.

To keep the chief secretary posted of the happenings, I rang up P.H. Vaishnav. He said he would get back to me, which he did at about 5.45 p.m. on 29 April to convey the chief minister's directions after consulting him. Vaishnav quizzed me, 'Have you understood what the chief minister wants?' I responded, 'Yes sir, no entry into the temple.' Almost as an afterthought Vaishnav added, 'Double your chase outside, these guys cannot disappear into thin air.'

Between 5.45 p.m. on 29 April 1986, when the chief secretary conveyed the chief minister's instructions of 'no entry' into the Golden Temple complex, and 12.30 a.m. on 30 April, when Barnala arrived at Raja Sansi, the chief minister changed his mind. He was in Delhi and the Central government pressed him to conduct an operation to clear the militants from the temple complex. Barnala acquiesced reluctantly. To ensure that he did not rescind, Arun Singh and Arjun Singh accompanied him at midnight to Amritsar from Delhi.

Sitting inside the small aircraft at Raja Sansi, Virk and I apprised them of the situation, and confirmed that the panthic committee and other known terrorists had left the complex apprehending State action. Police intervention in the temple complex would not yield militants at this stage. But Arun Singh was emphatic—a signal must go to the extremists and to the common citizen of the government's zero tolerance of secessionist activities, he said. The police, therefore, must enter the temple.

But, it was not the first time that Khalistan had been declared from the temple precincts. On 12 January 1984, Balbir Singh Sandhu, the self-styled secretary general of the Council of Khalistan, who had made room number 32, Guru Nanak Niwas, in the temple complex, his home since 1980, held a press conference announcing that on India's Republic Day, 26 January 1984, the Council of Khalistan would hoist the Khalistan flag and notify its constitution. On 26 January, a flag purportedly of Khalistan was duly unfurled atop Guru Nanak Niwas and a document titled 'Constitution of Republic of Khalistan' was released to the public. Punjab was under President's Rule, but neither the advance information given on 12 January nor the subsequent actual declaration of Khalistan on 26 January stirred Delhi or Chandigarh. This, even though the Akali Dal chief Longowal had unequivocally condemned the release of the 'Constitution of Khalistan' by Balbir Singh and called it a 'stunt'.

However, more as a formality rather than any effective affirmative action, two communications were issued, one by A.S. Pooni, home secretary, and the other by Ajay Pal Singh Mann, SSP, Amritsar, supplicating the SGPC to 'hand over' Balbir Singh Sandhu to the police in the two cases registered against him. One of the communications implored the SGPC to discourage such activities in the future. Avinashi Singh, the assistant secretary, SGPC, replied to the government that Balbir Singh had not been seen in the temple complex since 27 January. That was the end of the matter. This, in fact, epitomized the state response to Khalistani manoeuvres prior to Blue Star, and some political commentators have imputed motives to this ambivalent approach.

Now, however, the government instructed prompt entry into the temple to apprehend the militants. Virk needed time—he was short of manpower and sought forty-eight hours to mobilize police and paramilitary forces. The Government of India had anticipated this and sent Nagrani, the director general of the NSG, along with Barnala. While ordering the NSG–police entry, Barnala, however, unequivocally qualified that the forces shall not go inside the Harmandir Sahib or fire towards it.

That settled the scope of the operation—flushing out the militant elements and illegal weapons simultaneously from the Golden Temple precincts, Gurdwara Baba Deep Singh in Amritsar and the historical gurdwara at Tarn Taran. Barnala and the others flew back to Delhi at 4.15 a.m. on 30 April, and we got working on the operational plan for what is popularly known as Operation Black Thunder I.

30

Operation Black Thunder I

Operation Black Thunder was on. The NSG commandos, led by two major general—Naresh Kumar and Mankotia—landed at the Raja Sansi airport on the afternoon of 30 April 1986. In fourteen sorties, the aircrafts ferried about 1,500 men, eighty officers and 180 JCOs. NSG commandos numbered 300 and the rest belonged to the paramilitary forces.

It was to be a joint operation of the NSG, paramilitary forces and the Punjab Police. The Punjab Police and the paramilitary forces were assigned to deal with any possible militants in Gurdwara Baba Deep Singh, the gurdwara at Tarn Taran and the buildings in the Sarai complex of the Golden Temple that included Guru Ram Das Sarai, Guru Nanak Niwas and the Teja Singh Samundri Hall that housed the administrative branches of SGPC and the residential accommodation for visiting pilgrims. The NSG had a more onerous assignment: to flush out militants, if any, from the main temple complex, which included the langar building, Manji Sahib Diwan Hall, Ramgarhia Bunga, Parikrama and the sacred spaces including the Akal Takht.

Starting at 3 p.m., curfew was imposed in the eighteen localities around the Golden Temple. The forces encircled the entire area in a layered cordon. As far as possible, we wanted to avoid the physical entry of forces into the temple, and therefore made repeated announcements, appealing to all those inside to come out.

The first leg of the operation commenced in daylight, around 5 p.m., as the Punjab Police and paramilitary forces carried out a thorough search of the Akal Rest House, Sri Guru Ram Das Sarai, Teja Singh Samundri Hall and Guru Nanak Niwas. A few small weapons—revolvers and pistols and one 12-bore gun with a few cartridges—were recovered and about 120 people were taken into custody. Most of them were released after screening. Not a single bullet was fired and this part of the operation was over peacefully by 7 p.m.

Half an hour later, fresh announcements on the public address system were made around the Parikrama, appealing to the pilgrims and others to come out. Bhai Gurdev Singh Kaunke, jathedar of Akal Takht Sahib, reacted to the appeals and asked the pilgrims not to leave the temple. He prodded them to resist the forces and if need be sacrifice their lives in the tradition of the Khalsa. Fortuitously, his chivvy had little impact. About 100 persons, mostly pilgrims, walked out of the complex from the Ghanta Ghar Deori.

The NSG established a control room on the rooftop of the three-storey building of the Braham Buta Akhara (encampment), with the cooperation of its head, Mahant Sant Sarup. This akhara of the Udasi sect (literally meaning a stoic or a mendicant) abuts the Parikrama near the Ramgarhia Bunga and provides a panoramic view of the temple complex. We—the two NSG major generals, Julio Ribeiro, D.S. Mangat, IG, operations, P.C. Dogra, DIG, Jalandhar, C. Paul, DIG, CRPF, S.S. Virk and a few other officers—assembled at the control room by 8 p.m. The NSG demanded a formal requisition and Ribeiro signed it on behalf of the state government, with a copy endorsed to the district magistrate. Ribeiro's missive read, 'I, hereby, on behalf of the Punjab Government, requisition the services of personnel of National Security Guard in aid of Civil Authority on 30 April 1986, in Punjab, to assist in countering the terrorist activities in the state.'

The NSG commandos in black dungarees, their heads and faces covered with dark scarfs, looked menacing. They were to enter the Parikrama barefoot at 10.30 p.m. Electricity supply was turned off and it was pitch dark. However, the operation was halted due to a message from G.S. Bhatti, the executive magistrate on duty at Police Station Kotwali. He reported that the observation posts around the temple had spotted the movement of men in large numbers on the roof of the Harmandir Sahib, which has a high parapet that provides perfect cover. Harjit Singh, SP, CID, confirmed that Gurdev Singh Kaunke and his men had moved from the Akal Takht to the sanctum sanctorum; they were armed and could fire at the troops. We shared the information with the NSG.

P.C. Dogra cautioned the generals that the NSG commandos would be vulnerable to sharpshooters from the rooftop but should not fire back towards the Harmandir Sahib. He requested the generals to sensitize his men on the issue before they entered the Parikrama. This invited a sharp reaction from the NSG officers, who were not willing to constrict the options of the troops. An argument followed. The NSG general lost his cool and retorted, 'My men are not statues. If fired upon, they shall fire back.'

My intervention and reasoning about the sensitivity of Sikh sentiments did not help either; the general had his reasons but as the tempers heated up I had to tell him, 'I, as district magistrate, withdraw the state government's requisition. You pack up and go back from where you all came.' There was palpable disquietude.

Ribeiro, however, was wiser. He put a call through to Barnala and to Delhi, who endorsed our standpoint. That, in any case, was Barnala's brief to us. The generals now fell in line. The operation, which was to begin at 10.30 p.m., was delayed by over an hour.

The commandos entered the langar building and Manji Sahib simultaneously. They fired stun grenades—these are non-lethal, high-resonance projectiles producing blast-like sounds and occasional flashes and sparks, akin to high-calibre weapons. They shook up the area; the pitch and timbre were frightening. In the darkness, the occasional blinding flare accompanying the blasts could momentarily disorient anyone and that was the objective: to catch the terrorists off-guard. The commandos trudged through the two buildings, but in an anticlimactic end, there was not a soul inside. The place had been abandoned.

The second leg of the operation in the Parikrama, however, was tragic. The commandos footslogged from two sides. The first group entered from in front of the langar building and the second went towards the Akal Takht from the side of Bazar Muniaran. As the first group advanced along the Parikrama, Gurdev Singh, a young boy of about sixteen–seventeen years, ran out from near the memorial of Baba Deep Singh Ji. He failed to respond or halt to the calls of the commandos, and was fatally fired at.

Four others who suffered bullet injuries were lucky to escape death. Sotin Das was a blind vagrant who had taken shelter for the night near the Dukh Bhanjani Beri. Munir Alak, a thirty-five-year-old Bangladeshi Muslim, was biding his time in the complex for an appropriate opportunity to attempt an illegal crossover to Pakistan. Bangladeshis came in hordes and the temple complex was an agreeable, free boarding house. The BSF would push them across the international border, at times by providing diversionary cover fire, in retaliation to attempts by Pakistan to push in smugglers and terrorists. Often, Pakistanis would frustrate attempts by the Bangladeshis to cross over, landing them in the Amritsar jail; we didn't know what to do with them. Repatriation procedures were agonizingly slow.

The two others injured, Nishan Singh and Harjit Singh, were SGPC sewadaras on duty. The commandos had challenged Nishan Singh to raise his hands but he instead slipped his hand in the side pocket to pull out his SGPC identity card, which the commando mistook as a move to pull out a weapon. Harjit Singh was on duty at the Darshani Deori. He pushed open the wicket gate to step out and invited a burst of fire, but was lucky and survived. There was no loss of property inside the temple complex, except minor damage to the two doors of the rooms in the Parikrama. However, sparks from a stray stun grenade gutted a shop owned by one Tejinder Singh which abutted the complex. He was suitably compensated, as were the injured and the heirs of the deceased.

The NSG completed the combing operation of the Parikrama and the rooms along the verandah around the circumambulatory passage by 1.30 a.m. and wanted to hand over charge to the local administration. Their task, they said, was over. However, the men ensconced in the sanctum sanctorum, reportedly armed, were yet to be dealt with. We could feel the general's glee over our predicament when he brushed us aside saying, 'Deal with them yourself. My mandate was not to fire or enter the sanctum sanctorum.'

That mandate applied equally to us. Stuck, we resorted to making appeals. The public relations van parked outside the Ghanta Ghar Deori made ardent announcements on the public address system to those inside the Darbar Sahib not to defile the sanctity of the Harmandir Sahib and to come out. The repeated announcements, however, had no effect.

The Risky Task

We had two options: either allow the NSG into the sanctum sanctorum, after withdrawing the 'no firing' caveat, or linger with the siege, waiting for the militants' endurance to run out. Neither of these alternatives was appealing. Any delay in ending the operation would have given an opportunity to the radical elements to provoke people to march towards the temple, and that would have further complicated the sensitive situation.

At this stage, Virk and I decided to take a risk. Together, we stepped into the Parikrama, unarmed and unaccompanied by anyone. Carrying a hailer pulled out from the public relations department van, we climbed down the Ghanta Ghar Deori stairs into the open, white-marbled expanse. Two of us, both over six feet tall, stood there exposed from all sides, in direct line of fire of the militants—one sharpshooter could have got both of us.

I rested the loudspeaker on the edge of the sarowar and in chaste Punjabi disclosed our identities and announced our intent. I emphasized the imperative of maintaining the maryada and sanctity of the temple and assured the militants that no harm would come to anyone. With the preliminaries over, I concluded, '*Me Sangat nu benti kar da ha ke Darbar Sahib to bahar aa jaan* [I request the congregation to come out of Darbar Sahib].' No response came from the other side.

In the still of the night, I feared the worst, but kept repeating my appeal at the interval of a few minutes. By now it was around 4 a.m. Suddenly, we noticed some movement on the roof of the sanctum sanctorum. Someone was waving a cloth to catch our attention in the darkness of the night and yelled, 'We have no faith in you. Call Giani Puran Singh.'

Puran Singh, a temple priest, was held in high esteem by the extremists. His house was near Kaulsar Bazar, not far from the complex, but he did not respond when a police officer was deputed to summon him. Finally, Virk and I went to his house and brought him with us to the Parikrama. With Giani Puran Singh standing next to us, I made fresh announcements from across the sarowar. There was no response. Giani Puran Singh was, therefore, persuaded to go inside the Harmandir Sahib as an emissary, and to Giani's credit he was courageous enough to go alone. He failed to secure a surrender, but was successful in convincing Jathedar Gurdev Singh Kaunke to depute his representatives for negotiations with us.

Sitting in the Parikrama, Virk and I, assisted by Puran Singh, impressed on the five representatives the futility of holding on inside the Darbar Sahib. Religious ceremonies had already been disrupted and Waheguru would hold them accountable, we said. Our persuasion paid off and they agreed to bring all the people out. In the Sikh tradition of '*panch parvan panch pardhan*' (decision of the five chosen ones is final), all 135 persons walked out of the sanctum sanctorum in a single line, without anyone firing a shot. It was a peaceful end to a perilous situation. Gurdev Singh Kaunke, along with his aides, was arrested and the temple was cleared of the radicals.

Those who came out were made to sit in rows in the open in front of the Akal Takht Sahib. Thirty women and children emerged and were set free. The men, however, were detained for screening. They had been inside the Harmandir Sahib for over eight hours, and now made a beeline for ablutions. As the first group went out of the gate near the Nishan Sahib, the CRPF pickets on the roofs of adjoining buildings opened fire—they thought the militants were escaping. Providentially, no one was hit.

The operation was over by 6 a.m. and the temple's religious ceremonies were restored. Giani Kirpal Singh, who was 'sacked' from his post on 26 January 1984 by the Damdami Taksal's Sarbat Khalsa and had not been able to enter the complex since then, paid his obeisance for the first time on 2 May, along with Giani Sahib Singh, head priest of the Darbar Sahib, and Giani Pritam Singh, head priest of the Akal Takht.

These three high priests in a signed press statement welcomed the restoration of maryada in the temple complex. It was an indirect endorsement of the action, an implied linking of NSG entry into the temple to a decision taken at the Sarbat Khalsa held at Anandpur Sahib on 16 February 1986, where it had been decided to evict the militants and radicals who had occupied the temple forcefully. Barnala and a few of his Cabinet colleagues and Kabul Singh, president of the SGPC, also visited the temple on 2 May.

The security forces withdrew from the precincts before daylight. However, plainclothes policemen inside the Golden Temple complex were retained for over two months. The frisking of pilgrims by the police before entry into the complex continued for even longer.

The operation netted fifty-five persons of various hues of extremism. The police registered FIRs against them under the IPC and the TADA Act, including against the militant-appointed jathedar of the Akal Takht, Gurdev Singh Kaunke, and Surat Singh Khalsa, former secretary, United Akali Dal.

The operation at other gurdwaras, including Tarn Taran, yielded two grenades and a few small arms but no terrorists. Some unauthorized occupants were evicted from Gurdwara Ramdas Ji and its control was restored to the local management committee.

An unintended yield of the operation was the invaluable experience gained by NSG commandos on how to operate in the sacred space—it was this familiarization with the temple precincts, sensitization to the religious sensibilities and exposure to the foolhardiness of the militants that came in handy when they were recalled in May 1988 to execute operation Black Thunder II. The government had not given any sobriquet to the present swoop, but as a precursor to the 1988 operation, it is popularly called Operation Black Thunder I.

31

Barnala Excommunicated

THERE WAS A TREMBLE IN HIS HANDS. CHIEF MINISTER SURJIT Singh Barnala sat on the ground, cross-legged, his head bowed and hands folded before the high priests. He had been accused of sacrilege and had submitted himself before the ecclesiastical court of the Akal Takht. His offence: He had ordered the NSG and the police operation in the Golden Temple on 30 April 1986, and thus defiled the sanctity of the sacred space.

Barnala had been summoned by Giani Kirpal Singh to tender an explanation. The irony was that Jathedar Kirpal Singh himself was persona non grata till 30 April and could not venture inside the temple precincts for months.

Operation Black Thunder I had restored normalcy within the Golden Temple precincts, at least for the time being, without the bloodbath that sullied Blue Star. Unlike Blue Star, which had provoked a strong reaction in the Sikh community, there was no pronounced public outcry against Operation Black Thunder I.

After all, it had reinstated the high priests to their legitimate positions and re-established the institutional authority of the statutory body, the SGPC.

But post–Operation Black Thunder I, the circumstances changed almost overnight and with that the normal political manoeuvring and factional politics was back in full strength. The SGPC-appointed priests were back in the saddle and had now summoned the chief minister, whose action had enabled them to resume their duties as priests.

This was the story of Punjab; whenever terrorism peaked, the overground leadership, both political and religious, would capsize or duck and make itself unavailable. However, once some semblance of normalcy was restored, the traditional factions of Akalis would launch into power struggles against each other. And that is what they were up to now: Barnala's political opponents were targeting him, or rather his chief ministership, and they had a plausible theological justification of the police and NSG entry into the temple to pull him down.

Initially reluctant to proceed against Barnala, the high priests were targeted by the radicals. They buckled under their pressure and summoned Barnala to the Akal Takht to explain his conduct. On 8 May, the high priests, stung by media reports that accused them of having colluded with the government for ordering police entry into the hallowed space, released a joint press note denying that the NSG operation had had their tacit approval. They dubbed the operation 'tragic and unfortunate' and emphatically denied that they had 'justified the police entry'. The statement emboldened Barnala's political opponents and religious zealots, who increased pressure on the priests to proceed against Barnala for the sacrilege.

On 15 May, the jathedars met and issued a show-cause notice to Barnala, holding him 'personally accountable' for the 'untoward incidents' that had occurred inside the complex. He was summoned to Amritsar on a notice of two days. Giani Kirpal Singh spoke his heart out to me: It was imperative to silence the zealots and political dissidents for the sake of unity of the Akali Dal and more importantly for the institutional dignity and sovereignty of the Akal Takht, he said. Harking back to history, he recalled that even Maharaja Ranjit Singh had surrendered to the supremacy of the Takht. Who, then, was Barnala? Barnala was in trouble.

On the appointed day, 17 May, the chief minister, accompanied by some of his Cabinet colleagues, appeared before the five high priests[1] at the Jhanda-Bunga Gurdwara and pleaded his innocence. He submitted a written plea signed by him in his capacity as president of the Akali Dal, stating that the Sarbat Khalsa held on 16 February 1986 had resolved to restore the dignity of the temple complex and put an end to the unlawful interference of militants in the management of Sikh affairs by the SGPC. He pleaded that he had only complied with this decision by clearing the precincts of militants and restoring the authority of the SGPC.

His pleas were: Terrorists had declared war against the Indian Union on 29 April, and things had gone too far. He submitted that the lives and properties of Sikhs could have been at peril in various parts of the country as a reaction to the declaration of Khalistan. He bemoaned that his political opponents were exploiting the incident for their selfish interests and concluded by submitting that as a humble Sikh and a servant of the house of the Guru he would gladly undergo any punishment, should the priests hold him guilty of any religious breach.

While Barnala's trial proceedings were in progress, there was a commotion outside the Ghanta Ghar Deori. A crowd had gathered to protest against Barnala. Virk and I had stationed ourselves outside the Darbar Sahib for security reasons. We made an earnest effort to calm down the crowd, but our intervention invited louder sloganeering and aggression.

Then, suddenly, the Parikrama resounded with anti-Barnala slogans. A motley group of about thirty people, mostly women, had managed to slip in. Performing '*siapa*' of Barnala (wailing and shrieking, with hand gesticulation), they shouted 'Khalistan Zindabad' slogans.

As the crowed pushed forward menacingly, the CRPF had to be called in. The uniformed and armed men entered barefoot from the side of Gurdwara Thara Sahib and pushed the crowd back towards the Darshani Deori. The CRPF formed a protective ring around Barnala and escorted him out after he had finished with the proceedings.

The five priests gave Barnala a patient hearing and after he finished making his submissions, they were ready with the verdict within fifteen minutes. Their hukamnama pronounced Barnala guilty of ordering the 'tragic' and 'painful' police operation. Importantly, the verdict referred to Barnala as the president of the Shiromani Akali Dal and to his official designation as chief minister. Therefore, the verdict was against the chief minister of the state—in any case it was his official conduct in that capacity that had provided the cause of action against him.

The jathedars awarded him tankha, directing Barnala to undertake five *sevavan* (services) as atonement for his misconduct. The sevavans were: performing one akhand path at the Akal Takht; undertaking daily recitals of the Japji Sahib twenty-five times; offering Rs 501 at the Akal Takht; dusting the shoes of devotees for one week at any gurdwara; and offering karah prasad of Rs 102 at the Akal Takht at the time of ardas. With folded hands, Barnala accepted the verdict.

On reaching the Circuit House, Barnala held a press conference. He claimed that he was not declared guilty or awarded any tankha, but merely assigned sevavan, which he had accepted as a devout Sikh and as the president of the Akali Dal, carefully avoiding any reference to his official position as chief minister. Kabul Singh, the president of the SGPC who was present at the venue, showered praise on Barnala for upholding the glory of the panthic traditions.

Barnala's political opponents cried foul and alleged that he had been let off mildly by the priests; he should have been removed from the twin posts he held. They even protested against the sevavan he had been given, dubbing it as benign and accommodating, not equivalent to his transgression. Jathedar Kirpal Singh dismissed these as accusations of the ignorant. The Takht awards religious punishment, not temporal or political and profane penalties, he said. Besides, the Takht was supreme and no one could question its verdict. That would amount to contempt of the ecclesiastical court.

For seven days, Barnala performed the atonement services, including cleaning shoes of devotees at gurdwaras at Anandpur Sahib, Chandigarh, Fatehgarh Sahib and Delhi. After a week-long compliance with the directions of the Akal Takht, Barnala again appeared before the congregation, paid his obeisance, and thereafter stood discharged of his religious blemish. But the dissident Akali leaders had managed to discredit and delegitimize his rule in the eyes of the Sikh masses. The Congress leadership, however, was happy, as they had been waiting for the right opportunity to deal with Barnala—he had served their purpose and outlived his utility.

Political Dissidence

The challenge to Barnala now came not only from militants, but from dissident moderate Akali leaders of his own hue. Barnala had provided his political opponents an opportunity to paint him as a traitor of the quam. Black Thunder I was described as Barnala's Blue Star; his opponents alleged that there was no better affirmation of Indira Gandhi's foray into the temple than Barnala's iteration.

There were, of course, vital elementary differences between the two operations. In sheer scale of the carnage, and in death and destruction, Blue Star was horrendous. Black Thunder I was a deft operation, with minimal human suffering. The issue, his opponents argued, was not the human agony the two operations caused, but the sacrilege of the temple. The dissident Akalis believed and publicly propagated that Operation Black Thunder I had extenuated the trauma and alienation of Sikhs. They were now to split the Akali Dal (Longowal) into two factions.

But a tactical failure on the part of Barnala helped the opponents within his party. After reaching Chandigarh on 30 April from Amritsar, he had convened his Cabinet. The ministers discussed the emerging situation at Amritsar threadbare and unanimously resolved to fight terrorism to the finish. However, in a bid to maintain the secrecy of Operation Black Thunder I, Barnala did not disclose to his colleagues the sally he had commandeered into the temple. The Cabinet met and dispersed, in ignorance of what was brewing in Amritsar. Secrecy was a security imperative, but nevertheless a constitutional impropriety—a Cabinet swims or sinks together.

A few hours later, when the news of NSG entry into the temple became public, Amarinder Singh, agriculture minister, who had in 1984 resigned from the Congress in protest against Blue Star, complained that he learnt about Operation Black Thunder I from his tailor! Amarinder resigned from Barnala's ministry and so did the education minister, Sukhjinder Singh, and Sucha Singh, minister of state. Tohra and Badal quit the executive committee of the Akali Dal in disapproval of the police action.

Barnala made desperate attempts to win over the dissidents. Amarinder had rushed to Amritsar in a private vehicle from Patiala. Barnala was frantic to trace him, but no one knew his whereabouts, not even the CID. My general assistant captain, Narinder Singh, who had served in Amritsar district for long and had his contacts at the right places, located Amarinder and Ravi Inder Singh, former Speaker, and shared the information. But Amarinder was firm—his conscience did not permit him to serve the sacrilegious Barnala government.

Late in the night on 2 May, Amarinder and Ravi Inder Singh drove to my official residence. A journalist had alerted me that Amarinder was inquiring as to who had taken the decision to storm the temple, and which of the Central ministers had accompanied Barnala to Amritsar from Delhi. It was too close to the event and my bureaucratic duty inhibited me from sharing the information with anyone outside my official hierarchy. So, I decided that the best course of action was to not meet Amarinder Singh and Ravi Inder Singh. They had to return from my house without meeting me. Amarinder is not the kind to forget, nor did he, when he became chief minister years later. But that is a tale for another book.

On 8 May, Amarinder was dismissed from the Akali Dal for anti-party activities. A group of twenty-seven Akali MLAs led by Badal formed an independent group in the Legislative Assembly and emerged as the Akali Dal (Badal). The Barnala group, reduced to a minority with only forty-six MLAs, became dependent on Opposition parties, primarily the Congress, for survival.

Badal, Tohra, Amarinder and other dissident moderates now joined the AISSF, Damdami Taksal and some militant groups on the second anniversary function of Operation Blue Star on 4 June 1986 in the temple complex. The congregation expressed a lack of confidence in the SGPC-appointed high priests and endorsed the militant-appointed Gurbachan Singh Manochahal as jathedar of the Akal Takht.

Badal and Amarinder were to again keep company with the militants at the Fatehgarh Sahib Jor Mela on 27 December 1986, where 'a resolution demanding Khalistan was adopted by the AISS (Gurjit Group) endorsed by a show of hands at a highly charged venue', as Amarinder's biographer describes, and that 'the decision made it clear that the objective of the Sikhs was attaining "Khalistan" and the moderate Akali leaders who came in the way would meet the fate of Longowal'.[2] The ideological lines were clearly redrawn in the battle to gain political supremacy—if it meant cohabiting with the radicals and militants as a strategy, so be it.

Earlier, on 30 November 1986, Tohra was re-elected the president of the SGPC, defeating Barnala's candidate Kabul Singh by seventy-four to fifty-eight votes with the support of the Badal faction. In this power struggle, Barnala, dubbed '*Rajiv de chele* (protégé of Rajiv)', lost one more moral battle to lead the panth. His tragedy was that even Rajiv opted for politicking and, as we saw later, Barnala was abandoned by the Congress too.

Kabul Singh had taken a public stand that 'there could not be a blanket ban on the entry of police in Sikh religious places' and 'the police entry depended on the circumstances'.[3] The SGPC had raised a task force of about 134 men, mostly ex-servicemen, to police the temple complex. The SGPC and the district police armed these men with licensed weapons and a retired army officer, Brig. Mohinder Singh, mentored the force. It was to deter the militants and keep them out of the temple.

How with time the roles had changed. Brig. Mohinder Singh, now accommodated as chairman of the local improvement trust by Barnala, only two years ago was part of an ex-army cabal along with Brig. Jaswant Singh, Maj. Gen. Narinder Singh and Shabeg, guiding Bhindranwale.

Retired Sub. Maj. Joginder Singh was in charge of the task force in the temple; its deployment eliminated the need for presence of plainclothesmen inside the temple, which was always an irritant with the sangat. The task force performed well and helped to nab a few radicals from the complex. However, one of its personnel, Avtar Singh, was hacked to death inside the temple complex by the militants.

On Tohra's election as president, SGPC, on 30 November, one of the first announcements he made was to disband the task force under pressure by radical elements. Consequently, weapons and militants slowly seeped back into the complex. Tohra's election as president of the SGPC was not correlated to the killings, but on the same day, as if to sound a victory bugle, a group of terrorists massacred twenty-four Hindu bus passengers near Khudda in Hoshiarpur district, and injured many more.

Outside the temple, the militants had all along been active. Earlier, on 10 August 1986, General Vaidya was murdered in Pune. He was

Chief of Army Staff during the 1984 Blue Star operation. Ribeiro was fired at from automatic weapons inside the secure Punjab Armed Police complex at Jalandhar on 3 October 1986 by jeep-borne militants in police uniforms. He was lucky to escape but a CRPF constable, Kuldeep Raj, was killed.

In December 1986, the Tohra-led SGPC sacked the high priests as they were perceived to have let Barnala off the hook lightly. In their place, Prof. Darshan Singh, who, unlike the earlier jathedars, was not an employee of the SGPC but a well-respected ragi, was appointed the jathedar of the Akal Takht, while Giani Puran Singh, the pro-radical priest, joined as the head priest of the Golden Temple. The two other jathedars—Giani H.S. Mahalon of Keshgarh Sahib and Giani Lakha Singh of Damdama Sahib—departed a month later, in January 1987. With this, the high priests of Blue Star vintage faded into history.

On 26 January 1987, yet another Sarbat Khalsa was organized at the Golden Temple, in the presence of the newly appointed high priests led by Prof. Darshan Singh. It re-affirmed the earlier declaration of Khalistan. Prof. Darshan Singh genuinely believed that he could unite not only the different factions of the Akali Dal but also the multiple militant groups by adopting a radical posture. So he actively dabbled in politics and justified it in the historical context of the indivisibility of Miri and Piri.

On 5 February, as a process to unite all Sikh political groups, Prof. Darshan Singh announced the formation of a Unified Akali Dal (UAD) under Simranjit Singh Mann, who was languishing in jail then. He disbanded all the Akali factions and directed them to merge with the UAD. Barnala, however, refused to oblige and was declared tankhaiya on five grounds, the primary charge being that he did not resign, as directed by the priests, by 5 p.m. on 5 February 1987. Barnala perceived the jathedar's move as an attempt to remove him not only as president of his party, but also from chief ministership.

He was ex-communicated from the Sikh panth on 11 February 1987 by the jathedars.

Barnala ignored his ex-communication for nearly two years but submitted before the Akal Takht on 5 December 1988 after dissolving Akali Dal (L). This time, Prof. Darshan Singh, who had been reappointed jathedar of the Akal Takht for a second time, made an example of Barnala. He was fastened to a pillar with a placard around his neck, wherein Barnala declared himself the sinner and the Akal Takht the *bakshanhaar*, the pardoner. Barnala was directed to perform five akhand paths, and to teach him humility, made to scrub langar utensils, clean shoes of devotees and mop the gurdwara floor for seven days. He was finally readmitted to the panth on 25 December, with Prof. Darshan Singh removing the placard from his neck. Ironically, Prof. Darshan Singh was also ex-communicated from the panth by the Akal Takht in January 2010 for religious misconduct.

The unintended outcome of Prof. Darshan Singh's initiatives was the reassertion of militancy in the temple complex. This time, on their return to the complex, the militants relaunched the 'extortion operation' with greater precision. They would dispatch threatening letters, posing a challenge to the State.

In fact, the militants had never really left the precincts; they would temporarily disappear under police pressure, only to reappear. The police had raided the residential part of the temple on 18 January 1987 and rounded up a few suspects, but it was always only a pro tem suspension of militant activities—within days they would be back in business. Plainclothesmen on surveillance duty often became their victims.

On 7 March 1987, Davinderejit Singh, a head constable on duty, was kidnapped and detained in Room No. 47 of the Parikrama. He was tortured and when four unarmed plainclothesmen were sent in to rescue him, after taking the SGPC into confidence, they were fired at. Head Constable Sukhdev Singh died. Constable Sucha Singh and Lakhwinder Singh lay bleeding in the Parikrama, while the injured Constable Gurinder Singh managed to escape and inform the superiors waiting outside. The police entered the complex and on conducting a search, recovered ammunition. The militants were using the room as a torture chamber.

The gains of Operation Black Thunder I, if any, had clearly been lost. The competitive politics of the moderate Akali factions contributed to it as much as Khalistani asseverations of the militant groups and the political manoeuvres of the Central government.

32

The Do-Gooders

Baba Amte lay flat on a stretcher in a van, with an impaired spine. That is how he had traversed nearly 5,000 kilometres from Kanyakumari, covering an average 50 kilometres per day, starting late in 1985. The assassination of Indira Gandhi and the violence that followed had set this octogenarian disciple of Late Vinoba Bhave on a 'Bharat Jodo' campaign, to foster public opinion for peace, culminating in his mission in 1986 coinciding with the United Nations' International Year of Peace.

He held roadshows, public symposiums and corner conclaves, persuasively cautioning his audience that the struggle for Independence had been a comparatively straightforward affair because Indians knew who the enemy was, but the challenges of national integration were far more complex. It was a fight 'within ourselves', he would say. Punjab worried him. He covered the state extensively during the 'Bharat Jodo' tour and came back to Amritsar in July–August 1986, to initiate a dialogue with the terrorists, to convince them and to persuade them to take the path of peace. He genuinely believed he could do that.

I offered to organize an interaction with some militants in custody in the Amritsar jail, but he wanted to have face-to-face sessions with the free, gun-wielding ones. At grave personal risk he reconnoitred the countryside, hoping to meet the militants and persuade them to bring about peace.

He camped for a few nights at Fatehabad, Tarn Taran sub-division, then the hotbed of militancy, at the home of a farmer perceived to be a hardliner, hoping the militants would get in touch. I was concerned about his safety and met him a couple of times to persuade him to accept a discreet security cover, but he declined. By the time he left the district, he had met a large number of people, including local leaders, opinion-makers, peasants, relatives of bereaved families and victims of terrorism.

However, the terrorists shunned him. He went to Delhi and met the Prime Minister, but was disappointed that the government had only a police solution to the problem. He returned to Amritsar again and called it a 'lonely mission of love', but was soon disillusioned with the lack of response from all parties. His peace efforts were recognized with the Padma Vibhushan in 1986. He left Amritsar distressed, only to plunge himself into his next mission: the Narmada Dam.

The Hero

A man who evoked an enthusiastic response was matinee idol Sunil Dutt. His family had left its home in Jhelum district of Pakistan's Punjab for Bombay, but this Bollywood hero's heart was with the Punjabis—a '*dard ka rishta*', as he liked to say. His superstar status and the Congress connection evoked a ray of hope. He had joined the Congress in 1984, and was an MP. No one thought a busy actor would footslog from Bombay for seventy-eight days, covering 2,000 kilometres without the mandate of his party high command.

Or that Priya Dutt, his daughter, would miss her final-year BA examination at Sofia College, Bombay, to stride along with her father for nothing.

So, when on 11 April 1987, Dutt reached Rayya, the entry town to Amritsar district on his Maha Peace Yatra, with badly blistered feet and after losing 15 kg, there was an air of expectancy. Hindus and Sikhs alike swarmed the roads to cheer him. He spent the night at the ramshackle British-era Canal Rest House at Rayya, where I met him. My tactful queries failed to elicit if his mission had the blessings of Delhi. 'I am on a pilgrimage,' was all he said. The impression I got was that he would fizzle out, the way Amte had, though in the end Dutt did do a little better.

On 13 April, Dutt left for the Golden Temple early in the morning, supporting a saffron patka on his head. He was received by a large crowd, the air reverberating with cries of '*Bole so nihal*'. After attending the akhand path near the Dukh Bhanjani Beri that had been started for the success of his mission, he held an open session with Prof. Darshan Singh and some of his colleagues in the presence of acting SGPC chief Harinder Singh.

Dutt proposed a negotiated settlement with the government. Prof. Singh agreed, but qualified that the negotiations be held with the 'boys', meaning the militants. The jathedar also wanted that the right environment be created first, which meant a ceasefire before the talks, release of the Jodhpur detainees, reinstatement of the dharmi faujis, etc. Looking meaningfully into his eyes, the jathedar told him that if Delhi does not listen, 'you join us'.

Dutt's second scheduled meeting was an hour-long, closed-door affair with Baba Thakur Singh, Bhindranwale's successor at the Damdami Taksal. The third meeting in the negotiations was also a closed-door do with the 'boys' of the KCF, who provided security cover to the MP inside the temple. In those days the KCF held full sway in the temple complex and had emerged as the most dominant weapon-wielding group under the umbrella of the panthic committee, with strong links to the Gurjit Singh faction of the AISSF. Gurjit Singh was in direct touch with Pakistan's ISI. Later, Julio Ribeiro was to accuse the professor of letting the gun-toting militants surround Dutt, while the radicals objected to Dutt having accepted the police security while he was, they claimed, their protectee.

In the three meetings he held, Dutt engaged with the three power centres of the Sikh struggle—the jathedars–SGPC, the Damdami Taksal and the militants. However, before facing the press and the public, he wanted to be sure of what would be acceptable to the government. So he telephoned the Prime Minister seeking a settlement with the militants, but was instead advised to restrict himself to the usual diplomatic homilies. In the few interviews and the public congregations that followed, Dutt diagnosed the Punjab problem as a hurt Sikh psyche that needed a healing touch and appealed for national unity. Before leaving Amritsar, he stated that he had firmed up the terms and conditions of talks with the militants and the jathedars, and was ready to play negotiator between them and the Central government.

The Jain Saint

In conflict situations, resolving disagreements is never easy, but for the politicians, rather than the resolution, it is often the credit for it that is more crucial. Buta Singh, the home minister, had been the prime mover for the Congress in Sikh affairs. So, how could Sunil Dutt be allowed to steal the show? So, Buta Singh pushed forward Acharya Sushil Muni, the Jain saint, in the negotiation game. The acharya landed at Amritsar close on the heels of Dutt's sojourn, on 6 May 1987, accompanied by the old warhorse, Tarlochan Singh Riyasti, a former state minister.

When I met them at the Circuit House, Muni admitted that he was not an emissary of the Central government, but that he did have the blessings of the Prime Minister to negotiate and prepare the ground for a final settlement between the Centre and the militants. To establish his credentials with the militants, he got the CRPF men deployed around the Golden Temple withdrawn from within 200 metres of the temple. That was a precondition put up by the militants for talks. The order came directly to the CRPF through its own channel. Having thus established his credibility and earned goodwill among the radicals, Muni and the jathedar of the Akal Takht, Prof. Darshan Singh, met with much bonhomie.

The congeniality did not last long. Ribeiro, who was in Amritsar that day, ordered the redeployment of the CRPF. On 7 May, the uniformed policemen were back at their pickets before dawn. In protest, the jathedar refused to meet Muni the next day. Muni had to spend the better part of the day pulling strings with Delhi to get the CRPF men withdrawn a second time from the periphery of the temple. Capt. Satish Sharma, a close aide of Rajiv Gandhi, rang up, and instructions were conveyed to the force to keep their distance from the temple complex, without sharing a raison d'être, though almost everyone of any standing knew the reason.

The jathedar and Muni met again on 7 and 8 May, this time Justice A.S. Bains, a retired judge of the Punjab and Haryana High Court who had chaired a government-appointed committee to screen the cases of detained militants, and Baba Thakur Singh of the Damdami Taksal were also present. It was decided to hold talks between the Central government and the militants to resolve the Punjab tangle in the spirit of 'forgive and forget'. Muni agreed to the preconditions that all detainees in jails would be released unconditionally, army deserters would be rehabilitated and all paramilitary forces would be withdrawn from the state. Muni was to revert after confabulating with the Prime Minister.

In the meantime, a section of the state police, wary of these developments, fired a torpedo. A case of sedition was registered on 8 May against Prof. Darshan Singh for a speech he had given at Khalsa College on 27 February. The provisions of the TADA and IPC were applied. The official explanation for this sudden but much-delayed move by Izhar Alam, SSP, was that the legal opinion in the matter had been pending and had only been received now! Muni and Riyasti left grumbling for Delhi on 9 May, though Riyasti returned to Amritsar with Muni's secretary, Tej Parkash, in mid-June to carry the talks forward.

Barnala's government was dismissed on 11 May 1987, and Punjab remained under President's Rule till February 1992. Prof. Singh refused to meet Muni or his representatives again. He insisted that Muni should first fulfil the agreed preconditions for the talks now that the Union government directly administered Punjab. Despite Muni's assurance, there was obviously a lack of faith in Muni's capacity to get his word honoured by Delhi. That was the last we heard of Muni in Amritsar.

Tarlochan Singh Riyasti, unfortunately, met a gruesome end. A group of militants, who felt betrayed by an abortive peace deal, burnt him alive in his car in Ludhiana in June 1988. Sushil Muni, it seems, had sold a fresh peace dream to Prime Minister Rajiv Gandhi towards the end of 1987. An operation code-named 'Needle' was launched, involving Riyasti as a go-between. Through his underworld contacts, Riyasti had organized a meeting of Maloy Krishna Dhar, joint director of an intelligence agency, with a group of terrorists, namely Atinderpal Singh, Gurjit Singh of the AISSF, Avtar Singh Brahma, a dreaded killer, and some others. These facts are now in the public domain.

Under an agreement, the militants were escorted to Delhi and harboured at Sushil Muni's ashram, waiting for an appropriate time for a conclave with the Prime Minister. The meeting, however, did not materialize, but Sushil Muni and Satish Sharma met them. An understanding was reached that the Government of India would honour the Anandpur Sahib Resolution, comply with the unfulfilled terms of the Longowal–Rajiv Accord, grant general amnesty to the militants and strangely make an upfront preliminary payment of Rs 2 million to Gurjit Singh, to be delivered at Ludhiana.

Riyasti was to return to Delhi to collect the money, and when he contacted Satish Sharma, he is said to have backed out from the deal. Dhar wisely withdrew but Riyasti had no option; he had to return home to Punjab. When Riyasti met the militants at a pre-appointed rendezvous, he and his driver were both burnt alive in the car. To quote Dhar, 'Gurjit had gone mad not only over money but deliberate leakage of his trip to Delhi by some highly placed sources in Delhi.'[1] Dhar accused a member of the Rangreta Dal, a covert set-up floated with the blessings of Union Home Minister Buta Singh, for leaking the information to the panthic committee regarding the peace efforts. 'That was the height of treachery,' said Dhar. That, sadly, has been the tragedy of the cloak-and-dagger games played in Punjab.

There were also a few other men of God who made sanguine efforts to untangle the complex Punjab situation. One such person was Vishvesha Tirtha Swamiji of Udupi, who in March 1987 led nearly 400 sadhus from Har-ki-Pauri at Haridwar to Har-ki-Pauri at the Harmandir Sahib on a goodwill mission. He prayed for peace and on his return from Amritsar submitted a report to the Prime Minister, pleading for implementation of the unhonoured clauses of the Longowal–Rajiv Accord, greater autonomy to states and talks with the extremists. Sadhu Mohan was another such godman who came to Amritsar in July 1987 after undertaking a five-day fast at Delhi to seek release of the Jodhpur detainees. He met Prof. Darshan Singh, but without any outcome.

The valiant endeavours of these well-meaning men raised hopes and provided a much-needed diversion to the people from the daily news of death and destruction. However, these efforts did not yield a solution to the Punjab problem. Probably, the time for negotiation was not ripe yet. There was no unified command among the multiple terrorist groups, nor a central figure that could discipline the splinter groups and enforce any agreement that may be arrived at with the government. Prof. Darshan Singh's ability to bring them together was only nominal. The terrorists felt no pressure to negotiate, nor was the law and order establishment ready to give in. On both sides, the approach followed was bullet for bullet. But the oft-repeated refrain was to keep open lines of dialogue.

Prof. Darshan Singh earnestly strived to unite the Akali factions and bring the militant groups together. His endeavour was to bring a unity of thought around the common objective short of Khalistan. To this end, he organized a congregation at Amritsar on 4 August 1987, but was marginalized by the militant groups. The panthic committee and other militant groups thwarted his successive efforts and he had to abdicate his position; he tendered his resignation from the post of jathedar of the Akal Takht on 17 November 1987, which was later accepted by the SGPC.

The Militant Jathedar

The moderate high priests and even the pro-radical Prof. Darshan Singh had failed to unite the militant groups. Without such a unity, the chances of any negotiated settlement were dim. Maybe it was time to try one of their kind—a militant as the jathedar of Akal Takht? In 1988, that was the strategy adopted by the government.

Jasbir Singh Rode, nephew of the late Bhindranwale, was the militants' choice for the post of the jathedar of the Akal Takht in the Sarbat Khalsa organized on 26 January 1986, when the SGPC was 'dissolved' and its appointee high priests were 'removed'. However, Rode could not assume office at that time as he was underground. He had travelled to Dubai in 1977, ostensibly for business, and post–Blue Star had surfaced in Pakistan and London, indulging in radical activities. He was finally traced in Manila, from where he was arrested, brought to India and detained at Sagar and later in Tihar Jail, Delhi.

The intelligence agencies had a 'hook' in Rode from the early 1980s. Dhar has disclosed that in May 1981 he was mandated to establish links with Bhindranwale, and Jasbir Singh Rode became the conduit.[2] In a deal with Rode, he was released on 3 March 1988, armed with licensed weapons, and escorted on 5 March by Kalyan Rudra and Dhar, the two undercover officers, to Amritsar in a Second World War vintage Dakota.

On arrival at the temple, the militants, led by Nirwair Singh, welcomed him by indiscriminate firing in the air from an assortment of weapons amidst shouting of slogans like 'Khalistan Zindabad' and 'Bhindranwale Zindabad'. Seemingly, the militants were elated over his arrival in the temple, but some of them suspected Rode of being a government plant or otherwise regarded him as a threat to their pre-eminence. Consequently, conflict emerged within the militant movement within days of Rode's arrival in Amritsar.

To accord legitimacy to the accession of Rode, the SGPC was 'persuaded' to formally appoint him as the Akal Takht jathedar, which the executive committee did in its meeting on 8 March. To send a signal of its intent for the peace initiative, the Government of India also released forty Jodhpur detainees. Rode assumed office on 9 March 1988 on a positive note of support from the Government of India, SGPC, Akali Dal and a section of the militants. His brief was to persuade all the terrorist groups, including those seeking Khalistan, to arrive at a settlement.

Therefore, on arriving at the temple, to carry all the combatants along, Rode talked of 'Khalsa Raj' and 'Puran Azadi' for the Sikh quam, without defining what he meant by these. He kept his stand ambiguous and declared that it was up to the Government of India whether it would like to give 'Khalsa Raj' within or outside India.

The Khalistani groups with links to Pakistan were guided by their handlers to not fall in line with Rode. His ambivalent stand on Khalistan brought Rode into direct conflict with these strident sections of ISI-supported militants. The panthic committee and KCF chief Labh Singh openly accused Rode of being a government agent, while others like the Khalistan Liberation Organization questioned his motives.

To survive in this factionalized militant movement, Rode needed teeth and these were provided by a dedicated 'shaheedi' group that was propped up and armed with weapons, including AK-47 rifles, to support him. Rode was delegated to assert his way within the militancy's power structure; if weapons were required for that purpose, they were made available.

But, before this strategy could succeed, the inexorable dynamics of multi-combatant groups operating independent of each other overtook the plan and the Rode project came a cropper, as another NSG operation, named Black Thunder II, had to be launched inside the temple complex.

33

Operation Black Thunder II

Operation Black Thunder II was precipitously triggered on 9 May 1988, around 1 p.m., when DIG, CRPF, S.S. Virk's jaw was shattered by an AK-47 bullet fired by the terrorists from the periphery of the Golden Temple precincts.

Virk had just returned to Amritsar from Harsha Chhina village where the terrorists had massacred four persons the previous night. He received intelligence that the militants were constructing a battlement on top of a building in the temple area to gain a locational edge. The intrepid Virk proceeded for an on-the-spot inspection, accompanied by an equally committed Suresh Arora, then SSP, Amritsar (he retired as DGP, Punjab, in 2018), and a few other officers.

The spot where the militants were building the fortification is accessible through the narrow serpentine lanes at the western end of the temple. These streets are not negotiable by car, so the security forces abandoned their vehicles at a distance and proceeded on foot. As they approached a narrow lane in Chowk Darbar Sahib, the CRPF jawans manning a picket on top of a private building alerted them. Baldev Singh, SP City, Amritsar, who was also accompanying Virk, saw the militants take firing positions on another rooftop. He ducked and yelled, but it was too late for Virk—a bullet hit him in the face. He was evacuated from the narrow lanes on a borrowed scooter that Suresh Arora drove to the hospital.

The militants had always gravitated to the temple complex for religious reasons and because the precincts provided a degree of security against any sudden police action. By the beginning of 1988, most terrorist groups had a presence in the temple—the panthic committee had established 'Daftar Khalistan' in Room No. 14 in the Parikrama, the Babbars had their office in Room No. 26, the Bhindranwale Tiger Force of Khalistan operated out of Room No. 29 and the AISSF, KCF and KLF had also occupied numerous rooms.

Becoming bolder by the day, they had started erecting fortifications, reminiscent of the pre–Blue Star days. Observation posts that doubled as encampments were established on top of the twin towers of the Ramgarhia Bunga, which provided a commanding view of the entire area. The terrorists were facing the security forces at least at fourteen places on the high-rise buildings around the temple, which were manned by 49 Battalion of the CRPF under the command of Nand Lal. How the situation had been allowed to deteriorate under President's Rule—imposed a year earlier—and despite the level of maximum alert demonstrates the complexities of policing religious spaces perceived as existing beyond the temporal jurisdiction.

A flash point occurred on 29 April, when a suspected militant managed to slip into the complex from CRPF custody and in the resultant crossfire between the CRPF and the militants, one Swaran Kaur of Dhotian village, a devotee, was injured. In this skirmish, the terrorists suspected that the police-sponsored counter-insurgency group, the Panthic Tiger Force led by Santokh Singh Kala, had helped the security forces. This prompted them to hold a meeting inside the temple on 2 May, where they established a 'disciplinary committee' to maintain order that consisted of the representatives of KCF, Babbar Khalsa, KLF, AISSF and a nominee of Rode.

But unity remained elusive. A few groups opposed the move—Karaj Singh Thande of the Bhindranwale Tiger Force of Khalistan (BTFK), Jagir Singh and Nirwair Singh, the two well-known militants, a section of the Babbars and some in the panthic committee were not well-disposed towards the 'disciplinary committee'. The conflicts amongst these competing groups complicated the situation in the temple.

The stand-off with the security forces deployed around the temple complex could have lingered, but for the Virk incident. The ISI-sponsored Khalistani hardliners were not happy with the government initiative to formally induct Rode as a jathedar, as it had the potential to derail the separatist movement by uniting the militants and bringing them to a settlement.

Secondly, these hardliners were unhappy that criminal gangs had infiltrated the separatists and that was earning the ethno-national movement a bad name. These criminal elements—fortune-hunters, as I like to call them—had turned a section of the panthic crusaders into mercenaries. These elements were using the temple complex to indulge in crime—bodies were disposed of in the gutters behind the temple or just buried under the debris of the Akal Takht. After Operation Black Thunder II, several skeletons were recovered from under the rubble. Police entry into the Golden Temple, the hardcore Khalistanis perceived, would outrage the Sikh sentiment, and that would help to swing the focus of the movement back to the religious-ethnic leitmotif. Building of battlements in and around the temple was part of this design to provoke the security forces, and Virk became a victim of it.

The intelligence agencies had prior information, though not specific, of the terrorist plan to create trouble. Jasbir Singh Rode was tipped off about a possible strategy of the Babbars and the KCF 'to engage the police forces in action'.[1] Whether it was by design or a coincidence, Rode was removed from the scene of action in the temple complex on 8 May. He was summoned to collect a fresh consignment of weapons from Ludhiana to induct another fifty-odd armed men into his squad in the temple.

Rode was still in a rendezvous with the undercover operators somewhere in Ludhiana district when Virk was shot at. That is how he escaped the siege of the temple complex. He returned to Amritsar on 10 May, and at one stage the administration considered sending him inside the temple to persuade the holed-up militants to surrender; he consented to it. On 11 May, six emissaries carrying food went inside the temple to negotiate with the militant groups, but they weren't amenable to surrender.

Thereafter, a few journalists were allowed to go in and they interacted with Nirwair Singh and Jagir Singh, the two militant leaders, who, however, told the newsmen that 'they would continue to follow the path of Sant Jarnail Singh Bhindranwale and would struggle for Khalistan. The two warned that anyone who became an obstacle in the way of their struggle would be removed with a bullet.'[2]

On 12 May, the plan to allow Rode to go inside the temple was abandoned. The strategy now was to drive the trapped terrorists to fatigue. Rode, the other high priests, along with twenty-six followers, attempted to march into the temple, but they were arrested on 12 May following a scuffle with the officers. They accused the deputy commissioner and police officers of 'treachery', for having backed out from their commitment to permit them to enter the temple.

The SGPC authorities, in any case, were not happy with Rode and were waiting for an opportunity to remove him. The present developments provided them with a pretext. He was sacked on 30 May by the SGPC against the wishes of the administration. A rather aggressive last-minute intervention by Sarabjit Singh, my successor, and K.P.S. Gill to save Rode failed—it merely strained relations between the SGPC and the state at such a sensitive time.

The Operation

When Virk got shot at, the security forces deployed around the temple spontaneously opened retaliatory fire, and it continued intermittently till 6 p.m. on 9 May, killing three inside the complex and one in Chowk Muniara. A few more were injured.

Seven journalists, including the local BBC reporter, were trapped inside the temple due to the crossfire. They were escorted out of the Ghanta Ghar Deori with their hands raised by Swaran Singh Khalsa, office secretary of the AISSF, after nearly six hours of what must have felt like a nightmare. With them, a few devotees walked out too. Many more were still inside and the administration was concerned about their safety. Allowing the journalists to come out indicated that the militants were not planning to hold hostages.

As a precautionary measure, Sarabjit Singh imposed curfew in the walled city around 3 p.m. on 9 May, but there was no clarity on the plan of action, nor was there any coherence in the response of the security forces. Suresh Arora, once he was free from the hospital after leaving Virk in the safe hands of the doctors, sought Ribeiro's approval to storm the temple to apprehend the culprits, but was told to hold on for instructions from Delhi. The Central government continued to do a remote-control management of law and order in Punjab.

In the meantime, a crisis-management meeting chaired by Buta Singh, the Union home minister, at his office at Parliament House, decided to rush NSG officers to Amritsar. The troops were battle-ready and started arriving in Amritsar on the night of 9 May, under the operational command of Brig. Sushil Nanda. Maj. Gen. Naresh Kumar, who had led the NSG in Operation Black Thunder I two years earlier, was asked to monitor the operation from the headquarters at Delhi. The NSG established its tactical headquarters in a high-rise hotel that provided a panoramic view of the temple, while the CRPF and Punjab Police had their operational headquarters at the Braham Buta Akhara that overlooks the Parikrama.

Ribeiro and P.G. Halarnkar, DG, CRPF, arrived in Amritsar on the morning of 10 May. K.P.S. Gill, who till then was not contactable, arrived on the scene later. Gill had taken over as DGP on 20 April, when Ribeiro was elevated as adviser to the governor, but Gill was not traceable on 9 May. 'It was quite common for Gill to disappear in this manner without intimation to anyone. We overlooked this foible on the grounds that his security demanded total secrecy in movement,' writes Ribeiro in his autobiography.[3]

In the meeting with the local officers chaired by Ribeiro, a consensus evolved to tire the militants out by laying a siege for a few days. Ribeiro carried this recommendation to the Prime Minister and in a meeting attended amongst others by the governor, Punjab, P. Chidambaram, M.K. Narayanan, director, IB, K.P.S. Gill and Ved Marwah, DG, NSG, it was decided not to rush the forces into the temple. Marwah describes the strategy, 'To pin down the militants in their hiding places inside the complex by accurate long-distance sniper fire, and then step-by-step advance towards the Temple by first occupying the sarai and then the other strategic places.'[4]

This strategy wasn't different from the way Operation Black Thunder I was executed, except now the siege was to stretch over a few days. How many days? No one knew. The decisions were taken ad hoc, as the situation evolved, in brainstorming sessions among the officers. The local officers at Amritsar were constantly in touch with each other, while a core committee under the chairmanship of B.G. Deshmukh, the Cabinet secretary in Delhi, monitored the operation. The Prime Minister personally reviewed the developments, almost on a daily basis. He was wary of any adverse fallout of the operation, given the bitter history of Blue Star.

On the morning of 10 May, a ceasefire was announced to get the pilgrims out of the precinct. The militants made no move to prevent the people from exiting, and from what Sarabjit Singh told me, about 940 of them came out, mostly from the Sarai end. About twenty of them were suspected to be extremists and were detained for intensive interrogation. It was presumed that all the devotees had come out, but it was discovered later that some of them were still trapped inside.

Operation Black Thunder II was carried out by the NSG under the direct command of Brig. Nanda, who reported to Maj. Gen. Naresh Kumar. The request of K.P.S. Gill to place the NSG under his command was not agreed to. Nevertheless, Gill played an eminent role due to his domineering but perspicacious persona and understanding of ground reality. He emerged as the public face of the operation, and by the time it ended, his stature had grown taller than his 6-foot-plus frame. This helped the Punjab Police recover its public image, while the NSG stayed in the background.

Ved Marwah, DG, NSG, in a bid to find out what his men were going up against in the temple precinct, approached the Indian Air Force on 10 May to fly sorties, and identify and photograph the militants' battlements. As it turned out, there were only a few fortifications, unlike during Blue Star, when all the buildings in the entire periphery and inside of the complex had been fortified.

The militants' observation-posts-cum-encampments on top of the two towers of the Ramgarhia Bunga posed the greatest challenge to the NSG. The sky-high towers provided the militants perched on top a direct line of fire in all directions. These proved impregnable to the snipers and the LMG fire of the NSG commandos. Heavy machine guns were, therefore, flown from the army's Jabalpur ordnance depot to silence the towers. The troops also fired from portable anti-tank RCL rifles, making orifices in the bungas. These were the only military highlights of the entire operation. The militants, after the initial bluster and heavy firing on 9 May, had receded into a silence that was shattered only by the occasional NSG sniper fire.

The maryada at the Harmandir Sahib was disrupted from the afternoon of 10 May. The non-stop singing of hymns and recital of the gurbani, which commences daily early in the morning and continues till the departure of the palki sahib from the Harmandir Sahib to the Akal Takt at night, had stopped. And this was a matter of concern, since it could invite an adverse reaction from the Sikhs. The siege had not yielded the expected surrender till 13 May, despite the intermittent firing killing about twenty-four people. Six militants in a bold move even attempted to fight their way out of the temple on the night intervening 12 and 13 May, and two of them succeeded in escaping.

Considering the delay in winding up the operation, Governor Ray came to Amritsar on 13 May for a first-hand assessment and then flew to Delhi to reassure the Prime Minister that there was no backlash from the Sikh masses. Rather, people were critical of the conduct of the militants. The intelligence feedback endorsed this.

The Akali factions—Barnala, Badal and the UAD—did threaten to march to Amritsar to liberate the temple from the security forces, but these protestations were more to mark their political presence than to instigate an agitation. The Sikh masses were indifferent and Punjab did not witness any mass mobilization against the operation. The NSG, therefore, was permitted to persist with the siege.

Unlike Blue Star, when all telephones were disconnected, this time the lines were kept alive and even used for negotiations with the holed-up militants. Consistent communication with the militants conveyed the sincerity of the security forces to end the siege peacefully, and acted as a multiplier to win the battle of public perception.

On 13 May, the militants were sounded out in advance of a proposed ceasefire planned for the afternoon of 14 May, in consultation with Baba Uttam Singh of kar sewa fame. The Baba was supervising the gold plating of the Akal Takht dome and some of his men on watch duty over the gold were stranded inside. However, repeated surrender calls to the militants during the ceasefire between 3.30 p.m. and 4 p.m. on 14 May evoked no response—only four devotees came out of the temple. Nevertheless, the ceasefire reaffirmed the State's intent on a peaceful outcome of the operation.

On the night of 14 May, the Prime Minister again summoned Governor S.S. Ray, Ribeiro, K.P.S. Gill, Narayanan, Ved Marwah and a few others. In a strategic shift, he ratified to clear out the militants from the peripheral buildings of the precincts and to eliminate any armed militants seen moving around the complex. It paid dividends. The langar and Manji Sahib were cleared of terrorists by the NSG. The dreaded terrorist Jagir Singh and his companion were killed in sniper fire outside Daftar Khalistan—Room No. 14—their bodies lay in the open, reminding others of their likely fate. To build psychological pressure, the NSG exploded high-pitched light-and-sound-producing ammunition, which is otherwise not noxious.

This demonstrative firing of high-calibre weapons that created blasts and splashes of light worked. To give the militants a chance, Chaman Lal, IG, and Sarabjit Singh, who were stationed at Braham Buta Akhara abutting the Parikrama, announced another ceasefire on 15 May. This was followed by an appeal by Sarabjit Singh to the militants to come out. The men and women who had earlier been incommunicado now emerged from the rooms in the Parikrama. They were directed to walk towards the Guru Ram Das Sarai and 146 of them adhered to the announced instructions and reached the sarai, but about forty-seven militants deviated from the announced route.

A key catch among those who surrendered was Surjit Singh Penta, a dreaded terrorist of the BTFK responsible for nearly forty killings. His wife, Paramjit Kaur, had surrendered and was recognized by one of the intelligence sleuths. As the troops approached her to identify her husband in the crowd of those who had surrendered, Penta could foresee that his end had come. He was swift to take his own life—he consumed the cyanide capsule which most dreaded militants carried on their person. Before the CRPF doctor could reach him, Penta lay dead.

The forty-seven militants who did not follow the instructions to reach the Guru Ram Das Sarai swerved towards the Darshani Deori. Sarabjit made repeated announcements from the Braham Buta Akhara, directing them to stick to the specified route, but they ignored his calls and instead entered the Harmandir Sahib. The security forces were not permitted to fire towards them; not even warning shots or blank bullets that may have possibly deterred them from deviating from the prescribed route.

In the subsequent interrogations, it was revealed that Karaj Singh Thande had threatened to shoot anyone who did not follow him to the sanctum sanctorum. He was an ex-sergeant and had deserted the army in anger over Blue Star. On 18 May, when the militants finally came out from the sanctum sanctorum, he swallowed cyanide and died.

With the militants lodged in the sanctum sanctorum, the administration had a serious situation on its hands, the kind I had faced during Operation Black Thunder I, when the militants were ensconced inside the Harmandir Sahib, an area out of bounds for security personnel. Any damage to the hallowed sanctum sanctorum would have hurt religious sensibilities and evoked strong anti-State emotions. The saving grace was that none of the militants who entered the Harmandir Sahib were seen carrying guns, though the possibility of small weapons hidden under the togas could never be ruled out.

As the situation evolved, this setback turned out to be the tipping point to discredit the holed-up militants and their movement. In their three days of self-imposed confinement inside the sanctum sanctorum, the militants besmirched their cause by defecating within the confines of the holy place, the very divinity in whose name they were fighting. An unbearable stench of human excreta hung about the place by the time it was cleared of militants. The militants, and not the NSG, were now seen as the culprits who had defiled the sacred space. The uniformed personnel, in any case, did not enter the Parikrama throughout the operation, and the media persons perched on top of the high-rise buildings around the temple were witness to the restraint exercised by the NSG.

When the holed-up militants finally surrendered on 18 May and meekly plodded out of the temple in a single-file formation with their hands raised above their heads in broad daylight, the seemingly indomitable terrorists appeared infirm as the world watched their timid capitulation on their TV screens.

For the faithful, the desecration of the sanctum sanctorum and the kharkoos' servile surrender was a disgrace. Sociologist Dipankar Gupta rationalized that the surrender of the militants, the 'warriors of the faith', who were expected to fight to the finish, turned the panth's 'vicarious martyrdom' into 'vicarious disgrace'. This facilitated the isolation of the militants and a loss of the confidence the ordinary faithfuls had placed in them.

The interrogation of the captured militants further helped to delegitimize the ethno-national movement—they revealed stories of murder, torture, extortion, rape, etc. These accounts were shared with the media and a few select journalists even interviewed some of the captured militants. *Ajit,* the leading Punjabi daily, interviewed Bhai Nirwair Singh, 'who disclosed that incidents of extortion and rapes took place in the rooms around parikrama, Darbar Sahib'.[5] During the search operations that subsequently followed, forty-one bodies of those who had been put to death by the militants inside the temple precincts were recovered from under the rubble, some of these neatly packed in polythene sheets after covering them with sodium chloride to stifle the stench. The bodies wore signs of torture.

The damage to the complex during the operation was minimal—a few holes in the towers of the bunga an a blackening of the clock tower due to a fire which had broken out on the morning of 15 May. However, '. . . [T]wo stray bullets hit Harmandir Sahib—one just at the entrance to the sanctum sanctorum and the other is said to have ricocheted and kissed a rumala covering the handwritten holy book which lies on the first floor above the Har-ki-Pauri.'[6]

Thirty militants were killed in the operation and only three security men suffered injuries. A cache of arms and ammunition was recovered—about fifty-five weapons of disparate kinds and bores, including AK-47s, over 3,000 rounds of ammunition, a few hand grenades, etc. About fourteen rooms around the Parikrama that were being used as 'torture chambers' by the militants were cleared of 'torture tools' like leather straps and rubber spatulas used to thrash the victims.

The SGPC agreed to the demolition of the rooms on the verandah around the Parikrama, a condition insisted upon by the administration. This was to change the architectural design of the verandah that runs parallel to the Parikrama. To start with, the outer doors of these rooms were removed so that they could never again be used as extortion and torture chambers. The government also decided to demolish the buildings in the immediate periphery of the temple complex to provide a wide security-cum-aesthetic corridor. It was the precursor of the Galiara Scheme that beautified the temple surroundings.

This was the last time the militants were to make the Golden Temple their headquarters or appropriate the hallowed space for their cause. The false veil of divinity they operated under had been removed. The operation was, in that sense, both a tactical and a psychological victory.

The maryada at the temple was restored on 21 May, on the initiative of the deputy commissioner, and the DGP and SGPC were given possession of the entire complex on 26 October 1988, after the withdrawal of the security forces.

The Honours

The success of the operation boosted the morale of the forces. The NSG instituted a special medal, the Garaj Star, to embellish all its men. Maj. Gen. Naresh Kumar was decorated with a bar to PVSM (Param Vishisht Seva Medal), while Brig. Sushil Nanda was awarded a VSM (Vishisht Seva Medal). Suresh Arora was conferred the Gallantry Medal. The 1989 Republic Day declaration of the Padma awards bore the indelible imprint of Black Thunder—K.P.S. Gill, Sarabjit Singh, DC, Amritsar, and Ved Marwah, DG, NSG, were conferred the Padma Shri.

The Padma award to K.P.S. Gill and Sarabjit Singh had a twist in the tale—the two just about escaped from an impending charge sheet and swivelled to the honour. The Prime Minister was annoyed with them; he even ordered Ved Marwah to not let Gill enter the temple complex.[7] Buta Singh, P. Chidambaram, Gopi Arora, IAS, and Narayanan, director, IB, were dispatched to Amritsar at the unearthly hour of 1 a.m. on 20 May, and the two ministers grilled Sarabjit Singh and K.P.S. Gill at the Circuit House for a couple of hours.

The case against them was due to them handing over the valuables, including gold, recovered from the temple to the SGPC. Earlier, a joint team led by the two upright additional district magistrates, Suresh Kumar and H.S. Pawar, had prepared an inventory, sealed the valuables and affixed their official seals on it in the presence of SGPC functionaries. The gold and cash had been brought to the temple for kar sewa of the Akal Takht, but the government viewed it as case property.

Gill and Sarabjit had conducted a few eminent citizens to the sanctum sanctorum to show them the desecration and defilement committed by the militants. It was a well-intentioned move to build public opinion against the terrorists. However, when the media sought the reactions of these citizens, it was alleged that the statements were not complimentary to the operation. This annoyed the authorities.

In 1986, I had installed a teleprinter of UNI (United News of India) at the residential office of the DC. The device proved to be useful, as at times the media was ahead of the Police Control Room in reporting terrorist incidents. Sarabjit, in his defence, quickly retrieved the teleprinter clippings of the statements made by the eminent Sikh citizens to the media and obtained similar copies from the Press Trust of India (PTI) and read these out to the two ministers on the wee hours of 20 May. It turned out that the citizens who were escorted into the temple had made no adverse comments about the operation. They had merely declined to give statements to the media.

In those days people would not dare publicly deride terrorists as the retribution was usually fatal.

The third charge was specific to Gill—he did not permit the Doordarshan crew to adequately shoot inside the sanctum sanctorum, and consequently the defiling and defacement of the holy place by the militants could not be appropriately projected on TV. The Doordarshan crew was summoned to the Circuit House to endorse this charge, but they denied that Gill had stopped them from filming. The lifespan of the batteries of the camera flash was just two minutes and there was no electricity in the temple to recharge it. Hence Doordarshan's failure to capture images of the defilement and contamination of the holy space.

This exonerated them of all charges, but it left Sarabjit bitter. R.P. Ojha, the chief secretary, had confided in him that he was asked to keep papers for his compulsory retirement ready— Sarabjit had only a few more years of service left. When I visited Amritsar to call on the recuperating Virk and met Sarabjit too, he said to me, 'I have learnt the lesson of my career. Never take initiative.' This wisdom dawns on all civil servants at some stage or the other during service!

Sarabjit and Gill's tribulation, however, was redeemed by a DO letter from the Cabinet secretary to the chief secretary, conveying the Prime Minister's appreciation of the performance of Punjab officers, and the two of them were conferred the Padma Shri award.

However, what had ignited their ordeal? Sarabjit Singh insinuated it was Buta Singh, who had been ex-communicated from the Sikh panth in 1985, and apparently wanted to leverage the present situation to seek his exoneration. Allowing the re-entry of SGPC functionaries into the temple and handing over the valuables, including gold, to them, weakened Buta Singh's bargaining capacity. This had annoyed the minister, who, in turn, alleged Sarabjit, provoked the Prime Minister.

Gill and Sarabjit's initiative also negated a move to abolish the SGPC and constitute a board to manage the temple's affairs.

The government had consulted Opposition parties on the issue and the Prime Minister deliberated on its consequences at a high-level official meeting held on 28 May. The move was ultimately dropped, weighing the likely adverse reaction among Sikhs.

Buta Singh's nine-year ex-communication tribulation, however, was to end only in March 1994, when he submitted himself before the Akal Takht, accepted his 'sins and guilt' and sought pardon, which was granted after he had undergone tankha.

The Retaliation

The militants had suffered a great blow and many thought that Black Thunder would stem the tide of terrorism. But fighting militancy is not a one-time operation. It is war.

The militants, in a move to re-establish themselves and demonstrate their prowess, stepped up violence. The bulk of their cadre was intact—the number of those arrested in Black Thunder was not even 5 per cent of their cadre strength, as most of the terrorists were based outside the temple complex, operating from across the state. These elements now resorted to brutal mass murders, particularly of Hindus in Hindu-dominated areas to provoke communal clashes.

The list of killings is long and blood-curdling. The militants launched several attacks on innocent men and women. The SGPC officials were also to pay the price with their lives— Bhan Singh, secretary of the SGPC, and Sohan Singh, priest of the Golden Temple, were shot dead, and Mal Singh Ghuman, general secretary, was critically injured on 25 July 1988 in Ludhiana.

The militants had accelerated the acquisition of weapons in 1987–88. In March 1988, for the first time, fourteen anti-tank rocket launchers of Russian origin were recovered from an underground bunker at Kulla village in Patti, apart from AK-47s, thirteen grenades, timing devices, plastic bombs and over 6,000 rounds of ammunition of different calibres. A similar stockpile of weapons and ammunition was found at Mallanwalla village in Ferozepur. The security forces were in for the long haul in the battle propped up by Pakistan.

The Acquittals

Inexplicable as it is, none of those arrested from the temple during Black Thunder II and prosecuted for grave offences such as waging war against the State, sedition and committing offences under the Arms Act got convicted of these offences.

A special court acquitted them of the charges after a prolonged trial of about three years. It was common those days for the militants to convert to what was known as 'police-cats', or police agents. This has caused some to surmise if there was a quid pro quo with the surrendered terrorists. Your guess is as good as mine!

34

Mainstreaming the Militants

It is a well-acknowledged strategy tried across the world in many places to deal with civil strife and secession movements: Assimilate the secessionists into main polity; if you cannot break or bend them, win them over. The game plan in Punjab was to engage the militants in the electoral process and bring them into the democratic fold.

In March 1989, Prime Minister Rajiv Gandhi announced a 'package of hope' for Punjab. Among the provisions of the package were declarations to hold elections to the panchayats by June the same year, and to restrict the operation of the Punjab Disturbed Areas Act and the Armed Forces (Special Powers) Act to only the heavily militant-affected parts of the state. Most importantly, it was promised that the Jodhpur detainees—the men who had been arrested following Blue Star—would be released. They had been in jail for five years and their release had repeatedly figured in all negotiations between the government and morcha leaders, starting with the

Longowal–Rajiv Accord in 1985. Now, except for about eighty-six detainees against whom court proceedings were in progress, all others were freed. On 6 March 1989, an Indian Air Force plane brought 104 detainees from Jodhpur to Amritsar to a rousing public welcome.[1]

This was part of a carefully calculated move by the government towards the normalization process in Punjab. However, the proposed election to the panchayats in June could not be held because the local Congress leaders, particularly Beant Singh, were opposed to them. Elections to Parliament were due in November 1989, and Punjab had only thirteen seats in the 544-member Lok Sabha. The Central government believed that the entry of a few militants from Punjab into Parliament would not make much difference at the national level, but it could go a long way in conscripting the militants into the constitutional political process. That radicals would get elected was a fair assumption because of the then-prevailing anti-establishment sentiment among Sikhs and because the moderate Akalis were a divided and discredited lot.

Post Operation Black Thunder, several attempts to unite the various Akali Dals—Longowal, Talwandi and Mann—had failed, ostensibly due to ideological differences between them, but more due to the personal ambitions of these leaders. The leadership was split and that was the bane of Sikh politics. They indulged in competitive ethno-religious rhetoric, with each faction adopting a more belligerent approach to score over their rival dals. This weakened the collective capacity of the Akalis to bargain with the Central government, which had the option to choose from among multiple Akali Dals, play one against the other or even leave them behind. There were three main panthic committees, the Damdami Taksal, the AISSF divided into factions, apart from moderates who were also divided into many Akali Dals. There was no dearth of factions to choose from and bolster the ones that were more amenable to the government.

The Government of India narrowed down two groups, the UAD (M) and the AISSF, to help 'constitutionalize' the radicals.

Their top-rung leadership was in jail at that time. The two groups were bellicose, but not brutal or bloodthirsty. In fact, the head of the UAD (M), Simranjit Singh Mann, had gone on record against the bloodshed in Punjab. He had been detained under the National Security Act in 1984, kept in solitary confinement and allegedly flailed in captivity. After his arrest, he was accused of a conspiracy to wage a war against India and for conspiring 'to murder Smt. Indira Gandhi'; a twenty-four-page formal charge sheet was submitted in a special court on April 1989, nearly four months after Satwant Singh and Beant Singh, the two assassins of a Prime Minister, had been hanged to death on 6 January 1989. However, now that the government had decided to support the UAD (M)'s entry into the Lok Sabha, steps to free Mann were set in motion.

The move caught Basudeo Prasad, the special public prosecutor, by surprise. When he heard of the manoeuvre to free Mann, initially he opposed his release, but eventually fell in line to formally move the court to discharge Mann and his co-conspirators. After all, if Prime Minister Rajiv Gandhi, whose mother was assassinated, was the prime mover for Mann's acquittal, who was he to object? Special Judge Hari Krishna Verma in a judgment dated 2 December 1989 ordered the freeing of Mann, bringing his ordeal of five years to an end.

The charges against Mann, in any case, were vastly exaggerated. But these very charges had turned him into a hero of sorts among Sikhs. He had given up his high-profile IPS job, had languished in jail and confronted the Delhi Darbar, thereby fulfilling the cardinal criteria of leadership in traditional Sikh politics—sacrifice—and, therefore, was considered worthy of leading the quam. Prior to his acquittal, Mann was flown in a BSF Beechcraft to Delhi and confined in Tihar Jail. He swore allegiance to the Constitution of India and its integrity in a signed letter addressed to the Chief Justice of India[2] and this established, in official record, his loyalty to the nation.

The two AISSF leaders, Manjit Singh, president, and Harminder Singh Sandhu, general secretary, who were also under detention in

Jodhpur, were shifted to Punjab jails in June to facilitate negotiations with them. This also provided these two with an opportunity and elbow-room to manoeuvre themselves in a leadership role among the militants. Manjit Singh was set free in July 1989 through the judicial process after about five years of detention, and Harminder Sandhu was released a little later. Manjit Singh received the unstinted support of the Damdami Taksal and Baba Thakur Singh. He had the right lineage to claim leadership—he was the brother of Bhai Amrik Singh, the AISSF president who was killed in Operation Blue Star. His father, Sant Kartar Singh, was the thirteenth head of the Damdami Taksal. Despite this genealogy, the AISSF (Manjit) did not contest the election to Parliament and instead extended support to the candidates of UAD (M).

Elections to the ninth Lok Sabha were held in November. Three Akali factions entered the elections fray—UAD (M), which was not a recognized political party, Akali Dal (Talwandi) and Akali Dal (Longowal). In another calculated move, Badal and Tohra, who were also under detention, were not released till the run-up to the elections. They were the only two moderates left with some semblance of a popular base and that was probably what weighed in the authorities' decision not to release them before the polls. They could have cut into the votes of the radical groups, even defeating some of them, which would have run counter to the government's strategy of mainstreaming the militants; the moderates were anyway considered as lying within the constitutional boundaries, despite their occasional rhetoric against the State. Therefore, their release came only on 2 December 1989.

The well-established moderate Akali leaders who were aligned with Badal, such as Gurdev Singh Badal, who contested from Bhatinda, Sukhdev Singh Dhindsa from Sangrur and Charanjit Singh Atwal from Phillaur, suffered humiliating electoral defeats. The two traditional Akali Dals— Longowal and Talwandi—could not win a single seat; together they got less than 10 per cent of the votes polled. It was an unqualified triumph for Simranjit Singh Mann and his party.

As if to herald Mann's arrival on the political scene, the poll day, 26 November, passed off without any violence, although there had been a spurt in killings in early November, after the election was announced. In fact, while the government was taking calculated political manoeuvres—pitching one faction of the Akalis against the others, releasing a few kharkoo (militant) leaders while keeping some of the moderate leaders in detention—the killings on the streets of the state had not ceased. After months of uncertainty and bloodshed, the election day was peaceful. The voter turnout and voting percentage was respectable, considering the backdrop of violence in the state, and the results were what the government had hoped for. The radicals won nine seats out of the thirteen Lok Sabha seats.

Mann polled a record 89 per cent of the votes, winning the Tarn Taran seat with a huge margin of 4,80,417 votes over his nearest rival from the Indian National Congress. The five other candidates from his party also won with convincing margins. Notable among the victorious were Bimal Kaur and Sucha Singh, widow and father respectively of Beant Singh, one of Indira Gandhi's assassins.[3]

The elections had bestowed the opportunity of a lifetime to Mann. Akali leaders of all hues accepted his leadership and stood behind him. Baba Joginder Singh, father of the late Bhindranwale, formally transferred the charge of the party office of the Unified Akali Dal to Mann in the first week of December at a solemn ceremony at Manji Sahib Gurdwara, in the presence of Manjit Singh of the AISSF. G.S. Tohra extended his support and the leaders of other Akali Dal factions followed suit. Mann was now the undisputed leader of the panth. All he needed to do was seize the moment and lead Punjab out of a long decade of mayhem, but destiny deemed otherwise.

V.P. Singh as Prime Minister

The result of the Lok Sabha election and the changes it brought at the national level suited Mann. The Congress party failed to get a majority in the ninth Lok Sabha. Rajiv Gandhi demitted office on

2 December, and V.P. Singh took over as Prime Minister. Within days of assuming office, he reached Amritsar to pay obeisance at the Golden Temple. Punjab was a priority for him and he wanted to send a message of goodwill. Devi Lal, deputy prime minister, Mufti Mohammad Sayeed, home minister, and I.K. Gujral, external affairs minister, accompanied him to Amritsar.

V.P. Singh addressed the sangat in front of the Akal Takht. It was the first time that a Prime Minister had taken the stage inside the temple complex. The crowd was exuberant and V.P. Singh responded to the spontaneous public reception by riding from the temple in an open jeep through the packed roads of Amritsar. The militants posed no danger to the Prime Minister. It was bonhomie all over—all was set to go well for Punjab.

To push his Punjab initiative, the Prime Minister held an all-party meeting (the Congress and Mann abstained) in Delhi on 17 December, and hammered out a consensus agenda for Punjab. Broadly, they resolved that the excesses by security forces must end; law and order must be toned up and a healing touch employed. Prime Minister Singh followed this up with another all-party meeting in Ludhiana on 11 January 1990, but Mann again abstained from the public rally, though he had a private audience with Singh. The broad contours of an attenuating Simranjit Singh Mann emerged within days of his triumph—his own ambivalent conduct and the assertive militants were to lead him to insignificance.

The AISSF that had supported Mann in the election now created roadblocks. It retreated that Khalistan was its goal and demanded that the newly elected MPs should not enter Parliament till the government fulfilled the demands of the Sikhs. There was an internal struggle for supremacy within the AISSF. Harminder Singh Sandhu, who had escaped death during Blue Star, was killed at his home in Amritsar in the wee hours of 24 January 1990, allegedly by the militants of the Dr Sohan Singh Panthic Committee, though some pointed fingers towards Manjit Singh. Sandhu was suspected by the militants to be a government agent. His death further split the AISSF, with two of its leaders, Amarjit Singh Chawla and Rajinder Singh Mehta, forming still another faction—AISSF (Mehta–Chawla). With his leadership within the AISSF under challenge, Manjit Singh's attitude turned flinty on the separatist demands.

Under religious sentimentalism, Mann refused to take oath of office as MP unless he was allowed to carry the 3-foot-long kirpan inside the Lok Sabha. That was not permitted due to security reasons and as a result he stayed away from Parliament and resigned from the Lok Sabha in October 1990 without even stepping inside.

Mann was following the dictates of his faith, or so he claimed. Guru Gobind Singh had created the Khalsa in 1699, and ordained every Sikh to have five articles of the faith, the kirpan being one of them. The Punjabi word kirpan is made of two words: '*kirpa*' meaning compassion and '*aan*' meaning honour. The kirpan, therefore, is considered a symbol of mercy, grace and honour in Sikhism. Article 25 of the Constitution of India, which confers on every citizen the fundamental right 'freely to profess, practise and propagate religion', provides that 'the wearing and carrying of a kirpan shall be deemed to be included in the profession of the Sikh religion', thus making it a fundamental right.

However, neither the Constitution nor the Sikh rehat maryada (code of conduct) prescribes the length of the blade of kirpan. In practice, it is observed that baptized Sikhs carry kirpans with a blade length that varies from a few inches to 3 feet. Even Sikh priests, ragis, kirtanias, pathis, sewadars, etc., may carry short kirpans in a *gatra*, that is, a cloth strap usually worn around the neck from shoulder to hip. The high priests, however, usually carry siri sahib, the full-length sword. Mann followed in their tradition and hence declined to enter Parliament House.

Some of Mann's party colleagues, however, took oath of office as MPs and participated in the proceedings of Parliament. He, in fact, had little hold over his own MPs. Mann also lacked a cadre-based organizational structure to sustain the mass support he had received in the elections. He did not have the required party set-up or a systemic support mechanism to balance between the terrorists and their front organizations on one hand and the compulsions of a well-intentioned Prime Minister who had opted for a slow, evolutionary process to address the Punjab problem. V.P. Singh's options were constrained by the coalition government he headed. He was dependent on the support of communist parties and the BJP, which had strong views on terrorism, and that limited his choices. Consequently, V.P. Singh's pro-Punjab rhetoric was short on substantive delivery.

Mann also made the Prime Minister's task arduous by taking a complete U-turn and careening towards the militants. In April 1990, he shifted his stand by seeking a plebiscite under the aegis of the United Nations for a right to self-determination for Sikhs. His demand did not evoke any support, and even pro-Sikh newspapers like *Ajit* denounced it. A belligerent Mann, under pressure from the militants, even petitioned the American ambassador to India to support the Sikhs' right to self-determination. These actions, along with the militant's unyielding stand on Khalistan, aborted any possible chance of holding elections to panchayati raj institutions and the State Legislative Assembly that could have broad-based further induction of the radicals into democratic constitutionalism.

The underground terrorist outfits had never recognized Mann as their leader. They tolerated him and used him as a 'democratic facade' to further the goal of Khalistan. Mann too espoused a separatist cause, but his means were democratic. As mentioned earlier, his daughter Pavit Kaur has confirmed, 'Bhindranwale shared an ideology with my father: a separate homeland for the Sikhs.'[4] The difference between the militants and him was he stood against bloodshed.

The moderate Akalis who had tactically rallied behind him slowly deserted him. Tohra publicly insinuated that Mann was propped up by Rajiv Gandhi to marginalize the traditional Akalis. Each side accused the other of being government agents. Tohra, who had often acquiesced to militants in the past, became a target; he was lucky to escape a murder attempt on his life on 14 May 1990 in Ludhiana district.

Apparently shaken, Tohra was eager to project a pro-militant image. He got Bhai Ranjit Singh, the assassin of Baba Gurbachan Singh, the Nirankari chief, appointed as the jathedar of the Akal Takht in June 1990. Since Bhai Ranjit Singh was still in jail, Prof. Manjit Singh was asked to officiate in his place. The Akali Dal (Longowal) underwent a change in leadership with Surjit Singh Barnala moving out as governor of Tamil Nadu on 24 May 1990, and this further weakened the moderate factions of the Akali Dal.

Pakistan, it seems, had seen through the plan to constitutionalize the radicals. In August 1990, the Pakistan-based panthic committee virtually torpedoed the initiative to induct the militants into the mainstream by announcing their opposition to any Akali faction that opted for the electoral process. Akali leaders like Amarinder Singh, who dared to question the panthic committee, were censured and publicly denounced by the militants. The traditional Akali leadership, including Tohra and Badal, preferred to play it safe and lie low.

However, in 1999, when Mann was again elected MP from Sangrur by defeating Barnala, he attended the Lok Sabha wearing a short kirpan in a gatra. The inevitable inference is that in 1989–90, it was the radical elements that kept him out of the Lok Sabha. A massive public mandate was wasted. And except for the 1999 Parliament election from Sangrur, he never won an election again. The people were unsparing—all the members of Mann's party soon faded into history. Mann lost his security deposit in the 2014 election to the Lok Sabha from Khadur Sahib, his erstwhile seat that had elected him with a record margin in 1989. The separatists were decisively rejected by the electorate; their ideology and credentials stood delegitimized in the public eye by their own conduct.

The well-intentioned Nirmal Mukarji, who had taken over as governor in December 1989, exerted himself to end police excesses and extra-judicial killings. He wanted to build an environment of mutual trust. However, the unabated violence and Pakistani support to the terrorists resulted in the continuation of the muscular policy of the police. Consequently, Mukarji failed in building the people–government conviviality he tried so hard to promote in Punjab.

The security establishment found Mukarji 'too civil' and therefore he resigned on 1 June 1990 at the behest of the Central government. He was succeeded by Virendra Verma, a Janta Dal MP. He was sincere and wished Punjab well, but lacked Mukarji's sophistication and gubernatorial acumen. He soon got involved in open wrangling with senior state officers, both civil and police, damaging his own and the administration's image in the public eye.

Militant violence increased and I found Verma's belief that terrorism could be ended by exhibiting well-meaning intent and good wishes rather puerile. Punjab had been continuously under President's Rule since May 1987, and Verma wanted to hold elections to the state assembly before it ended on 10 November. It was an encouraging aspiration in the face of the upswing in terrorist violence. The inexorable historical forces, however, willed otherwise.

Chandra Shekhar as Prime Minister

Following the Mandal Commission agitation, V.P. Singh's government fell and Chandra Shekhar became Prime Minister on 10 November 1990. The change in the Central government provided cause for bureaucratic changes in Punjab. Governor Verma was moved out to Himachal Pradesh in December 1990, and K.P.S. Gill was sent to Delhi as DG, CRPF. The real reason behind their transfers, however, was that the security establishment under Gill and the political set-up under Governor Virendra Verma were pulling in different directions. They had dissimilar, in fact, incongruent strategies to deal with Punjab. Gill believed in never sparing the rod, while Verma was all for winning hearts. The Central government held both accountable for not pulling together and their removal was just a matter of time.

Gen. O.P. Malhotra, former Chief of Army Staff, was sworn in on 18 December 1990 as Punjab governor. He brought along an upright Punjab-cadre officer, D.S. Mangat, as the police chief.

Chandra Shekhar had a pro-Sikh persona. Post–Blue Star, he had participated in kar sewa at the Golden Temple and even interacted with a group of radicals a few weeks before Operation Black Thunder II. He had shown willingness for a direct dialogue with the militants within constitutional parameters. The various Akali factions mandated that Mann negotiate with the Prime Minister, including for the 'right to self-determination'—a term interpreted differently by different groups.

However, one or the other underground cabal in the highly splintered ethno-national movement would sabotage talks each time such an initiative appeared imminent by announcing obstructive prerequisites for a dialogue. Illustratively, Dr Sohan Singh's panthic committee demanded that the talks with the Central government be held in New York under the United Nations or in Geneva, and the militants be given a safe passage to these places.

It was impossible for Chandra Shekhar to concede to these secessionist conditions. Besides, his party did not have the required majority in Parliament. Chandra Shekhar's breakaway group of MPs had the strength of fifty-four in a house of 542; its existence was tethered to Congress support. He went through the motions of peace talks, but these were reduced to a stop-gap strategy to 'stabilize' Punjab, rather than a real chance of settlement of militant demands. He, therefore, directed Gen. Malhotra to build the right environment to hold elections as a tactic to keep hopes alive.

Malhotra worked on a two-pronged strategy. First, he toured the state extensively, addressing public meetings and public grievances in a bid to build a pro-state public opinion. He directed the officials, particularly the field-level functionaries, to do the same. I, as secretary of the Department of Information and Public Relations, was asked to regularly organize *sadbhavna* public rallies and *padyatra*s in support of peace efforts. Leaders of the political parties who were willing to speak out against violence addressed these rallies. Tejinder Khanna attended some and led a padyatra in the border town of Ferozepur. The two frequent political speakers at these rallies were the late Chief Minister Beant Singh and former Deputy Speaker of the Vidhan Sahba Bir Devinder Singh, and some leaders of the left.

My department also launched a campaign to win over the diaspora—the separatists had succeeded in garnering support among the Sikhs abroad, who funnelled funds for the terrorist movement. We printed literature and published glossy magazines that were dispatched to Indian embassies abroad for circulation among Punjabis to highlight the developmental work in the state.

The second leg of Malhotra's strategy was to contain terrorist violence. The army had been called in December 1990 to launch Operation Rakshak in aid of police and paramilitary forces. The troops spread out in the border districts and other sensitive areas, apparently for military exercises, but discreetly assisted the security forces in anti-terrorist operations. Night curfew was imposed in the border belt to restrict the militants' mobility and many militants were killed in the encounters. There were a few setbacks too, like the incident in Nathu Ke Burj village, under the jurisdiction of the Sarhali police station, on 26 February 1991, when some farmers on their way to fetch diesel were mistaken to be terrorists and fired at by the army, resulting in the death of six persons, including a retired BSF official. There was also tension in some villages in Amritsar district due to the brusque behaviour of a few soldiers.

Such instances do tend to alienate the public, but overall, the army earned appreciation and the much-needed goodwill of the people. The welfare activities it carried out in the border belt helped it overcome the memories of Operation Woodrose. The army completely sealed the border, which snapped the supply of weapons from Pakistan. It had a two-fold effect: militants started thinning out from the areas where the army was deployed, and secondly, some of the overground abetters of the militants surrendered to the police and were absorbed in the mainstream. In March, the Amritsar administration symbolically 'presented' about fifty such surrendered militants before the governor at the Circuit House. This demonstration helped thwart fresh recruitment to the militant cadres. The surrendered boys were also a valuable source of intelligence about the terrorists—their identities, hideouts, helpers, weapons, etc.

However, Chandra Shekhar resigned on 6 March 1991, forejudging the Congress (I)'s withdrawal of support to his government. He recommended dissolution of the Lok Sabha, which the President accepted. But Punjab's hopes were not extinguished as Chandra Shekhar's caretaker government recommended elections in the state along with the rest of the country. Polling was scheduled for 31 May in Punjab, and from 20–26 May in the rest of the country. However, T.N. Seshan, the chief election commissioner, shifted the polling date for Punjab to 22 June, to allow time for deploying extra forces. That provided an additional three-week period for campaigning to the candidates, but also perilously exposed the electoral process to terrorist attacks for that much longer.

The poll notification set the slumbering political forces into motion, and Akali factionalism was back in full play. The various factions of the Akali Dal that had acceded a leadership role to Mann were now keen to abandon him in a fresh assertion of their respective factional identities. With the announcement of the polls, the contrived tactical unity among the Akali factions cracked, and faction after faction deserted Mann in the race to gain power. Akali Dals mushroomed—UAD (M), Badal, Longowal, panthic committee of Amarinder Singh, Panthic-Rajdev and a little later Baba Joginder Singh. For the 1991 elections, none of the traditional Akalis partnered with any of the militant groups, nor did Mann, who had earlier been supported by the radical AISSF (Manjit) in the 1989 elections.

The political stratagem of the Congress (I) and the leftists was inexplicable. They decided to boycott the polls even though these parties had actively participated in government-sponsored public rallies for peace and mass contact. The presence of multiple Akali Dals would have split the rural votes to the advantage of the Congress, but for some reason the leadership were not ready to exploit it. The BJP, confined to cities as it was, stepped in to cash in on the Congress's absence in urban areas.

The radicals and the underground terrorist groups were also divided into two camps on the issue of participation in the election. The AISSF (Manjit), the panthic committee of Manochahal, KCF (Zaffarwal) and some smaller groups were pro-polls, and their logic, as theorized by Manochahal, was that wresting political power by the electoral process would earn their cause international recognition. Their candidates, who were mostly kin of killed terrorists, jumped into the election fray willingly. It was a major gain on the state's end to induct militants in the democratic process. It is a different matter that in the election campaign to protect their radical image and base, they projected a separatist manifesto. This gave an opportunity to the democratic forces opposed to the militants to create a disquiet—they argued that if these militants gained power, which then seemed likely, secessionist resolutions would be passed in the Legislative Assembly to lend legal heft to the demand for Khalistan.

The second group of militants consisting of the AISSF (Bittu), the panthic committee of Dr Sohan Singh, Babbars and a few more were adamant on not participating in the electoral process and called for a boycott of the election. They took to armed violence to sabotage the polls. Twenty-nine candidates contesting the assembly and Lok Sabha seats were killed by the militants despite the reinforced security cover extended to them by the state.

Even Subodh Kant Sahay, the Union minister of state for home, contesting for the Lok Sabha from Ludhiana, was targeted on 7 June, on the outskirts of the town, in a bomb blast. His bulletproof car saved him. He had been elected to the ninth Lok Sabha in 1989 from Ranchi in Bihar, but for the tenth Lok Sabha, he chose to contest from

Ludhiana, which has a large Bihari labour vote. Besides, Sahay was negotiating with some of the militants through his special assistant, Maloy Krishna Dhar. Sahay banked on the militants covertly supporting him, particularly the AISSF (Manjit).[5]

The common citizens, however, had no bulletproof shields to save them. On 15 June 1991, in coordinated attacks on two trains, terrorists at Baddowal and Kila Raipur in Ludhiana district killed about 100 passengers. In one train, Hindu passengers were segregated for selective slaughter, while in the other it was indiscriminate carpet gunfire that got both Sikhs and Hindus alike.

The timing of the killings was aimed to coerce the administration to axe the election process, but braving all odds, both Chief Secretary Tejinder Khanna and Governor Malhotra announced that the elections would be held as per the notified schedule. On 19 June, the governor reassured the people of Punjab that the required arrangements for peaceful polls were in place and they should vote without fear. T.N. Seshan, when asked by the media on 19 June, reiterated that there was no plan to postpone the election in Punjab.

The army was put on alert and over 1,20,000 security personnel were deployed to ensure peace. The campaign period ended on the evening of 20 June and the polling parties were ready to move to the notified polling booths. However, Governor Malhotra was woken up in the middle of the night and informed that the election had been postponed in Punjab. He was directed not to dispatch the polling parties to the booths. It was a unilateral decision of the Election Commission, without consulting the governor. Malhotra was enraged and he resigned, much to the embarrassment of the government.

In a somersault, uncharacteristic of strongman Seshan, he declared that free and fair polling was not possible due to the prevailing fear psychosis in the state. Political pundits, however, imputed motives to the postponement.

The tenth Lok Sabha was constituted on 20 June. P.V. Narasimha Rao had been elected leader of the Congress (I) and was sworn in as Prime Minister the next day, on 21 June. Rajiv Gandhi had been assassinated by the Liberation Tigers of Tamil Eelam (LTTE) militants on 21 May at Sriperumbudur in Tamil Nadu, and that had paved the way for Narasimha Rao to step in.

The Congress under Rao was short of a clear majority in the Lok Sabha and therefore jittery over the survival of its government.[6] A modern-day Chanakya, as Narasimha Rao was known, strategized to postpone the scheduled elections in Punjab. The Congress had boycotted the elections, therefore, had they been held, all the seats would have gone to non-Congress candidates. Rao visualized that if the polls were rescheduled, the Congress could win a number of seats out of the thirteen in the state, and that would give him and his allies a clear majority in the Lok Sabha. It is believed that Rao, then designated to take over as Prime Minister, prevailed upon Seshan to postpone the polls in Punjab. Apart from the other fallouts of this decision, it certainly discredited militant organizations like the AISSF (Manjit) that were bold to enter the election arena despite opposition from the competing militant cabals. The cancellation was as much a tactical victory for Rao as a strategic gain for the secessionists who were opposed to mainstreaming the militants. The panthic committee of Dr Sohan Singh and the underground terrorists aligned with it viewed the postponement as their victory and resolved to oppose with greater belligerence any elections that may be held in future.

Beant Singh Becomes Chief Minister

The decision to postpone the scheduled elections in 1991 cemented the Sikh ethno-national movement. Sikh leadership of all hues felt that the Central government was playing politics and the panth must give a collective response by abstaining from the electoral process in future. For the first time, the moderate Akali factions coalesced with the myriad militant organizations to project a common front to boycott the prospective elections.

However, the motivation of the various factions to boycott the electoral process was different. The traditional Akalis felt cheated of their certain victory. They had faced bullets in the cancelled poll process—militants had killed twenty-nine candidates. Bitter and aggrieved, they took the stand that unless Punjab's basic demands were first met and the militants isolated, holding elections would serve no purpose. At the back of the mind of the moderates was also the realization that even if they were to win the election, they would not be able to contain the violence. Their panthic credentials and the ideological posturing constrained them from seeking muscular measures against the militants.

Militant groups such as the AISSF (Manjit) which had decided to participate in the postponed May–June polls felt let down by the government. Their decision to contest had marked them as stooges of the government and isolated them from other militant groups. Besides, the reality of the electoral process had dawned on them—winning votes was not a cakewalk. There were multiple candidates in the fray and very often, more than one competing candidate professed 'panthic' credentials, which resulted in competition among themselves.

Illustratively, the AISSF chief, Manjit Singh, was 'forced' to withdraw his candidature for the Lok Sabha from Tarn Taran by G.S. Manochahal in favour of his close confidant Resham Singh Malmohri, who was under detention. It was claimed that being in jail had earned Malmohri better credentials than Manjit Singh.[7] There were intelligence reports that the Babbars and the KCF had instructed their hit men to specially target Manjit and Manochahal's candidates. Their experience during the postponed election process had turned fratricidal and that inhibited the AISSF (Manjit) from joining in any future poll. Prime Minister Rao, when he was Union home minister, had established a dialogue with Manjit Singh, then under detention. Some reports indicate that Rao also played a role in persuading the AISSF to boycott the rescheduled elections, and the boycott chorus grew stronger.

Baldev Singh Sibia, the then SGPC president, took the lead in bringing a multitude of diverse Sikh groups on a common platform. He convened a congregation on 11 August at Anandpur Sahib that was attended by about thirty-six organizations of all hues, including human rights bodies, NGOs and farmers' organizations. Together, they resolved to oppose state repression and in a conference at Anandpur Sahib on 1 September decided to boycott the assembly elections as and when they were held. This decision was re-endorsed on different occasions and in different conclaves. Some of the Akali factions attempted to backtrack from the agreement. However, except for the Akali Dal (Kabul), which had been formed with the merger of the Shiromani Akali Dal (Longowal) and the Shiromani Akali Dal (Panthic) of Amarinder Singh, all others abided by the abstention resolve.

The elections in Punjab could not be postponed in perpetuity, nor President's Rule extended indefinitely. That would have required a constitutional amendment for which the new Central government did not have the required numbers in Parliament. Therefore, to build the right environment to hold elections, an attempt was made to address the political demands of the Akalis, like the transfer of Chandigarh to Punjab, but the process was aborted by the Central government. Had the Central government gone ahead with this initiative, it would have brought the moderate Akalis to the election arena. However, the matter was deferred by the Central government for further discussion, to be taken up only after the completion of elections to the Legislative Assembly. Consequently, the Akalis and the panthic organizations stuck to their boycott decision.

The state government had proposed to conduct elections around April–May 1992. However, once the Central government was sure of the Akalis and the militants boycotting the polls, Prime Minister Rao hurried to hold them. He had his compulsions: the Union Budget was to be approved by Parliament before the end of financial year 1991–92; President R. Venkataraman was finishing his term on 25 July, and the vice president in September, and election to both these offices had to be held. The Congress, therefore, needed to maximize the strength of its MPs and MLAs to ensure the victory of its candidates. Subsequently, the Prime Minister was enmeshed in a bribery charge for attempting to buy Jharkhand Mukti Morcha (JMM) MPs to secure a majority in the Lok Sabha when his government faced a no-confidence motion in July 1993. Rao and Buta Singh were prosecuted and convicted by the trial court, but were acquitted on appeal by a higher court.

In the middle of January, the Lok Sabha and Vidhan Sabha elections were announced for 19 February. The campaign period was reduced to fourteen days to minimize exposure of the candidates to terrorist violence. Unlike the June 1991 elections that saw gruesome violence, the poll proceedings this time around were largely violence-free, though the militants targeted a few BJP workers and poll staff like schoolteachers; consequently, a few employee unions threatened not to perform their duties. The state government had made alternative arrangements to induct government staff from other states, if required, but the need did not arise.

The Akalis condemned the decision to hold elections and announced protest rallies in the state and a demurral march from Anandpur Sahib. The government responded by mass arrests under the National Security Act and the Terrorist and Disruptive Activities (Prevention) Act. Top leaders like Badal, Tohra, Mann and Manjit Singh were detained. The electioneering turned out to be a very low-key affair and was largely confined to the cities.

Prior to the announcement of the election date, the militants created mayhem. On 26 December, a group of heavily armed terrorists killed about fifty passengers, mostly Hindus, and injured another thirty near the Chowki Mann railway station in the Ludhiana–Ferozepur section. Reminiscent of the 15 June 1991 train killings in

Ludhiana, the terrorists indiscriminately fired a few hundred rounds of ammunition, targeting a train. On 8 January about twenty-one industrial workers were killed and a few days later five employees of the electricity board were gunned down at Dhanaula in Sangrur. Another seven died in a bomb blast on 17 January at Samana.

However, unexpectedly, from 17 January to around 10 March—the election days—there was a comparative lull in violence. Some political pundits have attributed this sudden decline to behind-the-scenes deals with terrorists. The election boycott, informed sources say, was a 'managed' affair and this aspect has since been commented upon in the media. Some Congress leaders had even established a support system within a few militant groups.[8] Quoting instances, *India Today* reported that the Congress candidate for the Lok Sabha, Surinder Singh Kairon, son of the late chief minister Partap Singh Kairon, had the tacit support of BTFK chief Sukhwinder Singh and the KCF (Panjwar). In the Assembly constituency of Naushehra Pannuan, Congress candidate Master Jagir Singh had the support of Lt Gen. Gulwinder Singh Galna of the BTFK. In Tarn Taran constituency, Dilbag Singh Daleke of the Congress managed to get elected unopposed with the support of the BTFK. 'The few who had filed nominations against Daleke withdrew when his "boys" brandished his clout,' wrote *India Today*. Likewise, Gurchet Singh in Valtoha had his support base among the radicals. 'In one case, a hardcore militant, Gurinder Singh, shot dead in an encounter in Chandigarh on 13 May 1985, was found to have been a protégé of Santokh Singh Randhawa, then the Punjab Congress president. Randhawa had to quit office soon thereafter in a damage control exercise.'[9]

The happiest man at the outcome of the elections was Prime Minister Rao. His strategy had worked. The boycott of the elections by the Akalis resulted in the Congress winning twelve out of thirteen Lok Sabha seats. It gave Rao's government the much-needed, though wafer-thin, majority. The Congress (I) also did extremely well in the state assembly, winning a two-thirds majority—eighty-seven seats out of 117. With a numerically insignificant opposition in the Vidhan Sabha, the Congress now had a free hand to deal with the Punjab turmoil.

The Congress's mandate, however, was a sham and its legitimacy questionable. The boycott of the elections by the main Opposition political party and the fear of bullets had resulted in mass-scale abstention by the voters. The overall percentage of the votes polled in the state were only 23.82 per cent. The polling was particularly low in rural segments—15.1 per cent as against almost 69 per cent in the 1985 elections. Beant Singh, who became the chief minister on 28 February 1992, polled only 17.15 per cent of the votes in the largely urban constituency of Jalandhar Cantonment. His government was labelled '10 per cent administration', as the Congress had polled only 10 per cent of the total electoral votes in the state.

By boycotting the elections, the militants had missed the last opportunity to gain power through constitutional means. The political forces that emerged victorious in the election were all opposed to the policy of appeasement. The BJP, CPI(M) and CPI had won six, one and four seats, respectively, in the Vidhan Sabha, and like the Congress, they too were against adopting a soft policy towards the militants. The election outcome, thus, was heavily loaded against the radicals and the militants. The Akali Dal (Kabul), the only party that may have advocated a dialogue, won only three seats, including that of Amarinder, who romped in unopposed from Samana, as the Congress had withdrawn its candidate against him.

The years 1990 and 1991 were bloody—1991 recorded the highest number of killings in the entire period of Punjab's turmoil. In 1989, Governor Ray had publicly claimed that terrorism was confined to only sixteen police stations in the state, but by the end of 1991 it had spread to most parts of Punjab, and about forty-seven police stations were badly affected by violence. The Congress had blamed it on the 'mollycoddling' of militants by the previous two Prime Ministers. Containing terrorism, therefore, became the priority of the government under Beant Singh. The Congress had won the electoral mandate on the agenda to end violence and it was its democratic covenant with the people of Punjab to restore peace. And it did succeed.

Surendra Nath took over as Punjab governor on 7 August 1991 and continued in office till his death in an air crash on 9 July 1994. He had a congenial personality, but deep down he firmly believed that there was no 'peaceful' solution to terrorism—elimination of terrorists was the only way, he would say privately. He brought K.P.S. Gill back as DGP, Punjab, on 11 November 1991, who too strongly believed in the strategy of elimination of militants. He had a long tenure in office, till December 1995, to put his belief to practice.

With the elected governments in place in Punjab, from Delhi to Chandigarh there was unity of command and thought, a unanimity on the modus operandi to deal with the Punjab turmoil, both in political and administrative hierarchies. There was an unmitigated meeting of minds between Prime Minister Rao, Chief Minister Beant Singh, Governor Surendra Nath and DGP Gill on the method to finish terrorism. They all firmly believed that the time for negotiations and dialogue with the militants was over and uncompromising use of force was the only solution to end militancy. Gill would say that nothing encouraged terrorists to greater audacity than the spectacle of weakness in the political leadership and confusion in the security forces.

35

The War Cops

K.P.S. Gill would say a war is a war. The war against the militants had begun on 29 April 1986, with the panthic committee's declaration of a sovereign state of Khalistan and the launch of its armed force, the KCF, to take on the might of the Indian State and hoist the kesari flag on the Red Fort.

Post–Blue Star, the army withdrew to the barracks, and now the responsibility to fight the war rested on the then ill-equipped, low-inmorale and poorly trained Punjab Police. To its credit, it transformed itself into a fighting force and swiftly slipped into a military role, following what is known as the 'Gill doctrine'—the physical elimination of militants without conceding to any of their demands.

Gill's strategy succeeded in finishing off the militants, but it failed to address the fundamental causes and factors that had, in the first instance, given birth to the ethno-national movement. That, in any case, was the domain of political processes, not the police. The war cops were merely a by-product of the situation they faced and the

Government of India's military policy to deal with the Punjab problem and the political challenges it posed. Some scholars and authors have alleged that the muscular policy was a conscious response of the Central government to the Punjab problem. Kirpal Dhillon states:

> The state response to Sikh militancy consisted mainly of two components—political management and upgradation of law-and-order machinery. The first of these was primarily geared to marginalize the moderate political voices of Sikhs, the Akali Dal, and promoting extremist elements led by Bhindranwale at one level, and distorting the character of the Akali movement for the redress of mostly regional grievances into a manifestly religious agitation at another. In other words, what the Centre was trying to achieve in Punjab was the de-secularization of an essentially regional secular movement.[1]

Quoting sociologist Dipankar Gupta, Dhillon says that the Central government 'ethnicized secular issues in order to marginalize its opponents, one by one from the national mainstream'. Consequently, he writes, 'the repression let loose in the rural areas by an increasingly lawless police vastly aggravated the hiatus between the Indian state and the Sikh community.'[2]

The Punjab-Police-turned-war-cops and its militarization was an inevitable outcome. The police acquired military-type weaponry and upgraded its hardware to war-grade. LMGs, SLRs, Sten guns, AK-47s, mine detectors and the like progressively replaced the British-era .303 rifles. Bulletproof cars and jeeps with mounted machine guns replaced the earlier rickety automobiles. Improvised armoured carriers such as steel-lined tractors to access the intended targets without fear of being hit by militants' bullets were acquired. Communications and wireless networks were upgraded and new electronic gadgetry acquired. Bomb disposal squads became an integral wing of the force. Policemen acquired bulletproof jackets and commando-like dresses—red or black dungarees, with battle-ready black patkas as headgear. The police deployment for ground domination showed up in automatic weapon emplacements, fortifications and bunkers at strategic points in towns or around key establishments.

The acquisition of new weapons and gadgetry didn't happen overnight, nor was it easy. The police had to struggle within the governmental system for allocation of funds and acquisition of weapons like LMGs that was, at the initial stage, even opposed by the Union Home Ministry on the grounds that a civil force should not be equipped with military weapons. However, as the gravity of the threat was understood, everyone rose to the occasion. To facilitate the modernization and upgrade, the police budget went up from a paltry Rs 30 crore in 1981 to about Rs 322 crore in 1994. In the budget for the year 2020–21, the total allocation to the Punjab Police has gone up to Rs 6,466 crore.[3]

Secondly, the police organization was restructured to ensure ground domination and improve its response capability. The intelligence set-up was rejuvenated and new smaller police districts were carved out by dividing up militancy-infested larger revenue districts such as Tarn Taran, Majitha and Batala out of Amritsar and Gurdaspur, and placing them under young SSPs. For better coordination of anti-terrorist operations, officers from the paramilitary forces were grafted on deputation as SP, operations, in sensitive districts, and at one stage the IG, operations, was a CRPF officer, bringing greater coordination between the two forces. The strength of the Punjab Police was more than doubled over a period; it went from about 24,500 in 1975 to nearly 54,000 in 1990. For effective supervision, IG-rank officers were placed above DIGs in the police ranges.

However, de facto, within the police hierarchy the line of command was often blurred—the SSPs would directly report to the DGP, bypassing DIGs and IGs. The small size of the state and a good communication network facilitated the day-to-day and incident-to-incident supervision of field officers by effective DGPs.

K.P.S. Gill, in his heyday, while on a tour of the state, would promote perceived brave officers on the spot, grant higher ranks and perform pipping ceremonies for them. Formal promotion orders could follow. In some cases, they wouldn't, but the promoted officer discharged the duties of the higher rank. In war, procedures were dispensable.

Thirdly, new laws conferred greater powers on the security forces. Illustratively, the Terrorist and Disruptive Activities (Prevention) Act, 1985; the Armed Forces (Special Powers) Act, 1983; the Punjab Disturbed Areas Act, 1983; the Terrorist Affected Areas (Special Courts) Act, 1984; the National Security (Amendment) Act, 1984, etc., gave sweeping powers to security forces, including to conduct search and seizure, arrest and detention. The National Security Act was amended to empower the government to detain persons without trial for longer periods.

Fourthly, there was a conscious shift in the type of human resources chosen to man key positions. More aggressive types replaced the tranquil armchair police chiefs of the yesteryears. The two obvious names are Julio Ribeiro and K.P.S. Gill, though there were others who were equally plucky. Most of the Punjab Police chiefs were personally selected by Prime Ministers and that was so even when the state had an elected government headed by a party other than the one that ruled Delhi.

Julio Ribeiro's appointment as DGP, Punjab, is an example of collaborative federalism in the fight against militancy. A Maharashtra-cadre officer, he was serving on deputation with the Government of India in Delhi when Rajiv Gandhi summoned him in March 1986 to lead the Punjab Police. He was escorted by Arjun Singh and Arun Nehru in a special aircraft to Chandigarh and 'presented' to Surjit Singh Barnala, the Akali Dal chief minister of Punjab, who merely formalized the Prime Minister's selection of the new DGP by issuing the required notification appointing Ribeiro as the new police chief. Ribeiro himself was promoted as adviser to the governor while he was away in Bombay for a prostrate operation and replaced as DGP by K.P.S. Gill of the Assam cadre of the IPS. All the DGPs—P.S. Bhinder, K.S. Dhillon in July 1984, S.D. Pandey in 1985, K.P.S. Gill in 1988, and then again in 1991, and O.P. Sharma in 1996—were the Central government's choices.

In the districts, a set of committed war cops, mostly young, resolute, courageous, fiercely independent officers, opposed to any extraneous interventions, particularly by politicians, were deployed. Some of them came on deputation from other states. Without these gritty men, Ribeiro, Gill or D.S. Mangat could not have triumphed.

The fifth and more critical facet of the police's militarization, however, was the metamorphosed work culture, a new ethos, and the very attitude and approach to law itself. In the military strategy and tactics adopted by the police, the elimination of the enemy was the only objective. Procedural niceties were avoidable irritants. The war cops were not averse to transgressing the law and the seniors often overlooked the deviant conduct and aberrations among their subordinates so long as they were fighters. The culture was to protect the perceived brave ones under the alibi of not demoralizing the force by disciplinary action. The police omertà—a 'khaki code of silence'—prevailed.

The Police Sena

The ingenious among the war cops floated their own senas—bands of civilians, mostly ex-terrorists and criminals, operating either together or even independent of the police, to take on the militants.

It began in 1986 in Amritsar. Initially, the operation was confined to identify and capture militants on the principle 'set a thief to catch a thief', and based on this analogy, it was nicknamed Operation Cat. It involved using captured terrorists or smugglers with militant links as Cats, or police spies. They were used as spotters to identify their comrades-in-arms. The Cats would be positioned, usually in vehicles with tinted glasses, at strategic spots known to be visited by militants. Once identified by a Cat, the militant would be nabbed. This led to the capture and killing of some known terrorists but the militants soon caught on as the ever-probing media snooped around and published news stories on it.[4]

However, the Cat operations validated the utility of conscripting captured terrorists in counter-insurgency operations. Therefore, the scope of the operation was expanded from using the services of ex-militants as mere spotters to deploying them as actual armed combatants—men with a dubious past and terrorist links were enlisted to carry out covert armed operations.

This had many advantages. Unlike the uniformed forces, these armed civilian bands were not answerable to the law or people, media or courts; they had ease of mobility and were not constrained by legalities of territorial jurisdiction. They were knowledgeable about their targets, hideouts and terrain, and had local contact information. Their motivation was either money, pardon for their own crimes, rehabilitation or settling scores with rival militant groups.

However, criminal proclivity rarely disappears, and some of these armed bands resumed their criminal conduct. One such instance was of constable Dalbir Singh, dismissed in 1983 and surreptitiously reinducted in 1986 for covert operations with then-DGP Ribeiro's endorsement. Dalbir delivered. He eliminated some known terrorists; however, he and his band also indulged in extortions and dacoities and one such daring heist was in the neighbouring state of Jammu. When he was summoned by the SSP, Patiala, Sital Das, in the presence of SP Baldev Singh Brar, Dalbir Singh got enraged over his questioning, pulled out his revolver and shot both Sital Das and Brar dead before shooting himself.

Apart from being a tragedy, this incident blew up the covert operation and earned the government a bad name. Nevertheless, the trend of undercover operations survived and some of these gangs continued to indulge in extortion and crime against innocent citizens. This, too, helped, as in the public eye these were the acts of terrorists, which discredited the militant movement, leading to the loss of goodwill and public sympathy for it.

Policemen like Gurmeet Singh Pinky operated at will. A few counterfeit small militant bands such as the Panthik Tiger Force led by Santokh Singh Kala, a cop, the Khalistan Armed Force of Shamsher Singh, the Rangreta Dal and the Khalistan Liberation Army of Bhai Kanwar Singh, etc., suddenly surfaced to take on the real militants. These spurious militant bands triggered inter-gang wars among already factionalized militants, helping criminalize the movement and diluting the ideological moorings of the ethno-national struggle. Their success boosted police morale and conversely marginalized ideologically committed militants and their handlers in Pakistan.

K.P.S. Gill's Defence

K.P.S. Gill would like us to believe that, 'there was, at no stage in the Punjab operations, a state policy or strategy based on arbitrary violence, intimidation, human rights violations or the lawless "elimination" of alleged terrorists by the police'.[5] Gill is right to the extent that no formal policy of extrajudicial measures or violation of human rights was notified by the state. Anyway, that could not have been done in a constitutional democracy. The de facto reality, though, was quite different from the de jure stand.

Gill's predecessors, however, were more forthright. Birbal Nath (DGP from September 1980 to 1 October 1982), admitted to institutional approbation for fake encounters during the period of Chief Minister Darbara Singh. He accused the authorities above him 'of the view that unless the terrorists were liquidated, the Government would continue to be accused of lack of firmness. Thus, those authorities started asking Superintendents of Police, bypassing me, to stage fake encounters. I protested vehemently. They had to give up this policy'.[6]

K.S. Dhillon, DGP, was even more candid to confirm the war methods, including 'staged encounters' with the 'tacit approval of the top brass in the state police'.[7] He publicly stated that suspects were routinely rounded up, often detained illegally and dealt with 'appropriately', not necessarily judicially. Dhillon has disclosed, 'As the end of the decade drew near, administrative and political disarray became even more glaring, the state police growing more and more unaccountable and resorting to rampant killings of innocent persons and branding them as terrorists.'[8]

The liquidation of pre-notified terrorists was incentivized by grants of monetary benefits, recognition and promotions. Snaring or killing terrorists would fetch lakhs in awards—much higher than the monthly salary of even senior police officers—critics called it a 'cash for corpse' scheme. 'Corruption, extrajudicial killings, extortions, abductions and other such illicit practices thrived; many officers acquired huge properties around Chandigarh and other cities overnight.'[9] The annual outlay for cash awards was Rs 100 million.[10] There were unannounced awards for killing unlisted militants. The award money varied from Rs 40,000 to Rs 5 lakh. '. . . [S]ome 50,000 to 60,00 awards had been given to men of the regular police force for the period 1991–1993.'[11]

Not all the encounters turned out to be genuine; there were instances of prize money being claimed while the dead terrorist resurfaced. Gurnam Singh Bandala was declared killed in an encounter in July 1994. However, he resurfaced in 1998, much to the embarrassment of the establishment.

Such encounters were problematic, but due to the intensity of the ongoing battle they were ignored. With the unabated killings of innocents by terrorists, police-in-war tactics were tolerated, and it became the de facto operational mantra, the modus operandi to deal with Pakistan's sponsored separatist struggle, particularly from the days of Julio Ribeiro and later accentuated during the tenure of K.P.S. Gill as DGP.

The war measures naturally created in the public a fear psychosis of false encounters, and often magistrates would receive requests from the detained that they be brought to court or taken out of prison only after handcuffing so that an 'escape story' was not cooked up. There were instances when I received entreaties, at times written ones, from parents or relatives that their suspect wards be arrested and put in prison, otherwise they feared they might be killed in a staged encounter.

K.S. Dhillon has accused the two super-cops—K.P.S. Gill and Ribeiro—of pursuing 'strategies that tended to promote a culture of illegitimate, brutal and possibly venal policing among their subordinates'.[12] There were, however, vital differences between the approach of Ribeiro and Gill. While Ribeiro believed that the turmoil triggered by ethno-religious nationalism could be contained but not eliminated by police, and that it would need a final political settlement to resolve the issue, Gill was clear that militant attrition and not any political process would end terrorism. Ribeiro was also against the indiscriminate use of force and even alleged that the problem was that Gill failed to appreciate that the common law-abiding citizen had to be 'brought over to our side'.

This police-at-war approach relied on the principle of maximum force. Gill went for physical termination of terrorists without waiting for political processes to manage the ethno-religious-nationalism issues. He was conscious that the competitive politics in Punjab ruled out meeting the Akalis' demands, which could have possibly marginalized the militancy. It would also be problematic to attempt to deradicalize the ecclesiastically indoctrinated warriors, as a counter-terrorist strategy would also be time-consuming. This left few time-efficient alternatives for Gill to pursue and he chose the police-at-war strategy.

The strategy inflicted a long-lasting scar on the Sikh psyche. There were collateral damages—it embedded an extrajudicial culture in the administrative system. A recent survey, 'Status of Policing in India Report, 2018' by Common Cause and the Centre for the Study of Developing Societies, reported that in India, Punjab showed the highest 'police dread'. Extracts from the report, carried by the *Times of India*, Chandigarh, on 12 June 2018, showed that '37 per cent of Sikhs were highly fearful of the Police—over double the national average' and went on to say that 'Punjab, according to the report, ranks last among the states on the states on the Index of Police Fear'. This is possibly due to 'the connection to the particular history of Punjab in the last four decades'.

The death statistics of the war strategy were chilling. The Punjab Police lost about 1,772 men. In addition, security personnel lost a couple of hundred of their near and dear ones in targeted killings; by the end of 1991, about 119 kin of policemen were killed. August 1992 was particularly heartrending when more than sixty family members of police personnel were killed in one month alone. From 1983 to 1990, the death count for the BSF was fifty-eight and for the CRPF ninety. Two police chiefs—Ribeiro and Mangat—were lucky to escape bids on their lives in 1986 and 1991, respectively. But Mangat's son, Dr Manjit Singh, was killed by militants in Patiala.

In fact, the cost of war was calamitous—starting 1981, Punjab lost about 21,660 people, including nearly 11,787 innocent civilians, out of which over 60 per cent were Sikhs.[13] The number of terrorist fatalities was around 8,112.[14] The economic and social cost was even more punishing.[15]

Manifestation of War Strategy: The Amritsar Experience

The law requires that each encounter, each death in police custody, be reported to the area magistrate. However, in Amritsar district initially no reports were sent. Then suddenly, in December 1984, a bunch of requests was received for magisterial inquests in all the old cases where the bodies had already been disposed of. Under Section 174/76 of the CrPC, 'there can be no inquest in the absence of the dead body', according to the district attorney whose legal opinion I had sought.

I referred the matter to the home secretary in December 1984 for seeking the advice of the legal remembrancer on two issues: Whether the death of a civilian in a police encounter is death 'in custody of police' and, secondly, whether a magisterial inquest under Sections 174/176 of the CrPC can be conducted in the absence of a dead body which is not traceable and cannot be disinterred. Despite over twenty-four reminders from 1984 till the second half of 1987, when I moved out of Amritsar, the home department had not given any direction or legal opinion.

In most cases, the practice of irregular reporting of deaths in encounters to the concerned SDM or district magistrate continued, despite SSP Bua Singh having issued directions to the SHOs on my asking. I had to remind Singh's successor, Mohammad Izhar Alam, that under the law it was mandatory to report such deaths immediately to the SDM and district magistrate, and non-compliance was a violation of the law. The situation improved only marginally.

The hue and cry over staged encounters became louder as the Punjab situation normalized. The abduction and subsequent 'disappearance' of Jaswant Singh Khalra, a human rights activist, gained international notoriety. Khalra had compiled details of about 2,000 persons who had 'disappeared' after being arrested during the 1980s and 1990s. On 6 September 1995, by when terrorism had been eliminated and normalcy returned to Punjab, Khalra also 'disappeared'. Kirpal Singh, a key eyewitness in his alleged kidnapping by police, was later framed in a rape case, allegedly to dissuade him from giving evidence, but was acquitted of the charge in 2007.

Kirpal Singh pursued his tormentors in the courts and ten years later, in January 2017, a court in Patiala held that he had 'suffered mental tension, agony, harassment and irreparable loss'. The court awarded him a compensation of Rs 49 lakh, to be paid by seven persons—four of them police officers, including a retired DGP and IGP. Police officers were not alone in framing Kirpal Singh for rape—a journalist and the complainant woman were among the others directed to compensate him.[16]

One of the police officers involved in the rape case against Kirpal Singh was a young, intrepid officer in Amritsar with me. I recall that in July 1987, he had brazenly threatened H.R. Megh, the magistrate, for granting seventeen days' police remand to an accused involved in a case under the Arms Act and Terrorist and Disruptive (Activities) Act, while the police had pleaded for thirty days. Megh complained in writing. The matter, however, was patched up; those days such aberrations were not taken sternly if the intent otherwise was not mala fide.

However, the most despicable conduct was reported to me in March 1987 by three judges—N.S. Kundra, judicial magistrate, and his two colleagues, J.S. Chawla and Kuldip Singh—all posted at Tarn Taran. They expressed fear for their lives, not from the terrorists but from Sita Ram, SHO of the Tarn Taran police station. Sita Ram had been summoned in several cases pending in the courts, but would not appear despite repeated summons; even the warrants against him remained unexecuted. He was declared a proclaimed offender and one of the judges ordered attachment of his salary. This annoyed Sita Ram no end. Infuriated, he threatened to get them bumped off. The judges complained that he had the tacit backing of his local superiors. The district and sessions judge endorsed these facts.

In another incident of abuse of power, the then vice chancellor of Guru Nanak Dev University complained that he was directed by the SHO, Sadar, Amritsar, to 'surrender' at the police station by the evening because a student had been shot dead by some terrorists on the university campus. In still another incident of misbehaviour with the SDM, Tarn Taran, his security cover was withdrawn because the local police found him non-cooperative.

These were aberrations, and got sorted out at my level, but were enough to send a wrong signal to the public that if such things could happen to high public functionaries, what would be the plight of the common man? Therefore, I deemed it appropriate to keep the home department informed. Demi-officially, I conveyed to the home secretary that the police was exceedingly becoming high-handed with common citizens in its fight against militancy. I wrote, 'The general feeling among the officers, particularly the judicial magistrates, is that they have to fear for their lives not only from the terrorists but also from the "uniformed terrorists", that is, the Amritsar Police.' My letter was leaked to the press in Chandigarh, and Kanwar Sandhu carried a story in the *Indian Express*. But media reports or DO letters made little difference, if any, to the police-at-war.

In those days, the home department, the controlling authority of police, was marginalized or chose to diminish its own authority. There were four kinds of home secretaries. A.S. Pooni, the home secretary in 1984, was unhappy with the happenings and therefore moped and withdrew, proceeding on leave. R.P. Ojha, N.N. Vohra, Ajit Kumar and a few others who succeeded Pooni were upright officers, and in the larger public interest played acquiescent and cooperative with the prevailing police-at-war ethos. They, in the typical bureaucratic mould, moved the files upwards to the governor or his adviser, where the reported digressions of the force would often rest unresolved, if not ignored, and the matter would die a natural death; so wrongdoings and deviant behaviour often went unpunished. However, subsequently, a few of the gentlemen officers who succeeded these worthy home secretaries ended up eclipsing the supervisory role of the department.

Then there were the likes of M.S. Chahal, the questioning home secretary who, for this reason, got marginalized in the then prevailing ethos. The successive police chiefs, with larger-than-life images, established direct communication with the governors and chief ministers and, not infrequently, the home department was bypassed. Even the DGP, K.S. Dhillon, complained that the governor became 'overtly tolerant' of daily happenings of 'brutality and extortion' and would 'gloss over even clear cases of lawlessness by security forces', the apparent alibi being not to demoralize the forces in the fight against terrorism.[17]

In this vitiated atmosphere, only those with guns mattered. The executive magistracy became ineffectual. K.R. Lakhanpal, the then serving district magistrate at Ludhiana, at a state-level meeting of the governor to review the law and order situation, said, tongue-in-cheek, that, in the law and order, the 'law' has gone to the judiciary and 'order' to the police. The executive magistracy is left with the 'and'.

De facto, the administrative system—executive, judicial and law enforcement—had coalesced, reminding one of the British-era 'Punjab school of administration', the difference being that the fulcrum of the state system was no more the district magistrate but the police. The ascendency of police power began early but by the time Gill took over as DGP, the boundaries of functional accountability had been marginalized, leading to the emergence of militarized policing. Where this strategy failed, however, was that unlike during the British times, when the support of rural intermediaries had been secured—the rural elites, sants and deras—Gill and his men found these powerful surrogates on the antagonistic side of the administration. That made policing difficult and resulted in excessive reliance on force.

The environment therefore transformed into one where abusee of power was not questioned. Let me illustrate with a few incidents I encountered during my stay in Amritsar. On 28 December 1986, we were managing an irate crowd protesting the killing of Sudesh Kumar, a Congress (I) leader, by the terrorists, when we received worrisome information about happenings at Brahampura village. P.C. Dogra, the then DIG, Jalandhar, Izhar Alam, SSP, and I rushed to the spot and found that on the night of 27 December, Avtar Singh Brahma, a dreaded terrorist who belonged to this village, had arrived there and using a hailer challenged the CRPF men and threatened to teach them a lesson if they failed to heed his reprimand that they should not humiliate and harass residents or hurt their religious sentiments. Fifteen minutes later, firing gunshots in the air, he left the village with his men, who were all armed to the teeth.

The CRPF contingent of 29 Battalion stationed at the village school heard the firing by Brahma but, fearing an ambush, did not step out.

The company headquarters of the CRPF was located at the nearby Canal Rest House, but it also did not react. After the militants had left, CRPF men barged into about fifteen residences and conducted a search operation. The houses of Daljit Singh, sarpanch, Sadha Singh, headmaster, and Charan Singh, a member of the panchayat whose pet dog was shot dead because it did not stop barking, were among those searched. They were all beaten up.

Some government personnel on leave—Lance Naik Gurmeet Singh, his brother-in-law Sudarshan Singh, a policeman posted at Central Jail, Amritsar, Gulbagh Singh, a CRPF naik, and Ajit Singh, a CRPF sub-inspector serving in Manipur—were roughed up even after they had shown their identity cards, which were torn up by the CRPF men. Three women were also pummelled—one was bitten on the cheek, and she showed the teeth marks and bloodstained shirtsleeve to us. Prem Nath, the veterinary doctor, was also not spared. In all, about twenty persons sustained injuries, and one of them, Gurdit Singh, succumbed on 30 December.

While searching the local gurdwara, suspecting that the terrorists had used its loudspeaker to make the announcements, the CRPF men allegedly set the Guru Granth Sahib on fire. We inspected the site—the Granth Sahib was completely burnt and the palanquin partially destroyed. In a gathering of about 300 villagers, we heard their version and both the DIG and I assured them of action against the guilty and compensation to the injured. A doctor was deputed to treat the injured and conduct their medical examinations. An entry of the incident was recorded in the daily diary, which was later converted into an FIR against thirty-five CRPF personnel to pacify the frayed sentiments of the people.

From 29 December, political leaders of all hues, including veteran leftist leader Satyapal Dang, MP Tarlochan Singh Tur, the SGPC president, the Akali Dal president and delegations of the CPI(M) and the Janata Dal and others visited the village. Governor Ray also came and consoled the victims. Ribeiro held a press conference on 3 January 1987 in Chandigarh and apologized for the excesses committed by the force.

I discussed the incident with K.P.S. Gill, who was then IG, CRPF, and it was his men who had committed the excesses. He recognized the wanton behaviour of the unit, but raised the proverbial concern of the morale of the force and the bugbear of demoralization of the men. Over a period of time, other happenings overtook Brahampura and the incident faded.

The incident, however, illustrates the work ethos of abusive policing. The CRPF had been stationed in the village for a reasonably long period, but it had made no effort to establish a relationship with the local community, earn their goodwill or engage with village-level organizations or create information sources. Consequently, when the situation arose, it resorted to breaking into houses and roughing up people because they were perceived to be passive harbourers. The approach was coercion and oppression, even against ordinary citizens. Even their own colleagues who had come to the village on leave were not spared by the CRPF.

Lack of oversight and failure to fix responsibility for aberrant conduct reinforced the rough and ready value norms. Once the boorish conduct and coercive methods became the operating strategy against terrorism, it did not take long for these methods to seep in and become part of the daily work culture, even against innocent citizens. The police-at-war syndrome had obliterated the differentiation between the innocent and not-so-innocent citizen. Let me narrate another telling incident from those days.

Mohammed Rafi was born at Kotla Sultan Singh in Amritsar district and every year his death anniversary is commemorated on 31 July by Amritsarias. In 1985, the memorial function was being held in a cinema hall packed to capacity. A crowd gathered outside and the police naturally had to disallow entry once the hall was full. Among the people stranded outside were two journalists—Balbir Singh Saggu of *Nawan Zamana* and Narinder Sharma of *Vir Partap*—

deputed by their newspapers to cover the function. They disclosed their identities and asserted their journalist credentials to demand entry. This infuriated the young police officer in charge, only a few years into his service, who then, to reproduce from *The Tribune* on 2 August 1985, '. . . asked his security guards to teach them a lesson. The guards gave them blows with rifles and butts and Mr Saggu and Mr Sharma were taken to the Kotwali. They were reported to be seriously hurt.' SSP Bua Singh and I rushed to the police station and got the journalists released.

Saggu had to be admitted in hospital with a serious eye injury. The local journalists went on a strike, only to lift the dharna on my assurance that a case would be registered. The young police officer was sent on leave, while A.A. Siddiqui, DIG, Jalandhar range, conducted an inquiry. On 25 August, Justice A.N. Grover, chairman of the Press Council of India, arrived in Amritsar and cautioned 'against such incidents'. The Red Cross picked up the hospitalization bills of Saggu and over a period the matter was compromised. The police officer involved in the incident went on to become an intrepid brand name in the fight against militancy, ending up as DGP, Punjab.

The then chief secretary S.S. Dhanoa's brother-in-law was once stopped for pillion-riding a motorcycle—it had been banned under Section 144 of the CrPC to prevent terrorists from using two-wheelers to commit crimes. To narrate the story in Dhanoa's own words, 'The police officer, not knowing him, gave him the treatment that is given to offenders in Punjab. While he was being roughed up, someone told the police officer that the person being roughed up was related to the Chief Secretary of Punjab. The police officer immediately booked him under TADA and sent him to the central jail, Ludhiana. We got him out of jail after two days.'[18]

The incident could be interpreted in two ways—the police was so fair that it did not spare even the chief secretary's relative. Or that it was another instance of high-handedness where for the offence of pillion-riding an innocent citizen was arrested under the

Terrorist and Disruptive Activities (Prevention) Act. It reflected the culture of 'I care two hoots', because the offending officers knew that no responsibility would be fixed or punishment awarded for the infraction of civil liberties, even when the victim had access to the state authority.

I recall that a court-appointed commission once recovered a number of men and women wrongly detained in a police station in Amritsar district. The then DGP, Kirpal Singh Dhillon, who believed in what he called an 'affirmative and positive approach', wanted to initiate action against the guilty officials but was advised by his IG, crime, against such a move. Dhillon writes in his memoirs that he questioned the IG, 'What do we do about the High Court direction?' The IG replied, 'That is a minor matter, sir,' and added, 'The same people who are supposed to have been recovered from illegal detention will present an affidavit that they were never detained nor rescued from any detention.' That is exactly what happened and the cases were finally disposed of in accordance 'with time-tested local policing tradition'.[19]

The well-meaning Dhillon was sucked in by the prevailing Punjab consternation and his earnest efforts to enhance the credibility quotient of the force went for a six. The rough and ready methods of illegal detention of relatives, including women, of suspect absconders, or seizing of their properties to secure surrender continued.

This kind of mindset and botched-up value system, however, is not the exclusive preserve of the police, nor has it transformed much since then. In 2007, as the chief secretary, Punjab, I was heading the state-level committee to prepare a draft of the new Punjab Police Act—the Supreme Court had directed all states to do so. The fair-minded Suresh Arora, who later became the DGP, Punjab, drafted the proposal in the police directorate and incorporated a provision for prosecution of police officers who may be found guilty of mala fide detention of innocent people or illegal seizure of their properties. N.P.S. Aulakh, the upright DGP, endorsed this move.

Guess who shot down this progressive proposal? The political leadership! A new government had assumed power—its leadership had been hounded and prosecuted en masse by the outgoing government for five years. When I presented the draft of the Act to a sub-committee of ministers, two members rejected this provision outright. One of them was honest enough to say, '*Hun sadi vary ayee hai, te hun tussi police they hath bunn rahe hon* [Now our turn has come and you are tying down the hands of the police].' The malady goes much deeper than just among the police establishment; it seems to be ingrained in the Punjabi politico-social ethos.

The Judiciary–Police Conflict

Separation of powers works on the principles of checks and balances, but when the established systems collapse, conflict is the invariable outcome. This is what happened to the executive–judiciary interplay in the face of terrorism.

To be fair to the police, the judicial system was not delivering in those days. The conviction rate was dismal and militants would often go scot-free. The judges justified the acquittals, attributing them to poor police investigation, lack of cogent evidence, non-production of reliable witnesses and tardy prosecution. The police officers, however, would allege that due to a fear psychosis—some judges had been killed in cold blood by terrorists—the scale of justice was tilting towards the accused. Consequently, the perceived inefficacy of the judicial processes became the justification to tackle militancy extrajudicially.

'. . . [O]ut of 17,890 offences registered in Punjab until then (2001) only 10,562 were charge-sheeted. By the end of that year, merely 190 were convicted and the rest acquitted; the rate of conviction was being as low as 0.2 per cent.'[20] The data reflects the collapse of justice system and mirrors the methodology adopted by the state to deal with terrorism. Prolonged detention of suspects was considered a solution in itself, not necessarily their conviction in a court of law.

The police's modus operandi and the judicial response are tellingly illustrated by a case that came to my notice involving Gurbinder Singh, an agriculture inspector with the government.[21] The police had shown that he was arrested at a naka near Mahal village on the night intervening 22 and 23 October 1984. One unlicensed .32 bore revolver and two live cartridges were recovered from his person. He was prosecuted under the Arms Act, but acquitted by the sessions court that found irreconcilable discrepancies in the evidence.

The defence version, upheld by the court, was that police had raided the house of Gurbinder Singh with the intent to arrest him, but he was not found at home. Subsequently, the village panchayat produced him at the Lopoke police station on 18 October. He was detained for interrogation and kept in confinement. Subsequently, it was shown that he had been arrested by the naka party at Mahal.

Gurbinder was lucky that, unknown to the police, when the Lopoke police did not release him on 19 October, the sarpanch sent telegrams to higher authorities providing details of his alleged wrongful detention. The village panchayat passed a resolution on 20 October seeking his release. The police story of the arrest at a naka on the night of 22 October naturally fell apart in the court and Gurbinder was acquitted.

Gurbinder Singh was a radical and suspected to be involved in militancy. The police arrested him on suspicion and made up a story, because they had no credible proof against him. This was the police dilemma—lack of credible evidence and unwillingness of independent witnesses to depose. In the absence of evidence, the police would make up stories and produce stock witnesses. The investigation of cases was sloppy, and prosecution even poorer. Consequently, even genuine cases involving terrorists would fail.

The hard-pressed and overstretched police often failed to produce the accused in courts, the judges complained that the prisoners were not brought to court from jails on the dates of hearings, resulting in frequent adjournments and delays. The jails were choked and overflowing with undertrials, but the judges at times sat idle in courts due to non-production of the accused. I called for a report in the matter from the jail superintendent, Amritsar, and found the situation alarming. Illustratively, 219 prisoners were not produced before the trial courts on 15 April 1985, seventy-three on 16 April, fifty-eight on 17 April and sixty-seven on 18 April.

The police attributed this to the non-availability of manpower to provide escorts to take prisoners from the jail to the court. The government also took long to establish special courts at Amritsar, and even longer to appoint judges to man the two courts of additional special judges. In the meantime, the accused had to be transported to the special courts at Jalandhar. The lawyers complained to the governor when he visited Amritsar on 10 and 11 January 1986 and initially two judges from Uttar Pradesh were proposed to be posted in Amritsar on deputation, but they declined to join.

Thus, it was a vicious circle—the police, judiciary and executive all blaming each other. It also reinforced the police tendency to rely, more and more, on the extrajudicial police-at-war methods. A war is a war, so went the rationale for all wrongs; malfeasance was viewed as unavoidable, projected as unintended peccadillos, and hence pardonable.

The Police at the Receiving End

The police officers who breached the law in the fight against militancy—and this number was large—later found the system that had tacitly encouraged and awarded them for such conduct abandoned them once normalcy was restored. The courts resurfaced.

K.P.S. Gill, however, stuck to his stand that the state had not asked any officer to violate the law. To a question on the allegation of officers having killed people in custody by journalist Shekhar Gupta in *India Today*, 15 April 1983, his reply was: 'My orders to my officers are clear—stay within the law. Still, if an officer has done something wrong, it is between him and his maker.'

The state, however, it was alleged, abandoned the perceived intrepid policemen it had set after the militants. The 'fearless' officers of the yesteryears, the likes of Ajit Singh Sandhu, decorated twice for gallantry, found themselves being hounded by the CBI and the courts, pushing him under the wheels of the Himalayan Queen in May 1997. He chose death by suicide—he was facing investigation and prosecution for excesses in over a dozen cases. At least four more officers died by suicide: Vivek Mishra, SP, on 23 May 2007; Swaran Singh, DSP, on 2 February 2008; Mohan Singh, inspector, on 1 April 2011; and Jagsir Singh on 27 June 2013.

By one count, a few hundred cases were registered against policemen and nearly 2,000 writ petitions and complaints were filed in the Supreme Court, the high court and the National Human Rights Commission (NHRC) by the aggrieved private parties, seeking justice. Some of these cases have concluded and others are pending. As of January 2022, eighty-six officers have been convicted for transgressing the law and are in jail or out on bail. Another thirty-five cases are pending in the trial courts.

The state government created an independent litigation cell in the police directorate under an IG to pursue these cases, with appropriate allocation of resources. Litigation costs are high, lawyers charge huge sums, and it was financially and psychologically crippling for many officers to fight legal battles despite state assistance.

The state had to dish out crores as compensation awarded by courts. The NHRC and the courts took cognizance of the furtive cremation of bodies and directed the state to recompense the kith and kin of those killed.

The Punjab Police eliminated militancy—it won the undeclared war for the nation, but in the process disabled many citizens and the State alike.

36
The Foreign Hand

THEY WOULD WAIT FOR HER IN THE LOBBY OF THE LAHORE HOTEL, their eyes fixed on the elevator. As soon as she stepped out of the lift, the men would rise in unison from the corners of the hotel foyer, leaving no room for doubt that they had indeed been waiting for her. They would tail her wherever she went, bumper-to-bumper and shoulder-to-shoulder.

These were men from the ISI, Pakistan's dreaded spy agency, shadowing my IFS batchmate, Neelam Dhamija Sabharwal, who was the liaison officer, deputed by the Government of India to coordinate the visit of the jatha (group of pilgrims) to Sikh shrines in Pakistan. My wife and I were devotees in the jatha and preferred the spartan gurdwara accommodation, while Neelam was entitled to a five-star hotel. The mistake we committed was to visit her at her hotel in Lahore—this helped them identify me, and thereafter we too were subjected to aggressive surveillance.

The objective of the intrusive reconnaissance of the Indian officials was to deter and restrict the Indian officials to their rooms, while ISI-sponsored men freely moved around spreading pro-Khalistan propaganda among the pilgrims. Neelam and I were fortunate to escape being roughed up, but two officials of the Indian embassy in Islamabad—S.B. Jain, counsellor, and Ravi Nair, first secretary, weren't as lucky. The ISI-sponsored groups, in two separate incidents, physically assaulted these officials while they were on visits to the gurdwaras to attend to the welfare of the visiting jathas. Another Indian official, who had served with me in Amritsar in 1985, and later was posted in our embassy at Islamabad, was also beaten up, his face badly bruised. He suffered trauma and had to be recalled.

The gurdwaras in Pakistan became the overground contact points for the ISI and radical Sikhs. There are a large number of historical gurdwaras in Pakistan and pilgrim jathas regularly visit Nankana Sahib, Panja Sahib Hasan Abdal and Lahore on the birthday of Guru Nanak Dev, the martyrdom day of Guru Arjan Dev and death anniversary of Maharaja Ranjit Singh. Militant groups based in the US, the UK, Canada and some other countries descended in hordes, distributing among Indian devotees pro-Khalistan literature and exhibiting videos to highlight the alleged human rights violations in Punjab.

The ISI men would be in tow to identify possible new recruits. Those who fell for the propaganda were watched and those who showed promise or susceptibility to the 'Sikh cause' were recruited for the movement. Subsequently, some of them would be encouraged to illegally cross over into Pakistan for training in subversive activities, including learning to make IEDs and bombs, handle weapons and carry out targeted killings. General Akhtar Abdul Rehman, who was head of the ISI for about eight long years starting in 1979, successfully penetrated some Sikh militant organizations, laying a strong network of spooks. His successor, the Pashtun General Hamid Gul, was equally virulent.

The semblance of a veil that intelligence agencies usually maintain on spy operations was lifted in 1999 when the former ISI chief General Javed Nasir was appointed chairman of the then newly formed Pakistan Sikh Gurdwara Parbandhak Committee. And this sabotage continues by inducting pliable Pakistani Sikhs on Pakistan's Sikh Gurdwara Parbandhak Committee (PSGPC). An example of this is Gopal Singh Chawla, the then general secretary of the PSGPC, 'admitting to involvement in the "Khalistan movement" and hailing Muslim terrorist outfits like LeT'.[1]

Indira Gandhi and her home minister, P.C. Sethi, often referred to the 'foreign hand' in Punjab, both inside and outside Parliament. The reference was obviously to our Western neighbour, but they refrained from naming Pakistan, probably for reasons of diplomacy and international imperatives. Such covert cloak-and-dagger games are played by nations with such circumspect canniness that though you always know who the players are behind the curtain, the operations are stealthy and leave little evidence of the masterminds behind them.

When the US supplied arms to the mujahideen in Afghanistan, these were not weapons made in America, which would have directly implicated the US, but mostly Soviet-made armaments procured from communist Czechoslovakia and even Egypt. Likewise, in the initial stages of militancy in Punjab, most of the small arms smuggled into India from Pakistan were originally of Indian ancestry—arms captured by Pakistan in the two wars it fought with us, and rechannelled to the militants.

I learnt of Pakistan's involvement in Punjab in the very first week of joining at Amritsar. The men of 26 Madras regiment apprehended Kuldip Singh, a young boy from Tarn Taran sub-division, and during interrogation he admitted to crossing over to Pakistan and receiving arms training in February–May 1984. On return, he joined the extremists in the temple complex. During my tenure, I came across many more instances of such misguided youth exploited by Pakistan.

The top leadership of the Khalistan movement, in any case, had ISI links.

Hein G. Kiessling, who has chronicled the ISI, discloses, 'Balbier Singh Sandhu, Subegh Singh and Amrik Singh, all three prominent heads of Khalistan movement, had made at least six trips to Pakistan between 1981 and 1983.'[2] Sandhu was the secretary general of the Council of Khalistan, while Amrik Singh was the president of the AISSF, and Shabeg Singh a cashiered Indian Army general and the military adviser of Bhindranwale.

Post–Blue Star, there was an exodus of young boys to Pakistan, partly due to outrage against the army action and partly due to fear of being caught by the army in Operation Woodrose. In 1985, they returned war-trained and accelerated violence, creating mayhem. Dr Sohan Singh, a Sikh ideologue; Bhai Kanwar Singh of the Akal Federation; Wadhawa Singh of the Babbar Khalsa; Atinder Pal Singh of the AISSF; and Gurjit Singh of the Damdami Taksal, to name a few, had frequently crossed the border. Dr Sohan Singh, after he was arrested on 4 November 1993, during his interrogation disclosed that he was based in Pakistan from February 1990 to April 1991, and again slipped across for a short trip. He had met Hekmatyar of Afghanistan and plotted a radio station out of Pakistan for anti-India propaganda, apart from strategizing with the ISI on behalf of the militant organizations and the panthic committee.

A porous 553 kilometres of Punjab's international border (240 kilometres with Amritsar district) that had not been fenced or lit till then made it easy for the radicals to cross over to Pakistan. No wonder that the worst affected districts of Punjab were the ones that share a border with Pakistan—Amritsar, Gurdaspur and Ferozepur. It is also no coincidence that an overwhelming number of Khalistani proponents and heads of various militant organizations either hailed from these three border districts or were based there. Familiarity with the topography, particularly in the riverine belt, and links with the local people facilitated their cross-border movement.

In Pakistan, militant organizations were provided bases, financial resources, weapons and training by the ISI, besides strategic direction. The ISI would set up special training camps and often shift these for security reasons. The places included Gujranwala, Kot Lakhpat Jail, Faisalabad, Attock, Peshawar, Kasur, Sheikhupura, Sialkot, Abbottabad, Dalla Kothi and many other places. Safe houses in urban conglomerates of Rawalpindi, Islamabad, Lahore, Karachi and other towns were used to house the militant leadership. Militant organizations like the Babbar Khalsa International, KCF, BTFK, Khalistan Liberation Force, Dal Khalsa and a few others had established their own regular bases in Pakistan to coordinate with the Pakistanis and carry out militant operations in India.

The weapons training was mostly traditional in nature, but the ISI was innovative and audacious enough to target strategic objectives. Had its design succeeded, it would have carried out an attack similar to the 9/11 attacks of 2001 in India almost a decade earlier. Kiessling refers to an abortive attempt to train a Babbar Khalsa activist as a pilot at a flight training school in Bombay. 'At an advanced stage of his training, during a solo flight he was to crash his plane into an offshore oilrig.'[3] A flying club in India was preferred for training as it provided cover to the Pakistani link; even operationally, it would have been uncomplicated to divert a flight from Bombay to Bombay High, a distance of about 170 kilometres, rather than fly from a foreign base. To hide its association, Pakistan has often launched operations in India from countries such as Nepal and other South East Asian nations.

India had become the primary target of such Pakistani operations soon after Independence. During the period of Ayub Khan, the second President of Pakistan, the ISI established a covert division for this purpose but at that time its target was India's north-eastern region. After the 1965 war, the ISI attempted to expand operations to Punjab but soon realized that the ground conditions were not fertile for it. It, therefore, redirected its focus towards Sikhs settled outside

India, and among the first to be supported by it was London-based Charanjit Singh Panchi of the Sikh Homeland Movement. In the early 1970s, Dr Jagjit Singh Chauhan, a former Punjab minister, then based in London, stepped into Panchi's shoes, with a rechristened Khalistan movement.

By the time Zia-ul-Haq assumed the presidency in 1978, the ground conditions in Punjab were turning favourable for intervention. India's internal politics had created the circumstances that facilitated Pakistan's designs. The Punjab turmoil, let there be no doubt, was wholly of our own creation, not Pakistan's. It was an indigenous brew, domestically fermented. However, an unsettled internal environment invariably invites hostile external forces for covert, if not overt, interventions. We did it in Sri Lanka by arming the LTTE,[4] and in Bangladesh by supporting the Mukti Bahini.[5] Pakistan paid us back in Punjab and Jammu and Kashmir.

The changed geopolitical environment in our neighbourhood also offered Pakistan the opportunity it needed to launch covert operations in Punjab. India was perceived as pro-Russia—these two countries had signed a cooperation agreement to defend each other's territorial integrity in August 1971. The US, on the other hand, had a 1959 Defense Agreement with Pakistan. When the Red Army invaded Afghanistan, the US viewed it as a prelude by Russia to capture the Persian Gulf oil. According to the US, it was a threat, not just to Afghanistan but also to Pakistan and Iran, where its ally, the shah of Iran, had been overthrown by an Islamist revolution. US President Jimmy Carter's national security adviser, Zbigniew Kazimierz Brzezinski, a hardliner, feared that the Russians would create a separate Balochistan, 'which would give them access to the Indian Ocean, while dismembering Pakistan and Iran'.[6]

The US, therefore, launched an intense clandestine operation in Afghanistan, and Pakistan as the frontline state became an arm of the US policy 'to make the Soviets bleed for as much and as long as is possible', as publicly stated by Brzezinski. The ISI became the conduit for the supply of money, material and arms and ammunition to the Afghan rebels fighting the Red Army.

To provide legitimacy to Pakistan's involvement in Afghanistan, as a strategy, the anti-Soviet operations were given the colour of Islam-versus-communism. The tribal militant groups of Afghanistan were catapulted overnight as the mujahideen, Muslim freedom fighters. Gen. Zia-ul-Haq went on record in an interview with Selig Harrison of the *New York Times* to say, '. . . [W]e will not permit it [Afghanistan] to be like it was before, with Indian and Soviet influence there and claims on our territory. It will be a real Islamic State, part of a Pan-Islamic revival that will one day win over the Muslims in the Soviet Union, you will see.'[7]

Punjab became an ancillary objective of Pakistan in this game plan. It quietly diverted a part of the resources provided by the US for fighting the mujahideen to Punjab to trigger and support the militancy. Initially, the US kept its eyes closed for it felt that the domestic turmoil in India would keep it internally occupied, and India would not be able to breath down Pakistan's neck on its eastern border while it carried out America's war against Russia on the western front. Lt. Gen. Hamid Gul, the ISI chief who was particularly active in supporting the Khalistan movement, would often boast that Pakistan-sponsored terrorism would 'tie down at least two divisions of the Indian Army' at no cost to the Pakistani taxpayer.

It is no coincidence that the nine years of Soviet occupation in Afghanistan somewhat corresponded with Punjab's decade of terrorism. The Soviets invaded Afghanistan in December 1979, and completed the withdrawal of its forces by February 1989. The Punjab violence began with the murder of Nirankari chief Gurbachan Singh in April 1980 and terrorism subsided in the early 1990s.

The ISI, to accelerate its clandestine intervention in Punjab, created three sections within its set-up—the psychological warfare section to focus on pro-Khalistan propaganda, highlight the alleged human rights violations and plant stories of success of the militants in Punjab; the logistics section to equip the terrorists with weapons, ammunition, money, etc.; and an operations section to focus on intelligence-gathering, recruitment, training and giving direction to the ethno-national movement.

Pakistan, however, was not sincere to the Khalistanis. Its objective was restricted to bleeding India by converting Punjab into 'Hindu Kush'—*kush* means 'killer'—and thus trigger cross-migration within India. The plan was to divide the Hindu–Sikh communities, and then follow it up by large-scale killings of innocents that would result in mob protests, public outcry and cross-migration. For this reason, Pakistan's supply of weapons to the terrorists was primarily of small arms.

In 1987, the deadly AK-47 and Russian Kalashnikovs were inducted to scale up violence. Heavier weapons like anti-tank rockets and Stinger missiles that were supplied in abundance to the Afghan mujahideen were not on Pakistan's Punjab inventory—for one, the intended target in Punjab was not the Indian Army but innocent civilians, and second, Punjab's terrain was not conducive to deploying heavier weapons. Pakistan's strategy was to emasculate India's 'sword arm', Punjab, by flooding it with weapons and narcotics. It encouraged drug cartels to smuggle and supply weapons to the terrorists. Once the drugs–weapon link was established, these money-spinning operations continued to supply drugs even after militancy ended. That was Pakistan's way to of avenging Bangladesh.

The Khalistanis, however, failed to discern the ISI's real intent. Pakistan was neither capable of nor acquiescent to creating a separate Sikh state because that would imperil its own territorial integrity. When some of the terrorist organizations published maps of Khalistan that showed parts of Pakistan as an integral part of it, Gen. Zia reportedly went into a rage. Lahore was the capital of Maharaja Ranjit Singh and no Sikh militant outfit could afford not to include it or sacred Sikh sites like Nankana Sahib, the birthplace of Guru Nanak, within the boundaries of imagined Khalistan. Sikhs in their daily prayers, ardas, beseech the Akal Purakh (Almighty) for free darshan of these sacred places in Pakistan—the separatists would lose credibility if they were ever to exclude these holy places from Khalistan.

The Sikh separatists realized too late that Pakistan's game plan was to foment communal violence and political instability in India, not Khalistan. They now openly accused Pakistan of betrayal. Dr Sohan Singh, after his arrest in 1993, in his interrogation stated, 'Pakistan has only been manipulating us.'[8] K.P.S. Gill interrogated him, it was recorded on video and shared with Indian journalists. Singh further disclosed, 'The ISI men told me in Pakistan that to promote terrorism in Punjab was their national policy irrespective of change of political leadership', and added that 'Pakistan-directed strategy is to avoid confrontation with security forces . . .'[9] Pakistan encouraged militants to target innocent civilians to create a communal divide and not confront the Indian Army establishment to create Khalistan.

Jagjit Singh Chauhan was even more forthright in expressing his frustration to Shekhar Gupta and Nirupama Subramanian[10] when he said, 'All they [Pakistan] have given Sikhs is less than *gobar* [rubbish].'

However, the ISI at times was blatant and strikingly imprudent. In a rather reckless design, it attempted to pillory the image of Prime Minister Indira Gandhi while she was on a state visit to the UAE in May 1981. Mysteriously, audiotapes containing insulting jokes against the Indian Prime Minister came in circulation in the high-flying social circles of Dubai. Their origin was traced to Pakistani sources. The UAE foreign office summoned the Pakistani ambassador and warned him not to misbehave with their honoured guest.

Again in Dubai, sometime in 1984, both the Pakistani ambassador and the consul general tried to block the repatriation of a Sikh terrorist using their official position; they urged the Dubai police not to send him back to India, but their undiplomatic intercession did not succeed.

The four cases of hijacking of Indian aircraft during 1981–84 highlight the most blatant involvement of Pakistan in Punjab militancy. On 5 July 1984, Indian Airlines flight 405 which had left Srinagar at 4.22 p.m. with 278 passengers for Bombay was hijacked as it neared Amritsar. I was in office when I got the message that Pakistani authorities were not permitting the flight to land at Lahore. The aircraft had fuel for only half an hour and we expected that it would have no option but to land at Raja Sansi, Amritsar. We rushed to the airport and as a precaution all measures for its landing were taken. After it had hovered over Lahore for a while, it was allowed to land at 6.40 p.m. A long wait of protracted negotiations with the hijackers followed. The seventeen-hour ordeal in Lahore was part of Pakistan's plan to lend international publicity to the hijackers and their demands.

Earlier, on 29 September 1981, five knife-wielding Dal Khalsa radicals had hijacked an Indian Airlines plane with 111 passengers and a crew of six. Pakistani authorities invited the Indian ambassador, Natwar Singh, to negotiate with them but refused to repatriate them to India. Again, the objective was to give the widest publicity to the hijackers and the Sikh separatist movement.

Two more hijackings took place in August 1982, but probably the worst abetment of the hijackers by Pakistan was on 24 August 1984. Seven militants had diverted an Indian Airlines flight from Chandigarh to Srinagar to land in Lahore. From there it was taken to Karachi and finally to Dubai. The defence minister of the UAE played a noteworthy role and succeeded in getting the passengers released. The hijackers were repatriated by the UAE to India, and along came a Walther PPK pistol, handed over to the hijackers by Pakistanis at the Karachi airport.

Initially, Pakistan denied its involvement, but the German intelligence service, the BND, confirmed to Interpol that the weapon was part of the consignment sold to the Government of Pakistan by the German manufacturer. Faced with the truth, Pakistan cooked up the story that the pistol was somehow lost and that it had no clue how the weapon had reached the hijackers.

When the Russians commenced withdrawal from Afghanistan in 1988, Pakistan cleverly shifted the focus from Punjab to Kashmir. The well-armed and trained mujahideen, having defeated communism, were now ready to take on 'Hindu imperialism'. They were conveniently redirected to Kashmir and imbued with a new ne plus ultra—jihad, a fight for the freedom of their Muslim brethren. Indian security forces were caught napping when on 31 July 1988, the first bomb blast in Jammu and Kashmir at the Srinagar club near the Central Telegraph Office sounded the beginning of a shift of ethno-religious terrorism from Punjab to Kashmir.

37

The Fourth Estate

The Genesis

THE TWO SANTS, LONGOWAL AND BHINDRANWALE, WERE ASTUTE enough to understand the pivotal role the media plays in building public opinion, and both were keen to set up their own newspapers. Both, however, abandoned the idea, though for different reasons. Longowal had seen *Akali Patrika,* a pro-Sikh newspaper, published from Jalandhar totter and realized the operational pitfalls of managing a media house.

Bhindranwale, however, stole the show. He had co-opted a few media advisers from among like-minded journalists, the most influential among them being Dalbir Singh of *The Tribune*, who was posted in Amritsar for a few years. When Bhindranwale consulted him to launch a newspaper, Dalbir Singh advised him to raise a few crores of rupees that would be required to set up a new media house.

Bhindranwale is said to have retorted: One Sten gun costs eight thousand rupees, how many could be acquired in one crore? If one magazine is emptied in a day, all radio stations and newspapers *baan baan karde reh jaan ge*—they will crawl to fall in line.[1]

And that settled the militant's media policy, though Bhindranwale was media-savvy. National and international journalists vied to interview him, often romanticized him and built his image larger than life. Longowal's frustration was captured by Sunil Sethi, a journalist and TV anchor, when Longowal bluntly told him, 'What viewpoint? Go ask your friend [Bhindranwale] next door for viewpoints. We are not worth much given the space we get on your cover. I mean you shoved us all into the bottom of his beard.'[2]

Post–Blue Star, Dalbir Singh went underground and faced several criminal charges and arrest warrants under the National Security Act. His services were terminated by *The Tribune*. Many other journalists 'friendly' to the movement, however, survived and some reoriented their leanings. The most scathing comment on the Punjab media came from another journalist, Abhinav Nayar. He alleged that in Punjab, journalism had become a 'mercenary profession', where some journalists became a 'willing tool in the hands of the extremists or the police'.[3] The state and the militants both were using journalists and at times some of them acted as informers.

The strategy to terrorize the media was adopted by the militants from the very beginning of the movement. Lala Jagat Narain of the *Hind Samachar* group was killed on 9 September 1981, and his son Ramesh Chandra on 12 May 1984. Journalists covering the Golden Temple faced subtle pressure, with occasional acts of violence. On 3 February 1984, Sanjiv Gaur, the Amritsar-based correspondent of the *Indian Express*, was stabbed outside the Golden Temple, and the same day a grenade was lobbed at the TV centre at Jalandhar, damaging the building.

Earlier, in June 1983, a parcel bomb sent to *Daily Partap* in Jalandhar exploded, killing two of its employees. On 25 January 1984, a grenade was thrown at *The Tribune* building in Chandigarh. Again, on 14 February 1984, Yash Pal Billa, who represented *Siyasi Jung*, was shot at in Amritsar and injured while his gunman Mohinder Singh died. On 22 February 1984, Sumit Singh Shammi, editor of *Preet Lari*, a literary Punjabi magazine, was shot dead at Lopoke in Amritsar. Sukhraj Khaddar, editor of *Chingari*, a leftist magazine, was killed in Gurdaspur on 11 April 1984.

While the militants targeted the media in Punjab, intensifying the state's predicament, the role of a section of the national press was also a matter of concern. Some of the leading national newspapers obfuscated the problem by equating terrorism and Sikhs, as if they were one and the same. They blurred the distinction between a political party's (Akali's) right to seek its demands through democratic agitation and the violence unleashed by the weapon-wielding militants.

The Telegraph, as early as 13 October 1982, wrote, 'These demands are superfluous but certainly lead to the basic objective of the present Akali leaders, which is to make Sikhism the state religion of Punjab and to convert it into a theocratic state. In many respects the Akalis are a Sikh version of Khomeinism.'[4]

On 27 March 1984, Girilal Jain of the *Times of India* wrote, 'I sincerely believe the agitation is misconceived because Sikhs cannot, in my opinion, possibly have any genuine grievance.'[5] He, in fact, was conveying a veiled warning of what was to follow a few months later, after the assassination of Indira Gandhi, when he wrote, 'It is 11 p.m. in the history of the Sikh community. It must reverse the clock. It is still possible to do so. But time is running out.'[6] Some historians have interpreted such write-ups as an attempt to manufacture public consent and a 'national consensus' for military action.

Kewal Verma, the chief of bureau of *The Telegraph*, warned in the *Mainstream* that had there been no military action, there would have been a military mutiny, with Hindu soldiers launching an assault on the Golden Temple. 'There would have been a massacre of Sikhs outside Punjab. The possibility of some sort of coup and the army marching into the Golden Temple with the battle cry "Har Har Maha Dev" could also not have been ruled out.'[7]

During and immediately after Blue Star, the government had enforced a media lockdown. All news was either blacked out, or carefully screened handouts were issued and the media faithfully carried them. The journalists became what is called embedded media. There was little, if any, independent or investigative reporting and journalists even lapped up the stories that were plants. Illustratively, a section of the media carried stories that women and used condoms were found inside the temple complex, hinting at immoral conduct, which was a manufactured story.

The journalists who violated the lockdown laws landed in trouble. Brahma Chellaney of *The Times*, London, was one who stayed on in Amritsar despite directions to the foreign media to move out of Punjab. A few days later, on reaching Shimla, he filed a story on telex on 13 June 1984. It was published the next day in *The Times*, London, under the heading 'Sikhs Tied Up and Shot'. It sensationalized the military operation and on 30 July a case was registered against him for offences that included sedition.

After Blue Star

Starting from 1989 and through 1990 and 1991, the militants targeted not just the journalists, but also their distribution network such as news agents, newspaper hawkers, newspaper distributers and even the concerned government departments and its agencies, accentuating the then prevalent fear psychosis.

What helped the terrorists was the fact that the media itself was a divided lot. Freedom of the press, in its classical formulation, presupposes the existence of diverse perceptions—though facts are always sacred. In Punjab, however, even facts at times became tainted by pre-existing biases so that the same news would bear a different nuance, if not slant, depending upon which section of the media carried the story. This was particularly true of the vernacular newspapers, a section of which was often acerbic in editorial comments and sensational in its headlines, further sharpening the communal divide.

The communal slant of the vernacular media was best highlighted when Santokh Singh Dhir, a Punjabi poet-novelist, wrote two open letters pleading for restraint—one implored the Sikhs and the second the Hindus. He sent both these letters to the vernacular newspapers. The one that implored the Sikhs got published in all the pro-Hindu newspapers, while they omitted the second letter addressed to the Hindus. The letter that beseeched the Hindus was published only by newspapers considered pro-Sikh while they blacked out the letter addressed to the Sikhs.[8]

In fact, the origin of the vernacular newsprint media in Punjab bore a communal ethos that prevailed in British India and it continued to dominate its responses even post-Independence. The ownership pattern was based on family proprietorship. The management structure of these newspapers largely rested on poorly paid stringers rather than regular staffers and their commercial interests, and still more importantly the readership constituency they addressed—these determined their approach to the Punjab problem.

The militants exploited this divisive posturing of the media, and a section of the print media was used by the militants to spread fear. A new practice—*spashtikarans*, or explanations—surfaced; the print media would print these spashtikarans of citizens threatened by the militants for alleged misdemeanours or violations of the code of conduct enforced by them. The threatened individuals and organizations would explain their conduct or seek militants' forgiveness by placing advertisements in newspapers. The media became a mode of communication between the terrorists and the terrorized. It suited the militants, who got publicity, and the newspapers, which earned revenue from advertisements.

The terrorists also used newspapers to eulogize their leaders. When a militant was killed, obituary advertisements with photographs of the 'martyred' militants would be inserted in the media with an appeal to people to attend their bhog ceremonies. They would also give calls to organize bandhs or shutdowns in various towns of the state, in remembrance of their fallen brethren.

The situation became so bad that when *The Tribune*, a 'neutral' English daily, declined to carry a bhog advertisement of an A Category terrorist, two gun-wielding men walked into the office of its editor-in-chief, V.N. Narayanan, in Chandigarh on 14 June 1990 and threatened him. *The Tribune* capitulated. The terrorists' edicts, codes of conduct, bhog obituaries, bandh calls, warnings and spashtikarans became a regular feature in newspapers.

The media capitulation was complete when Jinda–Sukha, the two assassins of Vaidya, the former army chief, issued a twenty-one-page letter to the newspapers with a directive to publish the full text or face bullets. UNI and PTI, the two leading news agencies of the country, circulated the letter on 26 July 1990, and many newspapers, including the national dailies, carried its extracts on 27 July.

In Chandigarh, the *Punjabi Tribune* carried the entire text of the letter, covering about three pages, while its sister publications *The Tribune* and the *Dainik Tribune* published only an abridged version. Narayanan, the editor-in-chief of *The Tribune*, had the memory of 14 June 1990 fresh in his mind when the two armed militants had walked into his office. So, when he received fresh threats, he fell in line and published the entire text of the letter on July 28 1990. The *Dainik Tribune*, which had continued to defy the warning, also succumbed on 30 July and published the entire letter with an apology on its front page for the delay in publishing it.

On 22 November 1990, the panthic committee (Sohan Singh) issued an elaborate code of conduct with a threat to inflict memorable punishment on journalists who violated it. The code prohibited the media from using the term 'terrorists' and instead they were to be addressed as 'militants'. A succession of other codes followed. On 1 December 1990, the panthic committee issued the 'language code' that enforced the use of Punjabi in the state.

Any non-compliance was punished by the militants. On 6 December 1990, A.K. Talib, the handicapped station director of AIR, who was home on leave for his daughter's marriage, was shot dead. Later, one Harminder Singh Happy, a terrorist, was arrested by Gurdaspur police and he confessed to the murder. The police wanted his confessional statement to be captured on camera to telecast it, but the Doordarshan camera crew did not dare turn up.

M.L. Manchanda, station director of AIR at Patiala, was next to be killed. Terrified, the radio station complied with the militant edict and discontinued its Hindi news bulletin and shifted its Hindi broadcast to the Rohtak station. Suddenly, the Doordarshan women announcers started wearing salwar kameez, covered their heads with dupattas, and spoke in chaste Punjabi.

Worst affected was the Hind Samachar group of newspapers. In a fresh offensive against the paper on 18 July 1990, the van carrying its newspapers to Ferozepur was ambushed near Jagraon and all its five occupants, including three police guards, were killed. Its editorial staffers: Inderjit Sood, news editor, Bant Singh, chief sub-editor, two reporters, Jagjit Singh and Parduman Singh, and its vendors, agents and hawkers, numbering about forty-four, were killed.

The government too buckled under the threats. The worst instance of it was when Governor Virendra Verma, without consulting K. Rajendran Nair, the secretary of the Department of Information and Public Relations, informally decided that the department may temporarily discontinue government press releases in Hindi and also suspend the release of advertisements to Hindi newspapers.

Verma's intent was to avoid confrontation with the militants who had imposed a ban on the use of Hindi in the state. His decision naturally invited criticism. In the very next meeting of the Press Relations Committee, a member bluntly told him, 'Khalistan aa gaya hai.' The governor, rather than owning up to the decision, blamed Nair. He repeated the same the very next day in a press conference at Chandigarh when confronted by the media. Not to take the false indictment, Nair stood up in the middle of the press conference, narrated his version to the media and walked out, leaving the governor red-faced. Later, he proceeded on deputation to the Government of India and I was brought in as secretary of the department.

The informal decision of the governor was formalized by adopting a new policy that curtailed advertisements to the Hindi press. Now 50 per cent advertisements were to be given to Punjabi papers, 26 per cent to English papers and 14 per cent and 10 per cent, respectively, to Hindi and Urdu papers. The official explanation was that it was to promote Punjabi, the official state language, in conformity with the Punjabi language policy, and it was 'not a discriminatory advertisement policy'.

The fear among government officials was so deep and widespread that Punjabi typewriters, which earlier were rarely used, suddenly became prized possessions—some departments even took policy decisions to buy only Gurmukhi typewriters. English made an exit from offices. The officials who were used to writing notings on files in English struggled to brush up their Punjabi. The English–Punjabi dictionaries that were little in demand earlier became valued accessories. Most secretaries would dictate official notes in English, the language they were used to, and then get it translated to Punjabi, pushing up the demand for translators. In February 1991, the Zaffarwal Panthic Committee issued another code of conduct directing the media to boycott government functions and its alleged misleading news items.

Strange as it may appear, most of the codes and edicts issued in the name of panthic committees and well-known militants were in fact the handiwork of overground 'intellectuals' sitting in cities like Chandigarh. These press notes, edicts and codes of conduct were often hand-delivered at newspaper offices and even at the residences of individual journalists, with their name and address written on the envelopes. Some press notes even carried attached warning notes to publish the news faithfully and in full, or be ready to face swift retaliation.

The Press Council of India noted, 'What newsmen found particularly disturbing would be scarcely veiled threats to their wives, and children whose names, ages, schools and classes might sometimes be mentioned to suggest that their movements were known.' It observed that 'moles are suspected everywhere'. It was a great intelligence failure otherwise, such a fear-mongering band of pseudo-intellectuals could not have surfaced and survived as long as the militancy lived.

Their lives and liberty in peril, most workers in the media opted for the policy that discretion is the better part of valour. Consequently, journalism survived on press handouts, whether of the militants or of the police. Investigative journalism or independent stories of terrorist violence or alleged police excesses were few and far between.

Gobind Thukral, who worked for the *Indian Express*, *India Today* and *Hindustan Times* from 1978 to 1996, in his seminal study done for the Indian Institute of Advanced Studies, Shimla, was candid to admit that the media was 'mostly dependent upon the police version and no questions were asked at the district level'.[9] Other sources of information such as eyewitnesses or public accounts, in any case, would rarely come forward to confirm or deny the respective claims of the terrorists or of the police.

Some courageous correspondents who tried to investigate either got compromised or were bumped off, like Balbir Singh Saggu, the Amritsar-based reporter who had gone to meet a source and was killed on 12 November 1990. However, stories of 'disappearance', a euphemism for staged encounters, were carried by a few journalists, particularly towards the end of the militancy. The two names that stand out are Naveen Grewal of *The Pioneer* and Manmoydass Gupta of *The Telegraph*.

Another aspect of Punjab's media noted by the Press Council of India was the unhealthy competition among them. It manifested in a dirty war of numbers; at times the body count of those killed by terrorists were inflated by news agencies to get better space in the newspapers. The council noted, 'It is demoralizing and spreads terror as numbers are inflated.'

It was this sort of reckless, competitive reporting that worsened the situation and one such instance that influenced the course of Punjab turmoil was a misleading sit-rep sent by UNI correspondent Akhil Gautam, after the failure of negotiations between the Akalis and the Central government. The morcha dictator, Longowal, while addressing his followers, announced in November 1982 from Manji Sahib that the Akali Dal had decided to court peaceful arrests at Delhi during the Asian Games as the next step of the ongoing agitation. He said the objective was to attract global attention to the non-fulfilment of their demands. The UNI correspondent, however, reported that the Akali Dal had announced plans to disrupt the Asian Games.

The PTI sit-rep that was dispatched an hour or so later gave a clear picture of the statement; Longowal had never said that the Akali Dal would disrupt the Games. However, UNI had beaten PTI on time, and its report was carried by most of the media. The damage had been done. Alarm bells rang in Delhi, and Rajiv Gandhi, who was then the general secretary of the Congress and supervising the Games, alerted Chief Minister Bhajan Lal of Haryana. What happened thereafter is too well known to be repeated here.

Government Response

The government's first response to the capitulation of the media to the directives of terrorists was an appeal to resist the onslaught. The governor met the Press Relations Committee at Jalandhar, extended government cooperation and offered security cover where required. Thereafter, on 10 August 1990, an advisory was issued to all newspapers not to carry 'objectionable advertisements and subversive writings', cautioning that it would attract penal provisions of the Indian Penal Code and the Terrorist and Disruptive Activities (Prevention) Act, which the government did not want to resort to. It wanted the press to exercise self-discretion and restraint.

The Press Council also appointed a sub-committee in December 1990 to study the media environment and it gave its first report titled 'Overcoming Fear' on 16 January 1991. As the state government acted on the report, the governor sought the help of Justice R.S. Sarkaria, chairman of the council, on 4 February 1991 to deal with the 'crude form of censorship' accepted by the media under terrorist threats. The Press Council, however, was critical of the government response. It observed, 'The Government too had no overall media strategy within Punjab strategy. Its actions are uncoordinated, faltering and ad hoc.'

But the terrorist threat proved mightier than the government's advisories or the Press Council's interventions, and subversive news and advertisements continued to regularly appear in newspapers. Therefore, the state had two options: It could either proceed under the Punjab Press (Special Powers) Act, 1956, and impose pre-censorship, or alternatively rely on Section 95 of the CrPC under which any newspaper, book or document that incites disinfection, disharmony, feelings of enmity, religious hatred, etc., could be seized. The government picked the second option, and on 20 February 1991, instructions were issued to district magistrates to institute a system of surveillance of all publications and proceed against the defaulting ones. The Chandigarh administration also issued a similar order under Section 95.

The government's instructions were that all subversive news items, obituary notices for bhog ceremonies that depicted terrorists as 'martyrs' in the struggle for Khalistan, publication of threats and warnings by them or giving justification for killings, news regarding any 'code of conduct', etc., were to be forfeited. Even hawkers and newspaper distributors were made liable if they sold newspapers containing such news items—they were expected to scan newspapers before distributing the same.

These instructions invited protests from journalists. On 4 March 1991, about seventy of them marched to the Raj Bhavan and sat on a dharna, and repeated it on 17 March. They alleged that the media was under a 'pincer attack' and that it was being badgered by both sides—by the militants who had a code of conduct for journalists and by the Punjab administration, which was resorting to penal provisions.

Expressing shock and anger at the action of the government, they set up an eleven-member committee 'to secure for newspapers and their employees the right to function in an atmosphere of greater freedom' and appealed to the government and the terrorists to 'lift all restrictions forthwith and allow the press to function independently'.

On 17 March, *The Tribune*'s employees' union organized another protest, calling Section 95 'Damocles' Sword'. They appealed to journalists to 'boycott all [government] functions and not to use press handouts' from the government for three days from the day copies of any newspaper were seized.

The government notification was also challenged in the High Court, which, however, upheld action under Section 95 of the CrPC on 30 July 1991, with the caution that these were extraordinary powers and 'must be used with care and circumspection, as it constitutes an inroad into enjoyment of the right guaranteed' for freedom of speech and expression.[10]

The Seizures

However, despite the notification under Section 95, newspapers did not stop the publication of objectionable news items and advertisements. Therefore, both Punjab and the Chandigarh administration resorted to physical seizures of newspapers that carried such items. Barring the leftist newspapers like *Nawan Zamana* and *Lok Lehr* and what was called Mahasha press—the Hind Samachar Group, *Vir Partap* and *Partap*—virtually all other major newspapers faced seizure at one point or the other.

In February 1991, the Chandigarh administration seized copies of the early-morning edition of *The Tribune* carrying an ultimatum issued by one of the panthic committees, naming a few officials as its target for dire punishment if they failed to implement its directive on the use of Punjabi. The paper dropped the news item from its subsequent editions of the day and this invited a three-page warning from the militants to all editors in Punjab and Chandigarh that they may be killed if they did not resist the government's 'censorship' under Section 95.

On subsequent dates, the Chandigarh administration acted against the *Indian Express*, and the Tribune Group a second time. Some of the newspapers, for example, the *Indian Express* dated 16 January 1991, protested and carried stories announcing 'police raids' on their premises and that the government had 'censored' news. *Ajit* and the *Times of India* were, in fact, also proceeded against under TADA by the Chandigarh administration.

In Punjab, *Ajit* faced the most government ire. Barjinder Singh Hamdard, its editor-in-chief, returned the Padma Shri award conferred on him in 1991 in protest against the media policies of the government. *Ajit's* stand was that it represented all sections of the people and that even militants' viewpoints should not be shut out completely. Consequently, the state proceeded against it on several occasions.

Aaj Di Awaz of Jalandhar was another newspaper that faced seizure of its copies on 3 March, 20 March, 23 March, 16 April, 18 May and 30 May 1991. *The Hindu* dated 20 February 1991 was also proceeded against.

The government strategy worked. The sub-committee of the Press Council in its second report noted that Section 95 of the CrPC 'has quite clearly worked and the militant's counter censorship had proved an empty threat'. It accepted the state's stand that the news items acted against did not represent 'news' by any test of public interest.

It, however, observed that 'it would not be desirable to shut out the militants' point of view completely . . . people in democratic society have a right to know what the militants stand for the basis of their argument . . . To label action taken to prevent such stories being published as censorship or attack on the freedom of press is perverse . . . those who violate reasonable laws reasonably applied must be prepared to face the consequences . . . there can be no doubt whatsoever that freedom of the press is threatened not by the government, whether in Chandigarh or Delhi, but by terrorist organizations. The press must stand up to this threat.'

The government action under Section 95 had provided the media an alibi not to carry subversive stories or advertisements. Using this as a pretext, over a period of time, the newspapers, even the pro-radical ones, put a stop to the publication of spashtikarans, bhog advertisements, bandh calls, threats, etc., easing the prevailing environment of fear and thus diminishing the publicity the militants had been gaining. In the end, the government edict proved more potent than the terrorist's gun.

38

Militancy: The Beginning and the End

The ethno-national movement in Punjab originated from matters of faith. Its objective, when it surfaced in the early 1980s, was limited to retribution—to set right the heretical Nirankaris.

The targeted killings began with the murder of the Nirankari chief on 24 April 1980. Sukhdev Singh of the Babbar Khalsa in a press statement made on 20 December 1983, while condemning the murders of innocent Hindus in Punjab, publicly acknowledged that his group had killed thirty-five Nirankaris. Apart from the Babbars, there were the '*mundey*', or boys, of Bhindranwale and the AISSF, who had their own hit list of heretics.

At that stage, the number of the kharkoos or combatants was minuscule and they were either the boys of Bhindranwale and the AISSF, or they belonged to the Babbar Khalsa. They were religious zealots determined to take on the enemies of Sikhism. The tradition of shaheedi in Sikhism and the deeply embedded historical predilection to take up arms against perceived injustice reinforced their resolve to eliminate the adversaries of the panth.

These kharkoos were foolhardy and audacious, and their mindset was reflected in the operative motto that Talwinder Singh Parmar had coined for the motorcycle gangs he had formed—'*Jo Ade So Mite*', or whosoever obstructs will be eliminated. However, they lacked the expertise needed to be assassins or sharpshooters and, not surprisingly, they co-opted skilled shooters from among the police and former Naxalites to augment their squads.[1]

Because the foundation of the ethno-national movement lay in theology, the kharkoos could claim a certain canonical legitimacy, and using it they placed themselves above worldly laws. It was this ecclesiastical context that created empathy with their cause or, if I may call it, 'a popular will' that meshed with the kharkoos on the issues of the Nirankaris' blasphemy. After all, the Nirankaris were apostates and therefore blasphemous in the eyes of the kharkoos as much as they were for the ordinary faithful. This, in turn, provided the kharkoos with an alibi and a sense of self-righteousness in their actions. The panth, therefore, tended to perceive them as kharkoos or combatants for the faith and not as terrorists. To use guerrilla leader Che Guevara's terminology, it was the 'absence of sufficiently antagonistic social contradictions' in Sikh ethos that facilitated the kharkoos to grow.

Viewed through the militant–religious lens, the predictable course of action was that the kharkoos would restrict the killings to only the heretics. However, the state response to their violence lacked effective deterrence or retribution. This facilitated the expansion of the 'killer boundaries' from the apostates to include whoever came in their way.

The arrest of Bhindranwale and what had transpired earlier in the attempt to arrest him at Chando Kalan, where holy books got burnt, and at Chowk Mehta, where about seven people were killed, enraged the kharkoos. For the first time, they executed mass killings of the innocent in the bazars of Jalandhar and Tarn Taran on 20 September 1981. It was a challenge to the state—and it failed to rise to it and stub out terrorism in this nascent phase.

At this stage, Khalistan was not the objective of the kharkoos, though a few independent individuals like Gurmeet Singh Aulakh, Dr Jagjit Singh Chauhan, Balbir Singh of the National Council of Khalistan and organizations like the Dal Khalsa had already appeared on the scene, and they did indulge in separatist propaganda. The number of kharkoos was also small, and they had a limited number of weapons, mostly small arms like rifles, 12-bore guns, pistols, revolvers and very few automatic weapons. For this reason, they were usually 'issued' arms for specific assignments and were expected to deposit these back after accomplishing the task. They exploited religious places for logistical support and carried out selective killings, their targets being the 'enemies of the panth'. In 1981 and 1982, the total number of civilians killed was thirteen in each year, and these included both Hindus and Sikhs. The number of terrorists killed was fourteen in 1981 and seven in 1982.

Violence, however, has its own intrinsic logic, and it was only a matter of time before brutality, which the combatants perceived as bravery for seeking their *hak*, or rights, transcended the kharkoo ethos. They had transformed from religious warriors to terrorists and to expand their reach they now executed a planned 'consternation strategy' to demoralize the security forces and paralyse the state administration. They aimed to gain international recognition, particularly among the Sikh diaspora.

Money was required to fund the acquisition of arms, and although Pakistan extended support, it was not enough. So, they resorted to the large-scale looting of banks. Starting 27 January 1983, when a branch of the Syndicate Bank in Amritsar was robbed, till the end of the year when the Punjab and Sind Bank on the Guru Nanak Dev University campus in Amritsar was looted on 6 December 1983, there were about twenty-one daylight bank dacoities in the state.

Communal polarization became a catalyst in the evolution of militancy. It had begun in 1981, when slogans like '*Kachh, kara, kirpan, dhak diyange Pakistan*' by Hindu radicals and counter-communal vociferations like '*Dhoti topi Jamna paar*' were heard on the streets of Amritsar. This oral spitfire and sloganeering against each other by the two main communities of the state soon turned into physical acts of desecration as severed cow heads were planted near temples or cigarettes were found in gurdwaras or the Guru Granth Sahib was set on fire at a few places.

When a gurdwara was set on fire at Churu in Rajasthan by the Jai Hindu Sangh with a call for Sikhs to leave Rajasthan, Bhindranwale retaliated that should anything happen to Sikhs, Hindus in Punjab would be slaughtered. As Mark Juergensmeyer, a professor of sociology at the University of California put it, the Punjab tragedy happened due to the 'coalescence of a peculiar set of circumstances—political, social and ideological—when religion becomes fused with violent expression of social aspirations, personal pride and movement of political change'.[2]

The Ethno-National Movement

Two tragic happenings—Operation Blue Star in June 1984, and the anti-Sikh carnage following the assassination of Prime Minister Indira Gandhi—coalesced the Sikh community into a common bruised psyche. The Sikh panth, which had prided itself on being the sword arm of India, found itself a terrorized minority, lynched or burnt alive on the streets of the nation, including its capital, Delhi. The carnage 'personalized the conflict' and 'nationhood became a defining part of the Sikh rebellion in Punjab'.[3]

These tragic happenings resurrected the historical martial trait of retribution among the radical elements and several young boys took to the gun to avenge the public ignominy and disgrace the community had faced. However, this backlash was not a secessionist response, nor a quest for territorial independence. It was a reaction to violence against Sikhs—a certain solidification of the Sikh identity, an expression of anguish and a quest for justice.

In fact, the Khalistan demand had not resonated with the panth—it was the stillborn aspiration of only a few fringe outfits. Jitinder Kaur, a professor from the University of Delhi who conducted a survey in 1985 in Punjab, found that the demand for Khalistan was a myth—only 6 per cent of the surveyed people sought secession, while among the elite the percentage dropped further to 2 per cent. The study concluded that the majority of those who supported the demand for Khalistan were in the age group of twenty-one to thirty and 'were by and large either illiterate or literate without any formal schooling'.[4] It was this microscopic number of young radicals that picked up the thread from what Bhindranwale had said—the foundation of Khalistan would be laid the day the government attacked the Golden Temple.

There was a long incubation period after Blue Star and the anti-Sikh carnage before a formal declaration of Khalistan was made from the Golden Temple in 1986. In fact, 1985 had seen a comparative calm in Punjab—sixty-three innocent people were killed, compared to the 359 killed in 1984. There were two reasons for this comparative lull. First, the community was in distress, awaiting justice and due process to take effect, which had evaded it as no one was punished for the anti-Sikh violence. Secondly, the radicals were on the run as the army conducted Operation Woodrose, following Blue Star. Many young hotheads crossed over to Pakistan to evade arrest.

During this interregnum, while the militants were on the run, religious preachers, folk singers, bards, *kavishari jatha*s and *dhadhis* stepped in to consolidate the panth's conscience with a tacit message to seek resistance and retribution. They would recapitulate the glorious Sikh struggle against oppression and simulate the community to fight back. Illustratively, the jatha of Nabhe Wallian Bibian, an all-women's group of parsons, became very popular with their vaars and ballads of courage and sacrifice, imparting a message to defy and confront those who wronged the community.

By the time Longowal was released from detention in March 1985, after his arrest in Operation Blue Star, he and his ilk had ceased to be relevant. The moderates tried to recapture the panthic imagination and even adopted an aggressive anti-government imagery, but they had lost credibility and the trust of the community. The panthic space had been captured by the martyrs of the quam. The radicals and gun-wielding militants represented the shaheeds, not traditional Akalis. The marginalized Akali moderates, therefore, either laid low or allied with the radicals to make separatist noises as a survival tactic. One such example is Longowal's public statement, 'Our doubts have now become a conviction. Now we are convinced that the government really does not want us to stay in the country.'[5] If anyone dared to question the militants, they were threatened or eliminated. The militants gained enough legitimacy to even use theological sanctions to silence the traditional leadership—several edicts and hukamnamas were issued, and many Sikhs were declared tankhaiya.

Once the army withdrew from Punjab in 1985, the terrorists reappeared. Those who had slipped across to Pakistan returned, armed and well-trained, ready to take on the Indian State. The Damdami Taksal provided the lead and the first militant organization, the Khalistan Commando Force, was formally launched from the Golden Temple in April 1986 by the panthic committee aligned with the Damdami Taksal. This sounded the bugle for the ethno-national armed struggle to achieve independence from 'Brahmanwad' and 'Baniawad' (read Hindu imperialism) and its perceived onslaught on Sikhs.

Violence, thus, acquired a reason, a justification and an objective—the creation of Khalistan. The targets were government institutions, innocent Hindus, Sikh leaders who were perceived to have 'betrayed' the quam or facilitated the Delhi Darbar and the Patit Sikhs, the apostate. In fact, more Sikhs than non-Sikhs were killed after 1986. The main objective, however, was to demobilize the state machinery by terror and violence by enforcing the militant's 'code of conduct' and floating parallel institutions like the Khalsa Panchayat and panthic committees to replace the statutory bodies and to create communal division.

The Mushrooming of Terrorist Groups

In 1986, there were only two militant organizations—the KCF, its associate the AISSF, and the Babbar Khalsa, whose thrust was theological. The total number of militants was hardly a thousand or so, and there were discernible signs of division among them. However, the first formal split in the panthic committee came in November 1986, when Aroor Singh was removed from its membership and within days of his dismissal, he launched a parallel organization—the Khalistan Liberation Force. To announce its birth, it massacred about twenty-two Hindus travelling in a bus.

With time, these militant modules mutated, mushroomed and splintered to multiply. In April 1987, another member of the panthic committee, Gurbachan Singh Manochahal, quit the committee and floated a new militant outfit, the Bhindranwale Tiger Force of Khalistan, and thereafter, in April 1989, he floated a separate panthic committee. Earlier, in November 1988, Dr Sohan Singh, who was to play a key role in directing the ethno-national movement, had formed yet another panthic committee.

The Babbar Khalsa formed its own equivalent of a panthic committee—the Akali Dal (Babbar), which was to act as its political front. Over a period, not one or two but five independent panthic committees or their equivalent emerged with their own operational armed wings and affiliate militant organizations. By 1992, the militant organizations numbered no less than seventeen, including some women's groups such as the Mai Bhago Regiment and the Mata Sahib Singh Commando Force led by Bibi Bhag Kaur and Bibi Harsharan Kaur, respectively. Most of these organizations, in turn, had their own gangs, modules and sub-units.

Except for some organizations like the KCF, KLF and the Babbars, which had a pan-Punjab presence, the other organizations were led by local chiefs who dominated a particular geographical area, usually close to their villages or region. These areas were not mutually exclusive jurisdictions as often more than one organization was active in the same area. While some of these set-ups were autonomous, the others operated in a loose confederacy with one or the other panthic committee. There was no single or central command for these militant organizations. The militancy was not monolithic in structure, operations or mandate—the only commonality among them was violence. In fact, there was inter-organizational strife among them, and inter-gang killings were not uncommon. They even suffered from an internecine struggle to gain leadership. The Khalistan movement, thus, was not a unified struggle against the state but one that consisted of multiple independent groups, with a few hundred militants in each organization, who had tasted the power of the gun and the riches it brought, creating bloodshed and havoc under the cloak of an ethno-national war.

Scholar Cynthia Keppley has observed that Khalistan was 'an opaque slogan rather than an articulated plan' that 'leaves us with the particular quandary of explaining just what was that all those young lives perished for'; it was 'the rallying cry at which Sikhs so excel, rather than at the level of an articulated concept or political philosophy'.[6]

The militant organizations, nevertheless, projected themselves as warriors seeking a Sikh state. The movement needed a political objective to gain respectability and therefore they made ideological statements and issued literature from time to time that relied heavily on the Sikh historical tradition of fighting oppression and routinely invoked the Gurbani.

But neither the members of the various panthic committees nor the so-called generals of its armed wings were theorists or thinkers (with a few exceptions like Dr Sohan Singh) with the intellectual capability to conceptualize. Therefore, they used like-minded 'intellectuals', mostly professors, a few journalists—even a colleague of mine, a Sikh ideologue—who drafted ideological edicts, dictates and press notes for various underground organizations.

These co-opted ideologues[7] operated from behind the scenes to philosophize and project an ideological base. But this division of labour between terrorists and thinkers, by its very nature, was dichotomous; there was a huge gap between philosophical theory and the unmitigated violence unleashed by the terrorists, particularly as the induction of new terrorists was not based on the ideological moorings of the new recruits or their commitment to the Sikh religion or even to the cause of Khalistan, but on friendships, family and clan affinity, social connectivity or proximity to a known militant. It is not surprising that out of more than 12,000 villages in the state, nearly 75 per cent of terrorists came from just about 225 villages.

The movement also lacked a charismatic leader to bind and discipline the cadres. The members of the panthic committees and the self-styled generals were all obscure pygmies, little known beyond the areas or region to which they belonged, till they hijacked newspaper headlines by bloodshed.

Pakistan encouraged the multiplication of terrorist organizations and opened separate supply chains to these diverse bands. The reasons were many. First, it was perceived that this way the ethno-national movement would proliferate much faster, and the larger the number of terrorist modules, greater would be the violence.

Secondly, penetrating multifarious groups would be more arduous for the state agencies. A monolithic, single militant organization, if successfully penetrated by government spies at any level, could be smashed in one go, but multiple groups that were operationally independent would pose a larger, more significant challenge. For this reason, the bigger militant outfits like the KCF and KLF had a highly decentralized command-and-control mechanism. The territorial jurisdiction for operations was loosely divided among various modules and sub-units, each under the command of a self-styled general, who in turn would command smaller amoebic groups. These smaller groups were given enough elbow room to choose their target, time, place and method of strike, and therefore, even if a module was compromised, it would not affect the other sub-groups. In fact, the only reason that united them or kept them together was the weapon supply chain—otherwise they were independent.

Thirdly, it was a pragmatic operational choice, given the Punjabi propensity towards individualism: Everyone considers himself a leader, born to command rather than follow. The Punjabi character is best described by the idiom '*Daduan De Panseri*', or an army of frogs—frogs even when put together in a sack jump out and hop in different directions. Keeping them together is not easy. Therefore, organizing the movement in a multi-module structure that operated in fragmented amoeba cell formations made it easy for that many more individuals to fulfil their leadership ambitions and thus was better suited to the Sikh psyche.

Lastly, Pakistan's objective was not to create Khalistan, but to foster communal polarization and the consequent social conflict and violence. This objective was better served by multiple localized militant formations.

The Post–Blue Star Militant

The bulk of the militancy were young boys, mostly in the age group of twenty to thirty years, though some of them were as young as seventeen or eighteen years. They were largely unemployed or facing disguised unemployment, belonging to peasant families with small holdings, were semi-literate, some even had a criminal past, and thus they constituted the fringe of the rural society. The unemployment rate in rural Punjab was higher than the all-India average. 'The register of employment exchange in Punjab in 1991, had 6.92 lakh job seekers, out of which 56.51 per cent (3.91 lakh) were educated up to matric and above. The 38th Round of the National Sample Survey, 1983, revealed that the unemployment rate for males with secondary education and females with graduation and above were higher in rural Punjab. These figures were higher than the all-India level.'[8]

However, once they had acquired weapons, it conferred upon them gun power, and with that came recognition, grudging respect and riches. During those days, the presence of the state machinery in rural Punjab was fragile. The lure to fill this void was seductive, and many a marginalized, unemployed youth or those driven by police 'excesses' or those wanting to settle personal family feuds joined the militancy, and augmented the ranks of those who had responded to the anti-Sikh carnage or Blue Star. For example, army deserters floated the Khalistan National Army and a small band of ex-armymen joined it. The jails, strangely, became another source of recruitment, as criminals and small-time convicts were inducted by their militant inmates. An overwhelming majority of militants came from rural Punjab, and this was an important facet of why peasants were stoic if not apathetic to violence initially. Secondly, the ethno-national movement did not undermine the agro-economy of the state. In 1984, the paddy output in Amritsar increased by 20 per cent and in 1985 wheat by 27 per cent, with a spurt in Basmati exports that touched hundred crore rupees from the district. These high yields and production were repeated year after year.

The three districts of Amritsar, Gurdaspur and Ferozepur, located on the international border, were the bulk suppliers of the militants. Majha region, among the three regions of Punjab, contributed over 60 per cent of the militants. A study found that 81.73 per cent of the participants were Jat Sikhs by caste, with Mazhabi (Scheduled Caste) Sikhs constituting the second-largest group at 7.42 per cent. There was even a small sprinkling of Hindu and Christian militants.[9] That is equally true of Mazhabi Sikhs, whom Guru Gobind Singh called '*Rengrete Guru ke bete*', that is, children of the Guru. Their martial trait was recognized by the British who raised an exclusive regiment—the Sikh Light Infantry, previously known as the Royal Sikh Pioneers—consisting of Mazhabi and Ramdasia Sikhs.

The average life span of a militant was about three to four years. Punjab has no forests or mountains to serve as hideouts. So the militants used the 'population jungle'—they looked no different from any other man on the street; they would commit a crime and just disappear into the crowds. The safe houses were provided by like-minded radicals, but often they managed food, shelter and hideouts by force. They survived by exploiting their knowledge of local areas, people, lanes and pathways. In rural Amritsar, the hub of militancy, farmers often lived in dhanis, that is, farm dwellings, outside the villages and these were usurped by militants, often by inflicting violence and butchery on the inmates. They extensively used couriers, including women, to camouflage their operations and to carry and deliver weapons near a target site, or act as spotters to survey targeted areas to avoid police roadblocks. After committing a crime, they would often disperse in different directions to evade arrest.

I remember Devinder Singh, a Pakistan-trained militant, entered the premises of Ram Lubhaiya in a thickly populated colony of Tarn Taran early in the morning, killed him and coolly walked away. After turning a few lanes, he passed on the weapon to a woman courier, bought a newspaper, and stood outside the police station pretending that he was enjoying the newspaper post his morning walk. In his interrogation later, he disclosed that he even attended Ram Lubhaiya's funeral!

The Beginning of the End

The militants' credibility, however, suffered a serious blow during Operation Black Thunder II. People realized that the terrorists were indulging in loot, rapes, extortions, abduction, land grabs and forced licentious hospitality. The image of the ethno-national struggle as projected by Khalistani ideologues slowly transformed. The people saw these 'warriors of faith' as the criminalized conglomerates they were. They were wielding guns not for a panthic cause, but for personal avarice and pleasure. This resulted in loss of public goodwill. The hideouts, shelters and peasant support that had come their way easily now abated. There were growing incidents of resistance from the common man, and those who were forced to capitulate under the fear of the gun often retaliated as informers. Many terrorists met with death due to tip-offs. Take the example of the dreaded terrorist Sukhwinder Singh and his two accomplices who were killed in May 1991 with the help of a tip-off given by a family from Basoya. The militants had been forcibly living in that household. Gurbachan Singh Manochahal, who was a dismissed ex-soldier, owned about an acre of land but by the time he was killed in February 1993, the family's assets had expanded to include about 17 acres, a big house, trucks and a brick kiln, apart from cash and other assets. The Babbar Khalsa, an organization that had the image of being 'holy warriors', was exposed when its chief Sukhdev Singh Babbar was found living in a palatial house in Patiala with a second wife, owning not one but three houses in Patiala and Rajpura. Gill has disclosed, 'In 1991 a confidential survey of the socio-economic profile of terrorists, including 205 hardcore terrorists, indicated that a majority of those who joined voluntarily did so for the lure of easy money and the benefits attached to being a terrorist; more than a third of the non-hardcore terrorists . . . were identified as having amassed great fortunes. Even the lesser terrorists gained immensely in social significance.'[9]

Dr Sohan Singh and a few other hardcore Khalistanis felt concerned by this degeneration of the struggle and appealed to the militants, but their attempts to regulate and reform the felons failed. The moral code of conduct enforced by various militant outfits was part of this image-building exercise. The first code of conduct came in 1987, enforced by the KCF and the AISSF (Gurjeet). It contained thirteen commandments, including directions to girls to not wear fashionable clothes or pluck their eyebrows; men were not to trim their beards; the sale or consumption of intoxicants like liquor or tobacco, and meat was banned; music or dance at weddings was prohibited and the allowed number of *baraatis* was restricted to eleven. School-going children were to wear only saffron, black and white.

Corrupt government officials were warned and people were asked to report their names to the AISSF (Gurjeet). The militants burnt liquor shops and terrorized businesses—almost anyone could be a potential target. A poster issued by the KCF warned that violators of the code would be burnt alive. They banned beauty parlours, wearing of jeans and saris, singing of the national anthem in schools, and also enforced a dress code. Sikh women were directed to keep their heads covered and not wear bindis or sindoor. Sikh men were not to trim their beards. Kesari turbans became the colour of Punjab.

In this puritanical drive, it was the ordinary citizen who was targeted—their day-to-day lives were restricted by the militants' codes. They randomly picked up their victims and brutally killed innocents. In one such instance, they shot the female principal of a school in Rajpura. Such acts created a fear psychosis in Punjab and alienated the people. The latter-day codes—such as those issued by the panthic committees of Dr Sohan Singh and Zaffarwal in December 1990 and February 1991, respectively, targeted journalists and imposed the use of Punjabi even on vehicle number plates; this further estranged people—for example, the truckers who plied pan-India faced operational difficulties.

The cumulative effect of all these activities was the loss of a popular base that was essential for the militants' survival. Consequently, the police was able to penetrate these organizations and intelligence operatives were able to establish 'contact' with key decision-makers in militant hierarchies, either directly or indirectly, including the heads of the three panthic committees—Dr Sohan Singh, Manochahal, and Zaffarwal. Even foreign-based Khalistanis like Ganga Singh Dhillon had been neutralized. Gurdev Grewal, who was joint secretary, internal security, during the critical period has disclosed that Dhillon was 'nurtured as an agent with a view to using him' to de-escalate the tension.[10] The success of the security establishment had a demoralizing effect on the movement. The militant leadership lost steam. Consequently, fresh inductions and the number of new recruits abated. The overground support mechanism of couriers, informers, weapon carriers and spotters, etc., disintegrated.

Given that the number of hardcore listed militants at any given time was never more than 1,500, physical liquidation and attrition depleted the militant cadres and finally ended the movement. In 1988, about 372 militants were killed, in 1989 about 703, in 1990 about 1,335, in 1991 about 2,300, and in 1992 about 2,110. About 916 militants surrendered to the police till 1993.

The utility of captured or surrendered terrorists to infiltrate militant groups was assessed, and those considered 'valuable' and cooperative were kept in protective custody, and deployed for counter-terrorism operations. Once they had outlived their relevance, the police helped them adopt new identities and start a fresh life, including migrating to foreign countries. This became an unwritten government policy and over 300 militants were rehabilitated. They reappeared in society with new identities. Local senior police officers exercised discretion in this regard—who to rehabilitate, where and how. These operations did raise questions regarding the legality and constitutionality of the practice, but extraordinary circumstances demanded out-of-the-box solutions; it was a sagacious move, though not necessarily constitutional, to reabsorb these terrorists into the mainstream. Post their rehabilitation, their conduct has not belied the faith reposed in them—though the covert strategy has caused occasional embarrassment to the administration.

Sukhwinder Singh 'Sukhi' of the KLF, who had several serious criminal cases against him, was given the identity of one Harjit Singh Kahlon and issued a passport on the address of a government housing complex under the occupation of CRPF men. He settled down as a travel agent and went abroad several times, but was exposed when he applied for the renewal of his passport in 2006, leading to many anxious moments for the then DGP, S.S. Virk. Similarly, Harpreet Singh of the Babbar Khalsa was captured in September 1992, declared dead but kept in custody and used as a counter-terrorist warrior. Once he had outlived his utility, he was packed off to Chennai with a new identity to start a new life. However, Chennai proved too taxing for him and he returned to move the Punjab and Haryana High Court in December 1995 to declare that he was alive. Such cases caused considerable disquiet.

The Pakistan Turnaround

Pakistan could foresee that the Khalistan movement was petering out and therefore shifted its focus from Punjab to Kashmir. Benazir Bhutto had taken over as Prime Minister in December 1988, and she thought she could bargain with Rajiv Gandhi on the Siachen glacier. When they met in Pakistan for bilateral talks during the SAARC summit in July 1989, she offered cooperation to tackle Sikh militancy. Apparently, an understanding was reached and she forced the ISI establishment to furnish the details of the militants, their bases and related intelligence inputs to India. Later on, she went on to complain that India did not honour its commitment on withdrawal from the Siachen glacier, even though she had helped curb Sikh militancy. She said:

> Does anyone remember those times or is public memory so short that no one recalls the extremely difficult conditions India faced during the Sikh insurgency twenty years ago? India was in a complete mess. Does anyone remember that it was I who kept my promise to Prime Minister Rajiv Gandhi when we met and he appealed to me for help in tackling the Sikhs? . . . Have they forgotten the results of that meeting and how I helped curb the Sikh militancy? . . . If anyone kept their word, it was me. Not Rajiv. He went back to India and then called me on his way to the Commonwealth to say that he could not keep his promise to withdraw from Siachen and that he would do it only after the election.[11]

Hein G. Kiessling, who has authored a book on the ISI, states that after the two Prime Ministers reached an understanding 'the ISI was not slow to respond' and Minister of Interior Aitzaz Ahsan passed on to India a list of all ISI contacts with militants in Indian Punjab. Kiessling calls it 'a betrayal which most of them [militants] paid for with their lives'.[12] This is confirmed by A.S. Dulat, former chief of India's Intelligence Bureau and Research and Analysis Wing (R&AW). In his book co-authored with Asad Durrani, former chief of the ISI, he has quoted Durrani as saying, 'Regarding the Sikh militancy, Indians were naturally grateful for the help provided by Benazir Bhutto's first government. I was quite surprised that the Indians took so long to make use of it.'[13]

The exact dates on which Pakistan provided intelligence inputs to Indian agencies is not in the public domain, but given the sequence of events it would have been towards the end of 1989 or early 1990. Why India took as long as it did to act on the information, as Durrani questioned Dulat, is probably because of the time taken to penetrate all the modules—there were too many of them, and not all were in direct touch with the ISI. Besides, it takes time to assimilate data and correlate it into a tactical operational plan.

Once terrorism was wiped out from Punjab, Pakistan provided three options to the militants it had anchored on its soil for years—stay on in Pakistan, go back to India or go to a third country. To facilitate the last option, Pakistan provided the militants with false identities and forged passports. Take the case of Wassan Singh Zaffarwal, a member of the original panthic committee (1986) who was based in Pakistan for eight years, guiding the movement. He was given a forged Canadian passport to migrate to Switzerland. He was brought to India in 2001, and after his acquittal in about a dozen cases pending against him, was released from jail in 2004. Similarly, Pakistan dispatched Dr Sohan Singh to Nepal, from where he was brought to Mohali and later, after following the due legal process, released.

However, a few of them chose to stay on in Pakistan and they are still there, occasionally launching militant modules for violence. Bhutto's gesture was a one-time exception; Pakistan has never stopped bankrolling covert terrorism and the ISI has continued its operations against India.

The End of Militancy

Operation Rakshak II, which commenced on November 1991, and its variants like Operation Night Dominance and Operation Final Assault that were launched in December 1992, heralded the end of militancy in Punjab. Earlier, from May 1990 to September 1990, and thereafter in March 1991, Operation Rakshak I had sent the militants on the run.

The Punjab Police drew up lists of the terrorists based on their ferocity and ranking in the militant hierarchy and then went for a focused chase. It involved intelligence-based search and seizure operations by the Punjab Police, with the army laying the outer cordon. Planned ambushes, night patrols, cordoning of known hideouts and search operations yielded results.

The scale of the operation may be gauged from the fact that troops numbering about 1 lakh from three army corps were deployed, apparently for field exercises but silently assisting the police. There were paramilitary forces numbering about 40,000 troops, in addition to the Punjab Police ranks. The army operation was overseen by Lt Gen. G.S. Grewal, GOC-in-chief, Western Command, and by 11 Corps led by Lt Gen. B.K.N. Chhibber and thereafter by Gen. V. P. Malik, who later rose to become army chief. During his tenure –April 1992 to 1994 – the army played a key role that saw the end of militancy in Punjab. Malik believed in minimal involvement of the army in civil affairs but it was the civil administration that depended more and more on military assistance. An IG-rank police officer was seconded to each corps, and an SP-rank officer was with each brigade for timely coordination and to reduce the response time of the army units.

For the first time, the army split its formations and deployed troops in section-level strength to cover every corner of the state. This instilled a sense of security among the people, who came forward to provide vital information. The army established a rapport with the common citizen by undertaking welfare activities in rural areas such as health camps, minor development works, even the supply of essential domestic consumables from the Canteen Store Department. When a village was cordoned off for a search that often lasted hours, it even served tea and langar to the residents who were asked to come out of their houses to facilitate the combing operation. By one count, about 400 villages were searched.

To ensure that the militants did not try to escape across the border or obtain a fresh supply of weapons from Pakistan, the entire Punjab border up to a length of 553 km was fenced with barbed wire and some areas were lit up. The deployment of the BSF on the international border was augmented, reducing the distance between checkposts substantially. The army laid a second line of deep cordon along the ditch-cum-bund—the bund runs along the entire length of the border, with a depth that goes up to about 5 kilometres from it. Night curfew was also imposed along the border belt to eliminate militants' movement at night.

With these measures, the militancy ended within two years, between 1992 and 1994. While in 1992, there had been 1,518 civilian deaths at the hands of terrorists, only two civilians died in 1994. In 1995, Chief Minister Beant Singh, along with those in his immediate security circle, were killed on 31 August 1995 by a human bomb. That was the last major act of militancy in Punjab.

Historians and scholars have interpreted the rise of militancy in Punjab in the context of the state's cultural milieu, religious fundamentalism, high rate of unemployment, economic inequities created by the Green Revolution, plateauing of agrarian prosperity and consequent peasant discontent, unethical power politics played by leading political parties, the foreign hand, etc. These factors, in varying degrees, did contribute to the tragedy of Punjab. However, all these fault lines persist even today, but militancy doesn't. Therefore, one must look beyond these for a critical factor explaining why the violence exploded into a full-blown ethno-national struggle. According to me, the foremost reason was a lack of good governance, poor law enforcement and an indifferent criminal justice administration. Punjabis, by character, are best governed when there is an effective and decisive administration—unjust or weak set-ups are often put to the test by them. There are historical reasons for this. Punjab as a frontier state has faced invasions, wars and bloodshed for centuries and this has militarized the Punjabi ethos and embedded in them an attitude that accepts violence as part of life. It is interesting to note what Maj. Gen. Sir Vincent Eyre, KCSI, CB, a British Indian Army officer, said, based on his experience in the state that they 'loved fighting for fighting's sake'. Lord Dalhousie, after the annexation of the Sikh empire, said, 'There never will be peace in Punjab so long as its people are allowed to retain the means and opportunity of making war.'[14]

One has to only look at the recent history of Punjab to validate Dalhousie's statement—Punjabis have never missed an opportunity to take on the State, whether the Mughal empire or the British. The Ghadari Babas, the Kukas, sixty-five of whom were blown up by cannons by the British, the Babar Akalis who in the 1920s took to the gun, or individuals like Bhagat Singh and Udham Singh; or in the post-Independence days the militant movement of the 'Lal Communist Party Hind Union' led by Teja Singh Swatantra for agrarian entitlements, when in 1949 its cadres routed the police at Kishangarh in PEPSU and the army had to be summoned to control the strife. Or a little later, the dacoits of PEPSU that were eliminated by the gun and the armed Naxalites in the 1960s or the tragic terrorism of the 1980s and the emergence of the present-day 'gangsters' in

Punjab. These are all reminders that Punjab will have peace only so long as the administration is effective and the state is perceived as just and delivers good governance. Otherwise, as the Punjabi saying goes, '*Jatt yamla, khuda nu lai gaye chor*'—the Jatt is crazy, thieves have stolen God, or, say, the government!

39

The Diaspora

In 1993, while on a visit to Switzerland, we were clicking photographs along the Zurich lake when a distant yell, '*Dekheyo, Sardar ji gir na jayo*', suddenly stopped me in my tracks. Two young boys with flowing beards and saffron turbans appeared from nowhere and said that they were on 'political', which meant they were asylum-seekers. Not knowing my identity, they were generous enough to offer assistance if I too was applying for asylum. Individuals facing persecution or threat to life for reasons of religion, race or political opinion, they said, were eligible. The prevailing conditions in Punjab then provided the legal alibi needed for that plea.

Across the Seas

Foreign lands have always held allure for land-locked Punjabis. This insatiable urge is best reflected by the Punjab Regiment's insignia of a galley with a bank of oars and sails. Raised by the British in

1761, it sailed overseas to fight alien battles. On its return, it inspired folklore of the offshore exploits, tempting many to venture out to these distant lands.

However, it was the Punjab Police that stole the lead over the faujis. A hundred Sikh policemen were the first to move to Hong Kong in 1890, with their British DSP, C.V. Creagh.[1] They manned the city and their number rose to about eight hundred by 1952. They were also deployed in Shanghai, China. From there, they drifted to greener pastures—the UK, Singapore, Malaysia, Australia and New Zealand, with their families and relatives in tow.

Canada, however, attracted the largest number of Punjabis—and it continues to do so. This migration story began in 1887, when a battalion of the Sikh Regiment that paraded in London to celebrate Queen Victoria's Golden Jubilee journeyed back via British Columbia. The soldiers brought back alluring tales of these distant lands. By the early 1900s, about 300 Sikhs had made Canada their home. The 1914 story of *Komagata Maru*, the ship that sailed from Hong Kong with Punjabis all the way to Canada, is too well known to be repeated.

The Pacific Coast was next, San Francisco, and from there, the agricultural lands of California state. It was not an effortless settlement as both Canada and the US enforced restrictive laws, but the indomitable Punjabis endured to add to their numbers. They were quick to set up gurdwaras, Singh Sabhas, Khalsa Dewans and even published weekly and monthly magazines in Punjabi to retain their culture, identity and religion.

In Africa, skilled Sikh Ramgarhia workers first went to Uganda in 1890 to construct railway lines and infrastructure projects. From there, they fanned out to other African nations, particularly Kenya. Soon, however, many of them joined the army. The very first modern regiment of the African Army, the East African Rifles, raised in 1895, with its headquarters at Mombasa, had a large Sikh contingent.[2]

The spurt to migrate was provided by Punjabi soldiers after the First World War. They had sailed across the sea and their number was sizeable. At the beginning of the war, the British Indian Army was 'Punjabi-ized' with 87 per cent of the artillery, 64 per cent of the cavalry and 47 per cent of the infantry soldiers coming from the state, mostly Sikhs and Muslims. After the world wars, a large number of them migrated to the lands they had fought for—the UK, the US and Europe. The second wave of migration came post-Independence, when professionals—doctors, scientists, techies, lawyers, teachers and small traders—joined the skilled and semi-skilled workers to augment the Punjabi presence on these foreign shores.

The Asylum Seekers

In the 1980s, the violence in Punjab provided a supplementary ground to go '*samundar paar*'. The numbers of asylum seekers from the state suddenly swelled. Young boys projected themselves as freedom fighters, as victims of the Sikh struggle, police atrocities and human rights violations, or said they were being religiously persecuted and they feared for their lives for their political opinions. Not all of them were radicals, kharkoos or *mulvadi*s (fundamentalists)—many were ordinary youngsters exploiting the prevailing circumstances in Punjab and the liberal provisions of the Geneva Convention of 1951 and its 1967 protocol. Those facing criminal charges, in any case, were ineligible for political asylum, nevertheless, a good number of them managed to settle in foreign lands, including some of the key figures of the ethno-national movement. In a few cases, the deep state facilitated them to go abroad to use them as deep assets. The modus operandi was simple. An aspirant had only to go beyond India, either on a valid visa or by adopting a false identity. Canada, the US, the UK, Germany, Belgium, Switzerland, France and the Netherlands were some of the preferred destinations, though the Far East, Thailand, Hong Kong, Philippines and Australia also got a sprinkling of migration-seekers. Once there, immigration lawyers would take over to exploit the liberal provisions of international law. In 1980, Canada received about twenty-five applications for political refuge benefits, but in 1981, the number of fresh Sikh arrivals from India went to over 2,000. The numbers swelled through the years.

Western countries were wary to accord them political asylum or refugee status, and only some requests were allowed, but the migrants mostly managed to stay on one or the other grounds or they got interim visas and then moved on to other countries. The generous diaspora in these countries extended help, shelter, sustenance and even legal aid to them. Once secure abroad, the radicals among them floated pro-Sikh organizations that, in fact, became an alibi, if not proof, of their political beliefs and hence the justification for allowing them to stay on. Bhindranwale's nephew Jasbir Singh Rode landed in the UK in July 1984 from Libya and formed the International Sikh Youth Federation (ISYF), allied with the All India Sikh Students Federation. He was later extradited to India, but his organization expanded with the express objective to establish the 'sovereign state of Khalistan'. His brother Lakhbir Singh Brar managed to reach Canada via Dubai, and took over command of the overseas operations. In Canada, one Surjan Singh set up a 'Republic of Khalistan' office in 1982; earlier in 1981 he had even moved the United Nations to seek observer status.

The Babbar Khalsa (International) and the Dal Khalsa with affiliation to their namesake organizations in India established branches in the US, Canada, Germany, Switzerland and Norway. The Khalistan Council with affiliation to the panthic committee of Zaffarwal was set up in the UK and some other countries. Maj. Gen. Jaswant Singh Bhullar, one of the military advisers to Bhindranwale, reached the US on a tourist visa but managed to stay on. He formed the World Sikh Organization (WSO) to rally Sikhs for the separatist cause. The WSO had its independent set-up in key Canadian towns. Bhullar, however, had to flee back to India due to internal group dissensions.

These radical organizations spread propaganda, built public opinion, organized rallies and collected money to fund the movement in Punjab, and even ran newspapers and magazines to support the Sikh cause. *Awaz-a-Quam* was the mouthpiece of the ISYF with editions from Toronto and Birmingham. *World Sikh News* was published from Stockton, and *The Sword* from Edmonton by the WSO. The Babbar Khalsa had its monthly mouthpiece, *Wangar*.

The migrants lobbied with opinion-makers, MPs, the Congress and local legislators, who, in turn, raised Sikh issues. Illustratively, Max Madden and Terry Dicks, both MPs in the UK, and a few Congress members in the US like Dan Burton, Robert Dornan and Jesse Helms, and political leaders like William Lipinski and George Miller, were active; in October 1995 as many as thirty-five Congressmen raised the issue of Sikh rights with the President of the US.

The radicals even imported violence with them to their new countries. Talwinder Singh Parmar, who had floated armed motorcycle gangs in India, reached Canada and led a violent movement. He returned to India via Pakistan and was killed in an encounter in 1992, along with a Pakistani militant, Intekhab Zia.

On 23 June 1985, a bomb was planted on Air India flight 182 that originated from Montreal for Delhi via London; 329 people were killed while the Boeing 743 was over the Atlantic Ocean. In a synchronized plot, the same day, a bomb was planted at Vancouver on Canadian Pacific Airlines flight 003 heading for Tokyo to link up with Air India Flight 301 from Tokyo to Bangkok. While transferring luggage at Tokyo's Narita Airport to the Air India aircraft, the bomb in the suitcase exploded, killing two baggage handlers. The passenger, one L. Singh, had never boarded the flight. In May 1986, another attempt to blow up an Air India flight to New York from Montreal was foiled and two Babbar Khalsa members were sentenced to life imprisonment.

Malkiat Singh Sidhu, a minister in Surjit Singh Barnala's Cabinet, while in Canada to attend his nephew's wedding was ambushed by four ISYF youth in Vancouver Island on 25 May 1986. He survived, but with a bullet lodged close to his spine which remained embedded in his body—he used to call it the 'Canadian souvenir'. Four militants, including one Jaspal Singh Atwal of the ISYF, were convicted by a Canadian court to undergo a twenty-year imprisonment. Atwal went on to embarrass Justin Trudeau, the Canadian Prime Minister, when he visited India in 2018. Atwal managed to get an invite to the official event in Mumbai hosted by the Canadian embassy for the visiting Prime Minister. Canada had declared the ISYF a 'listed terrorist entity' in June 2003.

In the UK, Tarsem Singh Toor, a moderate Sikh leader, was killed in January 1986, and Darshan Das Vasdev in 1987. The Dal Khalsa of Southall was established with the support of Jaswant Singh Thekedar after he got asylum in England and masterminded the struggle in the UK. Manmohan Singh, also of the Dal Khalsa, reached Dover in 1984 under a false identity after escaping from India via Kathmandu and travelled through many countries to settle in the UK. He managed to get asylum as a freedom fighter and worked for the Muslim Sikh Federation on the pretext of spreading inter-faith harmony.[3]

The radicals even ran drug trades to raise funds to sustain the movement. Their activities were cause for concern for the host countries and embarrassed India, such as when Ajit Singh Bhambra, who published a newspaper, *Sandesh*, was caught by police in the UK with heroin. He claimed in court that he was an Indian operative helping penetrate the militant groups. Babu Lal Gupta, then posted at India House, London, had to claim diplomatic immunity to escape the police dragnet.

In Canada in 1987, two Indian operatives who had successfully busted a few militant modules, however, had to leave for home after they were declared persona non grata. That temporarily soured relationships between our intelligence set-up and the Canadian Security Intelligence Service (CSIS). But success achieved by R&AW, our external intelligence outfit, and IB, which also operates in countries like Canada, was remarkable. They penetrated many foreign-based terrorist groups, busted some of them and even successfully forestalled several militant strikes by them in India.

International Clout

Hardeep Rai, a flourishing immigration lawyer settled in the US, made a casual remark to me, 'The epicentre of "Sikhi" has shifted abroad.' What Rai meant was the emergence of the Sikh diaspora as a political power. He reminded me that in March 2018, at the UN Security Council meeting of ministers, out of the ten delegates from Asia, Africa, Europe and the Americas, two were Sikhs—Nikki Haley Randhawa, former governor of South Carolina, and Harjit Singh Sajjan, the Canadian defence minister. The Sikh diaspora has indeed arrived internationally. And a few of them have radical ancestry—for example, Sajjan Singh's father was on the board of the WSO.[4]

The emergence of several countries with large ageing populations, globalization and liberal immigration policies has resulted in the proliferation of Indians abroad. In Canada, Sikhs today number about 5 million, or 1.5 per cent of the population, while in India they are around 2 per cent of the population. In places like Surrey in British Columbia, Sikhs are 42 per cent of the total population, 24 per cent in Brampton and 19 per cent in Abbotsford (Canada); 38 per cent in Richmond Hill and 36 per cent in Millbourne (US); and 12 per cent in Slough, 10.2 per cent in Wolverhampton and 10 per cent in Hounslow (UK).[5]

Their increased number and concentrated population in certain geographical areas has given the diaspora the critical mass to emerge as a political force.

But, frozen in the time when they migrated, many of them continue to be socioculturally unassimilated in the countries of their adoption. Facilitated by modern-day communication technology, they influence public opinion, finance elections in Punjab, remain active on Sikh issues in India and abroad, and inject indigenous ethno-national politics in the body politic of the country of their migration. They may not be heard in India, but the liberal democracies of the

West allow them the space and opportunity to internationalize Indian domestic issues, and this has ramifications for India.

Sikhs today have a significant presence in the public affairs and politics of their adopted countries. Gone are the days when there was a lone Sikh, Dalip Singh Saund, in the US Congress in 1956 or a Piara Singh Khabra in British Parliament in 1992. Today, they come in dozens. The Canadian Parliament in its 2015 election returned seventeen Punjabis, in the 2019 election eighteen Sikhs, and in the 2021 election seventeen Indo-Canadians out of which sixteen were Punjabis. The 2019 House of Commons elections had five MPs of Indian origin. Many became mayors of cities in the US—Preet Didbal of Yuba City, Ravi Bhalla of Hoboken in New Jersey and Manka Dhingra, a member of the state legislature in Washington, to name a few.

In South East Asian countries, particularly in Singapore, Malaysia and Thailand, Sikhs have a solid presence and they have done well for themselves. For instance, Malaysia has had several Sikh ministers. In Singapore, in April 2018, Pritam Singh, a Sikh MP, became head of the main Opposition party of the country—the Worker's Party—and he created history, not just for the panth, but for Singapore when Parliament in August 2020 officially designated him the country's first leader of the Opposition. Prime Minister Justin Trudeau in November 2015 cheerfully claimed that his Cabinet had more Sikhs (four) than Prime Minister Modi, who had only two—Maneka Gandhi and Harsimrat Kaur Badal.[6]

Some of these leaders have often courted controversy for outspoken remarks about Sikh affairs and human rights violations in India. In June 2017, Preet Kaur Gill became the first Sikh woman to enter the House of Commons, and was designated the shadow minister. She led several MPs to support the call given by Sikh organizations for an independent inquiry into the UK's role in Operation Blue Star. She said, 'I am deeply concerned with the findings of the report "Sacrificing Sikhs", which demonstrates that the Heywood Review was a whitewash.' She added, 'The British government, knowing fully well the contribution Sikhs made during both the First and Second World Wars, betrayed their trust and are indirectly involved in the persecution of thousands of Sikhs.'[7]

The Future

The demand for Khalistan, however, is long dead. It never enjoyed any mass appeal among the diaspora, and was confined to a vocal microscopic militant minority that was able to dominate the scene through aggressive lobbying and at times violence.

Organizations like the US-based Gurpatwant Singh Pannun's Sikhs for Justice still raise separatist noises, but these are one-man advocacy groups. Pannun called for a non-binding worldwide 'Referendum 2020' for Khalistan, which evoked no response. In August 2018, he held an international event at London's Trafalgar Square; the crowd was thin, and it was a Pakistani-origin member of the House of Lords, Nazir Ahmed, who made a shrill endorsement from the podium 'for Sikh brothers and sisters'. Pakistanis have still not stopped.

The diaspora's psyche, however, has moved from separatism to issues of Sikh identity and religion, violation of human rights, lack of good governance in India, etc. They raise voices against Indian officials abroad; gurdwaras in Canada clamped, for example, a ban on the entry of Indian officials alleging 'interference' in Sikh affairs, and some organizations in the UK proposed a similar measure against Indian diplomats.[8]

Some of these radical organizations have occasionally succeeded in painting a grim state of human rights in India; it required government intervention to get retired IGP Tejinder Singh Dhillon a Canadian visa that was denied to him in May 2017 on the grounds that he had served in the CRPF, a force alleged to have grossly violated human rights. My police batchmate, former DGP, Punjab, P.S. Gill, faced a similar refusal. Even Capt. Amarinder Singh and some other Punjab leaders were refused a visiting visa to Canada on political premises. Amarinder, as the chief minister of Punjab, reciprocated by refusing to meet Harjit Singh Sajjan, the Canadian defence minister of Punjabi origin, during his official visit to India in April 2017 on the grounds that he was supporting anti-India elements in his country.

In the US, some elements have often resorted to lawsuits for alleged human rights violations against visiting Indian dignitaries under Alien Torts Claims Act and Torture Victims Protection Act. Parkash Singh Badal, the former chief minister of Punjab, escaped one such case as the US federal judge in Wisconsin dismissed it on the grounds that the summons issued by the court had not been duly served on Badal while he was on US territory in February 2013. Congress leader Sonia Gandhi faced a similar suit for her alleged role in the anti-Sikh carnage in 1984 in a New York court in 2014—the suit was dismissed.

Issues like the 1984 anti-Sikh carnage and the failure to punish the guilty are invariably raised to highlight a non-performing justice system. The Ontario Legislature in April 2017 passed a resolution calling the 1984 anti-Sikh violence in India a genocide. Harinder Kaur Malhi of the ruling Liberal Party had moved the motion and the assembly condemned 'intolerance in India and anywhere else in the world, including the 1984 genocide perpetrated against the Sikhs throughout India, and call on all sides to embrace truth and reconciliation'.

In the US, the Assembly of Connecticut State passed a resolution 'recognizing' the anti-Sikh violence of 1984 as a 'Sikh genocide'. *The Times of India* further reported that the Sikh genocide day would be observed every year in November to remember the lives lost in the violence.[9] Resolutions have also been passed by the California State Assembly in 2015, by the Pennsylvania Assembly in 2018 and more recently in 2021 by the New Jersey Senate condemning the 1984 violence.[10]

A park in Fresno, California, was renamed on 31 August 2017 after Jaswant Singh Khalra, the human rights activist killed in a false encounter in Punjab, thus internationalizing the alleged police excesses during the days of militancy in Punjab.[11] Four Canadian cities—Burnaby, New Westminster, Regina and Brampton—and Manteca in the US issued proclamations to observe 6 September 2020 as 'Khalra Day' to commemorate his twenty-fifth death anniversary. Khalra is popular in the West as '*Laawaris laashan da waaris* (Guardian of unclaimed dead bodies)' and a song with this title on YouTube has gained popularity abroad.

Human rights causes appeal to Western liberal multiculturalism and we in India must keep our conduct and record straight to not provide an opportunity to others to exploit these issues against us. This requires reforming our own justice delivery systems and the State's response to human rights breaches. With a compelling transnational presence and having made a mark in the public affairs of their adopted countries, we need the diaspora on our side; apart from the intrinsic imperative to observe justice and human rights in India.

As for the Sikhs, *manas ki jat sabhe eke paihchanbo,* meaning all mankind is a single entity, and *sarbat da bhala*, meaning the good of all, are the guiding philosophies of Sikhism—a young living religion. Sikhs practise these principles in daily life. Gurdwaras and organizations like SikhAid have earned worldwide acclaim for humanitarian works, such as langar, and providing relief in natural calamities and the COVID-19 pandemic or in war zones. EcoSikh, another NGO, is known for its contribution to environmental preservation.

It is in this spirit that Sikhs must look beyond the Westphalian model of territorial sovereignty; Sikhs are an international community today—there are Canadian Sikhs, American Sikhs, English Sikhs, Spanish Sikhs, Australian Sikhs, etc. The panthic presence and consequently panthic sovereignty is not confined to any small geographical jurisdiction, but is territorially expanded and spread internationally. The community can leave its footprint, not by the force of the gun, but by achieving excellence and competitive merit in today's world.

Remember what historian Arnold Toynbee said, 'Civilizations die from suicide, not by murder.' The choice is ours.

PART II

The Historical Background

1

Beginning of the Divide

THE WEEKLY *KHALSA SAMACHAR* ON 24 JUNE 1909 CARRIED A STORY titled 'Ik Sikh Di Shaheedi' (Martyrdom of a Sikh).[1] It was the story of Lachman Singh, a Sikh sympathetic to the reformist Singh Sabha movement who was put to the gallows by the British administration on 10 June 1909. He had murdered three Muslims and was sentenced to death by the sessions judge.

What had inflamed Lachman Singh was the conversion of a Hindu *lambardar*—village revenue official—to Islam by local mullahs. Historians record that while Lachman Singh was being put to the noose in the jail premises, thousands of Sikhs and Hindus from near and far gathered outside in protest, seeking his release.

Such instances of a Khalsa taking to the sword or facing persecution at the hands of Mughal or Afghan rulers while defending the freedom of the faith are part of the common heritage of Indians. But there were interludes in this shared history when they forgot the composite past and were overcome by a communal consciousness. The 1980s was one such period when sectarian polarization was at its peak. A micro survey conducted post–Blue Star in 1985 found that 'the communal response of voters was so virulent that all class and caste differences were submerged in communal identity'.[2] The senseless killings of innocents in Punjab and the anti-Sikh carnage in Delhi and other parts of the country in 1984 were gruesome reminders of the sectarian frenzy. How and why did this happen?

For an ethno-national conflict to develop, at least two sides are needed. How did the erstwhile congruent communities of Punjab—Hindus and Sikhs—assume adversarial roles? I draw upon history in my attempt to trace the shift in the relationship between the two communities that ultimately led to mindless murders in Punjab and the massacre of Sikhs in 1984.

The Early Days

Muslim conquerors started their forays into India from the eighth century onwards. Punjab's geopolitical curse of being a frontier state placed its population at great peril. People lived in perpetual fear of invasions—Muslim invaders and Mughal rulers hounded Sikhs for the most part of their history.

In 1799, the advent of Ranjit Singh ended centuries of Muslim invasions. Ranjit Singh's Sarkar-e-Khalsa, though steeped in the Sikh ethos, was a benign, multi-communitarian regime and inter-religious antagonism was never allowed to dominate public discourse. Historians, including foreign nationals who visited Punjab, like French historian Jean-Marie Lafont, lauded the Punjabi ethos and pluralism that the maharaja nurtured. Ranjit Singh liberally donated to holy places of all the religions—including 6 quintals of gold to Hindu temples at Benares, and golden canopies to the Jawalamukhi and Kangra temples. He restored the doors of the Somnath temple looted by Mahmud Ghazni and banned cow slaughter in the parts of Afghanistan under his rule. He even funded the construction of mosques—for example, what is now known as the Mai Moraan Masjid in Lahore, built in 1824.

However, the annexation of Punjab by the British pushed Maharaja Ranjit Singh's agreeable multiculturalism into a period of competitive propagation of religions—not by the sword, but through pen, print and debate. Nothing suited the British better than the natives contesting with each other regarding their diverse canons and thus remaining continually divided.

Indians did not let the foreign invaders down and indulged in a relentless and often acrimonious preaching of their respective faiths. Those days were, if I may say so, a period of 'floating creeds'—almost anyone could come under the influence of any competing faith and get proselytized, though the number of actual conversions may not have been large.

At times, the religious diversity intruded into individual homes, as was the case of a Svetambara Jain of Dhudike village near Moga. His son, Lala Radha Kishan Agrawal, turned a practising Sunni Muslim while Radha's wife, Gulab Devi (mother of Punjab Kesari Lala Lajpat Rai), maintained Hindu sanctity at home. Lala Lajpat Rai himself was Arya Samaji and was associated with the Hindu Mahasabha.[3]

The advent of Christianity in the region happened with the annexation of the Sikh empire by the British in 1849—though the first Christian mission had already been set up in 1834 by John C. Lowrie at Ludhiana—which made the inter-faith contestation four-cornered. The first Sikh, a granthi named Kaiser Singh of Amritsar district, became Simeon, after his baptism to Christianity in 1853. The bugle was sounded by Punjab's Lt Gov. Donald McLeod, who in his presidential address to the Punjab Missionary Conference held in Lahore in 1862 said, 'If the Bible be the word of God and the books revered by the Hindus and the Mohammedan contain mere fables, then it must have been intended that the Christian rule prepare the way for the spread of the gospel.'[4] The missionaries established Christian colonies—the first one in 1868 near Lahore—to settle the converts, who were mostly from low castes, though the conversions were not confined to any caste or community. In 1873, four Sikh students of the Mission High School in Amritsar adopted Christianity. The proselytization crusade was so successful that an article in *The Tribune* in Lahore on 19 October 1892 extrapolated that Punjab would turn into a Christian region.

By 1921, there were over 3 lakh native Christians. Maharaja Duleep Singh, son of the famed Maharaja Ranjit Singh, and Raja Harnam Singh of Kapurthala were two prominent Sikh converts to Christianity in 1853 and 1860, respectively. These developments caused great concern to the natives who launched reforms and renaissance movements to restore the glory of their respective faiths and values. In the process, they generated inter- and intra-religious vying and strife. The Muslims had floated the Wahhabi and Ahmadiyya movements and many similar associations like the Anjuman-i-Himayat-i-Islam and the Anjuman-i-Islamia to propagate Islam. The Hindus formed a swarm of reformist orders such as the Brahmo Samaj, Dev Samaj, Sanatana Dharma, Ramakrishna Mission, Arya Samaj, Hindu Sabha, etc. The Sikhs launched the Singh Sabha movement in 1872; the first sabha was established in Amritsar, and the apex body, Chief Khalsa Dewan, came later. However, during those days, educated and urban Sikh elites participated in the Hindu renaissance movement as well, and were particularly active in the Brahmo Samaj and Arya Samaj.

Dayal Singh Majithia, an iconic Sikh who founded the liberal English newspaper *The Tribune* in 1881, was associated with the Golden Temple and was also leading Brahmo Samaj, a reformist movement based on the Upanishads and liberal values. His father, Sardar Lehna Singh Majithia, was a commander in Maharaja Ranjit Singh's army. *The Tribune*, on 12 April 1955, in its tribute to Dayal Singh, wrote, 'The flagstaff erected by Sardar Lehna Singh in front of the Akal Bunga [as the Akal Takht was known] in the Golden Temple at Amritsar still stands by the side of Maharaja Ranjit Singh's flagstaff.' Despite such a strong Sikh religious lineage, Dayal Singh's integration with the composite Hindu–Sikh social order manifested the robust bond that existed between the two communities. His newspaper *The Tribune* was seen 'as a Hindu organ'.[5]

Majithia, of course, was not the only one—Gurbaksh Singh Bedi, son of Baba Khem Singh Bedi, descendants of Guru Nanak, remained the president of the Punjab Hindu Sabha. Baba Khem Singh's great-grandfather, Sahib Singh Bedi, had performed the coronation ceremony of Maharaja Ranjit Singh by applying tilak in the traditional Hindu way of accession to the throne. Many Sikhs were active members and office-bearers of the Arya Samaj, a monotheistic Vedic faith opposed to idolatry that was founded by Swami Dayanand Saraswati, a Gujarati, in 1875.

The Arya Samaj had a modest following in Gujarat, but it proliferated among literate urban Hindus in Punjab. Swami Dayanand, the scholarly preacher, remained an understudy from 1860 for three years with Swami Virajanand Saraswati, a Punjabi, and thereafter returned to Punjab in 1877 to propagate Vedic philosophy. Bhai Jawahir Singh, a Sikh whose father was a granthi in the Golden Temple, assisted Swami Dayanand during his stay in the state and later rose to become secretary of the Lahore Branch of the Arya Samaj, vice president of the Paropkarini Sabha and was closely associated with the management of the first DAV College. Some other prominent Arya Samaji Sikhs were Giani Ditt Singh, Bhai Maya Singh and Lakshman Singh. 'The young Sikhs reacted to the Samaj with sympathy, interest and for a few, enthusiastic commitment' and 'educated Sikhs were viewed as new allies' of the samaj.[6] The intertwining of the urban Sikhs and Arya Samajis and the inter-faith cordiality is best illustrated by Mohan Singh Vaid (1881–1936), a leading light of the Singh Sabha at Tarn Taran. In the daily diary maintained by him, he has given his day's schedule: 'At 9 o'clock I attended the meeting of Arya Sabha and spoke for an hour on the Vedas . . . In the afternoon, I visited the

Golden Temple, and from there we went to the Singh Sabha. At this meeting I spoke for half an hour on the principles of the Arya Samaj.'[7]

The samajists had started a reconversion drive, and the Sikhs enthusiastically supported the Shuddhi Sabhas and joined purification ceremonies to readmit converts from Islam or Christianity. Kenneth W. Jones calls this period the 'Arya–Sikh Bhai' phase. The Sikhs, it seems, were more aggressive. 'The Shuddhi Sabhas under the leadership of militant Sikhs instituted a "pork test" for converts from Islam. If the eating of beef could transform a Hindu into a Muslim, then by similar logic the eating of pork would signify the return of a Muslim to Hinduism or Sikhism.'[8]

The first census of Punjab in 1855, in fact, made no distinction between Sikhs and Hindus as separate entities, and it was only subsequent censuses that segregated the two. The Hindu–Sikh relationship during that time is best reflected by a few lines in *The Tribune*, Lahore, on 27 August 1882:

> English writers, even Anglo-Indian editors, who might know better, always make a grave mistake when speaking of the Sikhs. They seem to think that Sikhs are a people totally different from the Hindus, with whom they have very little in common. While the fact is that practically what differentiates a Sikh from a Hindu is his long hair and unclipped beard. In many families one brother may be a Hindu and the other Sikh. As to religious belief, there is very little difference between the average Hindu and the Sikhs in Punjab, the Guru and the Granth being held in equal reverence by both.[9]

2

Parting of the Ways

THE PERCEPTION THAT 'THERE IS A VERY LITTLE DIFFERENCE between the average Hindu and the Sikh' was to change over a period of time. By 1885, the Sikh–Arya 'bhai-bhai' bonhomie was turning acerbic. Swami Dayanand in *Satyarth Prakash*, first published in 1875, had been critical of Islam, Christianity, orthodox Hinduism, Guru Nanak and Sikh practices. Some Arya Samajists picked up the thread and used hurtful expressions, like the following passage published in *Arya Samachar*, Lahore:

Nanak Shah Fakeer ne naya chalaaya panth
Idhar udhar se jor kar likh mara ik granth;
Pehley cheley kar liye, pichhey badla bhes
Sir par saafa bandh kar, rakh leeney sab kes[1]

[Nanak Shah Fakeer instituted a new panth
By picking up from here and there, he wrote a granth;

First he created a following, thereafter adopted a new form
He tied a turban, kept unshorn hair.]

Throughout 1887 and 1888, the Arya Samaj press was censorious of Sikhism.[2] At its anniversary celebrations in November 1888, Lahore, Lala Guru Datta in his address said, '. . . [I]t is difficult to say whether the Sikhs have any religion or not, but surely they have no knowledge of any kind . . . if Swami Dayanand Saraswati Maharaj called Guru Nanak a great fraud, what did it matter?'[3] The remarks caused the exodus of Sikhs from the Arya Samaj. The Chief Khalsa Dewan in 1888 submitted to the viceroy of India, Lord Dufferin, that 'they be no longer confounded with the Hindus but treated in all respects as a separate community'.[4]

Moderate Arya Samajis made earnest efforts for reconciliation. The editor of the *Arya Gazette* in its July 1897 issue wrote, 'Swami Dayanand had an imperfect knowledge of Gurmukhi and that the remarks made by him regarding Guru Nanak in the *Satyarth Prakash* are based on second-hand information and were not endorsed by the Arya Samaj.'[5] The hardliner Arya Samajis thwarted conciliatory initiatives; they dreamt of creating an Arya Samaji socio-religious order and claimed they were not Hindus but Arya Samajists. In competition to this, the Singh Sabha's aim was to restore the Sikh religion to its Tat Khalsa glory and purity. The issue of Sikh identity was central to it. Thus, the Samajists and Singh Sabhas were both set on different trajectories.

The introduction of the printing press in Punjab energized public debates on inter-religious disagreements, which often turned bitter. The acrimony is best demonstrated by *Rangila Rasul*, a disparaging pamphlet published by Arya Samajist Mahashay Rajpal in 1927, about the multiple marriages of Prophet Muhammad, apparently in response to a derogatory pamphlet published about Sita by some Muslims.

There was no statutory law to punish insult to religious feelings. Mahashay Rajpal, therefore, was acquitted by the court but was murdered in April 1929 by a Muslim zealot, Ilm-ud-din, who, in turn, was put to the noose by the court. However, the faithful honoured Ilm-ud-din as 'Gahzi' and responded by publishing a new book, *Muqaddas Rasool* or 'Pious Rasool'. The British, to cope with the law and order situations caused by religious dissensions, amended the law by inserting a new Section, 295-A, in the IPC, making deliberate and malicious insult to religion an offence.

In 1864, the first print edition of the Guru Granth Sahib was published and with that the inherent limitation of scribes and calligraphers to produce limited copies of handwritten volumes was overcome. Not every village had a gurdwara those days, unlike today when most have one, if not more. Some in rural Punjab those days believed in 'local' or 'popular religion' and that included Gugga-Mari, Shaheedan de asthan, Jathera or the place of elders, Sakhi Sarwar and many forms of folk religion, in addition to their principal faith, Sikhism. However, this was to transform soon, with the reform movement spearheaded by the Singh Sabhas. Gurdwaras proliferated, as more and more Guru Granth Sahibs were printed. Punjabi literature, the most prominent being Bhai Vir Singh's novels based on Sikh culture like *Sundari,* and newspapers like the *Khalsa*, *Gurmukhi Akhbar*, *Khalsa Akhbar*, *Khalsa Samachar*, *Khalsa Advocate* and many others helped to consolidate a distinct Sikh identity.

The Hindu–Sikh religious discourse resulted in the publication of a pamphlet titled *Sikh Hindu Hain,* which invited a counter response in the form of a book titled *Hum Hindu Nahin* by Kahn Singh Nabha in 1898. The first print of Kahn Singh's book was in Hindi, probably meant for a pan-Indian readership. Kahn Singh was careful to caution, 'After reading this book the reader must be able to understand that Sikhism is a distinct religion from Hinduism and other religions. However, it should not happen that you begin to oppose Hindus or abuse Hinduism.'[6]

Kahn Singh's cautionary observation was in light of the common bond that existed between the two communities—Hinduism and Sikhism were not antagonistic, but socioculturally congruous, with a strong umbilical cord. Secondly, for Kahn Singh, Sahajdharis—those with shorn hair but having faith in the Guru Granth Sahib—were constituents of the Sikh brotherhood. The inter se mobility is reflected by what the historian Grewal wrote, 'If some Sahajdharis insisted that they were Sikhs not Hindu, some Keshdharis insisted that they were Hindu.'[7]

In fact, the cleavage was not a Hindu-versus-Sikh issue but largely a conflict between Arya Samajists and Sikhs. Since Arya Samajists in appearance are Hindu, it got perceived as a divide between the two communities. The relations turned severely antagonistic in 1900, when the Arya Samaj initiated steps to reclaim and reabsorb Sikhs into the Hindu fold. In a public Shuddhi ceremony, a group of Rahtia Sikhs (of the weaver community) 'were seated on a pulpit and their heads were shaved by half a dozen barbers . . . By 12 a.m., however, the whole Sikh [community of] Lahore was mad with rage . . . The Rahtia purification and the resulting furore added new vigour and passion to the debate over Sikhs as Hindus' and 'propelled the Sikhs onward towards a separate Sikh consciousness'.[8] The Samajists continued with the conversion of Rahtias even subsequently.

Prominent Sikhs like Jawahir Singh and Ditt Singh left the Arya Samaj, became active in the Singh Sabha movement and Chief Khalsa Dewan. Ditt Singh wrote about forty books and pamphlets to propagate Sikhism and the Sikh cause, including the book *Mera Ate Sadhu Dayanand Ji Sambad.* The Sikh scholars focused on the philosophy of the Gurus; they emphasized the centrality of the Sikh identity as reflected by the five Ks and *pahul* (baptism). The number of sabat surat Sikhs with unshorn hair increased dramatically from 8,40,000 in 1891 to about 36,00,000 in 1931, and correspondingly the number of Sahajdharis went down to less than 3 lakh from about 5,80,000.[9]

The institutionalization of Sikhism started from the days of Guru Nanak, the founder of Sikhism, who had established the twin practices of sangat and *pangat.* He was born in a Hindu Bedi—Kshatriya—family. 'Bedi' means one who is knowledgeable about the Vedas. However, Nanak declared '*Ne me Hindu na Mussalman*', upholding universal brotherhood and unity of mankind and preached that there is One God. He is the Supreme Truth—the Creator, formless, omnipresent, transcendent and not encapsulated in human or idol form. He repudiated idolatry, questioned ritualistic practices and preached monotheism.[10]

Guru Gobind Singh, the tenth Guru, ordained, '*Guru Maneyo Granth*'—Sikhs are to worship the Guru Granth Sahib as a living Guru, and no one else. However, it takes time to break from well-entrenched social practices, and it was no different with Sikhs. The idol worship continued for a while, particularly in a few sects like the Udasis. It probably seeped back during the period the Sikhs were hounded by Ahmad Shah Abdali and the Mughals, when there was a price of Rs 50 for every Sikh captured alive and Rs 70 for a severed Sikh head. Sikhs were on the run, seeking shelter in forests and mountains, and their numbers fell to a few thousand.

The Mughals executed Bhai Mani Singh, the sewadar of the Golden Temple, in 1734, and from then onwards the Udasis and the Mahants, who professed Sikhism but also followed some Brahminical practices, looked after the Golden Temple till about 1764 and some other gurdwaras. They mismanaged the shrines and what *The Tribune* wrote about the Golden Temple was equally true of other Sikh gurdwaras: 'The management of the Golden Temple does not show any improvement. The Manager protected by the Government authorities is indifferent to all that is said against him.'[11]

During the period when the Udasis and the Mahants managed the Sikh gurdwaras, some of the idolatry practices percolated through. In the Parikrama of the Golden Temple, idols and icons were displayed and worshipped, in violation of the prohibition against idolatry.

However, with the new awakening and renaissance movement, Sikh reformers took serious objection to these practices and some of them, including Tikka Ripudaman Singh of Nabha, pursued the matter with Lt Gov. Sir Charles Rivaz, who referred the issue to the commissioner of Lahore, R.E. Younghusband, and C.M. King, the deputy commissioner, Amritsar. On 1 May 1905, on the directions of Arur Singh, the manager of the Golden Temple, all idols, icons and images were removed from the temple precinct.[12]

Sahajdhari or Sanatan Sikhs, as also many non-Sikh organizations like the Hindu Hitkari Sabha, Brahmo Samaj and Arya Samaj (who were otherwise opposed to idolatry) petitioned the government against the removal of the idols, but the directive of the temple manager prevailed. Interestingly, Maharaja Hari Singh of Nabha supported the Hindu Hitkari Sabha and others who were opposed to the removal of the idols; his son, Tikka Ripudaman Singh, however, campaigned for their removal.[13] The difference in the opinion and approach of the older and the younger generations of Sikhs over such religious issues was clearly reflected in the divide between the father and the son. The younger generation of Sikhs was leaning towards the Tat Khalsa tradition and the focus of the conflict now was not just Islam and Christianity but more the idolatry of Hinduism and Brahminical rituals.

Life cycle rituals are the signposts of a people; these define and delineate the boundaries of communities. The Singh Sabha movement, therefore, laid down norms of sociocultural rituals and community behaviour patterns for Sikhs. Its objective may have been to pull Sikhs out of superstitions and Brahminical rituals, but in the process, Sikhs were asked not to indulge in idol worship or observe 'shradhs' or believe in pandits and pirs, or pray at graves, tombs or cremation grounds or believe in miracles, etc.

The ceremonial rituals that are performed at birth, marriage and death and on other social occasions were defined and these now distinguished Sikhs from other communities, including Hindus.

The Chief Khalsa Dewan brought out an elaborate code of ceremonies and rituals, *Gurmat Parkash Bhag Sanskar*, in 1915, that clearly defined and thus differentiated Sikh ceremonies and practices from those followed by Hindus. As a symbol of separate identity, even the wearing of dhoti by Sikhs, then a common dress in north India, was discarded.

The process of demarcating the socio-religious boundaries was, in fact, an evolutionary process that had begun right from the days of the Gurus. Illustratively, historians tell us that a Randhawa Jat follower of Guru Amar Das (1479–1574) from present-day Tarn Taran district faced a boycott by Brahmins who declined to solemnize the marriage of his daughter as per Hindu rituals. The Brahmins felt that Randhawa, as a Sikh, had renounced the Hindu caste system, and hence forfeited the right to Hindu ceremonies. Thereupon, Guru Amar Das deputed Guru Ramdas to oversee the marriage ceremony and in due course of time the *laavan* became the marriage ceremony of the Sikhs.

Much later, in 1909, the Anand Marriage Act conferred a statutory validity to the laavan ceremony that had replaced the Brahminical marriage ceremonies of '*saat phere*' among Sikhs; it was a legal recognition of distinctiveness of the Sikhs from the Hindus. More such measures followed; for example the British government declared holidays for Sikh festivals and Gurpurabs, relaxed the Arms Act to allow the carrying of kirpan in public places in 1914, and conceded the right of Sikhs to sport turbans even at the London Inns of Law. These official recognitions ratified the socio-religious distinctiveness of Sikhs from de facto into de jure status.

3

Institutionalization of Sikhism

In October 1920, Sikhs faced an internal crisis of faith. The Gurus had eliminated the caste system, but a group of what we today call Scheduled Caste devotees faced hostile priests in the Golden Temple who refused to accept their offerings of karah prasad. Finally, in a compromise, it was agreed to seek the direction of Guru Granth Sahib, and a *vaak* (hukam or direction) was obtained by a random opening of the holy Granth. The Guru's mandate went against the priests and the offerings of the Scheduled Caste devotees were accepted. The incident, however, shook the Sikh consciousness—the temple priests were slipping back to the old ills of Hindu society long renounced by the Gurus.

Earlier, in a hurtful act the British-appointed *sarbrah* (manager) of the Golden Temple, Arur Singh, had bestowed a saropa on Gen. Dyer, the man responsible for the indiscriminate killing of peaceful people at Jallianwala Bagh. The Akal Takht had even issued a hukamnama against the leadership of the Ghaddar Party pronouncing that 'ghaddar heroes were not Sikhs'.[1] Such developments strengthened the Sikh resolve to purge gurdwaras of mahants and sarbrahs appointed by the British and restore Tat Khalsa values.

In November 1920, a few Sikh reformers met at the Akal Takht and announced the formation of the Shiromani Gurdwara Parbandhak Committee to manage the affairs of the historical gurdwaras by wresting back their control from the mahants and the managers appointed by the British administration. A month later they formed the Shiromani Akali Dal to coordinate and mobilize support for the reform movement. Leaders belonging to the middle class led this initiative. They had a mass appeal among the Sikh peasantry, unlike the earlier Singh Sabhas and Chief Khalsa Dewan, which were elitist set-ups of educated urban Sikhs. The Singh Sabha movement was conciliatory towards British rulers and their approach was 'petition' and 'prayer' to the administration to seek concessions. This changed now, with the SGPC and the Akali Dal adopting agitational methods.

A movement to liberate gurdwaras was launched, and over a period, nearly 300 gurdwaras were freed from the control of mahants. The success achieved by the Akalis attracted national attention and appreciation—Mahatma Gandhi and other prominent Congress leaders visited Amritsar and Nankana Sahib in support of the gurdwara movement.

The gurdwara reform agitation integrated the Sikhs in the national freedom struggle. The SGPC, which had registered itself as a corporate body in April 1921, formally resolved to support the national Non-Cooperation Movement on 11 May 1921. At this stage, the national focus was anti-imperialism and secular political forces had no reservation to join hands with the communitarian SGPC in the national struggle. Jawahar Lal Nehru courted arrest at Nabha in the Jaito Morcha launched by the Akalis to restore Maharaja Ripudaman Singh as the ruler of Nabha; he had been forced by the British to abdicate in favour of his minor son in 1923, and thereafter banished to Kodaikanal in 1928.

These agitations mobilized Sikhs as never before. In the five-year period of the gurdwara movement, about 400 Sikhs died, 200 were wounded, 30,000 courted arrest and a fine of Rs 15,00,000 was imposed on them. These agitations awakened the political consciousness not only of the Sikh masses, but even affected the Sikh soldiers serving in the British Army, some of whom started wearing kirpans and black turbans to protest the interference by the British in Sikh religious institutions. This alerted the empire and the 'British government made efforts to isolate them from other communities and then to create divisions in their ranks'.[2]

To sharpen the Sikh identity, the British enforced a strict code of sabat surat appearance for Sikh soldiers that markedly distinguished them from other communities. Nearly 1 lakh Sikh soldiers were recruited in the British Army, and they fought in the First World War. British intelligence officer D. Petrie has gone on record to say, 'Sikhs in the Indian Army have been studiously nationalized or encouraged to regard themselves as a totally distinct and separate nation. Their national pride had been fostered by every available means.'[3]

The divide and rule policy of the British by encouraging communal representation in public life and political institutions further sharpened sectarian awareness and inter-community conflicts, though it may be emphasized that Sikhs as a collective religious community were not and still are not a monolithic structure. Castes, sects and regions divide them as much as Hindu society.

The five-year-long gurdwara movement forced Malcolm Hailey, the then governor of Punjab, to concede a statutory status to the SGPC. The Sikh Gurdwaras Act, 1925, was enacted after dropping an earlier Bill circulated in 1921 that had not met with Sikh approval. The new SGPC Act recognized and conferred on Sikhs the legal right to manage their religious affairs through a democratically elected body—the SGPC. Section 2 (9) of the Act defined a Sikh as a person who professes Sikhism. And if a question arose whether a person is a Sikh or not, he had to declare that 'I am a Sikh, I believe in the Guru

Granth Sahib, I believe in the Ten Gurus and that I have no other religion'.

At that stage, the Sahajdhari Sikhs were not legally debarred from participation in the electoral process of the SGPC, but over time they and Patit Sikhs have been excluded from the gurdwara management hierarchy. However, there is complete parity between men and women; Sikh women aged twenty-one years and above have an equal right to vote in the gurdwara elections just as Sikh men. They have enjoyed the statutory right since 1925, three years before the right to vote in elections was conferred on women in England in 1928.

The SGPC law statutorily demarcated the boundaries of Sikhism from other religions. Historians mention that the very first resolution passed by the SGPC was to end the practice of applying a tilak on the Holy Granth in the mornings, a Hindu ritual.

The initial concern of the Akali Dal and SGPC was to liberate gurdwaras from the control of mahants. Once this objective was achieved and the will of the panth prevailed in religious affairs, it was opportune to focus on other challenges the panth faced in a divided, sectarian British India. Now, safeguarding the Sikh identity and representation of the community in public institutions and government services became an important concern. To achieve these and protect Sikh interests, the SGPC and Akali Dal needed an appropriate footprint in the power structure of the state. Guru Gobind Singh, through years of struggle and strife against Mughal atrocities, had taught the Sikhs that political power is the sine qua non to preserve religion—'*Raj bina na dharam chale hai* (Religion does not prosper without political power).' Political power is to be secured only on the strength of the community—'*Koi kisi ko raj na de hai, jo le hai nij bal se le hai* (Nobody gives political power as a gift, it is attained through one's own strength).'

In the process to gain a political foothold, the Akali Dal evolved as the undisputed political arm of the Sikh panth, and this would determine its political approach and agenda in future.

While the SGPC addressed the religious aspirations of Sikhs, the Akali Dal was to address their political hopes and dreams. Thus, the political and the religious coalesced in the historical tradition of miri and piri to provide leadership to the panth. The peaceful mass agitation during the gurdwara movement as a method of demand–resolution matured the panth for its political assertion in future struggles. Religion was not just a private matter of faith, but an all-encompassing motivational force that would also determine the community's asseveration in public affairs. The SGPC, thus, evolved as the pedestal for articulation and assertion of religious and even non-religious concerns of the community. With its massive resources and geographical spread, it has assumed the role of a mini-Parliament for Sikhs, a state within the state. The electoral process of the SGPC, however, has inducted competitive politics in the religious affairs of Sikhs, with all the concomitant ills of politicking. Political parties sponsor or support candidates who on paper are independent candidates but are de facto party nominees. The electoral politics has at times led to competing candidates adopting a radical approach to outwit each other, often with divisive outcomes.

4

Linguistic Dissensions

MAHARAJA RANJIT SINGH (1780–1839), WHO RULED OVER undivided multilingual Punjab, patronized all the languages of his empire and had no linguistic conflicts in his regime. He retained Persian as the language of the darbar, even though Punjabi was his mother tongue and the language of his faith, Sikhism.

However, in British Punjab, language conflicts divided Punjabis as much as their religions did. The western part of Punjab spoke Lahnda, a mix of Punjabi dialects. The eastern part (present-day Haryana that was merged with Punjab after the 1857 uprising) and the hill districts of present-day Himachal spoke dialects of Hindi. In the central districts or what is the present-day Punjab of India and Pakistan put together, the majority spoken language of Hindus, Muslims and Sikhs alike was Punjabi.

The 1881 census showed that the mother tongue of an overwhelming majority of the population in these central and southern districts of Punjab was Punjabi, even though Sikhs constituted only about 8 per cent of the population of the state. The district gazettes of the central and the southern districts published after the 1881 census depicted that 85–98 per cent of the population of these districts was Punjabi-speaking. As author Harjot Oberoi says, 'In mid-century Punjab the majority in the provinces—Hindus, Muslims and Sikhs—spoke a welter of Punjabi dialects without any religious distinction.'[1]

Urdu and English, however, were the official languages in British Punjab. The British preferred Urdu to Persian, as most of the British officers who had moved to Punjab after its annexation were not familiar with Persian but had earlier served in Urdu-speaking parts of India and were comfortable with the language.

For the first time, an Urdu–Hindi issue arose in Punjab in 1882, triggered by developments in Bihar.[2] In that year, the British administration of Bihar switched from Urdu in Persian script to Hindi in Devanagari script as the official language of the province. The pan-Indian ties of Hindus and Muslims, unlike Sikhs who were territorially localized in Punjab, spurred these two communities to lobby with the Punjab administration for Hindi and Urdu, respectively. In 1900, Hindi in Devanagari was inducted in the United Provinces as the official language, on a par with English and Urdu. This further spurred organizations like the Arya Samaj and a few other groups to promote Hindi in Punjab, while Anjuman-i-Islamia of Lahore opposed it and supported Urdu.

The irony, however, was that for most Hindus in central and southern Punjab, Hindi or Devanagari were not very familiar. The first mass-circulation Hindi newspaper, *Punjab Kesari*, commenced its publication only in 1965, from Jalandhar, because Devanagari had a narrow readership base to commercially sustain a daily newspaper.[3] This was despite the sectarian origin of print media in British Punjab—the four major communities commenced their own newspapers and journals corresponding to their religions and their reformist movements such as those in the Arya Samaj, Singh Sabhas and Brahmo Samaj, along with the Anjumans, Ahmadiyyas, Christian missionaries and Sanatanis. By 1905, there were 263 such publications, mostly in Urdu, a few in English and some in Punjabi and Hindi.

Hindi was introduced for the first time as an optional subject in Punjab's schools in 1917, while as M. Rose Greenfield, a Christian teacher in Ludhiana, noted that in 1882, many girls—Sikh, Muslim and Hindu—were already learning Punjabi in schools.[4] In 1882, there were 829 schools in the state teaching Punjabi and these included ten in Sirsa, seven in Ambala and one in Karnal, which are now part of Haryana and considered Hindi areas.[5]

The position of Hindi in Punjab may be gauged from what Paul R. Brass writes in his well-researched tome:

> The famous Arya Samaj leader and Punjab politician, Lala Lajpat Rai, who 'actually did not know the Hindi alphabet' entered political life in this controversy because he came to believe that Hindi could 'be the foundation for the edifice of Indian nationality'. From the Hindi–Urdu controversy, Lajpat Rai learnt his 'first lesson in Hindu nationalism' and 'became convinced that political solidarity demanded the spread of Hindi and Devanagari'.[6]

What was true of Lala Lajpat Rai was equally true of an overwhelming majority of Hindus in the state. They spoke Punjabi and were not well conversant with Devanagari, but a section, nevertheless, while supporting Punjabi, argued that 'for Punjab there should be no language other than Punjabi, but it should be written in Hindi characters instead of in Gurmukhi characters'.[7] Hindi had become the symbol of Hindu nationalism.

Gurmukhi got identified with Sikhs. 'Guru-mukhi' means from the mouth of the Guru. Guru Angad Dev had standardized the Gurmukhi script to write Punjabi, which is of ancient Indo-Aryan origin and linked to Sanskrit. The holy Guru Granth Sahib is written in Gurmukhi script, though its compositions, shabads, are rendered by Sikh gurus, Hindu saints and Muslim fakirs in a mix of languages such as Punjabi, Braj Bhasha, Lahnda, Khari Boli, Sanskrit and Persian.

Language, thus, got identified with religious communities—Urdu with Muslims, Hindi in Devanagari with Hindus, and Punjabi in Gurmukhi script with Sikhs, and this became a cause of inter-community conflict. Punjabi lost out the most. While everyone—Sikhs, Muslims, Hindus—continued to speak Punjabi, in the census operations they started reflecting their religiously congruent language as their mother tongue.[8]

The linguistic conflict that had surfaced in British India continued post-Independence, though its focus changed from Hindi-versus-Urdu to Hindi-versus-Punjabi. Logically, the migration of the Punjabi- and Lahnda-speaking population from Pakistan in 1947 should have increased the number of Punjabi-speaking people in Indian Punjab, but the percentage of the Punjabi-speaking population went down as reflected in the subsequent census figures. Punjabi became a minority language in Punjab because in the official census records a section of the Punjabi-speaking population disowned their mother tongue.

Paul Brass, in his analysis of the census figures, shows that in the 1911 census, the Hindi-speaking population of Punjab was only 13.94 per cent, Urdu-speaking 2.69 per cent, and Punjabi-speaking 64.13 per cent.[9] However, by 1961, the percentages (adjusted for boundary changes) changed to 55.64 per cent Hindi-speaking, 1.26 per cent Urdu and 41.09 per cent Punjabi. This switch in the mother tongue in the census records was to determine the future of Punjab and create conflicts.

5

1947: Partition

All Punjabis drank the same groundwater, but they drew it from different wells—Muslim or Hindu wells. At public places like railway stations, separate taps dispensed 'Muslim pani' and 'Hindu pani' (this was meant for Sikhs as well).[1] Religious demarcation was now deep and all-pervasive among the masses.

However, defying religious determinants at the lofty political level, Punjabi agrarian elites exhibited remarkable cohesion. With shared economic interests, the Muslim, Hindu and Sikh agrarian bourgeois came together to form the Unionist Party and together they protected the poverty-stricken peasantry of Punjab by instituting measures such as rural debt relief.

The Congress party was not part of the Unionist coalition, nor did it support the two legislations brought before the State Assembly by Unionists to address the rural indebtedness. Punjab Congressmen like Dr Gopi Chand Bhargava, Dr Satyapal, Bhimsen Sachar and Duni Chand, to name a few, were opposed to these measures and even called the Bills 'black laws' because the party's base was the urban population, primarily the Hindu trading community. This opposition of the Congress to the debt relief bills alienated it from 85 per cent of the peasantry, mostly Muslim, Sikhs and a few Hindus, and made it what historians called an urban 'Hindu Party'. It also determined the nature of the freedom movement in Punjab, 'the national movement in Punjab remained confined to the Sikh peasantry', so wrote the leftist icon Harkishan Singh Surjeet.[2] Sardar Vallabhbhai Patel, whose ancestors originally came from Punjab and migrated to Gujarat, wrote to Maulana Azad in December 1945 of 'how badly the Congress was messing up in Punjab' and bemoaned, 'I am afraid we have mishandled the whole Punjab situation . . .'[3]

The Congress was politically opposed to the Unionists, even though the Unionists had brought the overwhelming peasant population of all the communities together and bound them by common economic agrarian interests. Together, they opposed and resisted the partitioning of Punjab. Sikandar Hayat Khan, the premier of Punjab, and his Cabinet colleague Sir Chhotu Ram, the Jat leader, shooed away Muhammad Ali Jinnah from the state and rejected the proposal to create Pakistan. However, they died in 1942 and 1945, respectively. The successor premier of Punjab, Khizar Hayat Tiwana, also of the Unionist Party, was equally opposed to Partition.

Jinnah dubbed the Unionists as British stooges and called Punjab Premier Khizar Hayat Tiwana 'Sardar Khizar Singh', a 'thief' and a 'traitor'.[4] The sweeping communal fire that Jinnah had set ablaze finally forced Khizar to resign on 2 March 1947, and the Unionist coalition government fell, bringing Punjab under Governor's Rule. That is when Master Tara Singh of the Akali Dal drew out his Khalsa sword. On 3 March 1947, he stood on the steps of the Lahore Legislative Building, unsheathed his sword, and declared, 'Sikhs would not live under Muslim rule nor allow Pakistan to emerge.'[5] The Akali Dal had, in fact, consistently and strongly opposed the creation of Pakistan. In its memorandum to the Cabinet mission, it had opposed the division of India with the rider that if Pakistan was to be formed, Sikhs should also have the right to form a separate state. On 15 April 1940, Master Tara Singh stated, 'If the Muslim League wants to establish Pakistan, they will have to pass through the ocean of Sikh blood.'[6] He led an anti-Pakistan movement and opposed Pakistan till the last day.

However, as violence broke out in Punjab, the Congress in its Working Committee meeting held in Delhi on 8 March 1947 agreed to the demand of the Muslim League for the creation of Pakistan—Punjab was to be partitioned into two. The British had given the Sikhs the option to join India or Pakistan. Jinnah lured the Sikhs with the offer of 'autonomy' within Pakistan and 'offered to meet all their demands' if they joined Pakistan.[7] The Sikhs and the Akali Dal, however, threw their lot in with India. Thus, 'The East Punjab became, in a sense, a gift of Akalis to the Indian Union'.[8] Otherwise, India's international boundary may not have been the Ravi, but could have been the Ghaggar or even the Yamuna, considering that the boundaries of the Sikh princely states extended deep into present-day Haryana and included Mohindergarh, Narnaul, Jind and beyond. No wonder Quaid-e-Azam Jinnah disappointingly felt that Pakistan was a moth-eaten country.

Partition adversely affected all Punjabis but the largest sufferers were the Sikhs. By one estimate, about 40 per cent of the total Sikh population had to relocate, abandoning their homes and historical shrines. Caught in the insecurities of a minuscule minority in joint Punjab (12.99 per cent, as per the 1931 census), and having lost the separate electorate status and the communal representation they enjoyed in British India, they initially orchestrated the demand for a 'Sikh majority' state within India. Master Tara Singh, while emphasizing the Hindu–Sikh historical bond, said, 'The Sikhs are Hindus and I feel they are so. But I do not say so, as in that case the Hindus would absorb Sikhs.'[9]

It was a question of Sikh identity and fear of a majoritarian Hindu India submerging their diversity. Punjabi Hindus were no less apprehensive—the division of Punjab and the unparalleled violence that accompanied it had generated a fear psychosis. If the Muslims got Pakistan, what was stopping the Sikhs to demand a state of their own, many feared. A mutual distrust, more than anything else, was the inevitable outcome of the bloody Partition and it had sowed the seeds of suspicion, if not division, by sharpening their separate religious identities. One outcome was that fresh conversions to Sikhism from Hindus virtually stopped—the umbilical cord that had intertwined the two was wrecked long back. 'No more do Hindu families raise some of their children as Sikhs. Even Keshdhari Sikhs and Hindus in the same family have drawn further apart.'[10]

Interestingly, in British India, the Sikh population was on the ascendency. In the 1921 census, the Sikh numbers went up from 8.2 per cent of Punjab's population to 12.4 per cent, while Hindus declined from 43.8 per cent to 35.1 per cent of the population. This happened mainly because, as historian Rajmohan Gandhi puts it, due to Hindus giving self-descriptions as Sikhs. But that was now a thing of forgotten history; the Hindus had moved on, as the fear of Islamic challenge had abated in independent Hindustan.

6

Punjabi Suba

On 26 January 1950, we, the people of India, solemnly affirmed and adopted a secular, democratic Constitution. It was easy to establish the institutional framework but far more arduous to internalize a culture of democratic secularism in Indian society.

The British had injected communal representation deep in the body politic, and it had become the operating mantra in India's public life. The two major communities of Punjab—Hindus and Sikhs—continued with a sectarian approach even after Independence, and projected claims for space in the sociopolitical arena based on religious and communal identities. The trend was accentuated by the vote bank politics of the political parties.

The Akali Dal, to preserve Sikh identity and to secure a piece in the political pie, initially raised the demand for a Sikh majority state within India, but soon abandoned it to seek a unilingual Punjabi-speaking state—Punjabi Suba. This demand was challenged by a section of the Hindu leadership, and the way successive governments handled the issue precipitated a turmoil that lingered for nineteen years, from 1947 to 1966—it is a study in how not to resolve conflicts or how not to go about building nationhood.

In pre-Independence Punjab, Hindus were in a minority (35 per cent) and Muslims constituted 51 per cent of the population. The Muslims, the common bête noire of Sikhs and Hindus, however, migrated to Pakistan, barring a small number that continues to live in complete social harmony in Malerkotla. With the demographic relocation, Hindus became the majority community in Indian Punjab (about 62 per cent as per the 1961 census). The Sikhs had also overcome the handicap of a dispersed presence and improved their numbers in a much smaller Indian Punjab, but they were still a minority in the state. The Hindu leadership feared that the community would lose its majority status, and consequentially lose political power if Indian Punjab were to be further divided to exclude Hindi-speaking areas from the state. As a strategy to block Punjabi Suba, which they viewed as a linguistically camouflaged Sikh state, Punjabi Hindus opted for Hindi as the mother tongue (in the 1961 census, 11 million recorded Hindi as their mother tongue versus the 8 million who listed Punjabi). It was exactly the same fear—the fear of the submergence of Sikh identity and loss of power in a Hindu-majority Punjab that had prompted the Sikhs to seek Punjabi Suba.

The electoral politics of the two main political parties—the Akalis and the Congress—further sharpened the divide. The Akalis and the Congress have had periods of close cooperation and had even merged in 1948 and then again briefly in 1956. In 1956, the Akalis virtually adopted the Congress's political manifesto! However, the brotherly bonhomie was transitory and soon the two split to resume the unending power tussle that widened the sectarian strife. The electoral base of the Akalis was primarily the Sikh peasantry and that of the Congress were urban Hindus. Both parties were addressing their respective electoral bases in pursuing or opposing the demand for a linguistic state rather than building a consociational democracy or a spirit of 'Punjabiyat'.

During this period, the Congress ruled at the Centre in a hegemonic and asymmetric federal relation with the states. It opposed the Akali demand for a linguistic state and that, in the Sikh perception, made the Central government staunchly allied with the Hindu cause. To the Congress, it came naturally to oppose Punjabi Suba, because, as historian Rajmohan Gandhi puts it, 'the Punjab Congress remained too Hindu and too urban'.[1] There was also the historical retraction by the Congress from its publicly stated stand and that aggrieved the Akalis. In its 1929 Lahore session, the Congress had resolved that no future Constitution would be adopted without the satisfaction of the Sikhs. The Sikhs were demanding a 'homeland' within the Indian Union for protection of their identity and rights. As mentioned earlier, they had opposed the Partition of India, despite Jinnah luring them with the promise of 'autonomy' within Pakistan.

Mahatma Gandhi in 1931 addressed a Sikh congregation at Sis Ganj Gurdwara, Delhi, and declared that Sikhs had no reason to fear that the Congress would betray them. 'For the moment it does so,' he said, 'the Congress would not only thereby seal its own doom but that of the country too.' He added, 'Moreover, Sikhs are brave people. They know how to safeguard their rights by the exercise of arms.'[2] Pandit Nehru followed it up by a public assurance in July 1946: 'The brave Sikhs of Punjab are entitled to special consideration' and that he saw nothing wrong in an area set up in the north where 'Sikhs can also experience the glow of freedom'.[3] However, when the draft Indian Constitution was adopted, the Sikh representative in the Constituent Assembly, Hukam Singh, refused to affix his signature of approval as Sikh demands had not been met.

The seed for a separate Sikh state within India had, thus, been sown by the demand of Sikhs for a 'homeland' and the assurances given by the Congress and its leaders, with the accompanying open suggestion by Gandhi to take to arms if the Congress betrayed the community. Master Tara Singh, the Sikh leader who in February 1948, had reiterated the demand of a Sikh state within the Indian Union where the panth could enjoy the right of 'self-determination in matters religious, social and political',[4] felt betrayed.

The ruling government argued that once India's democratic, secular Constitution was adopted, the circumstances had changed—in secular India, religion could not be a territorial determinant to create a separate state. For the Akalis, it was perfidy of the solemn assurances.

What irked the Akalis additionally was that they were being denied even a linguistic state. The Congress had recognized language as the legitimate base to organize Indian states in its 1916 and 1920 sessions. In the Constitution that the Congress drafted for itself in 1920, Punjabi was recognized as the mother tongue of the people living in the tract between the Yamuna and the Indus rivers, and Punjab with Punjabi as a linguistic province.[5]

In independent India, the policy of linguistic states was reaffirmed by the Congress-led Central government on many occasions. The Akali Dal that had initially demanded a Sikh 'homeland' within the Indian Union now swiftly switched its demand to seek a unilingual Punjabi-speaking state.

Sikh insecurity sharpened when there was an institutional disowning of the Punjabi language by certain sections in Punjab. Illustratively, the Hindu-dominated municipal corporation, Jalandhar, in February 1949, resolved to have Hindi instead of Punjabi as the medium of instruction in schools. Punjab University, which was set up in 1882 at Lahore and had moved to Solan after Partition, on 9 June 1949, spurned Punjabi in favour of Hindi and English.[6]

The Central government had constituted a States Reorganization Commission in conformity with the policy to form linguistic states, but in 1955 it rejected the demand for a unilingual Punjabi state on the plea that it lacked the 'general support of the people'. Instead, PEPSU

(Patiala and East Punjab States Union), which was the only Punjabi-speaking state of India—Sardar Patel had referred to PEPSU as 'a Sikh homeland' on 15 July 1948 while inaugurating the new state[7]—was merged with multilingual Punjab on grounds of geographical and administrative compulsions on 1 November 1956, despite its Legislative Assembly's unanimous rejection of the proposal.[8] While most Sikhs felt betrayed, most Hindus welcomed the merger.

On getting wind that the States Reorganization Commission was likely to reject the demand for Punjabi Suba, Master Tara Singh launched a disobedience movement. He courted arrest on 10 May 1955. Before offering himself for arrest, he addressed a huge congregation of the devotees in the Golden Temple, where he stoked the Sikh sentiment of honour and discrimination against it:

> We are not satisfied with the present situation and ask for Punjabi Suba, but they stop us even from propagating the demand of Punjabi Suba. They have imposed a ban on raising slogan for the demand. Khalsa Ji! Understand this that all this is to finish our honour. This is all we have, if this is gone then all is gone. So, stake everything to maintain our honour. In the present time we should offer our heads peacefully like Guru Tegh Bahadur. The rivals are haughty rulers, but we have faith in Guru.[9]

His call was not in vain. About 12,000 people courted arrest within days. The Golden Temple became the hub of the agitation and for the first time in independent India, police entered it on 4 July 1955 to arrest the agitators inside the complex. The temple was cordoned off, and its residential and administrative blocks were searched. *The Tribune* in its 18 July 1955 edition wrote: 'What overshadows the entire situation is that every weapon in the armoury of the government has been brought into play.'[10] The police entry into the temple imparted a religious complexion to the linguistic temper of the agitation and it gained a fresh momentum. Finally, the state relented and Master Tara Singh was released on 8 September. The ban imposed on raising pro-Punjabi Suba slogans was withdrawn. Chief Minister Bhim Sen Sachar visited the Golden Temple to pay obeisance and apologized for the police entry. A few months later—in 1956—he was asked to resign and sent away as governor of a state. Partap Singh Kairon became the chief minister.

Parallel to the demand for a unilingual Punjabi state, a Hindi movement emerged. The Hindi Raksha Samiti, the Maha Punjab Samiti and Congress leaders like Lala Jagat Narain and a few others led the pro-Hindi movement. Some leaders of these organizations, for example Yagya Dut Sharma of the Jana Sangh and Swami Rameshwaranand, went on fasts unto death to oppose the Akali demand for Punjabi Suba. Demonstrations and strikes were organized in various cities of the state. The Hindi Satyagraha Committee led by Arya Samaj leader Swami Atmanand Saraswati, some Congressmen and a few others even opposed the Regional Plan which the Akalis had accepted as a compromise in 1957 and merged the Akali Dal with the Congress. The two parties had contested the 1957 elections as a single entity. The Regional Plan had endorsed the earlier Sachar Formula of October 1949, and recognized Punjab as a bilingual state. Both Hindi and Punjabi were to be taught in schools, either as a first or second language, depending upon which part of the state you lived in.

However, the opposition of some Hindu leaders to the formula, its apathetic implementation, and political conflicts between Master Tara Singh and Partap Singh Kairon soon caused the demise of this compromise, which could have potentially saved the state from division. It seems the Punjab Congress itself was a divided house. About fifty Congress legislators petitioned the Prime Minister and met him; fourteen of them resigned on the language issue, including Lala Jagat Narain who assiduously opposed all such moves in his newspapers.[11]

The agitation for a unilingual Punjabi province strained relations and brought the two communities in acrimonious conflict. In July 1957, cigarette cases were thrown into the sarowar of the Golden Temple and on 1 August torn parts of the Guru Granth Sahib were found scattered in Amritsar. Acts of sacrilege continued throughout the year at Amritsar, Patiala, Hisar and some other places. Such incidents were repeated in 1965 in various parts of the state.[12]

By then, the territorial reorganization of states in India had been implemented for all major regional languages of the country, except Punjabi. The demands of the Telugu, Kannada, Malayalam and Marathi people had fructified in the formation of Andhra Pradesh (where the Prime Minister had announced the separation of Andhra Pradesh from Madras immediately on the death of the fasting Potti Sreeramula; the state was created on 1 October 1953), Kerala (1 November 1956), Karnataka (1 November 1956), Maharashtra (1 May 1960) and Gujarat (1 May 1960).

The Akali Dal viewed the rejection of its demand as an act of discrimination against Sikhs. They asserted that the demand was not secessionist or anti-India; its focus was to safeguard Sikh identity and they wanted a cultural, linguistic, religious and political set-up to safeguard it. However, the opposition had successfully painted the demand as separatist and as a threat to Indian unity. Even senior leaders like Nehru while campaigning at Patiala rejected the demand and said as early as 4 January 1952, 'I will not allow India to be divided again.'[13] The memory of the bloody communal Partition of the country in 1947 was fresh and the opposition of the Hindus in Punjab made the Congress leadership view the demand for a linguistic state within India as secessionist. The Akali Dal had never sought a state outside India but the opposition of the Congress to the demand, as also the initial demand of Master Tara Singh for a Sikh homeland within the Indian Union, which was later abandoned for a linguistic state, was used to kindle misgivings of communal separatism.

The Tribune in an editorial on 1 June 1961 suggested that the Akali leadership try to win over the Hindus and 'remove the doubts and suspicions entertained by their fellow Punjabis', and later the paper was to compliment Sant Fateh Singh, who in a letter to Nehru wrote, 'We want a linguistic, and only a linguistic unit, where Punjabi culture and language [are] prevalent, regardless of whether Hindus or Sikhs are in a majority there.'[14] Sant Fateh Singh's stand was unambiguous—a composite Punjabi linguistic state.

In August 1965, Sant Fateh Singh declared his intent to go on a fifteen-day fast from 10 September, and if by then the Central government did not accede to the Punjabi Suba demand, to self-immolate on the sixteenth day. In the meantime, war broke out between India and Pakistan. Responding to the national emergency, Fateh Singh postponed the fast. The Akali Dal and the Punjabis, particularly the peasantry of the border districts, played a pivotal supportive role in the war effort. As a goodwill gesture in recognition of the patriotic role played by Punjabis in the war, the Central government agreed to reconsider its stand on Punjabi Suba; President Radhakrishnan more or less conceded it when on 11 November 1965 in a broadcast he said, 'I dare say he [Fateh Singh] will be satisfied with the eventual solution of this problem.'[15]

However, ultimately, the formation of Punjabi Suba was an outcome of inexorable historical serendipity. Hukam Singh, Speaker, Lok Sabha, a former Akali who had joined the Congress, was apathetic towards the demand and had even opposed it on the floor of the Lok Sabha.[16] So, when a Parliamentary Consultative Committee was constituted to consider the issue, Gulzarilal Nanda, the home minister, 'suggested Hukam Singh's name for Chairmanship of the Committee under the mistaken impression that [Hukam Singh] was opposed to the Punjabi Suba demand'.[17]

In the meantime, Hukam Singh, it seems, had a change of heart. When Indira Gandhi got an inkling of it, she tried to prevent him from giving a favourable report for a unilingual Punjabi state. She was a member of the Cabinet sub-committee to consider the Punjabi Suba issue, along with Y.B. Chavan and Mahavir Tyagi, the two other members. As the *Indian Express* reported on 11 April 1983, Hukam Singh was to later say, 'The intention of the government then was to use me against my community to secure an adverse report and then reject the demand.'[18] In its report published on 18 March 1966, the Parliamentary Committee recommended the reorganization of Punjab on linguistic grounds as specified in the First Schedule to the Punjab Regional Committee's Order, 1957, but this observation was ignored by the subsequent appointment of the Shah Commission, making the 1961 census data as the basis of the reorganization.

Indira Gandhi states in her autobiography, 'I had heard that Sardar Hukam Singh was going to give a report in favour of Punjabi Suba and that should be stopped.' She continues, 'I was very bothered and I went around seeing everybody. Of course, once the report came, it was too late to change it.'[19] 'Congress,' she states, 'found itself in a dilemma: to concede the Akali demand would mean abandoning a position to which it was firmly committed and letting down its Hindu supporters in the projected Punjabi Suba.' Indira Gandhi, it appears, was opposed to Punjabi Suba not on linguistic considerations but due to electoral concerns. She describes the Akali Dal as the 'party of militant Sikh nationalism',[20] and Hindus as supporters of the Congress.

Indira Gandhi became the Prime Minister in January 1966 after the death of Lal Bahadur Shastri and gave the impression of dragging her feet over the issue of the formation of Punjabi Suba. This invited a strong reaction from Sant Fateh Singh, who on 28 February 1966 declared that the Central government had only four weeks' time, and threatened to revive his fast unto death and self-immolation. The dynamics of the internal power struggle within the Akali Dal often led to ideological extremism. Master Tara Singh, who had lost the leadership to Sant Fateh Singh, now adopted a radical posture. In an open session of the Akali Conference in Jalandhar on 27 February, he made the accusation that 'powers are consistently being applied to discriminate against the Sikhs, to demoralize and degrade them with the ultimate object of submerging the Sikh people into the Hindu mass, and thus make the Sikhs pass out from the pages of history'. The conference resolved that 'the Sikh people are entitled to demand self-determined political status for themselves within the Republic of the Union of India'.[21] Patience was wearing thin and the demand had long ago assumed a communal colour. Finally, the Congress Working Committee, privy to the likely outcome of the Parliamentary Consultative Committee's report, on 9 March 1966, recommended the formation of Punjabi Suba to the Central government.

By this time, the Hindi-speaking population of Haryana and the Arya Samajists of Hindi-speaking areas had awakened to the prospects of their own state. They supported the carving out of a Hindi-speaking state before the Parliamentary Consultative Committee. The Jana Sangh, which had initially opposed the demand, also backed a Punjabi unilingual state—many Jana Sangh leaders declared that their mother tongue was Punjabi.

'Both Madhok and the RSS leader, Golwalkar, who toured Punjab in April 1966, urged the Hindus of the Punjab to acknowledge Punjabi as a legitimate language and Gurmukhi as a proper script for Hindus to accept.'[22] M.S. Golwalkar, the RSS chief, had in fact even in November 1960 while on a tour of the state advised Hindus to own Punjabi as their mother tongue, but at that time the Jana Sangh did not fall in line.[23]

Punjabi Suba was formed on 1 November 1966 by dividing the state into Punjab and Haryana and transferring the hilly areas to Himachal on the recommendations of the Punjab Boundary Commission. Chandigarh, which the commission had recommended go to Haryana, became a Union Territory and the common capital of Punjab and Haryana.

The Akali Dal had demanded an area of 35,458 sq. miles for Punjabi Suba and it included the districts of Ambala, Karnal (except Panipat tehsil) and the present-day districts of Sirsa, Fatehabad (then parts of Hisar) and Tohana, a few Punjabi-speaking hilly areas like Kangra, Dalhousie, Una and Nalagarh that were given to Himachal Pradesh during the reorganization by the commission, and Ganganagar of Rajasthan. However, this demand was not accepted due to the shift in the census statistics, which showed these areas to be dominated by Hindi speakers.

With the exclusion of these territories from present-day Punjab, the Central government created a Sikh majority state (about 63 per cent). The Akali Dal protested over the exclusion of these areas which it claimed to be historically Punjabi-speaking. Sant Fateh Singh, reacting to the recommendations of the Punjab Boundary Commission, called it 'communal' and said, 'The proposed Punjabi Suba will become lame without these areas. I will endeavour to get these areas for the Punjabi Suba.'[24] The Akali Dal abstained from the celebratory functions to commemorate the formation of the new Punjab and gave a call to observe 16 December as a protest day due to the non-fulfilment of all its demands.

The terms of reference of the Punjab Boundary Commission were broad-based. It was an empowered commission and therefore could cavort with the boundaries for the formation of the new state. Apart from the census-based linguistic data, it was to consider factors like administrative convenience, economic well-being, communication and geographical contiguity. However, the commission went primarily by the 1961 census linguistic data, in which the Punjabi-speaking Hindu population had declared Hindi as their mother tongue—the slight of statistics became the culprit, and the outcome was a truncated Punjab in what may be called a 'commissioned manoeuvre' of the Boundary Commission.

By doing so, the Punjabi Hindus had scored somewhat of a self-goal and become a minority in the new Punjab. Some historians, however, have recorded that the Central government wanted to keep the size of the new Punjab small, apprehending future national security concerns considering its geographical location with a hostile Pakistan. In hindsight, the move was counterproductive, because a bigger Punjab with a more balanced Hindu–Sikh population may have never witnessed the militancy and turmoil that affected Punjab.

In the new Punjab, the emphasis, however, was on Hindu–Sikh unity. The sharing of power by the Akali Dal and the Jana Sangh, which the Congress called 'an unholy alliance',[25] following the elections in 1969 helped to restore the confidence of the minority Hindu population in the new state. The Akali Dal had its base among Sikhs, and the Jana Sangh enjoyed a majority among Hindus and their political marriage enabled both to gain power—the outcome was equally beneficial to harmonize the inter-community friction of the past. In due course, the Akali Dal adopted a more inclusive electoral strategy, sponsoring Hindu candidates in elections and enlarging its base among non-Sikhs and Scheduled Castes, which were the traditional Congress vote banks. In the new Punjab, the Akali Dal mostly formed coalition governments, primarily with the BJP, even when it had a clear majority of its own in the Assembly.

In the new Punjab, the language disagreement was settled after a few hiccups, with the enactment of the Punjab Language Act, 1967. The Act accorded Punjabi in Gurmukhi script the status of official language, though in the higher echelons of government English continues to be the de facto official lingua franca. A three-language formula for school education, with liberty to private schools to decide the language of the medium of instruction, found wide acceptance.

Language is no more an issue today—in a unanimous decision that included BJP members of the Punjab Vidhan Sabha, the Punjab Learning of Punjabi and Other Languages Act, 2008, was enacted, making the learning of Punjabi compulsory in all schools in the state from classes 1 to 10. The decision was welcomed by all communities in Punjab.

However, the pruned 'Punjabi Subi', as the new Punjab was dubbed, created fresh territorial and river water disputes. The merger of Chandigarh and carving out Punjabi-speaking areas from Punjab, the distribution of river water from the Punjab and the control of the 'head works' are lingering to date, despite protracted political agitations and fasts unto death—Jathedar Darshan Singh Pheruman died on 27 October 1969, fasting for these causes. These unsettled issues have kept the political pot boiling.

What have been the gains of Punjabi Suba for Sikhs and Punjabis is a debatable issue—there are diverse perceptions. The Akalis credit themselves for saving the Punjabi language and culture from assimilation by the majority and its gradual extinction, as they say is visibly happening in Delhi.[26] Opponents, however, cite the loss of substantial geographical territory to Haryana and Himachal Pradesh and the resultant loss of economic opportunities these could have offered to Punjabis.

7

Post–Punjabi Suba

In a democracy, when politics degenerates into politicking, it devalues not only the constitutional institutions, but the entire politico-social ethos. That is what was to happen in Punjab.

The demographic profile of the new state had enhanced the electoral prospects of the Akali Dal as Sikhs were in a marginal majority in Punjabi Suba. However, communities do not vote en masse for a single political party, and that made it imperative for the Akalis to build alliances with other parties to gain power. Akali–Jana Sangh coalition governments, thus, emerged as an alternative to the Congress. This could have brought an end to Hindu–Sikh sectarianism, but a hegemonic federal structure ensured that between 1967 and 1987 the Akalis or their coalitions never ruled Punjab for a full term, not even after they won electoral majorities. The federal government either dismissed the state governments by subverting constitutional provisions, or engineered defections to bring down duly elected governments.[1]

Repeated dismissals of Akali governments frustrated its political aspirations and the party reverted to what it was good at—agitations. Consequently, the Punjab turmoil was kept alive to gain and retain political power and soon it turned into an ethno-religious struggle.

Arguably, the Congress executed similar 'dismissals of the state governments' and indulged in factional political manoeuvres in other states of the country too, but these did not result in terrorism. What made the difference in Punjab was the minority syndrome of the Sikhs and the perceived sense of discrimination engraved deep in their collective memory. An assertive historical lineage reinforced by a young living religion, in combination with other factors gradually birthed a sense of deprivation into the ethnic conflict, which was further accentuated by electoral politics.

To gain power, the Congress resorted to what for want of a better expression may be called 'religiosity manoeuvres', a race for religio-political domination. It became more pronounced in 1972, when it captured power in Punjab and Giani Zail Singh became chief minister. He was a Riyasti Praja Mandalist with impeccable nationalistic credentials, having suffered confinement in a 10x7-foot cell, grinding wheat daily and weaving *khes* and durries in the Faridkot jail during the freedom struggle.

However, he lacked formal education—he was a Giani, knowledgeable about religious affairs and Gurmukhi. That was both his strength and his limitation. The 'Sikh agenda' came naturally to him and as chief minister he gave the Akalis a run for the religiosity card. He would tee-hee the Akalis as '*aklon khali*' (without brains) and rationalize his government's acquired religious symbolism by surmising 'you can cut steel only with steel'. Zail Singh believed that the Akalis had no exclusive hegemony over the Sikhs and his government indulged in religiously loaded manoeuvres.[2] The coup de maître was importing pedigreed descendants from the lineage of the horses that Guru Gobind Singh is said to have ridden, from England. The horses were publicly paraded in processions taken out in different cities of the state. In a remarkable show of devotion to his faith, he set a trend by carrying the droppings of the horses over his head in a vessel. For days, as he paraded the horses, devotees packed the streets—old women even stooping to pick up the poop. Later, lounging on the Rashtrapati Bhavan lawns, Zail would laugh about the whole thing: '*Lohe se loha kate, zahar se zahar* [Steel cuts steel and poison kills poison].'

Stoking Sikh religiosity was Zail Singh's strategy to capture a base among the peasantry and the more religious urbanites. How did the Akalis meet the challenge? They 'retaliated by passing an ambiguous resolution at Sri Anandpur Sahib making many demands on behalf the Sikhs'.[3] To counter Zail Singh's excursions in the Akali agenda, the Working Committee of Akali Dal adopted a policy document, popularly called the Anandpur Sahib Resolution, in 1973. It was formally approved in the form of twelve resolutions at the party's eighteenth All India Conference held at Ludhiana in 1978. The resolutions were a political statement covering religious, political, agrarian and economic policies, and ideology of the party. The document highlighted asymmetrical federalism, hegemonic authority of the Central government and resultant discrimination against the states of the federation. Resolution 1 sought to 'recast the constitutional structure of the country on real and meaningful federal structure principles to obviate the possibility of any danger to national Unity and the integrity of the country and further, to enable the states to play a useful role . . .'[4]

However, different political parties interpreted the resolutions differently and that laid the foundation for conflict and agitation in the state. The confusion was also partly caused as there were at least three versions of the Anandpur Sahib Resolution in circulation. However, the official English version, duly authenticated by Harchand Singh Longowal, appears as Annexure III to the Government of India's 'White Paper on the Punjab Agitation' issued in Delhi on 10 July 1984. While the Akali Dal maintained that the resolutions were based on its experience of the asymmetrical federal relations it had encountered while running governments in Punjab between 1967 and 1971,[5] the Congress and some others branded the Akalis as secessionist for raising what was presented as an anti-national and divisive agenda.

The political slugfest was finally resolved in July 1985 by the accord signed by Rajiv and Longowal. The Anandpur Sahib Resolution was referred for consideration to the Sarkaria Commission on Centre–State Relations. The commission had been announced on 24 March 1983 by Indira Gandhi to examine the entire gambit of Centre–state relations. Longowal had welcomed its formation on 26 March, but the issues raised in the Anandpur Sahib Resolution were not referred to the commission. The Congress viewed the resolution as secessionist and for this reason the Union government declined to even discuss it with the Akalis, projecting itself as the saviour of the nation.

In 1985, however, the same Anandpur Resolution was viewed not as a secessionist charter but as a document of an affirmative assertion of regional aspirations against a hegemonic federal structure—an issue of Centre–state relations worthy of examination by the Sarkaria Commission. From 1973, when the resolution was adopted, till 1985 when it was referred to the commission, the Akalis used it to whip up anti-Centre sentiments, while the Congress used it as a weapon to nail the Akalis as secessionists. It was politicking for electoral vote banks which generated a fear psychosis and conflict in Punjab.

The Akali Dal, in fact, was not the only political party to demand the restructuring of Centre–state relations. The CPI(M), ADMK, Janata Party and some other regional parties had raised similar demands, but being a community-based party that stood for '*Khalsa ji de bol bale*' or pre-eminence of the Khalsa, it was easy to beat the Akalis with the stick of being anti-national. But what brought the Akali Dal and its leadership in direct confrontation with Indira Gandhi was the declaration of internal Emergency on 25 June 1975. The Allahabad High Court on 12 June 1975 held Indira Gandhi guilty of electoral malpractices and 'unseated' her. The Akali Dal joined the anti-Emergency national movement led by Jayaprakash Narayan to oppose 'the fascist' measure and on 9 August 1975 launched a 'Save Democracy' morcha.

The first to court arrest were the five Akali leaders—Badal, Tohra, Talwandi, Atma Singh and Basant Singh Khalsa. In all, about 60,000 Akali workers courted arrest by the time Emergency was withdrawn in March 1977.[6] The 1978 Anandpur Sahib Resolution also demanded from the then Central government action against the 'long tale of the excesses, wrongs, illegal actions committed by the previous Congress government, more particular during Emergency'.

Indira Gandhi, however, was not the kind of leader to forget the massive resistance put up by the Akalis in the hour of her personal crisis. K.S. Dhillon, the former DGP, Punjab, has disclosed, 'She strongly disliked the Akalis . . . In a one-to-one meeting this writer had with her in her office in Parliament House, sometime in August 1984, she expressed herself very strongly against the Akalis . . .'[7] She lost the parliamentary elections in 1977, and the new Central government in a blatant violation of the democratic norms dissolved the nine state governments in which the Congress was in the majority.

In the elections to the Punjab Assembly in March 1977, the Akali Dal declared its commitment for 'a secular democratic socialist society'—a marked shift from its Sikh-centred election manifesto of the previous years. It won a slim majority with fifty-eight seats but opted for a coalition government with the Janata Party (twenty MLAs) and the support of the CPM (eight MLAs) from outside. However, the government was dismissed on 17 February 1980 by the Congress-led Central government even when it had a clear majority in the Legislative Assembly.

8

Rise of the Radicals

In Punjab, the main political parties were peddling fundamentalism to gain political power. There was an inter-party struggle for power and within each political party the intra-group strife and rivalry led to radicalism and became a major contributing factor to create turmoil in the state. The leaders strategized to divide rather than integrate the people as they found it much easier to capture power via polarization. The very process of nation-building, thus, had become divisive.

While the Akalis relied on religion to retain their support base and adopted the tactic of mass agitations, some Congress leaders entered this race to create an alternate Sikh leadership which could compete with the Akalis' fundamentalism. In the process, they deployed religious symbolism, propped up parallel charismatic religious crusaders and surreptitiously supported radical organizations. The game plan was to outwit the Akalis in religiosity and fundamentalism, and the activities that the Congress as a secular party could not itself undertake were outsourced. Some of the prominent individuals and organizations are detailed below.

The Khalistanis

A two-man army—Dr Jagjit Singh Chauhan and Balbir Singh—appeared on the horizon in the early 1970s. They sowed the seeds of separatism not by firearms, but by propaganda. Stunts and symbolism were their weapons, and with Pakistan's help they attempted to create the dream of an independent country, Khalistan. They internationalized the cause of Khalistan and gave it the visibility it needed, before the gun-wielding militants appeared on the scene.

Chauhan, a good-looking dentist from Tanda in Hoshiarpur district, was an active leftist in his younger days, a comrade-in-arms of Harkishan Singh Surjeet. However, he was ambitious and to gain power he abandoned the Marxist cause and entered the state assembly in the 1967 elections and became the deputy speaker in the Akali government. He, however, soon broke off from the Akali Dal along with Lachhman Singh Gill, who became the chief minister with the outside support of the Congress. Chauhan became finance minister in the Congress-supported Lachhman Singh's Cabinet. That, however, was the last time he wielded political power in Punjab.

In 1969, Chauhan lost the election and shifted base abroad, from where he launched the 'letter-head' government of Khalistan, funded by Pakistan. However, the response of the Sikh community in Canada and the UK was poor. In fact, he encountered opposition from the traditional Akali leadership in these countries. In December 1971, the Khalsa Dewans of Vancouver and a gurdwara in Leeds in the UK passed resolutions against him and the Akali leader A.K.S. Aujla even remonstrated, 'Most Gurdwaras objected to Dr Chauhan's campaign and restricted his entry.'[1] Chauhan, however, received encouragement from Pakistan, which he visited in 1971. In November of the same year, Sant Fateh Singh suspended him from the Akali Party for anti-party and pro-Khalistan activities. In Pakistan, the title 'Father of the Sikh Nation' was bestowed upon him by President Yahya Khan. Chauhan was launched by the ISI internationally—he visited the US, where National Security Adviser Henry Kissinger is said to have motivated him to berate India for human rights violations.

The ISI bankrolled Chauhan in October 1971 to insert an advertisement in the *New York Times* announcing Khalistan as a separate Sikh state. He met Zulfikar Ali Bhutto in New York and was assured of Pakistan's support.[2] However, after Gen. Zia-ul-Haq seized power, Chauhan was given the cold shoulder, though he continued to be used by the ISI for anti-India activities.

Intriguingly, he commuted between India and the UK a couple of times, and his easy mobility within India and access to the top leaders may have peeved the Pakistanis, who began suspecting him to be a double agent. He founded a new party in India—the Akali Dal (Revolutionary)—to intensify radical activities, but met with little success. In November 1979, he installed a toy transmitter in the Golden Temple with a range of less than 200 metres, ostensibly to pressurize the Government of India to concede to the demand to relay gurbani from the temple, but his real objective was to dramatize the cause of Khalistan. He established links with Bhindranwale and other like-minded radicals. Strangely, while in the UK, his media adviser was a Kashmiri Brahmin named Pyare Shivpur, a former BBC employee.

In April 1980, he was allowed an audience with Prime Minister Indira Gandhi. 'Shortly, after that,' states Gen. V.K. Singh, the former Chief of Army Staff, 'at Anandpur Sahib, Chauhan declared the formation of the National Council of Khalistan with himself as the President and Balbir Singh Sandhu as its Secretary General.'[3]

Two journalists, Kuldip Nayar and Khushwant Singh, have revealed, 'Chauhan met Mrs Gandhi more than once at that time. Soon after her return to power, he met her again.'[4] What transpired in these meetings is not known, but the fact that a foreign-based proponent of Khalistan had a discussion with the Prime Minister of India more than once was enough to raise eyebrows.

After announcing the formation of the Council of Khalistan at Anandpur Sahib, Chauhan returned to the UK, where he headed the self-proclaimed government of Khalistan in exile out of a building called Khalistan House in Bayswater, London. A guard in Nihang regalia kept watch at the entrance, perhaps to lend a semblance of authenticity to the premises. He indulged in theatrical symbolism by making appointments to a Cabinet of the non-existent Khalistan and issuing passports and even currency notes. However, like most other radical outfits, Chauhan also got disillusioned with his fruitless chase of Khalistan and returned to India on 27 June 2001. It was a back-channel persuasive operation carried out by the intelligence agencies, perhaps motivated by the fact that his return would also mean an end of his secessionist activities, that facilitated his final return to India after due observance of the judicial process. Back in India, to rehabilitate himself, Chauhan floated the Khalsa Raj Party in 2002, but it was a political fiasco. In the twilight years of his life, he established a charitable hospital and died at the age of eighty in April 2007.

Chauhan's associate Balbir Singh was originally a school teacher, and he later joined Gulzarilal Nanda's Bharat Sevak Samaj at the bidding of Gurdial Singh Dhillon, a former Speaker of the Lok Sabha.[5] Around 1977, he came in contact with Chauhan and together they formed the National Council of Khalistan, with Chauhan as its president and Balbir Singh as its secretary general.

In 1980, Balbir Singh shifted to Room No. 32 of Guru Nanak Niwas in the Golden Temple complex and operated out of it till his death in Operation Blue Star. Some, however, claim that he slipped across to Pakistan. Ensconced in the secure confines of the temple complex, and uninterrupted by the government or the SGPC, Balbir Singh indulged in histrionics such as the release of Khalistani stamps and passports. In January 1984, he hoisted a kesari flag in the

Golden Temple precincts, and called it the Khalistani flag. Strangely, he was not arrested for anti-India activities even when the Akalis viewed him with suspicion. Longowal even told Kuldip Nayar, 'He is an agent of the Intelligence Bureau.'[6]

There were a few more individuals based abroad who played such pro-Khalistani games. One such person was Ganga Singh Dhillon, a wealthy Sikh from Washington. He was the head of the Shri Nankana Sahib Foundation. His association with the President of Pakistan, Gen. Mohammad Zia-ul-Haq, who had assumed power in 1978, brought him into the limelight. Their wives were friends from their pre-marriage Nairobi days and this connection was used by the ISI to woo Ganga Singh Dhillon and aid and abet his anti-India and pro-Khalistan activities.

'Dhillon was also in touch with Zail Singh,' wrote journalist Kuldip Nayar, though this liaison was explained by Zail Singh's supporters as an attempt to 'retrieve Dhillon'. Strangely, in a communication written by Dhillon to Gajinder Singh, a go-between, that has been quoted by Nayar in his book, reads, 'I had mentioned about my talk with Giani Zail Singh at Karnal in detail. You must have met him by now and he must have managed the finance and other required things. One fact must be taken care of that he is not to be seen often.'[7]

Another Khalistani, Gurmeet Singh Aulakh, the self-styled president of the Council of Khalistan, operated out of Washington. He lobbied at Capitol Hill, and with American press and politicians. Apparently, he had won the confidence of Edolphus Towns, who represented New York in the House of Representatives, and of Jesse Helms, a former senator. In the UK, Lord Avebury lent him an ear.

Over a period, the Khalistanis faded away as the Sikhs of Punjab remained aloof to the idea. Attempts by Pakistan-sponsored organizations like the US-based 'Sikhs for Justice' of Gurpatwant Singh Pannun notwithstanding, the generation of separatists has passed into oblivion or is on the verge of it.

Dal Khalsa

Dal Khalsa, a radical set-up formed on 6 August 1978 in a small congregation held at a gurdwara at Chandigarh, played a significant role in the ethno-national turmoil. The first set of its leadership—Gajinder Singh, Harsimran Singh, Jaswant Singh, Satnam Singh, Harbhagat Singh and others had strong, devout Sikh family backgrounds and were religiously motivated.

The trigger to form the Dal may have come from the April 1978 Nirankari clash at Amritsar, but the Dal Khalsa's objective was unambiguous: the formation of Khalistan.

The organization's ideological inspiration can be traced to Kapur Singh, a former civil servant and Sikh scholar who espoused the cause of Sikh sovereignty. The choice of the name, Dal Khalsa, reflected the historical lineage of the idea of Khalsa Raj. On 29 March 1748, in a Sarbat Khalsa at the Golden Temple, a gurmata or resolution had resolved to create a Khalsa state. Jassa Singh Ahluwalia was made the commander-in-chief of the Khalsa army, called the Dal Khalsa. The present-day Dal Khalsa emulated this tradition and its governing body that met at Gurdaspur in December 1979 formally resolved to establish Khalsa Raj. Politically, the Dal Khalsa posed a challenge to the Akali Dal's hegemony over Sikh affairs by espousing the radical cause.

The first head of the Dal Khalsa, Harsimran Singh, was a stenographer with Dr V.N. Tiwari, an eminent professor at Panjab University. Dr Tiwari, aligned to the Congress, had supported the Emergency and was nominated as a member of the Rajya Sabha in 1982. Kuldip Nayar has written more than once that Dr Tiwari had a hand in the foundation of the Dal Khalsa. 'He [Dr Tiwari] told me, when I was in Chandigarh looking after the *Indian Express* edition there, that what he and his mentors, Zail Singh and Sanjay Gandhi, wanted was to embarrass the Akali Party.'[8] 'And Tiwari, who later wrote a book defending Mrs Gandhi's excesses during Emergency, never made a secret of the fact that he had a hand in the foundation of the Dal Khalsa.'[9] Unfortunately, Dr Tiwari fell to the bullets of the militants in 1984.

Harsimran Singh was wanted in a few murder cases and was finally arrested in 1982 from the residence of one Harinder Pal Singh, the driver of a Congress minister. In his interrogation by the Punjab Police, he named 'Congress (I) leaders, administrators both at the Centre and the state as well Akali leaders who had given him shelter'. Among those named by him were Zail Singh, a few Congress ministers and Akali leaders Tohra and Talwandi.[10]

Historians have also chronicled Zail Singh's nexus with the Dal Khalsa. He 'paid the bill for its [Dal Khalsa's] first meeting at the Aroma Hotel at Chandigarh and who [Giani ji] used to ask journalists to give prominence to its activities'.[11] There is also an independent corroboration of Zail Singh's presence at Aroma Hotel provided by Jagtar Singh, a Chandigarh-based journalist, who saw Zail Singh at the hotel, though Jagtar has recorded that Zail Singh's offer to pay the bill was politely declined by the Dal Khalsa in public.[12]

Even at its peak, the membership of the Dal Khalsa never exceeded 300. Its initial activities were largely symbolic in nature and confined to holding seminars and conferences and raising occasional pro-Khalistan slogans, hoisting of the Khalistani flag and distributing pro-Khalistan literature at these gatherings. However, in the early 1980s, it started mobilizing Sikh youth and organized indoctrination camps, mostly in Himachal Pradesh, Rajasthan and Jammu and Kashmir. In 1981, a few acts of sacrilege and desecration of religious places such as planting of severed heads or tails of cows in temples were attributed to it. Its five activists led by Gajinder Singh Panch of Chandigarh hit the headlines when they hijacked the Delhi–Srinagar Indian Airlines flight IC-423 to Pakistan on 29 September 1981. Pakistan declined to repatriate them to India. Gajinder Singh, after completing his sentence in Pakistan, continues to live there, while two others—Jasbir Singh and Karan Singh—were granted asylum in

Switzerland. Tejinder Pal Singh and Satnam Singh, who moved to Canada and the US, respectively, from Pakistan, were repatriated to India and put on trial. Thirty-seven years after the hijacking, they were acquitted in August 2018, by Ajay Pandey, additional sessions judge, Delhi.

The authorities took serious cognizance of the organization only after the hijacking incident, and some of its prominent leaders were detained. Harsimran Singh, the mukh panch of the Dal Khalsa, was arrested on 12 February 1982, and the then DGP, Punjab, has disclosed that 'the Home Minister Giani Zail Singh called me to his residence . . . he was very upset that I had entrusted the interrogation of Dal Khalsa Pramukh Harsimran Singh to a Jat Sikh DIG' who wanted 'to see him disgraced'.[13] This panic, obviously, betrayed that Giani Ji had something to hide.

The state government under Darbara Singh, alarmed at the secessionist activities of the Dal Khalsa, had moved the Union home ministry a few times to ban the organization, but 'each time the request was made, the ministry turned it down'.[14] Giani Zail Singh was then the Union home minister but despite his demurral, the Dal Khalsa and the National Council of Khalistan were banned in May 1982, under the Unlawful Activities (Prevention) Act, 1967. It is relevant to note that most of its initial activities happened in Chandigarh, a Union territory, directly governed by the Government of India, for example, the congregation held at Panchayat Bhawan, Chandigarh, on 1 February 1981, chaired by Syed Abdullah Bukhari, Shahi Imam of the Jama Masjid, Delhi, in which a formal call for the creation of Khalistan was given.

Later, the Dal shifted its headquarters to Guru Nanak Niwas in the Golden Temple complex and slowly spread its wings and branches in the state and abroad. It played a significant role during the Punjab turmoil. The ban on the organization was lifted in May 1992, and it is active in promoting panthic issues.

9

Emergence of Bhindranwale

Sikh preacher Sant Jarnail Singh Bhindranwale was to dominate the religious–political discourse in Punjab for a short period of about six years (1978–84), but the forces he unleashed caused a tsunami. He defined the course of Sikh history as no other individual has done probably since Independence.

A high-school dropout—Bhindranwale dropped out of school after class 7—he was deeply influenced by the history of the Sikh struggle against Mughal and Afghan tyranny. He conveniently juxtaposed this historical struggle to modern times, substituting historical tormentors with what he called the Delhi darbar's Brahminical imperialists. Consequently, he triggered an ethno-religious turmoil, which, but for him, Punjab may have never seen.

With earthy intelligence and little exposure beyond the canons of the religion and Sikh history, he was a charismatic leader, reigning over his followers by a mix of dogmatic assertions and the sheer force of personality. Circumstances and destiny conspired to place him in a politico-religious role that transformed the man from a mere evangelist to an emissary of Sikh identity and ultimately led him to his death.

Bhindranwale was born in a Brar Jat Sikh family of Rode village in present-day Moga district in the Malwa region of Punjab. His father, Baba Joginder Singh, a marginal farmer, had seven sons and a daughter. At a very young age, Bhindranwale joined the Damdami Taksal, a respected Sikh seminary that traces its origin back to the days of Guru Gobind Singh. In the puritanical ethos of the Taksal, he studied the scriptures, Sikh history and thereafter dedicated himself to propagation of the religion. He was married and had two sons.

Bhindranwale was known for his dedication to panthic causes and the propagation of Sikh values and he became the fourteenth head of the Taksal. He focused on Amrit Parchar and preached preservation of sabat surat Sikh identity. His philosophy was simple: '*Amrit chakho, Sikh sajo, nam jappo and nasha chado*', that is, become baptized Sikhs, maintain the symbols of Sikhism, recite the gurbani and abjure intoxicants. He campaigned for the eradication of social evils and practices, and his reformist stance made him popular and famous.

In those murky days of politicking, political leaders were searching for an alternative Sikh persona of some standing who could pose a challenge to the established base of the Akali Dal among the Sikhs. A few independent chroniclers have also written about these developments, but of significant relevance is an acknowledgement of the Congress (I) in a volume on the history of the party, published to mark its 125th anniversary:

> Meanwhile, during their years in the wilderness, Zail Singh, in complete collaboration with Sanjay, picked up a relatively obscure, young and fundamentalist lay preacher named Jarnail Singh Bhindranwale with a view to building him up as a rival to the Akali leadership. It is inconceivable that they

> could have done so without Indira Gandhi's consent. Sanjay and Zail Singh believed that by advocating extremist causes the young preacher would embarrass the Akali Dal. [1]

Conformation of the Congress's claim about Bhindranwale came from none else than the then jathedar of the Akal Takht, Giani Kirpal Singh. On 21 July 1984, in an interview to Subhash Kirpekar, the jathedar, with discernible fear on his face, answered Kirpekar's question, 'He [Bhindranwale] was a Congress agent.'[2]

The journalist, the Late Kuldip Nayar, has also disclosed how Sanjay Gandhi and Zail Singh strategized to field some sant 'to challenge the Akali government'. Kamal Nath, the Congress leader, and former chief minister of Madhya Pradesh, disclosed to Nayar that the choice was Bhindranwale, who was 'strong in tone and tenor, seemed to fit the bill. We would give him money off and on.'[3]

Retired spy M.K. Dhar also divulged that Zail Singh was part of the plot. In May 1981, Dhar was mandated to establish links with a close relative of Bhindranwale and bring him to Delhi for a meeting with the then home minister, Zail Singh. Dhar writes that he picked up Bhindranwale's nephew Jasbir Singh and 'a personal aide to Jarnail Singh from Sardulgarh on the Haryana border and drove them straight to the official residence of the Home Minister'. After the meeting, they were back 'with two fat shoulder bags'. Dhar writes, 'I was asked to drop them at Mansa near Bhatinda. I did my job with the characteristic silence of a deaf, dumb and blind intelligence officer.'[4] What did the bags contain? Your guess is as good as anyone else's.

But Bhindranwale was not a 'creation' of the Congress party as alleged by a few— he merely collaborated with the Congress. The reason was his disenchantment with the then Akali government over its perceived inaction against the Nirankaris following the April 1978 clash. Bhindranwale felt that the Akalis were mere seekers of political power and not committed to promote Sikhism. The unfortunate killings in the Nirankari clash at Amritsar and the Sikh radical's perception that the Akali government was soft against the Nirankaris with the objective of retaining power with the support of right-wing Hindu parties provided an opportunity to the Congress to woo an indignant Bhindranwale. An entente with the Congress suited Bhindranwale to capture the SGPC, dislodge the Akalis and their hegemony over the religious parliament of the Sikhs. In collaborating with the Congress, Bhindranwale was merely pursuing his own objectives, while the Congress was 'using' him to marginalize the Akalis and polarize people for vote bank politics.

Then came the 31 March 1979 SGPC elections. As a secular party, the Congress would not directly contest elections to the religious body, but to strike at the power base of the Akalis it was vital to secure control over the SGPC. So it outsourced this task; it was not for the first time that this strategy to capture the SGPC through alliance groups had been tried. In 1960, Congressmen had joined hands with a few dissident Akalis and propped up the Sadh Sangat Board as a front to contest the SGPC elections, but they were routed by the Akalis.

This time, the Congress's choice was Bhindranwale and a few other radical Sikh groups who aspired to have a hold over the SGPC for their own reasons. Bhindranwale's objective was to undertake reforms and restore the Sikh religion to its Tat Khalsa purity, while groups like the Dal Khalsa and the Panth Khalsa, who joined hands, had designs to promote their declared objective: Khalistan. These organizations and the AISSF joined hands with the Baba Jiwan Singh Mazhabi Dal against the Akali Dal in the SGPC election. The Congress extended support to these groups from outside. Bhindranwale and these groups together fielded '70 candidates under the auspices of Panth Khalsa formed by him and Dr Jagjit Singh'.[5]

However, the election outcome was a big setback for Bhindranwale and the groups aligned with him. The Akali Dal won eighty-eight out of ninety-six seats it contested in the general constituencies and all the ten reserved constituencies. Jiwan Singh Umranangal, then a minister in Badal's Cabinet, resigned to contest the SGPC election against Bhai Amrik Singh, and defeated him. This was a personal blow to Bhindranwale.

Bhindranwale's alignment with the Congress continued even during the January 1980 Lok Sabha polls. As payback for the help in the SGPC elections, he extended support to Congress candidates in the constituencies geographically close to his headquarters, Mehta. These included the constituencies of Raghunandan Lal Bhatia in Amritsar, Gurdial Singh Dhillon in Tarn Taran and Sukhbans Kaur Bhinder in Gurdaspur. The sant is said to have shared the stage with Indira Gandhi during Sukhbans Kaur's election rally in Gurdaspur district in December 1979.[6]

Their association continued even after some of the radical groups had given a call for violence and Baba Gurbachan Singh Nirankari and journalist Lala Jagat Narain had been killed. Bhindranwale eulogized, 'Whoever performed these great feats deserves to be honoured by the Akal Takht . . . if the killers come to me, I would weigh them in gold.' Satyapal Dang, the leftist leader, rued, 'Congress, at least one faction of it, continued to nurture and support him [Bhindranwale] even after he openly called for murder of the Nirankari Baba and Lala Jagat Narain. The game obviously was to split or weaken the Akali Party, as yet the only rival in the bid to rule Punjab' and that 'this Sant was brought into politics by the Congress (I). The game was not given up even after Bhindranwale began organizing large scale terrorism and made serious efforts to bring about Hindu–Sikh riots.'[7]

By the end of 1981, Bhindranwale parted company with the Congress 'but the Congress did not fall out with him . . . Indira Gandhi maintained contact with Sant Jarnail Singh through R.L. Bhatia who remained in regular contact with Bhai Amrik Singh till April 1984'.[8]

What complicated the political stratagem was the dismissal of the Akali government in February 1980. The Congress had won the 1980 Lok Sabha election, and on assuming power at the Centre, it dismissed all non-Congress state governments, even when these were in a majority. The Akalis did not take long to declare their dismissal as an act of discrimination against Sikhs and added this instance to the long list of existing Sikh grievances. However, in the election to the Punjab Vidhan Sabha that followed in May 1980, the Akali Dal lost and the Congress formed the government with Darbara Singh as the chief minister.

Once out of power, it was the Akali Dal's turn to adopt a radical posture. On 19 August 1980, the general body meeting of the party described the killing of the Nirankari chief as 'the brave act' and a 'matter of pride' for Sikhs. The pot kept on simmering and in 1981 an All World Sikh Convention proposed to launch the Dharam Yudh Morcha to secure Sikh demands—forty-five in all. In September, a charter of these demands was sent to the Central government.

As they say, there are no permanent friends or foes in politics. With the launch of the Dharam Yudh Morcha on 4 August 1982, Bhindranwale joined hands with the Akali Dal. Bhindranwale, of course, was not a contender for political power and that suited both the Congress and the Akalis. If Bhindranwale could mobilize crowds for the morcha, it suited the Akalis, and if Bhindranwale polarized communities and consolidated Hindu votes, so much the better for the Congress. The Akalis and the Congress were now trying to ride a tiger that, in due course of time, would marginalize both the parties.

Bhindranwale soon captured the centre stage of the ethno-national movement and operated out of the Golden Temple independent of the Akalis or the Congress. He was a 'sant' and that imparted him canonical legitimacy while the Akali morcha provided him the political platform. The sacred space of the Golden Temple, with its never-ending flow of devotees, provided him with a reverential audience and the news-hungry journalists projected him as a larger-than-life figure in the national and international media. The guns of the armed militants conferred the required 'power' to complete the story of his ascendency.

Bhindranwale, as K.P.S. Gill said, 'was the brainchild of the Congress. He was an intelligence operation gone awry.'[9] Gill writes, 'It must be clearly recognized that it was the Congress party, under the leadership of Indira Gandhi, that brought this lunatic fringe to the dominant core of Sikh politics, and created the monster—Khalistan terrorism—that was to ravage Punjab for a decade and a half . . . The cynicism of the Congress-I leadership in supporting—indeed "creating"—Jarnail Singh Bhindranwale as a leader of Sikh militancy in its initial phase in order to undermine the political base of the Akalis, is unquestioned.'

Bhindranwale died in Blue Star, or attained shaheedi as many devout Sikhs perceive, but in his death he delivered to the Congress the success the party needed in the 1984 elections. If that also triggered an ethno-national struggle lasting over a decade with countless suffering, it was viewed as just collateral damage.

Notes

PART I

1: 'Rumours Have Wings'

1 Aeschylus, *Agamemnon.*
2 Pavit Kaur, *Stolen Years, A Memoir of Simranjit Singh Mann's Imprisonment* (Gurgaon: Random House India, 2014), p. 2.
3 Sarbpreet Singh, *The Camel Merchants of Philadelphia: Stories from the Court of Maharaja Ranjit Singh* (Chennai: Westland, 2019), p. 75; also see Maninder Dabas, 'Punjab Has Its Own Taj Mahal Called Pul Moran, a Memorial of Maharaja Ranjit Sing's Love for Moran, a Dancer', Indiatimes.com, 2 February 2017, https://www.indiatimes.com/news/india/punjab-has-its-own-taj-mahal-called-pul-moran-and-it-s-a-memorial-of-maharaja-ranjit-singh-love-for-moran-a-dancer-270753.html.

2: On to Amritsar

1 Wheeler M. Thackston, ed. and trans., *The Jahangirnama: Memoirs of Jahangir, Emperor of India* (New York, Oxford University Press, 1999), p. 59.

2 Pranab Mukherjee, *The Turbulent Years: 1980–1996* (New Delhi: Rupa Books, 2016), p. 5.
3 Mark Tully, *Amritsar: Mrs Gandhi's Last Battle* (New Delhi: Rupa Books, 1985), p. 146.
4 Jagtar Singh, *Khalistan Struggle: A Non-Movement* (New Delhi: Aakar Books, 2011), p. 170.

3: The Trigger

1 Illustratively, a clash had occurred in 1951 at Amritsar when Avtar Singh, the Nirankari chief, held a satsang. More recently, the two had clashed in 1972, on 15 September 1973 at Chowk Mehta, on 23 September 1973 at Ludhiana, in 1974 at Ghoman in Gurdaspur district, in September 1977 at Pathankot and also at Qadian and Sri Hargobindpur in the same district. N.S. Rattan, the then district magistrate, Ludhiana, had sent a detailed report to the home ministry over certain groups planning to demolish Nirankari establishments at Jagraon, but these specific inputs were also overlooked.

4: Bhindranwale Arrested

1 Birbal Nath, *The Undisclosed Punjab: India Besieged by Terror* (New Delhi: Manas Publications, 2008), p. 162.
2 Harkishan Singh Surjeet, *Deepening Punjab Crisis: A Democratic Solution* (New Delhi: Patriot Publishers, 1992), p. 95.
3 Nath, *The Undisclosed Punjab*, p. 177.
4 Ibid.
5 The meeting was attended by Sant Longowal, Tohra and Badal, among others from the Akali side, and the Prime Minister was assisted by Home Minister Zail Singh, Finance Minister Pranab Mukherjee, Cabinet Secretary S.R. Krishnaswamy Rao Sahib, Principal Secretary to the Prime Minister P.C. Alexander and Home Secretary T.N. Chaturvedi.

5: The Administrative Collapse

1 P.C. Alexander, *Through the Corridors of Power: An Insider's Story* (New Delhi: HarperCollins India, 2004), p. 270.
2 Birbal Nath, *The Undisclosed Punjab: India Besieged by Terror* (New Delhi: Manas Publications, 2008), p. 168.
3 K.P.S. Gill, *Punjab: The Knights of Falsehood* (New Delhi: Har-Anand Publications, 1997), p. 95.
4 Ghani Jafar, *The Sikh Volcano* (New Delhi: Atlantic Publishers and Distributors, 1988), p. 262.

5 B.D. Pande, *In the Service of Free India: Memoir of a Civil Servant* (New Delhi: Speaking Tiger Books, 2021), p. 253.
6 *The Tribune,* Chandigarh, 20 July 1983.
7 *The Tribune,* Chandigarh, 24 April 1984.

6: The Morcha

1 Harkishan Singh Surjeet, *Deepening Punjab Crisis: A Democratic Solution* (New Delhi: Patriot Publishers, 1992), p. 81; also see Government of India, 'White Paper on the Punjab Agitation' (New Delhi: Government of India, 10 July 1984), pp. 61–65.
2 *The Tribune*, Chandigarh, 1 November 1982.
3 R. Venkataraman, defence minister; P.C. Sethi, home minister; P. Shiv Shankar, petroleum minister; and Amarinder Singh, MP, apart from government officials, participated from the side of the government, while P.S. Badal, Balwant Singh, Ravi Inder Singh and a few others represented the Akalis.
4 Khushwant Singh, *Captain Amarinder Singh: The People's Maharaja: An Authorized Biography* (New Delhi: Hay House India, 2017), p. 125.
5 Ibid., p. 126.
6 Chand Joshi, *Bhindranwale: Myth and Reality* (New Delhi, Vikas Publishing House, 1984), p. 123.
7 Surjeet, *Deepening Punjab Crisis*, pp. 54–81.
8 B.D. Pande, *In the Service of Free India: Memoir of a Civil Servant* (New Delhi: Speaking Tiger Books, 2021), p. 294.
9 Amarjit Kaur, 'Akali Dal: The Enemy Within', in *The Punjab Story* (New Delhi: Lotus Collection, Roli Books, 2007), p. 31.
10 Gen. S.K Sinha, *A Soldier Recalls* (New Delhi: Lancer International, 1992), pp. 287–88.
11 Ghani Jafar, *The Sikh Volcano* (New Delhi: Atlantic Publishers and Distributors, 1988), p. 104.
12 Khushwant Singh, *A History of the Sikhs, Vol II: 1839–1988* (New Delhi: Oxford University Press, 1991), p. 332.
13 See Vandana Shiva, *The Violence of the Green Revolution, Ecological Degradation and Political Conflict in Punjab* (Dehradun: Research Foundation for Science and Ecology, 1989), pp. 128–29. She writes, 'A crisis that was economically and politically rooted in the Green Revolution rapidly expressed itself in communal overtones because of the contingent overlapping of the identity of the farming community in Punjab with a Jat Sikh identity. … Farmers in Punjab are largely Jat Sikhs, and the party representing their interests is the Akali Party, it was possible to represent Green Revolution related conflicts as communal

conflicts, and treat them as only having a religious base unrelated to the politics of technological change and its socio-economic impact. The Green Revolution failed to bring lasting peace and prosperity to Punjab.'

14 Giani Zail Singh, *Memories of Giani Zail Singh, the Seventh President of India* (New Delhi: Har-Anand Publications, 1997), p. 179.
15 Kuldip Nayar, 'Longowal Speaks Out His Mind', *The Tribune*, 1 April 1985.
16 Gurdarshan Singh Dhillon, *Truth about Punjab, SGPC White Paper* (Amritsar: Shiromani Gurdwara Parbandhak Committee, 1996), p. 239.
17 Kuldip Nayar, *Beyond the Lines: An Autobiography* (New Delhi: Roli Books, 2012), p. 290.
18 A.G. Noorani, 'A White Paper on a Black Record', in *The Punjab Crisis: Challenge and Response,* edited by Dr (Mrs) Abida Samiuddin (New Delhi: Mittal Publications, 1985), p. 227.
19 M.S. Deora, *Akali Agitation to Operation Blue Star* (New Delhi: Anmol Publications, 1991), p. 521.
20 Singh, *Captain Amarinder Singh*, p. 137.
21 Dr Gurmit Singh, *History of Sikh Struggles, Vol. 111* (New Delhi: Atlantic Publishers and Distributers, 1991), p. 49.
22 Mark Juergensmeyer, *The Logic of Religious Violence: The Case of the Punjab* (New Delhi: Sage Publications, 1 January 1988).
23 Gobind Thukral, 'Punjab: Growing Tension', *India Today*, 1982.
24 P.P.S. Gill, 'Dal, Bhindranwale Trade Charges', *The Tribune*, Chandigarh, 14 April 1984.
25 K.P.S. Gill, *Punjab: The Knights of Falsehood* (New Delhi: Har-Anand Publications, 1997), p. 93.
26 Ghani Jafar, *The Sikh Volcano* (New Delhi: Atlantic Publishers and Distributers, 1988), p. 143.
27 The committee consisted of the jathedar of the Akal Takht, Giani Kirpal Singh; head priest of the Golden Temple, Giani Sahib Singh; jathedar of the Takht Keshgarh Sahib, Giani Harcharn Singh Mahalon; jathedar of the Damdama Sahib, Sant Lakha Singh; and head granthi of the Akal Takht, Giani Pritam Singh. The committee evolved a code of conduct that included a ban on gunfire in the temple area, on any excesses or torture in the temple complex, on mutual character assassination, etc.
28 'Appendix IV', *The Punjab Crisis, Challenge and Response*, edited by Dr Abida Samiuddin (New Delhi: Mittal Publications, 1985), pp. 684–87.

7: The Army Marches On

1 Lt Gen. K.S. Brar, *Operation Blue Star: The True Story* (New Delhi: UBS Publishers' Distributors, 1993), p. 77.

2 Subhash Kirpekar, 'Operation Blue Star: An Eyewitness Account', *The Punjab Story* (New Delhi: Lotus Collection, Roli Books, 2007), p. 107.
3 Dr Baldev Singh was to disappear later, never to be heard from again. It is believed that terrorists killed him by inviting him to their hideout.

8: 'Who Moved My Army?'

1 B.D. Pande, *In the Service of Free India: Memoir of a Civil Servant* (New Delhi: Speaking Tiger Books, 2021), p. 295.
2 Ibid., p. 266.
3 S.S. Dhanoa, *Nothing to Hide: A Civil Servant Reveals* (New Delhi: Manas Publications, 2017), p. 176. Dhanoa, a former chief secretary of Punjab, has quoted Pooni's DO letter. Also see K.D. Vasudeva, 'The Congressmen Who Let Punjab Down', *Financial World*, 2011, and Canadian Punjabi paper *Quomantry Pardesi*, June 2011, and Vasudeva's TV interview to PTC, Mohali.
4 Lt Gen. V.K. Nayar, *Threat from Within: India's Internal Security Environment* (New Delhi: Lancer Publishers, 1992), p. 10.
5 'Appendix IV', *The Punjab Crisis, Challenge and Response*, edited by Dr Abida Samiuddin (New Delhi: Mittal Publications, 1985) pp. 684–87.
6 Zail Singh, *Memoirs of Giani Zail Singh, the Seventh President of India* (New Delhi: Har-Anand Publications, 2001), p. 178.
7 P.C. Alexander, *Through the Corridors of Power: An Insider's Story* (New Delhi: HarperCollins India, 2004), p. 322–23.
8 *India Today*, 'President: Dignified Demeanour', 30 June 1984, pp. 28–29. Also see M.S. Deora, *Akali Agitation to Operation Blue Star* (New Delhi: Anmol Publications, 1991), pp. 593.
9 Singh, *Memoirs of Giani Zail Singh*, pp. 177–78.
10 Pranab Mukherjee, *The Turbulent Years: 1980–1996* (New Delhi: Rupa Publications, 2016), p. 35.
11 *The Tribune*, 'Pranab: Indira Was Convinced of Op Blue Star', 14 May 2017.
12 Alexander, *Through the Corridors of Power*, pp. 294–96.
13 Lt. Gen. Nayar, *From Fatigues to Civvies*, p. 207.
14 Ibid.; Alexander, *Through the Corridors of Power*, p. 298.
15 Lt. Gen. Nayar, *From Fatigues to Civvies*, p. 207.
16 Ibid., pp. 186–217.
17 Ibid., p. 194.
18 Ibid.
19 Lt Gen. Nayar, *Threat from Within*.
20 Birbal Nath, *The Undisclosed Punjab: India Besieged by Terror* (New Delhi: Manas Publications, 2008), p. 184.

21 Ibid.
22 K.P.S. Gill and Sadhavi Khosla, *Punjab: The Enemies Within* (New Delhi: Bookwise India, 2017), pp. 35–36.

9: The Grand Mosque of Mecca

1 Pascal Menoret, 'Fighting for the Holy Mosque', in *Treading on Hallowed Ground*, edited by C. Christine Fair and Sumit Ganguly (New York: Oxford University Press, 2008), p. 131.

10: Operation Blue Star: Part I

1 Vani Sundarji, 'A Man Called Sundarji: A Wife Remembers', in *Of Some Consequence: A Soldier Remembers* (New Delhi: HarperCollins India, 2000), p. xv.
2 Government of India, 'White Paper on the Punjab Agitation' (New Delhi: Government of India, 10 July 1984), p. 44.
3 Lt Gen. K.S. Brar, *Operation Blue Star: The True Story* (New Delhi: UBS Publishers, 1993), p. 97.
4 Lt Gen. P.N. Hoon, *The Untold Truth* (Chandigarh: Mohindra Publishing House, 2015), p. 53.

11: Operation Blue Star: Part II

1 Dr Madanjit Kaur, *The Golden Temple, Past and Present* (Amritsar: GNDU, 2004), p. 10.
2 Lt Gen. K.S. Brar, *Operation Blue Star: The True Story* (New Delhi: UBS Publishers, 1993), pp. 91, 95 and 98.
3 Ibid., pp. 146–47.
4 Harminder Kaur, *Blue Star over Amritsar* (New Delhi: Corporate Vision Publishers, 2006), p. 46.

12: Operation Blue Star: Part III

1 Brig. Onkar S. Goraya, *Operation Blue Star and After: An Eyewitness Account* (Panchkula: self-published, 2013), p. 62.
2 Lt Gen. K.S. Brar, *Operation Blue Star: The True Story* (New Delhi: UBS Publishers, 1993), pp. 103–10.
3 Brig. Goraya, *Operation Blue Star and After*, pp. 70–71.
4 Surjit Singh Sokhey, 'Extremists Had Tried to Kill Longowal', in *The Punjab Crisis: Challenge and Response*, edited by Dr Abida Samiuddin (New Delhi: Mittal Publications, 1985), p. 349.

13: The Desertions and the Demurral

1 Birbal Nath, *The Undisclosed Punjab: India Besieged by Terror* (New Delhi: Manas Publications, 2008), p. 202.
2 Lt Gen. P.N. Hoon, *The Untold Truth* (Chandigarh: Mohindra Publishing House, 2015), p. 52.
3 Nripinder Rattan, *Operation Blue Star 84* (Ludhiana: Chetna Parkashan, 2021), p. 230.
4 Pavit Kaur, *Stolen Years: A Memoir of Simranjit Singh Mann's Imprisonment* (Gurgaon: Random House India, 2014), pp. 6-9.
5 Khushwant Singh, 'I Felt I Should Reaffirm My Identity as a Sikh', in *The Punjab Crisis, Challenge and Response*, edited by Dr Abida Samiuddin (New Delhi: Mittal Publications, 1985), pp. 321–22.
6 Bishan Singh Bedi, 'On India's Destiny', in *The Punjab Crisis, Challenge and Response,* edited by Dr Abida Samiuddin (New Delhi: Mittal Publications, 1985), p. 324.

14: Blue Star: A Blunder?

1 P.C. Alexander, *Through the Corridors of Power: An Insider's Story* (New Delhi: HarperCollins India, 2004), p. 308.
2 *The Punjab Crisis, Challenge and Response*, edited by Dr Abida Samiuddin (New Delhi: Mittal Publications, 1985), p. 307.
3 Lt Gen. S.K. Sinha, *A Soldier Recalls* (New Delhi: Lancer International, 1992), pp. 290–91.
4 Lt Gen. V.K. Nayar, *From Fatigues to Civvies, Memoirs of a Paratrooper* (New Delhi: Manohar Publishers and Distributers, 2013), p. 195.
5 Lt Gen. K.S. Brar, *Operation Blue Star: The True Story* (New Delhi: UBS Publishers, 1993), pp. 9–10.
6 Louis E. Fenech, *Martyrdom in the Sikh Tradition: Playing the Game of Love* (New Delhi: Oxford University Press, 2000), pp. 18, 43–44.
7 Fenech argues that Sikhs have suffered 'mass martyrdom' in Chhota Ghallughara in 1746 and Wadda Ghallughara in 1762. However, in Sikhism, martyrdom is not an act of aggression or vengeance, nor is it a jihad waged to conquer infidels. Sikhs don't have jannat or paradise as promised to jihadis. In Sikhism, it is what historians call a 'passive martyrdom' for a righteous cause and for the freedom of faith, where the 'victim' gladly embraces suffering and sacrifice. Guru Arjan Dev and Guru Tegh Bahadur sacrificed themselves without resistance or aggression—acts of embracing torture and death inflicted by the Mughals. Even after the militarization of the Sikh faith, Guru Gobind Singh qualified to resort to aggression only when all other means had failed: It is lawful to take to the sword not as a weapon of aggression, but only as a righteous recourse to the last resort. It is in this context

that historians question the aggressive violence resorted to by the militants—clearly, it was a non-Sikh ethos.

8 Subhash Kirpekar, 'Operation Blue Star: An Eyewitness Account', in *The Punjab Story* (New Delhi: Lotus Collection, Roli Books, 2007), p. 106.

9 'Truth about Punjab, SGPC White Paper' (Amritsar: Gurdarshan Singh Dhillon, Shiromani Gurdwara Parbandhak Committee, 1996), p. 249.

10 The Damdami Taksal seminary was pedigreed by the unparalleled martyrdom of Baba Deep Singh Ji, its first head. Ahmad Shah Durrani (Abdali) on his way back to Kabul from Delhi had demolished the Harmandir Sahib, levelled the holy sarowar with its debris, and slaughtered cows. To avenge the sacrilege, seventy-five-year-old Baba Deep Singh in 1757 fought near Amritsar with the forces of Timur Shah, who was then Abdali's governor for Punjab. Severely wounded, Baba Ji laid his head down but only on reaching the circumambulation of the Harmandir Sahib, where a gurdwara commemorates his supreme sacrifice. Bhindranwale, as the fourteenth head of the Damdami Taksal, had to keep up with this illustrious past.

11 Lt Gen. P.N. Hoon, *The Untold Truth* (Chandigarh: Mohindra Publishing House, 2015), pp. 51, 54.

12 General V.K. Singh, *Courage and Conviction* (New Delhi: Aleph Book Company, 2013), p. 152.

13 Lt Gen. Jagjit Singh Aurora (retd), 'Assault on the Golden Temple Complex: 5–6 June 1984', in *The Punjab Story* (New Delhi: Lotus Collections, Roli Books, 2007), p. 127.

15: The President and the Prime Minister Arrive

1 Lt Gen. K.S. Brar has erroneously mentioned in his book *Operation Blue Star: The True Story* that Giani Zail Singh visited the Golden Temple in the morning hours.

2 Giani Zail Singh, *Memoirs of Giani Zail Singh: The Seventh President of India* (New Delhi: Har-Anand Publications, 2001), p. 183.

3 Lt Gen. K.S. Brar, *Operation Blue Star: The True Story* (New Delhi: UBS Publishers Distributors, 1993), p. 120.

4 P.C. Alexander, *Through the Corridors of Power: An Insider's Story* (New Delhi: HarperCollins, 2004), p. 310.

16: The Treasure Trove: Toshakhana

1 Harjit Oberoi, *The Construction of Religious Boundaries: Culture, Identity and Diversity in the Sikh Tradition* (Chicago: University of Chicago Press, 1994), p. 363.

2 S.S. Dhanoa, *Nothing to Hide: A Civil Servant Reveals* (New Delhi: Manas Publications, 2017), p. 272.

17: Death and Destruction

1 Lt Gen. P.N. Hoon, *The Untold Truth* (Chandigarh: Mohindra Publishing House, 2015), p. 47.
2 *Ajit*, 'Professor Badungar Holds Closed Door Meeting with Simranjit Singh Mann', 30 May 2017.
3 B.D. Pande, *In the Service of Free India: Memoir of a Civil Servant* (New Delhi: Speaking Tiger Books, 2021), pp. 184 and 298.
4 Hoon, *The Untold Truth*, p. 51.
5 The district-wise break-up is: Amritsar, 405; sixty-five from Gurdaspur; fifty-five from Sangrur; forty-seven from Ferozepur; twenty-nine from Faridkot; twenty-three from Kapurthala; twenty-four from Ludhiana; twenty from Bhatinda; eighteen from Jalandhar; seventeen from Patiala; sixteen from Hoshiarpur; three from Ropar; and twenty from other states.
6 S.S. Dhanoa, *Nothing to Hide: A Civil Servant Reveals* (New Delhi: Manas Publications, 2017), p. 279.
7 *Indian Express*, 'Court Orders Damages for 40 Sikhs Held during Op Blue-Star', 10 May 2017.
8 *Kamaladevi Chattopadhyay v. State of Punjab and Another*; AIR 1984 SC 1895 and (1985) 1 SCC 41.

18: Thefts, Violence and Shortages

1 *The Tribune*, 'After 33 years, Op Blue Star Major Wins Battle of Honour', 30 August 2018; also see *Hindustan Times*, 20 August 2018.
2 The exit–entry points were: Chowk Ghanta Ghar, two openings from Thara Sahib—one opening towards Bazar Mai Sewan and another in Bazar Kathian towards Bazar Shivala, one gate from Thara Sahib towards Bazar Jhutha, entry towards Chowk Darbar Sahib, Gali Karah Parshad towards Chowk Darbar Sahib, three main gates towards Atta Mandi, two main openings towards Baba Attal Sahib, main gate of Baba Attal Sahib, entry to Baba Attal from Gali Sangla Wali, entrance to Kaulsar Tank from the Katra Dal Singh side, main entry for Sarai Guru Ram Das, two main gates from Langar Guru Ram Das towards Brahmboota, exit point between Akhara Brahmboota and Akhara Sanglanwala and exit through Bunga Baba Kharak Singh. The smaller entrances were: Through the reception office of the temple, four gates from the residential quarters of the granthis adjoining the reception, thirteen gates through the residential quarters towards Atta Mandi,

two gates from Guru Nanak Niwas towards Gali Bagha Wali, five exit points from Gali Bagha Wali to Sarai Guru Ram Das, five exit points from the old Akal Rest House to the new Akal Rest House, five exit points between the Bunga Kharak Sing and the Darshani Deori, and five gates through the residential quarters towards Chowk Darbar Sahib.

19: The Purge

1 Harkishan Singh Surjeet, *Deepening Punjab Crisis: A Democratic* Solution (New Delhi: Patriot Publishers, 1992), p. 72.
2 Ibid. After joining at Chandigarh, Bhinder made two statements, which he later denied, that there were neither any criminals hiding in gurdwaras nor any firearms. This was seen as appeasement of the militants.
3 Kirpal Dhillon, *Time Present and Time Past: Memoirs of a Top Cop* (New Delhi: Penguin Books, 2013), p. 224.
4 G. Jagathpathi, IAS officer of the Madhya Pradesh cadre, P.G. Gavai, IAS officer of the Maharashtra cadre, Harbans Singh, IAS officer of the Tamil Nadu cadre, and S.S. Sidhu, IAS of the Uttar Pradesh cadre, all demitted office. Surendra Nath, IPS, stayed on but had to surrender the security portfolio to Lt Gen. R.S. Dayal. R.V. Subramaniam was inducted as senior adviser but was sent home once Arjun Singh was sworn in as governor.
5 B.D. Pande, K.T. Satarawala, Arjun Singh, Hokishe Sema, S.D. Sharma, S.S. Ray, Nirmal Mukarji, Virendra Verma, Gen. O.P. Malhotra and Surendra Nath were governors, while K.D. Vasudeva, S.S. Dhanoa, P.H. Vaishnav, R.P. Ojha and S.L. Kapoor served as chief secretaries. G.K. Sawhney, P.S. Bhinder, K.S. Dhillon, S.D. Pandey, B.S. Dhaliwal, J.F. Ribeiro, K.P.S. Gill, D.S. Mangat and then again K.P.S. Gill were the police chiefs.

20: The Politics of Kar Sewa

1 Brig. Goraya, who was involved in the negotiations, has given a graphic account of the proceedings of the meetings in his book: Brig. Onkar S. Goraya, *Operation Blue Star and After: An Eyewitness Account* (Panchkula: self-published, 2013), pp. 116–125. Post-retirement, Oberoi was appointed Lt Governor of Andaman and Nicobar Islands, where he served from 1985 to 1989.
2 The Sarbat Khalsa on 26 January 1986 resolved that to 'rejuvenate the sublime democratic Sikh tradition, Sarbat Khalsa should be held twice every year, on Baisakhi and Diwali, without fail'.
3 For a detailed account of the evolution of the Khalsa, see Harjot Oberoi, *The Construction of Religious Boundaries, Culture, Identity*

and *Diversity in the Sikh Tradition* (Chicago: University of Chicago Press, 1994).

4 Dr Gurmit Singh, *History of Sikh Struggles: Vol I* (New Delhi: Atlantic Publishers and Distributors, 1989), p. 50.

21: 'The President Is Guilty'

1 Dr Gurmit Singh, *History of Sikh Struggles: Vol I* (New Delhi: Atlantic Publishers and Distributors, 1989), p. 197.
2 Dr Madanjit Kaur, *The Golden Temple, Past and Present* (Amritsar: Guru Nanak Dev University, 2004), pp. 54–55.
3 Giani Zail Singh, *Memoirs of Giani Zail Singh: The Seventh President of India* (New Delhi: Har-Anand Publications, 2001), p. 190.
4 Ibid., p. 191.
5 Ibid., p. 193.
6 Ibid., p.195.
7 P.C. Alexander, *Through the Corridors of Power: An Insider's Story* (New Delhi: HarperCollins India, 2004), p. 318.

22: The Garrison State

1 Brig. Onkar Singh Goraya, *Operation Blue Star and After: An Eyewitness Account* (Panchkula: self-published, 2013), pp. 133–46.
2 Tan Tai Yong, *The Garrison State* (New Delhi: Sage India, 2005), p. 229.
3 Samar Vijay Singh, *The Lasting Reflections: Incidents from the Life of a Police Officer* (New Delhi: Vikas Books, 2015), p. 76.
4 Yong, *The Garrison State*, p. 192.

23: Indira's Assassination

1 Vinay Sitapati, *Half Lion: How P.V. Narasimha Rao Transformed India* (Gurgaon: Penguin Random House India, 2016), p. 63.
2 Manoj Mitta and H.S. Phoolka, *When a Tree Shook Delhi: The 1984 Carnage and Its Aftermath* (New Delhi: Lotus Collection, 2007), pp. 215–16.
3 *Indian Express*, Chandigarh, 12 September 2018.

24: The Accord and Longowal's Assassination

1 Arjun Singh, *A Grain of Sand in the Hourglass of Time: An Autobiography* (New Delhi: Hay House India, 2012), pp. 195–96.
2 It is generally believed that the formation of the United Akali Dal was an initiative of Buta Singh. As father of the late Bhindranwale,

Baba Joginder Singh was considered suitable for the job. Two Congress leaders—Tarlochan Singh Riyasti and Inder Jit Singh Sekhon, an advocate from Faridkot—met Baba Joginder Singh and as a goodwill gesture assured him of the release of his son Jagjit Singh, who had been in detention post–Blue Star. Jagjit Singh was set free on bail and following this, Baba announced the formation of the UAD and the dissolution of the factionalized Akali Dals, the Longowal and Talwandi factions. In fact, Baba Joginder Singh was not the only member of the late Bhindranwale's family to be inducted into public life—Jagjit Singh, the brother of Bhindranwale, his nephews Gurjit Singh and Jasbir Singh and his uncle Harcharan Singh, all entered politics at different stages of the Sikh movement. Soon after its formation, the UAD ideologically aligned itself with militants. It organized a rally at the Golden Temple in June 1985 on the first anniversary of Operation Blue Star. The radicals captured the stage, raising slogans in favour of Khalistan and casting the traditional Akali leaders like Longowal, Tohra and Badal as *ghadar*s of the Sikh panth; they were charged with having 'surrendered' to the army without a fight. The formation of the UAD thus resulted in unifying the radical voices under one flag and they aligned themselves against the traditional political leadership of the Akali Dal and the Accord.

3 Surjit Singh Barnala, *Story of an Escape* (New Delhi: Penguin Books, 1996), p. 57.

4 Singh, *A Grain of Sand in the Hourglass of Time*, p. 211.

5 Ibid.

27: The Hindu Exodus

1 B.D. Pande, *In the Service of Free India: Memoir of a Civil Servant* (New Delhi: Speaking Tiger Books, 2021), p. 280.

2 M.S. Deora, *Akali Agitation to Operation Blue Star* (New Delhi: Anmol Publications, 1991), p. 429.

3 Chintamani Panigrahi gave this information to the Rajya Sabha in a written reply to a question by Pawan Bansal, MP. Chandigarh, *The Tribune*, 6 May 1987.

29: Declaration of Khalistan

1 Subhash Kirpekar, 'Operation Blue Star: An Eyewitness Account', in *Punjab Story* (New Delhi: Lotus Collection, Roli Books, 2007), p. 106.

31: Barnala Excommunicated

1 Giani Kirpal Singh, jathedar of the Akal Takht; Giani Harcharan Singh Mahalon; jathedar of the Takht Keshgarh Sahib Anandpur Sahib; Giani Lakha Singh, jathedar of the Takht Damdama Sahib Talwandi Sabo; Giani Pritam Singh, head granthi of the Akal Takht; and Giani Sahib Singh, head priest of the Golden Temple.
2 Khushwant Singh, *Captain Amarinder Singh, The People's Maharaja: An Authorized Biography* (New Delhi: Hay House India, 2017), p. 182.
3 *The Tribune*, Chandigarh, 30 November 1986.

32: The Do-Gooders

1 Maloy Krishna Dhar, *Open Secrets: India's Intelligence Unveiled* (New Delhi: Manas Publications, 2005), p. 329.
2 Ibid., p. 82.

33: Operation Black Thunder II

1 Maloy Krishna Dhar, *Open Secrets: India's Intelligence Unveiled* (New Delhi: Manas Publications, 2005), pp. 340–41.
2 *The Tribune*, 'Govt. Priest Talks to Effect Ceasefire', 12 May 1988.
3 Julio Ribeiro, *Bullet for Bullet: My Life as a Police Officer* (New Delhi: Penguin Books, 1999), p. 335.
4 Ved Marwah, *Uncivil Wars: Pathology of Terrorism in India* (New Delhi: HarperCollins India, 1995), p. 191.
5 Dr Joginder Singh, *Myth and Reality of Sikh Militancy in Punjab* (New Delhi: Shree Publishers and Distributers, 2006), p. 166.
6 *The Tribune*, 'Unholy Deeds at Holiest of Places', 22 May 1988.
7 Marwah, *Uncivil Wars*, p. 194.

34: Mainstreaming the Militants

1 Forty detainees had been released in March 1988, and 138 detainees in September 1988.
2 Pavit Kaur, *Stolen Years: A Memoir of Simranjit Singh Mann's Imprisonment* (Gurgaon: Random House India, 2014), p. 221.
3 Bimal Kaur, widow of Beant Singh, an assassin of Prime Minister Indira Gandhi from Ropar; Rajinder Kaur Bulara, widow of a PAU professor allegedly eliminated by the police, from Ludhiana; Rajdev Singh, a human rights activist from Sangrur; Sucha Singh, father of Beant Singh, the assassin of Prime Minister Gandhi, from Bhatinda; and Jagdev Singh Khudian, a close associate of Simranjit Singh from Faridkot, won.

Three independents who won also had radical credentials: Kirpal Singh, who won from Amritsar, was a sophisticated but an outspoken Sikh ideologue and had led the Chief Khalsa Dewan for about seventeen years; Dhian Singh Mand who won from Ferozepur had a family bond with the terrorist outfit KCF; and Atinder Pal Singh, who won from Patiala, was a former AISSF leader and had led the Khalistan Liberation Organization. I.K. Gujral, who got elected as the Janata Dal candidate from Jalandhar, was inducted as external affairs minister. He became Prime Minister in April 1997 and was hugely pro-Punjab. The Congress could get only two seats, of Sukhbans Kaur Bhinder who, in any case, was believed to have had an acquiescent political understanding with the Taksal, and Kamal Chaudhary from Hoshiarpur. Gurdaspur and Hoshiarpur have a sizeable Hindu population, which helped the Congress. Harbhajan Singh Lakha, BSP, bagged Phillaur.

4 Kaur, *Stolen Years*, p. 2.

5 Maloy Krishna Dhar, *Open Secrets: India's Intelligence Unveiled* (New Delhi: Manas Publications, 2005), p. 413.

6 With 231 MPs and eighteen allies, the Congress required twelve more MPs to gain a simple majority in the Lok Sabha.

7 Sarabjit Singh, *Operation Black Thunder: An Eyewitness Account of Terrorism in Punjab* (New Delhi: Sage Publications, 2002), p. 283.

8 *India Today*, 'Banking on Bullets', 29 February 1992.

9 Kirpal Dhillon, *Identity and Survival: Sikh Militancy in India, 1978–1993* (New Delhi: Penguin Books, 2006), p. 258.

35: The War Cops

1 Kirpal Dhillon, *Identity and Survival: Sikh Militancy in India, 1978–1993* (New Delhi: Penguin Books, 2006), pp. 158–59.

2 Ibid.

3 *The Tribune*, 'Rs 308 Crore More in Police Kitty', 29 February 2020.

4 Illustratively, Gurjant Singh Budhsinghwala, chief of the Khalistan Liberation Force, Sukhdev Singh Dasuwal, a leading Babbar, Sukhdev Singh Babbar, chief of the Babbar Khalsa, Gurbachan Singh Manochahal, a member of the panthic committee, etc., were killed in Cat operations.

5 K.P.S. Gill and Sadhavi Khosla, *Punjab: The Enemies Within, Travails of a Wounded Land Riddled with Toxins* (New Delhi: Bookwise India, 2017), p. 185.

6 Birbal Nath, *The Undisclosed Punjab: India Besieged by Terror* (New Delhi: Manas Publications, 2008), p. 176.

7 Kirpal Dhillon, *Identity and Survival: Sikh Militancy in India, 1978–93* (New Delhi: Penguin Books, 2006), pp. 111, 161, 243, 308.

8 Ibid., p. 306.
9 Kirpal Dhillon, *Time Present and Time Past: Memoirs of a Top Cop* (New Delhi: Penguin Books, 2013), p. 291.
10 Inderjit Singh Jaijee, *Politics of Genocide: Punjab, 1984–94* (Chandigarh: Baba Publishers, 1995), p. 75.
11 Ibid.
12 Dhillon, *Identity and Survival*, p. 310.
13 The figure of Sikh deaths given by K.P.S. Gill in his book (*Punjab: The Knights of Falsehood* [New Delhi: Har-Anand Publications], p. 76) is 7,139—or 61 per cent of the total civilian deaths.
14 Gill and Khosla, *Punjab: The Enemies Within*, pp. 179–80.
15 Starting June 1984, nearly 9,500 persons were detained under Section 107/51 of the CrPc in Amritsar district up to 18 August 1984, a sign of social strife. The normal life of citizens was often disrupted by a plethora of 'ban-orders', mostly issued under Section 144 of the CrPC. These included a ban on plying of yellow motorcycles, plying of 3 horsepower Bullet motorcycles, pillion-riding, assembly of five or more persons, use of loudspeakers, carrying of weapons and firearms in public places and night curfew in villages along the border belt that crippled free movement of men and material. Under Section 3 (1) of the Punjab Village and Small Town Patrol Act, 1918, services of all able-bodied males were requisitioned for watch and ward duty and to patrol the railway tracks, irrigation works including canal embankments, electricity transmission lines and sub-stations, etc., to protect public assets.
16 *The Tribune*, 'Khalra Murder: Rs 49 Lakh Damages for Key Witness', 21 January 2017.
17 Dhillon, *Identity and Survival*, p. 306.
18 S.S. Dhanoa, *Nothing to Hide: A Civil Servant Reveals* (New Delhi: Manas Publications, 2017), p. 281.
19 Dhillon, *Time Present and Time Past*, p. 238.
20 Dhillon, *Identity and Survival*, p. 248.
21 *State v. Gurbinder Singh*, Sessions Case No. 4/8.1.85 Trail No. 15/9.4.85, in the court of M.S. Sehmee, additional judge, Special Court, Judicial Zone Jalandhar, at Amritsar, decided on 19.4.85.

36: The Foreign Hand

1 *The Times of India*, 'Was Part of Khalistan Movement: PSGPC Gen. Secy', 21 October 2017.
2 Hein G. Kiessling, *Faith, Unity, Discipline: The ISI of Pakistan* (Noida: HarperCollins India, 2016), p. 156.
3 Ibid., p. 157.

4 Sabil Francis, 'LTTE and Tamil Nadu: A Nexus', *Institute of Peace and Conflict Studies*, 2000, http://www.ipcs.org/comm_select.php?articleNo=430. Also see 'Fact Box—India's Role in Sri Lanka's Civil War', Reuters, 17 October 2008.
5 Praveen Davar, 'Mukti Bahini: A Force for Freedom', *The Telegraph*, published 29 April 2021, https://www.telegraphindia.com/opinion/mukti-bahini-a-force-for-freedom/cid/1813965
6 Jagmohan Meher, *America's Afghanistan War: The Success That Failed* (Delhi: Kalpaz Publications, 2004), p. 88.
7 Ibid., p. 144.
8 *India Today*, 30 November 1993.
9 K.P.S. Gill, *Punjab: The Knights of Falsehood* (New Delhi: Har-Anand Publications, 1997), p. 19.
10 Birbal Nath, *The Undisclosed Punjab: India Besieged by Terror* (New Delhi: Manas Publications, 2008), p. 243.

37: The Fourth Estate

1 Jaspal Singh Sidhu, *Sant Bhindranwale De Ru B Ru, June 1984 Di Pattarkari* (Amritsar: Singh Brothers, 2016), p. 56.
2 Sunil Sethi, 'The Great Divide', in *The Punjab Story* (New Delhi: Lotus Collection, Roli Books, 2007), p. 175.
3 Gobind Thukral, *Troubled Reflections: Reporting Violence* (Shimla: IIAS, 2009), p. 64.
4 Bikash Chandra, *Punjab Crisis, Perception and Perspectives of the Indian Intelligentsia* (New Delhi: Har-Anand Publications, 1993), p. 137.
5 Ghani Jafar, *The Sikh Volcano* (New Delhi: Atlantic Publishers, 1988), pp. 165–66.
6 Chandra, *Punjab Crisis*, pp. 171–72.
7 *Punjab: The Fatal Miscalculation, Perspectives on Unprincipled Politics*, edited by Patwant Singh and Harji Malik (New Delhi: Patwant Singh, 1985), p.18.
8 Thukral, *Troubled Reflections*, p. 66.
9 Ibid., p. 121.
10 *Sadhu Singh Hamdard Trust v. The State of Punjab And Ors*, 1992 CriLJ 1002. Subsequently, however, on 11 March 1993, another writ petition filed by Barjinder Singh of *Ajit* against the seizure of its newspaper found favour with the court and the order issued by the district magistrate was held to be non-speaking as it did not disclose the grounds or the reasons on the basis of which the district magistrate had acted against the newspaper: *Barjinder Singh v. State of Punjab* CWP 15625 of 1991; (1993) 104 PLR).

38: Militancy: The Beginning and the End

1 There were more than thirty ex-cops who joined the militancy in Punjab. Bhindranwale's close circle included more than a dozen ex-policemen. Talwinder Singh Parmar, who was associated with the Babbar International and the Akhand Kirtani Jatha, inducted former Naxalites and police sharpshooters such as Tarsem Singh Kalasnghian and three head constables. Sukha Sipahi—popularly known as Gen. Labh Singh—a one-time chief of the KCF, was a former police head constable. It is interesting that the co-option of policemen continued almost till the end of the militancy. In 1995, Chief Minister Beant Singh was killed by Dilawar Singh and his co-conspirator Balwant Singh Rajoana—both were former Punjab policemen. Babbar International had co-opted them and provided logistical support in the mission. Former Naxalites were even larger in number in the militant movement—Nachhatar Singh, the killer of Lala Jagat Narain, was one of them; he had joined hands with Swaran Singh and Dalbir Singh, the other two involved in the murder.

2 Mark Juergensmeyer, *Terror in the Mind of God: The Global Rise of Religious Violence* (Berkeley and Los Angeles: University of California Press, 2001); and also, *The Logic of Religious Violence*, edited by David Rapoport (London: Frank Cass, 1988). pp. 172–93

3 Mark Juergensmeyer, 'From Bhindranwale to Bin Laden: A Search for Understanding Religious Violence', in *Religion And Conflict in South and Southeast Asia* (London: Routledge, 2007).

4 Jitinder Kaur, *Punjab Crisis: The Political Perception of Rural Voters* (Delhi: Ajanta Publications, 1989), p. 131.

5 *The Tribune*, 'Longowal Speaks Out His Mind', 1 April 1985.

6 Cynthia Keppley Mahmood, 'Khalistan as Political Critique', in *The Oxford Handbook of Sikh Studies*, edited by Pashaura Singh and Louis E. Fenech (New Delhi: Oxford University Press, 2016), pp. 571, 572.

7 Illustratively, the two assassins of Chief of Army Staff Gen. Vaidya issued an excellently drafted ideologically insightful letter to the President of India, rationalizing their crime. The letter, it came out later in the investigation, was drafted by two professors.

8 Birinder Pal Singh, *Violence as Political Discourse: Sikh Militancy Confronts the Indian State* (Shimla: India Institute of Advanced Studies, 2002), p. 201.

9 Harish K. Puri, Paramjit Singh Judge, Jagrup Singh Sekhon, *Terrorism in Punjab, Understanding Grassroots Reality* (New Delhi: Har-Anand Publications Pvt Ltd., 1999), pp. 59-60.

10 K.P.S. Gill, *Punjab: The Knights of Falsehood* (New Delhi: Har-Anand Publications, 1997), pp. 101–04.

11 Gurdev Grewal, *The Searching Eye* (New Delhi: Rupa and Co., 2006), p. 160.
12 T.C.A. Raghavan, *The People Next Door: The Curious History of India's Relations with Pakistan* (Noida: HarperCollins India, 2017), pp. 188–89.
13 Hein G. Kiessling, *Faith, Unity, Discipline: The ISI of Pakistan* (Noida: HarperCollins India, 2016), pp. 88, 160.
14 A.S. Dulat, Asad Durrani and Aditya Sinha, *Spy Chronicles: RAW, ISI and the Illusion of Peace* (Noida: HarperCollins India, 2018), p. 205.
15 Gurmit Singh, *History of Sikh Struggles: Vol. I* (New Delhi: Atlantic Publishers and Distributors, 1989), p. 47.

39: The Diaspora

1 Darshan Singh Tatla, *The Sikh Diaspora: The Search for Statehood* (UK: UCL Press, University of Washington Press, 1999), p. 86.
2 Ibid., p. 50.
3 Radhika Chopra, *Militant and Migrant: The Politics and Social History of Punjab* (New Delhi: Routledge, Taylor and Francis Group, 2015), pp. 101–03.
4 Terry Milewski, *Blood for Blood: Fifty Years of the Global Khalistan Project* (Noida: HarperCollins India, 2021), p. 70.
5 *Times of India*, Chandigarh, 4 September 2017.
6 Harjit Sajjan became defence minister, Navdeep Bains the minister for innovation, science and economic development, Amarjeet Sohi the minister for infrastructure and Bardish Chagger the minister for small businesses. However, two of Trudeau's Sikh ministers courted controversy in India for their alleged pro-Sikh separatist leanings. Amarjit Singh Sohi, before his migration to Canada, was imprisoned in Bihar for about two years in the 1980s for his alleged pro-radical and leftist credentials. Harjit Singh Sajjan's family leaned towards the WSO.
7 *The Times of India*, Chandigarh, 1 November 2017.
8 *Hindustan Times*, 'Now, UK Body to Bar Entry of Indian Officials at Gurdwaras', 6 January 2018.
9 *The Times of India*, Chandigarh, 17 July 2018.
10 *The Tribune*, 20 October 2018; and *The Tribune*, 12 January 2022.
11 *Sunday Times of India*, 'Park in Fresno Named after Slain Rights Activist Khalra', 3 September 2017.

PART II: The Historical Background

1: Beginning of the Divide

1 Louis E. Fenech, *Martyrdom in the Sikh Tradition: Playing the Game of Love* (New Delhi: Oxford University Press, 2000), pp. 178–79.
2 Jitinder Kaur, *Punjab Crisis: The Political Perception of Rural Voters* (New Delhi: Ajanta Publications, 1989), p. 2.
3 Kenneth W. Jones, *Arya Dharm: Hindu Consciousness in 19th Century Punjab* (New Delhi: Manohar, 2006), pp. 52–53.
4 Harjot Oberoi, *The Constructions of Religious Boundaries: Culture, Identity and Diversity in the Sikh Tradition* (Chicago: University of Chicago Press, 1994), p. 219.
5 Rajmohan Gandhi, *Punjab: A History from Aurangzeb to Mountbatten* (New Delhi: Aleph Book Company, 2013), p. 251.
6 Jones, *Arya Dharm*, p. 136.
7 Oberoi, *The Construction of Religious Boundaries*, p. 219.
8 Jones, *Arya Dharm*, pp. 202-03.
9 Jones, *Arya Dharm*, p. 202.

2: Parting of the Ways

1 Khushwant Singh, 'Genesis of the Hindu–Sikh Divide', in *The Punjab Story* (New Delhi: Roli Books, Lotus Collection, 2007), pp. 6–7.
2 Kenneth W. Jones, *Arya Dharm: Hindu Consciousness in 19th Century Punjab* (New Delhi: Manohar Publishers, 2006), p. 137.
3 Ibid., pp. 137–38.
4 Paul Wallace, 'Religious and Secular Politics in Punjab: The Sikh Dilemma in Competing Political Systems', in *Political Dynamics and Crisis in Punjab*, by Paul Wallace and S. Chopra (Amritsar: GNDU, 1988), p. 9.
5 Jones, Arya *Dharm*, p. 206.
6 Paramjit Singh Judge, *Religion, Identity and Nationhood* (Jaipur: Rawat Publications, 2005), p. 23.
7 J.S. Grewal, *The Sikhs of the Punjab* (New Delhi: Cambridge University Press, 1999), p. 146.
For an autobiographical story of a Sahajdhari family in the Sikh faith, see Reena Nanda, *From Quetta to Delhi: A Partition Story* (New Delhi: Bloomsbury, 2018).
8 Jones, *Arya Dharm*, pp. 205, 208, 209.
9 Grewal, *The Sikhs of the Punjab*, p. 138.

10 His concept of One Universal God is the essence of the Adi Granth that was first installed at the Golden Temple in 1604. There was a conscious departure from the orthodox Hindu tradition and philosophy. Bhai Gurdas compiled the Adi Granth under the directions of Guru Arjan Dev, and historians record that he made a number of trips to Varanasi and Agra for familiarizing himself with Sanskrit traditions. He was assisted, among others, by Jagana Brahmin of Agra, a disciple of Guru Arjan Dev.

11 *The Tribune*, 'Mismanaged Golden Temple', 5 January 1887.

12 Dr Madanji Kaur, *The Golden Temple: Past and Present* (Amritsar: Guru Nanak Dev University, 2004), p. 64.

13 J.S. Grewal and Indu Banga, *A Political Biography of Maharaja Ripudaman Singh of Nabha (1883-1942)* (New Delhi: Oxford University Press, 2018), pp. 302–03.

3: Institutionalization of Sikhism

1 Harkishan Singh Surjeet, *Deepening Punjab Crisis: A Democratic Solution* (New Delhi: Patriot Publishers, 1992), p. 15.

2 Mohinder Singh, *The Akali Movement* (New Delhi: National Book Trust of India, 2008), p. 85.

3 Surendra Chopra, 'Ethnicity, Revivalism and Politics in Punjab', in *Political Dynamics and Crisis in Punjab,* edited by Paul Wallace and Surendra Chopra (Amritsar: GNDU, 1988), p. 474.

4: Linguistic Dissensions

1 Harjot Oberoi, *The Construction of Religious Boundaries* (Chicago: University of Chicago Press, 1994), p. 348.; also see Farina Mir, *The Social Space of Language: Vernacular Culture in British Colonial Punjab* (Berkeley: University of California Press, 2010).

2 Paul R. Brass, *Language, Religion and Politics in North India* (London: Cambridge University Press, 1974), p. 287.

3 The *Akali Patrika*, a Punjabi daily started from Lahore in 1920 and shifted to Jalandhar after Partition, while *Ajit* was launched from Lahore first in Urdu in 1940 and after Partition from Jalandhar in 1955. Its circulation was reported to be around 1,70,00 copies in 1966. Interestingly, *Ajit*, under the influence of Giani Kartar Singh, who was a minister in Gopichand Bhargava's ministry in independent India, was critical of the demand for a Punjabi-speaking state advanced by Master Tara Singh. It, however, changed its stand later and supported the cause of the Punjabi Suba.

4 Rajmohan Gandhi, *Punjab: A History from Aurangzeb to Mountbatten* (New Delhi: Aleph Book Company, 2013), p. 257.
5 Oberoi, *The Construction of Religious Boundaries*, p. 136.
6 Brass, *Language, Religion and Politics in North India*, p. 282.
7 Kenneth W. Jones, *Arya Dharm: Hindu Consciousness in 19th Century Punjab* (New Delhi: Manohar Publishers, 2006), p. 210.
8 Ibid.; Brass, *Language, Religion and Politics in North India*, pp. 292–94.
9 Brass, *Language, Religion and Politics in North India*, pp. 294–95.

5: 1947: Partition

1 Rajmohan Gandhi, *Punjab: A History from Aurangzeb to Mountbatten* (New Delhi: Aleph Book Company, 2013), p. 316.
2 Harkishan Singh Surjeet, *Deepening Punjab Crisis: A Democratic Solution* (New Delhi: Patriot Publishers, 1992), p. 13.
3 Hindol Sengupta, *The Man Who Saved India: Sardar Patel and His Idea of India* (Gurgaon: Penguin Random House India, 2016), p. 264.
4 Gandhi, *Punjab*, pp. 325, 329.
5 Ibid., p. 337.
6 Krishan Gopal Lamba, *Dynamics of Punjabi Suba Movement* (New Delhi: Deep and Deep, 1999), p. 13; also see J.S. Grewal, *The Sikhs of the Punjab* (New Delhi: Cambridge University Press India, 1999, second edition), p. 173.
7 Ibid.; Gandhi, *Punjab,* p. 346.
8 Grewal, *The Sikhs of the Punjab*, p. 180.
9 Baldev Raj Nayar, *Minority Politics in the Punjab* (Princeton: Princeton University Press, 1966), p.72.
10 Ibid.

6: Punjabi Suba

1 Rajmohan Gandhi, *Punjab: A History from Aurangzeb to Mountbatten* (New Delhi: Aleph Book Company, 2013), p. 364.
2 Krishan Gopal Lamba, *Dynamics of Punjabi Suba Movement* (New Delhi: Deep and Deep, 1999), p. 54.
3 Ibid.
4 Baldev Raj Nayar, *Minority Politics in the Punjab* (Princeton: Princeton University Press, 1966), p. 98.
5 'Unilingual Punjabi State and the Sikh Unrest': A statement by Sardar Gurnam Singh (retd) judge of the high court and late chief minister of Punjab, p. 30.
6 Lamba, *Dynamics of Punjabi Suba Movement*, p. 64.

7 J.S. Grewal, *The Sikhs of the Punjab* (New Delhi: Cambridge University Press, 1999, second edition, reprinted in 2009), pp. 184–85.
8 Gurmit Singh, *History of Sikh Struggles: Vol. I* (New Delhi: Atlantic Publishers and Distributers, 1989), p. 410.
9 Nayar, *Minority Politics in the Punjab*, p. 242.
10 Ibid.
11 Lamba, *Dynamics of Punjabi Suba Movement*, p. 123.
12 Singh, *History of Sikh Struggles, Vol. I*, pp. 123, 157, 159.
13 Ajit Singh Sarhadi, *Punjabi Suba: The Story of the Struggle* (Delhi: UC Kapur and Sons, 1970), p. 221.
14 *The Tribune,* 'Sant Fateh Singh', 1 November 1972; and *The Tribune,* 'Master Tara Singh's Fast', 1 June 1961.
15 Ibid.; Sarhadi, *Punjabi Suba,* p. 414.
16 Lamba, *Dynamics of Punjabi Suba Movement*, p. 165.
17 Ibid., p. 150.
18 Ibid.
19 Indira Gandhi, *My Truth* (New Delhi: Vision Books, 1980), pp. 105–06.
20 Ibid., p. 104.
21 Sarhadi, *Punjabi Suba*, pp. 422–23.
22 Paul R. Brass, *Language, Religion and Politics in North India* (London: Cambridge University Press, 1974), p. 333.
23 Lamba, *Dynamics of Punjabi Suba Movement*, p. 111.
24 Sarhadi, *Punjabi Suba*, pp. 447–48.
25 Ibid., p. 467.
26 The attempts to change the name of Dyal Singh College, Delhi, to Vande Mataram College in 2018 is quoted as an example of an attempted cultural assimilation of Punjabi heritage by the majority community; it is argued that if this could happen to the 'secular' Dyal Singh in Delhi, while Dyal Singh College in Lahore still retains his name, Punjabi culture would have faded into the majoritarian ethos if Punjabi Suba was not carved out.

7: Post–Punjabi Suba

1 Gurnam Singh was chief minister for 262 days (8.3.67 to 25.11.67). Lachhman Singh, who had helped to bring down Gurnam Singh's government, lasted only for 272 days (25.11.67 to 23.8.68). Gurnam Singh's second term had a life of one year and thirty-eight days (17.2.1969 to 27.3.1970). P.S. Badal was chief minister for one year and seventy-nine days (27.3.1970 to 14.6.1971) when the Vidhan Sabha was dissolved on the recommendation of Badal due to defections within the Akali Dal and thereafter again for two years and 242 days (20.6.1977 to

17.2.1980). S.S. Barnala remained chief minister for one year and 255 days (29.9.85 to 11.6.87) before his government was dismissed.

2 Illustratively, Zail Singh created a new district and named it after Guru Gobind Singh's martyred son, Sahibzada Ajit Singh Nagar, held kirtan darbars in various parts of the state, got some hospitals named after the Sikh Gurus, and even helped to organize the centenary celebrations of the Singh Sabha, the pre-Independence Sikh reformist organization. Some of these initiatives were part of developmental schemes such as the Guru Gobind Singh Marg under which the pathway traversed by Guru Gobind Singh was metalled, but some others were symbolic populistic measures.

3 Inder Malhotra, 'Indira Gandhi: An Overview', in *A Centenary History of the Indian National Congress, Volume V: 1964–1984* (New Delhi: Academic Foundation, 2011), p. 58.

4 Government of India, 'White Paper on the Punjab Agitation' (New Delhi: Government of India, 10 July 1984), p. 73.

5 J.S. Grewal, *The Sikhs of the Punjab* (New Delhi: Cambridge University Press India, 2009, second edition), p. 212.

6 Surjit Singh Barnala, *Surjit Singh Barnala: Story of an Escape* (New Delhi: Penguin Books, 1996), p. 29.

7 Kirpal Dhillon, *Identity and Survival: Sikh Militancy in India, 1978–1993* (New Delhi: Penguin Books, 2006), p. 48.

8: Rise of the Radicals

1 Darshan Singh Tatla, *The Sikh Diaspora: The Search for Statehood* (Seattle: University of Washington Press, 1999), p. 104.

2 Birbal Nath, *The Undisclosed Punjab: India Besieged by Terror* (New Delhi: Manas Publications, 2008), p. 243.

3 Gen. V.K. Singh, *Courage and Conviction* (New Delhi: Aleph Book Company, 2013), p. 147.

4 Kuldip Nayar and Khushwant Singh, *Tragedy of Punjab: Operation Blue Star and After* (New Delhi: Vision Books, 1985), p. 51.

5 Nath, *The Undisclosed Punjab*, p. 122.

6 Nayar and Singh, *Tragedy of Punjab*, p. 78.

7 Ibid., p. 51.

8 Ibid., p. 38.

9 Kuldeep Nayar, 'Towards Disaster', in *The Punjab Crisis: Challenge and Response*, edited by Dr Abida Samiuddin (New Delhi: Mittal Publications, 1985), p. 115.

10 Chand Joshi, *Bhindranwale: Myth and Reality* (New Delhi: Vikas Publishing House, 1984), pp. 35, 99.

11 J.S. Grewal and Indu Banga, *Punjab in Prosperity and Violence, 1947–1997* (Chandigarh: Institute of Punjab Studies, 1998), pp. 71–72.
12 Jagtar Singh, *Khalistan Struggle: A Non-Movement* (Delhi: Aakar Books, 2011), p. 40.
13 Nath, *The Undisclosed Punjab*, p. 170.
14 Ibid., p. 120.

9: Emergence of Bhindranwale

1 Inder Malhotra, 'Indira Gandhi: An Overview', in *A Centenary History of the Indian National Congress: Volume V* (New Delhi: Academic Foundation, Darya Ganj, 2011), p. 58.
2 Subhash Kirpekar, 'Operation Blue Star: An Eyewitness Account', in *The Punjab Story* (New Delhi: Roli Books, 2007), p. 118.
3 Kuldip Nayar, *Beyond the Lines: An Autobiography* (New Delhi: Lotus, Roli Books, 2012), p. 282.
4 Maloy Krishna Dhar, *Open Secrets: India's Intelligence Unveiled* (New Delhi: Manas Publication, 2005), p. 279.
5 Birbal Nath, *The Undisclosed Punjab: India Besieged by Terror* (New Delhi: Manas Publications, 2008), p. 142.
6 Kuldip Nayar, 'Towards Disaster', in *The Punjab Crisis: Challenge and Response,* edited by Dr Abida Samiuddin (New Delhi: Mittal Publications, 1985), p. 117; also see J.S. Grewal and Indu Banga, *Punjab in Prosperity and Violence: 1947–1997* (Chandigarh: Institute of Punjab Studies, 1998), p. 84.
7 Satyapal Dang, 'Punjab in Crisis', in *Political Dynamics and Crisis in Punjab,* edited by Paul Wallace and Surendra Chopra (Amritsar: GNDU, 1988), p. 419.
8 Grewal and Banga, *Punjab in Prosperity and Violence*, pp. 84–85.
9 K.P.S. Gill in an interview to *Hindustan Times*, Chandigarh, 23 July 2015; also see K.P.S. Gill and Sadhavi Khosla, *Punjab: The Enemies Within* (New Delhi: Bookwise India, 2017), p. 1.

Index

About the Author

Ramesh Inder Singh, popularly known as R.I. Singh, is a distinguished civil servant of the Punjab cadre. He was awarded the Padma Shri in 1986, at the age of thirty-six, for his notable contributions in the field of public administration.

He was district magistrate, Amritsar, from 1984 to 1987, and dealt with the turbulence in Punjab from close quarters. The various army operations against militancy, including Operation Blue Star, Operation Woodrose and Operation Black Thunder I, were conducted during this period.

During his long career of forty years in public life, he has held many crucial appointments. He was principal secretary to the chief minister of Punjab for five years; chief secretary of Punjab for over two years; and from that position, he took premature retirement from the IAS in 2009 to serve for five years as chief information commissioner, the transparency watchdog under the Right to Information Act.

Before joining the IAS, he taught political science in a constituent college of Delhi University. He has an MA in Political Science and topped Panjab University, and is a law graduate (LLB) from Delhi University. He has also worked with the World Bank as a consultant.

He is currently retired.

OPERATIO
THE GOLDEN T

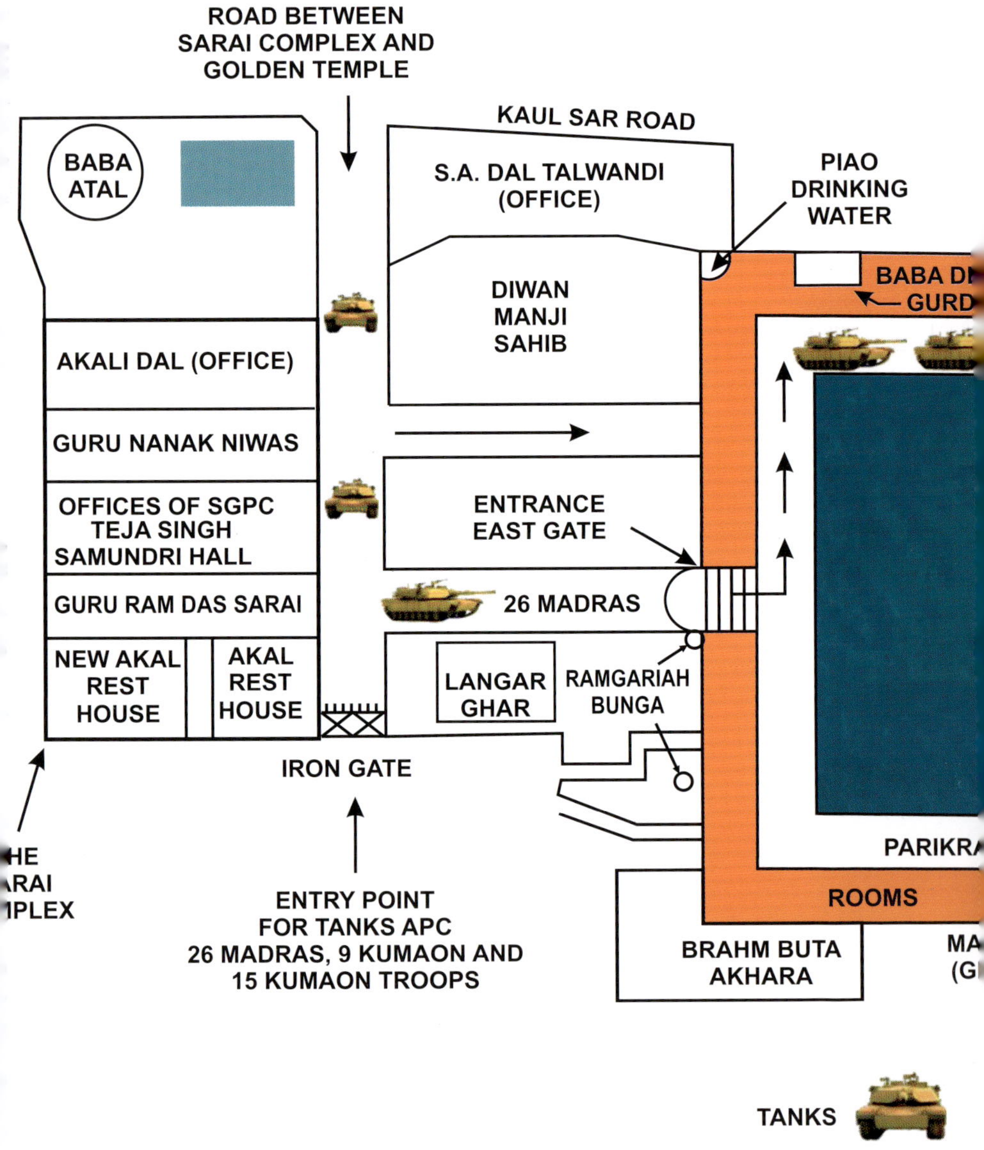

ROAD BETWEEN SARAI COMPLEX AND GOLDEN TEMPLE

KAUL SAR ROAD

BABA ATAL

S.A. DAL TALWANDI (OFFICE)

PIAO DRINKING WATER

DIWAN MANJI SAHIB

BABA D
GURD

AKALI DAL (OFFICE)

GURU NANAK NIWAS

OFFICES OF SGPC TEJA SINGH SAMUNDRI HALL

ENTRANCE EAST GATE

GURU RAM DAS SARAI

26 MADRAS

NEW AKAL REST HOUSE

AKAL REST HOUSE

LANGAR GHAR

RAMGARIAH BUNGA

IRON GATE

PARIKRA

HE
RAI
IPLEX

ENTRY POINT FOR TANKS APC 26 MADRAS, 9 KUMAON AND 15 KUMAON TROOPS

ROOMS

BRAHM BUTA AKHARA

MA
(G

BLUE STAR

MPLE PRECINCT

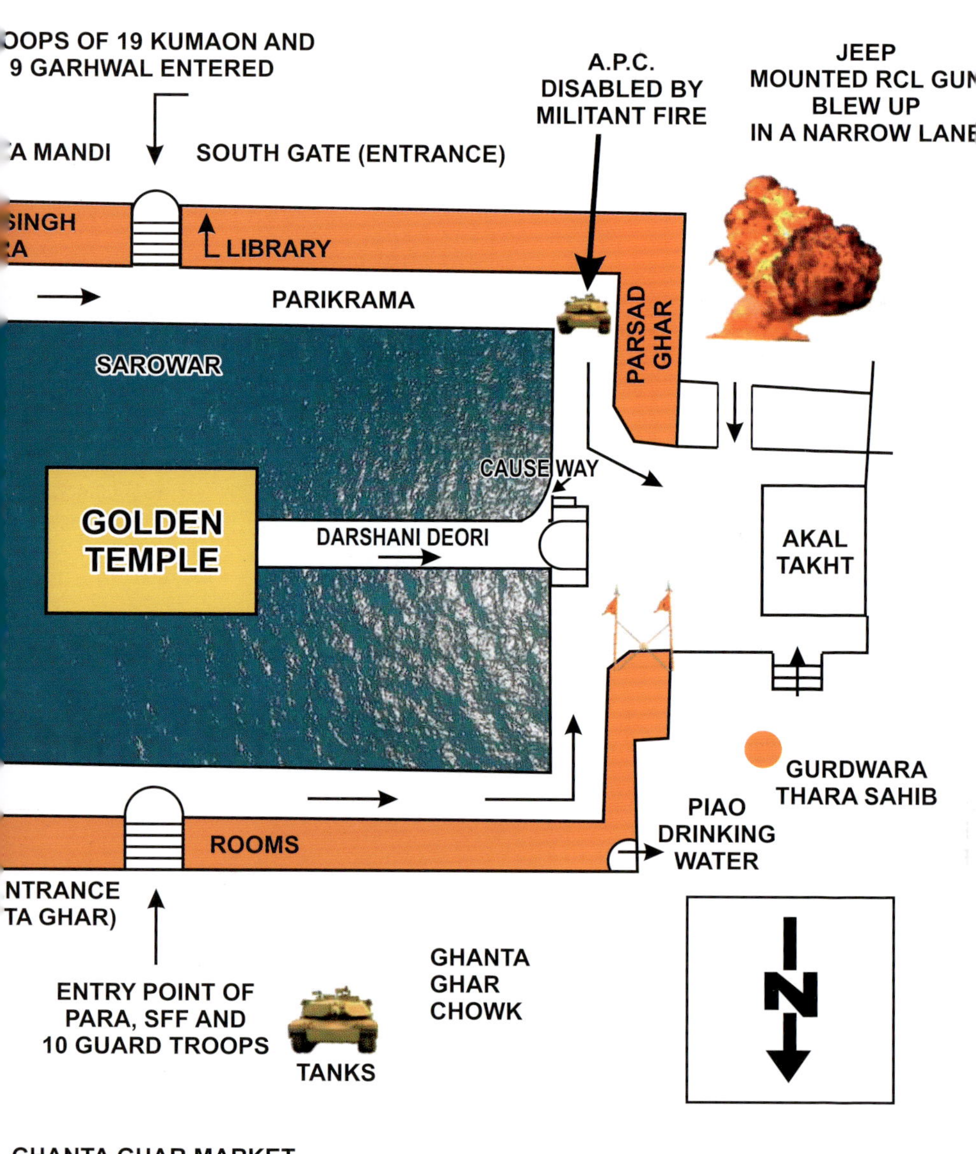